THE ADULT LEARNER

EIGHTH EDITION

How do you tailor education to the learning needs of adults? Do they learn differently from children? How does their life experience inform their learning processes?

These were the questions at the heart of Malcolm Knowles's pioneering theory of andragogy which transformed education theory in the 1970s. The resulting principles of a self-directed, experiential, problem-centered approach to learning have been hugely influential and are still the basis of the learning practices we use today. Understanding these principles is the cornerstone of increasing motivation and enabling adult learners to achieve.

This eighth edition has been thoughtfully updated in terms of structure, content, and style. On top of this, online material and added chapter-level reflection questions make this classic text more accessible than ever. The new edition includes:

- Two new chapters: Neuroscience and Andragogy, and Information Technology and Learning.
- Updates throughout the book to reflect the very latest advancements in the field.
- A companion website with instructor aids for each chapter.

If you are a researcher, practitioner or student in education, an adult learning practitioner, training manager, or involved in human resource development, this is the definitive book in adult learning that you should not be without.

Malcolm S. Knowles was one of the nation's leading authorities on adult education and training. He was the founding executive director of the Adult Education Association, and Professor of Adult and Community College Education at North Carolina State University.

Elwood F. Holton III, Ed.D., is the Jones S. Davis Distinguished Professor of Human Resource Development and Adult Education at Louisiana State University.

Richard A. Swanson is Professor Emeritus of Organization Learning, Policy, and Development at the University of Minnesota.

A Companion Website for this book is available at
www.routledge.com/cw/knowles

THE ADULT LEARNER

The definitive classic in adult education and human resource development

EIGHTH EDITION

Malcolm S. Knowles, Elwood F. Holton III, and Richard A. Swanson

Routledge
Taylor & Francis Group

LONDON AND NEW YORK

First published in 1973 by Butterworth-Heinemann, an imprint of Elsevier
Authored by Malcolm S. Knowles

This edition published 2015
by Routledge
2 Park Square, Milton Park, Abingdon, Oxon OX14 4RN

and by Routledge
711 Third Avenue, New York, NY 10017

Routledge is an imprint of the Taylor & Francis Group, an informa business

British Library Cataloguing in Publication Data
A catalogue record for this book is available from the British Library

Library of Congress Cataloging in Publication Data
Knowles, Malcolm S. (Malcolm Shepherd), 1913–1997.
    The adult learner/Malcolm S. Knowles, Elwood F. Holton III, Richard
    A. Swanson. – Eighth edition.
    pages cm
    Includes bibliographical references and index.
    1. Adult learning. 2. Adult education. 3. Training. I. Holton, Elwood
    F., 1957–. II. Swanson, Richard A., 1942–. III. Title.
    LC5225.L42K56 2014
    374 – dc23
    2014014309

ISBN: 978-0-415-73901-6 (hbk)
ISBN: 978-0-415-73902-3 (pbk)
ISBN: 978-1-315-81695-1 (ebk)

Typeset in Times New Roman and Franklin Gothic
by Florence Production Ltd, Stoodleigh, Devon, UK

Malcolm S. Knowles, the Father of Andragogy in the United States, died on November 27, 1997.

Malcolm was one of the world's leading scholar-practitioners of adult learning. He was a member of a generation that experienced the fullest range of character-building phases the United States has known: a massive influx of immigrants, several wars, an economic depression, waves of technological advances, the civil rights movement, the dominance of the knowledge worker, and an optimism about the human spirit. While Malcolm participated in all this, he was one of the thinkers and doers rising above the milieu and pointing the way for a dynamic democracy. Equivalent leaders of his generation, in such areas as economics, quality improvement, religion, and psychology, have finished their work and their legacy lives on in the next generation. Malcolm's early understanding of the importance of adult learning has provided insight that will guide the professions dedicated to adult learning into the next millennium.

This revised eighth edition of Malcolm's 1973 book is a testimony to his own learning journey and his personal confidence in the individual learner. In honor of Malcolm S. Knowles, the Academy of Human Resource Development has named its doctoral-dissertation-of-the-year award in his name. Those wishing to make a donation to this student-award endowment should contact the Academy.

CONTENTS

NOTES ON THE AUTHORS

Elwood F. Holton III, Ed.D., is the Director of the School of Human
Resource Education and Workforce Development and the Jones S. Davis
Distinguished Professor of Human Resource Development and Adult
Education at Louisiana State University. He is the author and editor of
numerous books and articles on adult learning and human resource
development, as well as the founding editor of *Human Resource
Development Review*. Dr. Holton is also a Past-President of the Academy of
Human Resource Development. He has been inducted into the International
Adult and Continuing Education Hall of Fame. He is an expert on adult
learning applications in public and private settings, and consults extensively
with organizations in both sectors.

Richard A. Swanson, Ed.D., is Professor Emeritus of Human Resource
Development and Adult Education at the University of Minnesota. He has
wide-ranging teaching and consulting experience, and has published
extensively in the areas of learning and human resource development. He
received the Distinguished Alumni Award from the University of Illinois
College of Education, and has been inducted into both the International Adult
and Continuing Education Hall of Fame and the Human Resource
Development Scholar Hall of Fame. Dr. Swanson is a leading authority on
how to develop and unleash human potential in organizations.

FIGURES

TABLES

PREFACE

Welcome to the newest edition of *The Adult Learner*. It is an honor for us to join with Malcolm Knowles in this updated and revised eighth edition. *The Adult Learner* has stood as a core work on adult learning for over 40 years. Our goal has been for it to remain a classic in the field of adult learning and human resource development.

We approached the task of continuing to update this classic book with care and thoughtfulness. In shaping this revision, we thought it was still important to preserve Malcolm's works and thoughts as close to their original form as possible. At the same time, we heard reader feedback loudly and clearly that it was time to give the book a fresh, updated feel. So while we have preserved all of Malcom's core material, we have also tried to make it more accessible and readable.

Highlights of the eighth edition include: Reorganizing the chapters for a more logical flow; significant editing on most chapters to improve readability; a new chapter on Neuroscience and Andragogy; and a new chapter on Information Technology and Learning. In addition, we have prepared a set of PowerPoint slides for each chapter which will be available to anyone adopting the book for classroom use. We hope you will agree that we have only improved upon the very successful seventh edition.

Each of the five parts of *The Adult Learner* has its own style. While the voices are varied, the messages are harmonious. The messages of lifelong learning, faith in the human spirit, and the role that adult learning professionals play in the adult learning process come through chapter by chapter.

Our hope is that this new edition of *The Adult Learner*, and its potential to advance adult learning wherever it is practiced, is realized and that Malcolm Knowles's vision continues to thrive in this new century.

We would like to thank several colleagues for their help at various points in this effort. John Henschke, Josh Reischmann, and Janis Lowe all contributed their work to this expanded edition. Finally, thanks to our families who continue to believe that our work is important and worth the sacrifices.

Elwood F. Holton III
Louisiana State University
Richard A. Swanson
University of Minnesota

PART 1
ADULT LEARNING

INTRODUCTION TO
ADULT LEARNING

1

When andragogy and the concept that adults and children learn differently was first introduced in the United States by Malcolm Knowles in the early 1970s, the idea was groundbreaking and sparked a great deal of research and controversy. Since the earliest days, adult educators have debated the essence of andragogy. Spurred in large part by the need for a defining theory within the field of adult education (AE), andragogy has been extensively analyzed and critiqued. It has been alternately described as a set of guidelines (Merriam, 1993), a philosophy (Pratt, 1993), a set of assumptions (Brookfield, 1986), and a theory (Knowles, 1989b). The disparity of these positions is indicative of the complex nature of adult learning. Regardless of what it is called, "andragogy is an honest attempt to focus on the learner. In this sense, it does provide an alternative to the methodology-centered instructional design perspective" (Feur and Gerber, 1988). Merriam, in explaining the complexity and present condition of adult learning theory, offers the following:

> Attempts at codifying differences between adults and children as a set of principles, a model or even a theory of adult learning have been, and continue to be, pursued by adult educators. However, just as there is no single theory that explains all of human learning, there is no single theory of adult learning. Instead, we have a number of frameworks, or models, each of which contributes something to our understanding of adults as learner. The best known of these efforts is andragogy.
>
> (Merriam et al., 2007, p. 83)

Despite years of critique, debate, and challenge, the core principles of adult learning advanced by andragogy have endured (Davenport and Davenport, 1985; Hartree, 1984; Pratt, 1988). Few adult learning scholars would disagree with the observation that Knowles' ideas sparked a revolution in

AE and workplace learning (Feur and Gerber, 1988). Brookfield (1986), positing a similar view, asserts that andragogy is the "single most popular idea in the education and training of adults." Adult educators, particularly beginning ones, find these core principles invaluable in the practical challenge of shaping the learning process for adults.

It is beyond the scope of this introductory book to address all the dimensions of the theoretical debate raised in academic circles. Our position is that andragogy presents core principles of adult learning that in turn enable those designing and conducting adult learning to build more effective learning processes for adults. It is a transactional model that speaks to the characteristics of the learning transaction, not to the esoteric goals and aims of that transaction. Thus, andragogy is applicable to any adult learning transaction, from community education to human resource development (HRD) in organizations.

Care must be taken to avoid confusing core principles of the adult learning transaction with the goals and purposes for which the learning event is being conducted. They are conceptually distinct, though as a practical matter may at times overlap. Critiques of andragogy point to missing elements that keep it from being a defining theory of the *discipline of adult education* (Davenport and Davenport, 1985; Grace, 1996; Hartree, 1984), not of *adult learning*. Grace, for example, criticizes andragogy for focusing solely on the individual, and not operating from a critical social agenda or debating the relationship of AE to society. This criticism reflects the goals and purposes of the discipline of AE. *Human resource development* in organizations has a different set of goals and purposes, which andragogy also does not embrace. Community health educators have yet another set of goals and purposes that are not embraced.

We see the strength of andragogy as a set of core adult learning principles that apply to all adult learning situations. The goals and purposes for which the learning is offered are a separate issue. Adult education professionals should develop and debate models of adult learning separately from models of the goals and purposes of their respective fields that foster adult learning. Human resource development, for example, embraces organizational performance as one of its core goals; whereas AE focuses more on individual growth.

It is important to note that these core principles are incomplete in terms of learning decisions. Figure 1.1 graphically shows that andragogy is a core set of adult learning principles. The six principles of andragogy are (1) the learner's need to know, (2) self-concept of the learner, (3) prior experience of the learner, (4) readiness to learn, (5) orientation to learning, and (6) motivation to learn. These principles are listed in the center of the model. As you will see in this and subsequent chapters, there are a variety of other factors that affect adult learning in any particular situation, and may cause adults to behave more or less closely to the core principles. Shown in the two outer rings of the model, they include individual learner and situational differences, and goals and purposes for learning. Andragogy works best in practice when it is adapted to fit the uniqueness of the learners and the learning situation. We see this not as a weakness of the principles, but as a strength. Their strength is that these core principles apply to all adult learning situations, as long as they are considered in concert with other factors that are present in the situation.

This eighth edition of *The Adult Learner* provides a journey from theory to practice in adult learning. Figure 1.1 provides a snapshot summary of considerations within the journey in displaying the six core adult learning principles surrounded by the context of individual and situational differences, and the goals and purposes of learning. The following chapters will reveal the substance and subtleties of this holistic model of andragogy in practice.

PLAN FOR THE BOOK

The first part of the book, Adult Learning (Chapters 1–5), presents the introduction to the book and adult learning (Chapters 1 and 2), the andragogical perspective on adult learning (Chapters 3 and 4), and the presentation of the andragogy in practice model (Chapter 5). Part 2, The Backdrop of Learning and Teaching Theories (Chapters 6–8), devotes Chapter 6 to exploring the realm of learning theory, presents theories of teaching in Chapter 7, and adult learning within human resource development in Chapter 8.

Part 3, Advancements in Adult Learning (Chapters 9–12), extends the boundaries to include new perspectives on andragogy (Chapter 9), beyond andragogy (Chapter 10), information technology and learning (Chapter 11), and neuroscience and andragogy (Chapter 12).

Part 4, Practices in Adult Learning (Chapters 13–18), covers the Whole–Part–Whole Learning Model (Chapter 13), facilitating learning (Chapter 14), guidelines for using learning contracts (Chapter 15), Core Competency Diagnostic and Planning Guide (Chapter 16), Personal Adult Learning Style inventory (Chapter 17), and effective technology-based adult learning (Chapter 18).

Part 5, International and Future Perspectives on Adult Learning (Chapters 19–21), looks beyond the boundaries of geography, context, culture, and time. Specific topics include: European perspectives on adult learning (Chapter 19), andragogy: international history, meaning, context, and function (Chapter 20), and the future of andragogy (Chapter 21).

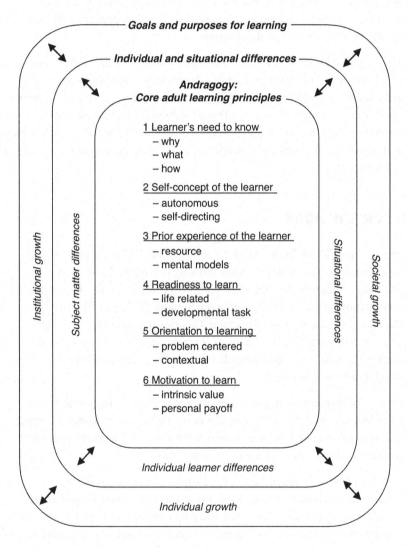

Figure 1.1 Andragogy in practice

Source: Knowles *et al.* (1998)

REFLECTION QUESTIONS

1.1 What are your general thoughts on how humans learn?

1.2 Based on personal experience, what key factors are related to adult learning?

1.3 Why is andragogy in practice (Figure 1.1) presented as a holistic learning model?

1.4 If you understood more about how adults learn, how would you use this information in your day-to-day life?

1.5 If you understood more about how adults learn, how would you use this information in your work as an educator/teacher/trainer?

EXPLORING THE WORLD
2 OF LEARNING THEORY

INTRODUCTION

While there still remains a great deal of mystery as to how human beings learn and the brain functions, we do know a great deal about this realm. Throughout history, there have been events and movements that have punctuated the knowledge base. Political enlightenment, world wars, and advance technology are just a few. Influential scholars and practitioners have led the way.

WHY EXPLORE LEARNING THEORY?

This is a good question. Perhaps you shouldn't. If you have no questions about the quality of learning in your organization, or if you are sure it's the best it can be, we suggest that you cancel your purchase of this book and get a refund. However, if you're a policy-level leader, a change agent, a learning specialist, or a consultant, you should seriously consider exploring learning theory. Doing so will increase your understanding of the range of learning theories, and your chances for achieving your desired results.

Policy-level leaders may have such questions as: Are our Human Resource Development (HRD) interventions based on assumptions about human nature and organizational life that are congruent with the assumptions on which our management policies are based? Are our human resource decisions contributing to long-run gains in our human capital, or only short-run cost reduction? Why do our HRD personnel make the decisions that they do concerning priorities, activities, methods and techniques, materials, and the use of outside resources (consultants, package programs, hardware, software, and university courses)? Are these the best decisions? How can I assess whether or not, or to what degree, the program is producing the results I want?

Managers may have all of these questions plus others, such as: Which learning theory is most appropriate for which kind of required learning, or should our entire program be faithful to a single learning theory? How do I find out what learning theories are being followed by the various consultants, off-the-shelf programs, and other outside learning resources that are available to us? What difference might their theoretical orientation make in our program? What are the implications of the various learning theories for our program development, selection and training of instructional personnel, administrative policies and practices, facilities, and program evaluation?

Learning specialists (instructors, curriculum builders, and methods, materials, and media developers) may have some of the previous questions in addition to the following: How can I increase my effectiveness as a learning specialist? Which techniques will be most effective for particular situations? Which learning theories are most congruent with my own view of human nature and the purpose of education? What are the implications of the various learning theories for my own role and performance?

Consultants (change agents, experts, and advocates) may have some of these saved questions plus others, such as: Which learning theory should I advocate under what circumstances? How shall I explain the nature and consequences of the various learning theories to my clients? What are the implications of the various learning theories for total organizational development? Which learning theory is most consistent with my conception of the role of consultant?

A good theory should provide explanations of phenomena as well as guidelines for action. But theories about human behavior also carry with them assumptions about human nature, the purpose of education, and desirable values. Understandably, then, a better understanding of the various learning theories will result in better decisions regarding learning experiences, more predictable outcomes, and more desirable results.

WHAT IS A THEORY?

It seems that most adult learning authors do not define the term theory, but expect their readers to derive its meaning from their use of the term. "A theory simply explains what a phenomenon is and how it works" (Torraco, 1997, p. 115). "Applied disciplines are realms of study and practice that are fully understood through their use in the functioning world" (Swanson and Chermack, 2013, p. 14). Adult learning is an applied discipline.

Webster's Seventh New Intercollegiate Dictionary gives five definitions: (1) the analysis of a set of facts in their relation to one another; (2) the general or abstract principles of a body of fact, a science, or an art; (3) a plausible or scientifically acceptable general principle or body of principles offered to explain phenomena; (4) a hypothesis assumed for the sake of argument or investigation; (5) abstract thought. Learning theorists use all five of these definitions in one way or another, but with wide variations in their usage:

Here, for example, are some definitions by usage in context.

> The research worker needs a set of assumptions as a starting point to guide what he/she does, to be tested by experiment, or to serve as a check on observations and insights. Without any theory, researcher activities may be as aimless and as wasteful as the early wanderings of the explorers in North America . . . knowledge of theory always aids practice.
>
> (Kidd, 1959, pp. 134–135)

> A scientist, with the desire to satisfy his/her curiosity about the facts of nature, has a predilection for ordering his/her facts into systems of laws and theories. He/she is interested not only in verified facts and relationships, but in neat and parsimonious ways of summarizing these facts.
>
> (Hilgard and Bower, 1966, pp. 1–2)

> Every managerial act rests on assumptions, generalizations, and hypotheses—that is to say, on theory.
>
> (McGregor, 1960, p. 6)

> Few people, other than theorists, ever get excited about theories. Theories, like vegetables and televised golf tournaments, don't trigger provocative reactions from people. Most theories, except those that are truly revolutionary, such as the contributions of Newton, Einstein, and Darwin, just do their jobs quietly behind the scenes. They may increase our understanding of a real-world event or behavior or they may help us predict what will happen in a given situation. But they do so without a lot of fanfare.
>
> (Torraco, 1997, p. 114)

From these excerpts and perspectives we can see that a theory can be a guiding set of assumptions (Kidd), an ordering system that neatly summarizes the facts (Hilgard and Bower), and/or assumptions, generalizations, and hypotheses (McGregor). Also, as Torraco points out, theories can be tacit. Yet, we must examine another important perspective: the fact that there are some psychologists who don't believe in theories at all. For example, Skinner objects to theories on the score that the hypothesis-formulation-and-testing procedures they generate are wasteful and misleading. "They usually send the investigator down the wrong paths, and even if the scientific logic makes them self-correcting, the paths back are strewn with discarded theories" (Hilgard and Bower, 1966, p. 143). Skinner believes that the end result of scientific investigation is a "described functional relationship demonstrated in the data." After reviewing the classical theories, he comes to the conclusion that "such theories are now of historical interest only, and unfortunately, much of the work which was done to support them is also of little current value. We may turn instead to a more adequate analysis of the changes which take place as a student learns" (Skinner, 1968, p. 8).

Similarly, Gagné (1965) writes, "I do not think learning is a phenomenon which can be explained by simple theories, despite the admitted intellectual appeal that such theories have" (p. v). He goes on to explain, however, that a number of useful generalizations can be made about classes of performance change, which he describes as conditions of learning.

Where does all this leave us in answering the question, "What is a theory?" As a practical matter it is important to determine the theoretical view of each author to understand their particular perspective. Perhaps the only realistic answer is that a theory is what a given author says it is. So here is our definition: *A theory is a comprehensive, coherent, and internally consistent system of ideas about a set of phenomena.*

WHAT IS LEARNING?

The simple definition of learning is "the acquisition of knowledge or skills through experience, study, or by being taught" (*New Oxford Dictionary*, 2010). Any deeper discussion of a definition of learning should be prefaced with an important and frequently made distinction between what is education and what is learning.

Education is an activity undertaken or initiated by one or more agents that is designed to effect changes in the knowledge, skill, and attitudes of individuals, groups, or communities. The term emphasizes the educator, the agent of change who presents stimuli and reinforcement for learning and designs activities to induce change.

> The term learning, by contrast, emphasizes the person in whom the change occurs or is expected to occur. Learning is the act or process by which behavioral change, knowledge, skills, and attitudes are acquired.
>
> (Boyd et al., 1980, pp. 100–101)

Having made this distinction, defining learning can still prove to be complicated. Some learning theorists assert that defining learning is difficult, while still others maintain that there is no basic disagreement about the definition of learning between the theories. Smith (1982, p. 34) summarizes the challenge of defining learning in these words:

> It has been suggested that the term learning defies precise definition because it is put to multiple uses. Learning is used to refer to (1) the acquisition and mastery of what is already known about something, (2) the extension and clarification of meaning of one's experience, or (3) an organized, intentional process of testing ideas relevant to problems. In other words, it is used to describe a product, a process, or a function.

In contrast, Ernest Hilgard, an interpreter of learning theory, concludes that the debate centers on interpretation and not definition:

> While it is extremely difficult to formulate a satisfactory definition of learning so as to include all the activities and processes which we wish to include and eliminate all those which we wish to exclude, the difficulty does not prove to be embarrassing because it is not a source of controversy as between theories. The controversy is over fact and interpretation, not over definition.
>
> (Hilgard and Bower, 1966, p. 6)

This generalization appears to hold with regard to those learning theorists who dominated the field until recently, although there are striking variations in the degree of precision among them. Let's start with three historic definitions by different authors as presented in *Readings in Human Learning* (Crow and Crow, 1963):

> Learning involves change. It is concerned with the acquisition of habits, knowledge, and attitudes. It enables the individual to make both personal and social adjustments. Since the concept of change is inherent in the concept of learning, any change in behavior implies

that learning is taking place or has taken place. Learning that occurs during the process of change can be referred to as the learning process.

(Crow and Crow, 1963, p. 1)

Learning is a change in the individual, due to the interaction of that individual, and his environment, which fills a need and makes him more capable of dealing adequately with his environment.

(Burton, 1963, p. 7)

There is a remarkable agreement upon the definition of learning as being reflected in a change in behavior as the result of experience.

(Haggard, 1963, p. 20)

The last notion implies that we don't directly know what learning is, but can only infer what it is. This idea is supported by Cronbach (1963), who stated, "Learning is shown by a change in behavior as a result of experience" (p. 71). Harris and Schwahn (1961) go back to "Learning is essentially change due to experience." They go on to distinguish between learning as product, which emphasizes the end result or outcome of the learning experience from learning as a process. Learning as a process emphasizes what happens during the course of a learning experience in attaining a given learning product or outcome. Learning as function emphasizes certain critical aspects of learning, such as motivation, retention, and transfer, which presumably make behavioral changes in human learning possible (pp. 1–2). Others take care to distinguish between planned learning and natural growth:

Learning is a change in human disposition or capability, which can be retained, and which is not simply ascribable to the process of growth.

(Gagné, 1965, p. 5)

Learning is the process by which an activity originates or is changed through reacting to an encountered situation, provided that the characteristics of the change in activity cannot be explained on the basis of native response tendencies, maturation, or temporary states of the organism (e.g., fatigue, drugs, etc.).

(Hilgard and Bower, 1966, p. 2)

The concepts of control and shaping lie at the heart of Skinner's (1968) treatment of learning: (1) "Learning is essentially change due to experience" [control]; and (2) "Once we have arranged the particular type of consequence called a reinforcement, our techniques permit us to shape the behavior of an organism almost at will" (p. 10).

Clearly, these learning theorists (and most of their precursors and many of their contemporaries) see learning as a process by which behavior is changed, shaped, or controlled. Other theorists prefer to define learning in terms of growth, development of competencies, and fulfillment of potential. Jerome Bruner (1966), for example, observes, "It is easy enough to use one's chosen theory for explaining modifications in behavior as an instrument for describing growth; there are so many aspects of growth that any theory can find something that it can explain well." He then lists the following "benchmarks about the nature of intellectual growth against which to measure one's efforts at explanation" (pp. 4–6):

1. Growth is characterized by increasing independence of response from the immediate nature of the stimulus.
2. Growth depends upon internalizing events into a "storage system" that corresponds to the environment.
3. Intellectual growth involves an increasing capacity to say to oneself and others, by means of words or symbols, what one has done or what one will do.
4. Intellectual development depends upon a systematic and contingent interaction between a tutor and a learner.
5. Teaching is vastly facilitated by the medium of language, which ends by being not only the medium for exchange but the instrument that the learner can then use himself in bringing order into the environment.
6. Intellectual development is marked by increasing capacity to deal with several alternatives simultaneously, to tend to several sequences during the same period of time, and to allocate time and attention in a manner appropriate to these multiple demands.

Still other theorists feel that even this emphasis on growth, with its focus on cognitive development, is too narrow to explain what learning is really about. For instance, Jones (1968) objects to Bruner's under-emphasis on emotional skills, his exclusive attention to extra-psychic stimuli, the equating of symbolism with verbalism, and his preoccupation with the processes of concept attainment to the seeming exclusion of the processes of concept formation or invention (pp. 97–104).

Nevertheless, Bruner is moving away from the perception of learning as a process of controlling, changing, or shaping behavior and putting it more in the context of competency development. One of the most dynamic and prolific developments in the field of psychology, humanistic psychology, had recently exploded on the scene (the Association of Humanistic Psychology was founded in 1963) and carried this trend of thought much further. Carl Rogers is one of its exponents. The elements of humanistic psychology, according to Rogers (1969, p. 5), include:

1. *Personal involvement.* The whole person, including his or her feelings and cognitive aspects, is involved in the learning event.
2. *Self-initiation.* Even when the impetus or stimulus comes from the outside, the sense of discovery, of reaching out, of grasping and comprehending, comes from within.
3. *Pervasiveness.* Learning makes a difference in the behavior, attitudes, perhaps even the personality of the learner.
4. *Evaluation by the learner.* The learner knows whether the learning meets personal need, whether it leads toward what the individual wants to know, whether it illuminates the dark area of ignorance the individual is experiencing. The locus of evaluation, we might say, resides definitely in the learner.
5. *Its essence is meaning.* When such learning takes place, the element of meaning to the learner is built into the whole experience.

Maslow (1970) sees the goal of learning to be self-actualization: "the full use of talents, capacities, potentialities, etc." (p. 150). He conceives of growth toward this goal as being determined by the relationship of two sets of forces operating within each individual:

> One set clings to safety and defensiveness out of fear, tending to regress backward, hanging on to the past. . . . The other set of forces impels him forward toward wholeness to Self and uniqueness of Self, toward full functioning of all his capacities. . . . We grow forward when the delights of growth and anxieties of safety are greater than the anxieties of growth and the delights of safety.
>
> (1972, pp. 44–45)

Building on the notion that "insights from the behavioral sciences have expanded the perception of human potential, through a re-casting of the image of man from a passive, reactive recipient, to an active, seeking, autonomous, and reflective being," Sidney Jourard (1972) develops the concept of independent learning:

> That independent learning is problematic is most peculiar, because man always and only learns by himself. . . . Learning is not a task or problem; it is a way to be in the world. Man learns as he pursues goals and projects that have meaning for him. He is always learning

something. Perhaps the key to the problem of independent learning lies in the phrase "the learner has the need and the capacity to assume responsibility for his own continuing learning."

(Jourard, 1972, p. 66)

Other educational psychologists question the proposition that learning can be defined as a single process. For example, Gagné (1972, pp. 3–41) identifies five domains of the learning process, each with its own approach:

1. *Motor skills*, which are developed through practice.
2. *Verbal information*, the major requirement for learning being its presentation within an organized, meaningful context.
3. *Intellectual skills*, the learning of which appears to require prior learning of prerequisite skills.
4. *Cognitive strategies*, the learning of which requires repeated occasions in which challenges to thinking are presented.
5. *Attitudes*, which are learned most effectively through the use of human models and "vicarious reinforcement."

Tolman distinguished six types of "connections or relations" to be learned: (1) cathexes; (2) equivalence beliefs; (3) field expectancies; (4) field-cognition modes; (5) drive discriminations; and (6) motor patterns (Hilgard and Bower, 1966, pp. 211–213). The significance of Tolman's work is his effort to integrate rival definitions and theories.

Bloom and his associates (1956, p. 7) identified three domains of educational objectives: (1) cognitive, "which deal with the recall or recognition of knowledge and the development of intellectual abilities and skills"; (2) affective, "which describe changes in interest, attitudes, and values, and the development of appreciations and adequate adjustment"; and (3) psychomotor. Later scholars expanded on the psychomotor domain to include all the human senses and their dimensions.

With major advances in neuroscience and information technology the definitions, theories, and methods of adult learning continued to be challenged. These challenges are presented in later chapters.

SUMMARY

Exploring learning theory can be beneficial to policy-level leaders, managers, learning specialists, and consultants by providing information that will allow better decisions, and ultimately more desirable learning experiences.

However, doing so is not a simple task. In order to explore learning theory, the key concepts of the definition of theory, the distinction between learning and education, and the complexities involved in defining learning must be understood.

We know that some learning theorists consider a theory to be a guiding set of assumptions, an ordering system that neatly summarizes the facts, and/or assumptions, generalizations, and hypotheses. Some psychologists, however, oppose the concept of learning theories. For instance, Gagné asserts that despite the "intellectual appeal," learning cannot be readily explained by theories. Analyzing the changes that occur as a student learns, according to Skinner (1968), produces more valuable information than the "wasteful" and "misleading" procedures generated by theories. Despite these objections, we conclude that a theory is a comprehensive, coherent, and internally consistent system of ideas about a set of phenomena. We also acknowledge the distinction between education and learning. Education emphasizes the educator, whereas learning emphasizes the person in whom the change occurs or is expected to occur. Although this distinction is easily understood, developing a working definition of learning is more complex. Key components of learning theorists' definitions of learning serve as the foundation for our discussion of the definition of learning. These components include change, filling a need, learning as product, learning as process, learning as function, natural growth, control, shaping, development of competencies, fulfillment of potential, personal involvement, self-initiated, learner-evaluated, independent learning, and learning domains. We define learning as the process of gaining knowledge and expertise.

REFLECTION QUESTIONS

2.1 What is the connection between theory and practice?
2.2 Why should practitioners care about theory?
2.3 What is the essential difference between the concepts of education and learning?
2.4 What key points about learning presented in this chapter have the most meaning to you? Why?
2.5 Which definition of learning presented do you prefer and why?

ANDRAGOGY

3

A THEORY OF ADULT LEARNING

INTRODUCTION

Until recently, there has been relatively little thinking, investigating, and writing about adult learning. This is a curious fact considering that the education of adults has been a concern of the human race for such a long time. Yet, for many years, the adult learner was indeed a neglected species.

The historical lack of research in this field is especially surprising in view of the fact that all the great teachers of ancient times—Confucius and Lao Tse of China; the Hebrew prophets and Jesus in biblical times; Aristotle, Socrates, and Plato in ancient Greece; and Cicero, Evelid, and Quintillian in ancient Rome—were teachers of adults, not of children. Because their experiences were with adults, they developed a very different concept of the learning/teaching process from the one that later dominated the formal education of children. These notable teachers perceived learning to be a process of mental inquiry, not passive reception of transmitted content. Accordingly, they invented techniques for engaging learners in inquiry. The ancient Chinese and Hebrews invented what we now call the *case method*; in which the leader or one of the group members describes a situation, often in the form of a parable, and together with the group explores its characteristics and possible resolutions. The Greeks invented what we now call the *Socratic dialogue*; in which the leader or a group member poses a question or dilemma and the group members pool their thinking and experience to seek an answer or solution. The Romans were more confrontational; they used challenges that forced group members to state a position and then defend them.

In the seventh century in Europe, schools were organized for teaching children, primarily for preparing young boys for the priesthood. Hence, they became known as cathedral and monastic schools. Since the indoctrination of students in the beliefs, faith, and rituals of the Church was the principal mission of these teachers, they developed a set of assumptions about learning and strategies for teaching that came to be labeled pedagogy, literally meaning "the art and science of teaching children" (derived from the Greek words *paid*, meaning "child," and *agogus*, meaning "leader of"). This model of education persisted through the ages well into the twentieth century and was the basis of organization for the educational system in the USA.

Shortly after the end of World War I, both in the United States and in Europe, a growing body of notions about the unique characteristics of adult learners began emerging. But only in more recent decades have these notions evolved into an integrated framework of adult learning. It is fascinating to trace this evolutionary process in the United States.

TWO STREAMS OF INQUIRY

Beginning with the founding of the American Association for Adult Education in 1926, and the provision of substantial funding for research and publications by the Carnegie Corporation of New York, two streams of inquiry are discernible. One stream can be classified as the scientific stream, and the other as the artistic or intuitive/reflective stream. The scientific stream seeks to discover new knowledge through rigorous (and often experimental) investigation, and was launched by Edward L. Thorndike with the publication of his *Adult Learning* in 1928. The title is misleading, however, for Thorndike was not concerned with the processes of adult learning but rather with learning ability. His studies demonstrated that adults could, in fact, learn, which was important because it provided a scientific foundation for a field that had previously been based on the mere faith that adults could learn. Additions to this stream in the next decade included Thorndike's *Adult Interests* in 1935 and Herbert Sorenson's *Adult Abilities* in 1938. By the onset of World War II adult educators had scientific evidence that adults could learn and that they possessed interests and abilities that were different from those of children.

On the other hand, the artistic stream, which seeks to discover new knowledge through intuition and the analysis of experience, was concerned with how adults learn. This stream of inquiry was launched with the publication of Eduard C. Lindeman's *The Meaning of Adult Education* in 1926. Strongly influenced by the educational philosophy of John Dewey, Lindeman (1926b) laid the foundation for a systematic theory about adult learning with such insightful statements as these:

> The approach to adult education will be via the route of situations, not subjects. Our academic system has grown in reverse order: subjects

and teachers constitute the starting point, students are secondary. In conventional education the student is required to adjust himself to an established curriculum; in adult education the curriculum is built around the student's needs and interests. Every adult person finds himself in specific situations with respect to his work, his recreation, his family life, his community life, etc.—situations which call for adjustments. Adult education begins at this point. Subject matter is brought into the situation, is put to work, when needed. Texts and teachers play a new and secondary role in this type of education; they must give way to the primary importance of the learners.

(pp. 8–9)

The resource of highest value in adult education is the learner's experience. If education is life, then life is also education. Too much of learning consists of vicarious substitution of someone else's experience and knowledge. Psychology is teaching us, however, that we learn what we do, and that therefore all genuine education will keep doing and thinking together. . . . Experience is the adult learner's living textbook.

(pp. 9–10)

Authoritative teaching, examinations which preclude original thinking, rigid pedagogical formulae—all these have no place in adult education. . . . Small groups of aspiring adults who desire to keep their minds fresh and vigorous, who begin to learn by confronting pertinent situations, who dig down into the reservoirs of their experience before resorting to texts and secondary facts, who are led in the discussion by teachers who are also searchers after wisdom and not oracles: this constitutes the setting for adult education, the modern quest for life's meaning.

(pp. 10–11)

Adult learning theory presents a challenge to static concepts of intelligence, to the standardized limitations of conventional education and to the theory which restricts educational facilities to an intellectual class. Apologists for the status quo in education frequently assert that the great majority of adults are not interested in learning, are not motivated in the direction of continuing education; if they possessed these incentives, they would, naturally, take advantage of the numerous free educational opportunities provided by public agencies. This argument begs the question and misconceives the problem. We shall never know how many adults desire intelligence regarding themselves and the world in which they live until education once more escapes the patterns of conformity. Adult education is an attempt to discover a new method and create a new incentive for learning; its implications are qualitative, not quantitative. Adult learners are precisely those whose intellectual aspirations are least likely to be aroused by the rigid, uncompromising requirements of authoritative, conventionalized institutions of learning.

(pp. 27–28)

Adult education is a process through which learners become aware of significant experience. Recognition of significance leads to evaluation. Meanings accompany experience when we know what is happening and what importance the event includes for our personalities.

(p. 169)

Two excerpts from other Lindeman writings elaborate on these ideas:

I am conceiving adult education in terms of a new technique for learning, a technique as essential to the college graduate as to the unlettered manual worker. It represents a process by which the adult learns to become aware of and to evaluate his experience. To do this he cannot begin by studying "subjects" in the hope that some day this information will be useful. On the contrary, he begins by giving attention to situations in which he finds himself, to problems which include obstacles to his self-fulfillment. Facts and information from the differentiated spheres of knowledge are used, not for the purpose of accumulation, but because of need in solving problems. In this process the teacher finds a new function. He is no longer the oracle who speaks from the platform of authority, but rather the guide, the pointer-out who also participates in learning in proportion to the vitality and relevance of his facts and experiences. In short, my conception of adult education is this: a cooperative venture in nonauthoritarian, informal learning, the chief purpose of which is to discover the meaning of experience; a quest of the mind which digs down to the roots of the preconceptions which formulate our conduct; a technique of learning for adults which makes education coterminous with life and hence elevates living itself to the level of adventurous experiment.

(Gessner, 1956, p. 160)

One of the chief distinctions between conventional and adult education is to be found in the learning process itself. None but the humble become good teachers of adults. In an adult class the student's experience counts for as much as the teacher's knowledge.

Both are exchangeable at par. Indeed, in some of the best adult classes it is sometimes difficult to discover who is learning most, the teacher or the students. This two-way learning is also reflected by shared authority. In conventional education the pupils adapt themselves to the curriculum offered, but in adult education the pupils aid in formulating the curricula. . . . Under democratic conditions authority is of the group. This is not an easy lesson to learn, but until it is learned democracy cannot succeed.

(Gessner, 1956, p. 166)

Table 3.1 Summary of Lindeman's key assumptions about adult learners

1. Adults are motivated to learn as they experience needs and interests that learning will satisfy.
2. Adults' orientation to learning is life-centered.
3. Experience is the richest source for adult's learning.
4. Adults have a deep need to be self-directing.
5. Individual differences among people increase with age.

These excerpts from the pioneering theorist are sufficient to portray a new way of thinking about adult learning, yet it is important to note that Lindeman (1926b) also identified several key assumptions about adult learners. His assumptions, summarized in Table 3.1, have been supported by later research and constitute the foundation of adult learning theory:

1. Adults are motivated to learn as they experience needs and interests that learning will satisfy; therefore, these are the appropriate starting points for organizing adult learning activities.
2. Adults' orientation to learning is life-centered; therefore, the appropriate units for organizing adult learning are life situations, not subjects.
3. Experience is the richest resource for adults' learning; therefore, the core methodology of adult education is the analysis of experience.
4. Adults have a deep need to be self-directing; therefore, the role of the teacher is to engage in a process of mutual inquiry with them rather than to transmit his or her knowledge to them and then evaluate their conformity to it.
5. Individual differences among people increase with age; therefore, adult education must make optimal provision for differences in style, time, place, and pace of learning.

It is interesting to note that Lindeman did not dichotomize adult versus youth education, but rather adult versus "conventional" education. The implication here is that youths might learn better, too, when their needs and interests, life situations, experiences, self-concepts, and individual differences are taken into account. The artistic stream of inquiry that Lindeman launched in 1926 flowed on through the pages of the *Journal of Adult Education*, the quarterly publication of the American Association for Adult Education, which, between February 1929 and October 1941, provided the most distinguished body of literature yet produced in the field of adult education. The following excerpts from its articles reveal the growing collection of insights about adult learning gleaned from the experience of successful practitioners:

By Lawrence P. Jacks, principal of Manchester College, Oxford, England:

Earning and living are not two separate departments or operations in life. They are two names for a continuous process looked at from opposite ends. . . . A type of education based on this vision of continuity is, obviously, the outstanding need of our times. Its outlook will be lifelong. It will look upon the industry of civilization as the great "continuation school" for intelligence and for character, and its object will be, not merely to fit men and women for the specialized vocations they are to follow, but also to animate the vocations themselves with ideals of excellence appropriate to each. At the risk of seeming fantastic I will venture to say that the final objective of the New Education is the gradual transformation of the industry of the world into the university of the world; in other words, the gradual bringing about of a state of things in which "breadwinning" and "soulsaving" instead of being, as now, disconnected and often opposed operations, shall become a single and continuous operation.

(*Journal of Adult Education*, *I*(1), February 1929,
pp. 7–10)

By Robert D. Leigh, president of Bennington College:

At the other end of the traditional academic ladder the adult educational movement is forcing recognition of the value and importance of continuing the learning process indefinitely. . . . But among the far-seeing leaders of the movement in the United States it is recognized not so much as a substitute for inadequate schooling in youth as an educational opportunity superior to that offered in youth—superior because the learner is motivated not by the artificial incentives of academic organization, but by the honest desire to know and to enrich his experience, and because the learner brings to his study relevant daily experience, and consequently the new knowledge takes root firmly, strikes deep, and feeds on what the day's life brings it.

There is gradually emerging, therefore, a conception of education as a lifelong process beginning at birth and ending only with death, a process related at all points to the life experiences of the individual, a process full of meaning and reality to the learner, a process in which the student is active participant rather than passive recipient.

(Journal of Adult Education, II(2), April 1930, p. 123)

By David L. Mackaye, director of the Department of Adult Education, San Jose, California, public schools:

A person is a good educator among adults when he has a definite conviction about life and when he can present intelligent arguments on behalf of it; but primarily he does not qualify as an adult educator at all until he can exist in a group that collectively disputes, denies, or ridicules his conviction, and continues to adore him because he rejoices in them. That is tolerance, an exemplification of Proudhon's contention that to respect a man is a higher intellectual feat than to love him as one's self. . . . There is positive evidence that no adult education system will ever make a success of collegiate methods of instruction to adults in the cultural fields. Something new in the way of content and method must be produced as soon as possible for adult education, and probably it will have to grow up in the field. No teacher-training-college hen can lay an adult education egg.

(Journal of Adult Education, III(3), June 1931,
pp. 293–294)

By Maria Rogers, volunteer worker, New York City Adult Education Council:

One type of adult education merits particular consideration and wider use by educators seeking new methods. Though meagerly publicized, it has proved effective in numerous instances. It has undertaken a far more difficult task than that assumed by the institutions for adult education which confine their concept of method to the sequence of procedure established for adults who enter classrooms to learn something already set up to be learned. Its prime objective is to make the group life of adults yield educational value to the participants. . . .

The educator who uses the group method of education takes ordinary, gregarious human beings for what they are, searches out the groups in which they move and have their being, and then helps them to make their group life yield educational values.

(*Journal of Adult Education*, X, October 1938,
pp. 409–411)

By Ruth Merton, director of the Education Department, Milwaukee YWCA:

In a day school, where the students are usually children or young adolescents, a learned teacher–ignorant pupil relationship is almost inevitable, and frequently it has its advantages. But in a night school the situation is entirely different. Here, so far as the class is concerned, the teacher is an authority upon one subject only, and each of the students has, in his own particular field, some skill or knowledge that the teacher does not possess. For this reason, there is a spirit of give and take in a night-school class that induces a feeling of comradeship in learning, stimulating to teacher and students alike. And the quickest way to achieve this desirable state is through laughter in which all can join.

And so I say again that, if we are really wise, we teachers in night schools will, despite taxes or indigestion, teach merrily!

(*Journal of Adult Education*, XI, April 1939,
p. 178)

By Ben M. Cherrington, chief of the Division of Cultural Relations, United States Department of State:

Authoritarian adult education is marked throughout by regimentation demanding obedient conformity to patterns of conduct handed down from authority. Behavior is expected to be predictable, standardized.
. . . Democratic adult education employs the method of self-directing activity, with free choice of subject matter and free choice in determining outcomes. Spontaneity is welcome. Behavior cannot with certainty be predicted and therefore is not standardized. Individual, critical thinking is perhaps the best description of the democratic method and it is here that the gulf is widest between democracy and the authoritarian system.

(*Journal of Adult Education*, XI(3), June 1939,
pp. 244–245)

By Wendell Thomas, author of Democratic Philosophy *and a teacher of adult education teachers in New York City:*

> On the whole, adult education is as different from ordinary schooling as adult life, with its individual and social responsibilities, is different from the protected life of the child. . . . The adult normally differs from the child in having both more individuality and more social purpose.
>
> Adult education, accordingly, makes special allowance for individual contributions from the students, and seeks to organize these contributions into some form of social purpose.
>
> (*Journal of Adult Education, XI*(4), October 1939, pp. 365–366)

By Harold Fields, acting assistant director of Evening Schools, Board of Education, New York City:

> Not only the content of the courses, but the method of teaching also must be changed. Lectures must be replaced by class exercises in which there is a large share of student participation. "Let the class do the work," should be adopted as a motto. There must be ample opportunity for forums, discussions, and debates. Newspapers, circulars, and magazines as well as textbooks should be used for practice in reading. Extracurricular activities should become a recognized part of the educational process. . . . There are some of the elements that must be incorporated in a program of adult education for citizens if it is to be successful.
>
> (*Journal of Adult Education, XII*, January 1940, pp. 44–45)

By 1940, most of the elements required for a comprehensive theory of adult learning had been discovered, but they had not yet been brought together into a unified framework; they remained as isolated insights, concepts, and principles. During the 1940s and 1950s, these elements were clarified, elaborated on, and added to in a veritable explosion of knowledge from the various disciplines in the human sciences. It is interesting to note that during this period there was a gradual shift in emphasis in research away from the highly quantitative, fragmentary, experimental research of the 1930s and 1940s, to more holistic longitudinal case studies with a higher yield of useful knowledge.

CONTRIBUTIONS FROM THE SOCIAL SCIENCES

Clinical psychology

Some of the most important contributions to learning theory have come from the discipline of psychotherapy. After all, psychotherapists are primarily concerned with re-education, and their subjects are primarily adults. (See Table 3.2 for summary.)

Sigmund Freud has influenced psychological thinking as much as any other individual, but he did not formulate a theory of learning as such. His major

Table 3.2 Major contributions of clinical psychologists

Sigmund Freud	Identified influence of subconscious mind on behavior.
Carl Jung	Introduced the notion that human consciousness possesses four functions: sensation, thought, emotion, and intuition.
Erik Erikson	Provided "Eight Ages of Man": Oral–sensory, muscular–anal, locomotion–genital, latency, puberty and adolescence, young adulthood, adulthood, and final stage.
Abraham Maslow	Emphasized the role of safety.
Carl Rogers	Conceptualized a student-centered approach to education based on five "basic hypotheses":

1. We cannot teach another person directly, we can only facilitate his learning.

2. A person learns significantly only those things which he perceives as being involved in the maintenance of, or enhancement of, the structure of self.

3. Experience which, if assimilated would involve a change in the organization of self, tends to be resisted through denial or distortion of symbolization.

4. The structure and organization of self appear to become more rigid under threat and to relax its boundaries when completely free from threat. Experience which is perceived as inconsistent with the self can only be assimilated if the current organization of self is relaxed and expanded to include it.

5. The educational situation that most effectively promotes significant learning is one in which (a) threat to the self of the learner is reduced to a minimum, and (b) differentiated perception of the field is facilitated.

contribution was in identifying the influence of the subconscious mind on behavior. Some of his concepts, such as anxiety, repression fixation, regression, aggression, defense mechanism, projection, and transference (in blocking or motivating learning), were adopted by learning theorists. Freud was close to the behaviorists in his emphasis on the animalistic nature of humans, but he saw the human being as a dynamic animal that grows and develops through the interaction of biological forces, goals, purposes, conscious and unconscious drives, and environmental influences. This is a concept more in keeping with the organismic model.

Carl Jung advanced a more holistic concept of human consciousness. He introduced the notion that it possesses four functions or four ways to extract information from experience to achieve internalized understanding; sensation, thought, emotion, and intuition. His plea for the development and use of all four functions in balance laid the groundwork for the concepts of the balanced personality and the balanced curriculum.

Erik Erikson provided the "Eight Ages of Man," the last three occurring during the adult years, as a framework for understanding the stages of personality development:

1. *Oral–sensory*, in which the basic issue is trust vs. mistrust.
2. *Muscular–anal*, in which the basic issue is autonomy vs. shame.
3. *Locomotion–genital*, in which the basic issue is initiative vs. guilt.
4. *Latency*, in which the basic issue is industry vs. inferiority.
5. *Puberty and adolescence*, in which the basic issue is identity vs. role confusion.
6. *Young adulthood*, in which the basic issue is intimacy vs. isolation.
7. *Adulthood*, in which the basic issue is generativity vs. stagnation.
8. *The final stage*, in which the basic issue is integrity vs. despair.

In fact, the central role of self-concept in human development and learning received increasing reinforcement from the entire field of psychiatry as it moved away from the medical model toward an educational model in its research and practice. The works of Erich Fromm and Karen Horney are particularly telling in this shift.

But it is the clinical psychologists, especially those who identify themselves as humanistic, who have concerned themselves most deeply with problems of learning. The humanistic psychologists speak of themselves as "third-force psychologists." In Goble's (1971) words, "By 1954 when Maslow published his book *Motivation and Personality*, there were two major theories dominant" in the behavioral sciences. They were Freudianism and behaviorism, in which "Freud placed the major motivational emphasis on deep inner drives (and) urges and the behaviorists placed the emphasis on external, environmental influences." But "like Freud and like Darwin before him, the behaviorists saw man as merely another type of animal, with no essential differences from animals and with the same destructive, anti-social tendencies" (pp. 3–8). Third-force psychologists are concerned with the study and development of fully functioning persons (to use Rogers's term) or self-actualizing persons (to use Maslow's term). They are critical of the atomistic approach common among the behaviorists; which is breaking things down into their component parts and studying them separately.

Most behavioral scientists have attempted to isolate independent drives, urges, and instincts and study them separately. Maslow found this to be generally less productive than the holistic approach that holds that the whole is more than the sum of the parts (Goble, 1971, p. 22).

Growth takes place when the next step forward is subjectively more delightful, more joyous, more intrinsically satisfying than the previous gratification with which we have become familiar and even bored; the only way we can ever know that it is right for us is that it feels better subjectively than any alternative. The new experience validates itself rather than by any outside criterion (Maslow, 1972, p. 43).

Maslow (1972, pp. 50–51) placed special emphasis on the role of safety, which the following formulation of the elements in the growth process illustrates:

1. The healthily spontaneous [person], in his spontaneity, from within out, reaches out to the environment in wonder and interest, and expresses whatever skills he has.
2. He does this to the extent that he is not crippled by fear and to the extent that he feels safe enough to dare.
3. In this process, that which gives him the delight-experience is fortuitously encountered, or is offered to him by helpers.
4. He must be safe and self-accepting enough to be able to choose and prefer these delights, instead of being frightened by them.
5. If he can choose these experiences, which are validated by the experience of delight, then he can return to the experience, repeat it, savor it to the point of repletion, satiation, or boredom.
6. At this point, he shows the tendency to go on to richer, more complex experiences and accomplishments in the same sector if he feels safe enough to dare.
7. Such experiences not only mean moving on, but have a feedback effect on the Self, in the feeling of certainty ("This I like; that I don't for sure") of capability, mastery, self-trust, self-esteem.

8. In this never-ending series of choices of which life consists, the choice may generally be schematized as between safety (or, more broadly, defensiveness) and growth; and since only that [person] doesn't need safety who already has it, we may expect the growth choice to be made by the safety-need gratified [individual].

9. In order to be able to choose in accord with his own nature and to develop it, the [individual] must be permitted to retain the subjective experiences of delight and boredom, as the criteria of the correct choice for him. The alternative criterion is making the choice in terms of the wish of another person. The *Self* is lost when this happens. Also this constitutes restricting the choice to safety alone, since the [individual] will give up trust in his own delight criterion out of fear (of losing protection, love, etc.).

10. If the choice is really a free one, and if the [individual] is not crippled, then we may expect him ordinarily to choose progression forward.

11. The evidence indicates that what delights the healthy [person], what tastes good to him, is also, more frequently than not, "best" for him in terms of fair goals as perceivable by the spectator.

12. In this process the environment [parents, teachers, therapists] is important in various ways, even though the ultimate choice must be made by the individual.

   a. It can gratify his basic needs for safety, belongingness, love, and respect, so that he can feel unthreatened, autonomous, interested, and spontaneous and thus dare to choose the unknown.

   b. It can help by making the growth choice positively attractive and less dangerous, and by making regressive choices less attractive and more costly.

13. In this way the psychology of *Being* and the psychology of *Becoming* can be reconciled, and the [person], simply being himself, can yet move forward and grow.

Carl R. Rogers, starting with the viewpoint that "in a general way, therapy is a learning process" (1951, p. 132), developed 19 propositions for a theory of personality and behavior that evolved from the study of adults in therapy (pp. 483–524) and then sought to apply them to education. This process led him to conceptualize *student-centered teaching* as parallel to client-centered therapy (pp. 388–391).

Rogers's student-centered approach to education was based on *five basic hypotheses,* the first of which was: *We cannot teach another person directly; we can only facilitate his learning.* This hypothesis stems from the propositions in Rogers's personality theory that "every individual exists in a continually changing world of experience of which he is the center" and "the organism reacts to the field as it is experienced and perceived." It requires a shift in focus from what the teacher does to what is happening in the student.

His second hypothesis was: *A person learns significantly only those things that he perceives as being involved in the maintenance of, or enhancement of, the structure of self.* This hypothesis underlines the importance of making the learning relevant to the learner, and puts into question the academic tradition of required courses.

Rogers grouped his third and fourth hypotheses together: *Experience that, if assimilated, would involve a change in the organization of self, tends to be resisted through denial or distortion of symbolization, and the structure and organization of self appear to become more rigid under threats and to relax its boundaries when completely free from threat. Experience that is perceived as inconsistent with the self can only be assimilated if the current organization of self is relaxed and expanded to include it.* These hypotheses acknowledge the reality that significant learning is often threatening to an individual, and suggest the importance of providing an acceptant and supportive climate, with heavy reliance on student responsibility.

Rogers's fifth hypothesis extends the third and fourth to educational practice. *The educational situation that most effectively promotes significant learning is one in which (a) threat to the self of the learner is reduced to a minimum, and (b) differentiated perception of the field is facilitated.* He points out that the two parts of this hypothesis are almost synonymous, since differentiated perception is most likely when the self is not being threatened. Rogers defined undifferentiated perception as an individual's "tendency to see experience in absolute and unconditional terms, to anchor his reactions in space and time, to confuse fact and evaluation, to rely on ideas rather than upon reality testing"; in contrast to differentiated perception as the "tendency to see experience in absolute and unconditional terms, to anchor his reactions in space and time, to confuse fact and evaluation, to rely on ideas rather than upon reality testing" (p. 1441).

Rogers sees learning as a completely internal process controlled by the learner and engaging his whole being in interaction with his environment as he perceives it. But he also believes that learning is as natural and required a life process as breathing. His Proposition IV states: *The organism has one basic tendency and striving—to actualize, maintain, and enhance the experiencing organism* (p. 497). This central premise is summarized in the following statement:

Clinically, I find it to be true that though an individual may remain
dependent because he has always been so, or may drift into
dependence without realizing what he is doing, or may temporarily
wish to be dependent because his situation appears desperate. I have
yet to find the individual who, when he examines his situation
deeply, and feels that he perceives it dearly, deliberately choose
dependence, and deliberately chooses to have the integrated
direction of himself undertaken by another. When all the elements
are clearly perceived, the balance seems invariably in the direction
of the painful but ultimately rewarding path of self-actualization and
growth.

(p. 490)

Both Maslow and Rogers acknowledge their affinity with the works of
Gordon Allport (1955, 1960, 1961) in defining growth not as a process of
"being shaped," but as a process of becoming. The essence of their
conception of learning is captured in this brief statement by Rogers
(1961): "I should like to point out one final characteristic of these
individuals as they strive to discover and become themselves. It is that the
individual seems to become more content to be a process rather than a
product" (p. 122).

Developmental psychology

The discipline of developmental psychology has contributed a growing body
of knowledge about changes with age through the lifespan in such
characteristics as physical capabilities, mental abilities, interests, attitudes,
values, creativity, and lifestyles. Pressey and Kuhlen (1957) pioneered in the
collection of research findings on human development and laid the
foundation for a new field of specialization in psychology known as *lifespan
developmental psychology*, which has been built on by such contemporary
scholars as Bischoff (1969) and Goulet and Baltes (1970). Havighurst (1972)
identified the developmental tasks associated with different stages of growth
that give rise to a person's readiness to learn different things at different
times and create "teachable moments." Sheehy (1974) provided a popular
portrayal of the *Predictable Crises of Adult Life* and Knox (1977) provided a
more scholarly summary of research findings on adult development and
learning. (See also Stevens-Long, 1979; Stokes, 1983.) Closely related to this
discipline is *gerontology*, which has produced a large volume of research
findings regarding the aging process in the later years (Birren, 1964;
Botwinick, 1967; Donahue and Tibbitts, 1957; Grabowski and Mason, 1974;
Granick and Patterson, 1971; Gubrium, 1976; Kastenbaum, 1964, 1965;

Neugarten, 1964, 1968; Woodruff and Birren, 1975) and their implications for learning and teaching (Burnside, 1978; Hendrickson, 1973; John, 1987; Long, 1972).

Sociology and social psychology

The disciplines of *sociology* and *social psychology* have contributed a great deal of new knowledge about the behavior of groups and larger social systems, including the forces that facilitate or inhibit learning and change (Argyris, 1964; Bennis, 1966; Bennis et al., 1968; Bennis and Slater, 1968; Etzioni, 1961, 1969; Hare, 1969; Knowles and Knowles, 1972; Lewin, 1951; Lippitt, 1969; Schein and Bennis, 1965; Schlossberg et al., 1989; Zander, 1982) and about environmental influences, such as culture, race, population characteristics, such as population density, on learning.

Philosophy

Philosophical issues have been prominent in the literature of the adult education movement in the United States since its beginning. Eduard Lindeman laid the foundation of this theme in his book *The Meaning of Adult Education*, published in 1926 (see also Gessner, 1956) and it was reinforced by Lyman Bryson in his *Adult Education* in 1936 and *The Next America* in 1952. But many of the articles in the periodicals of the American Association for Adult Education between 1926 and 1948 were also philosophical treatises, with the aims and purposes of adult education as a social movement as the predominant issue. The underlying premise of the argument was that achieving a unified and potent adult education movement required a common goal among all programs in all institutions—one side holding that this goal should be the improvement of individuals, and the other holding that it should be the improvement of society. Two attempts were made in the mid-1950s, under the sponsorship of the Fund for Adult Education of the Ford Foundation, to sway argument in favor of the latter position with the publication of Hartley Grattan's *In Quest of Knowledge* (1955) and John Walker Powell's *Learning Comes of Age* (1956). However, this issue and arguments over other issues continued to embroil the field.

Professional philosopher Kenneth Benne, president of the newly formed Adult Education Association of the USA in 1956, dedicated his efforts to bringing some order to the polemics. One of his first acts as president was to convene a national conference on the topic of "Philosophy of Adult Education," in North Andover, Massachusetts, in which 13 philosophers and adult educators from across the country spent three days addressing these issues:

- What is the purpose of adult education—adult education for what?
- What is the relationship between content and method in instruction?
- Should individual interests and desires prescribe the curricula of adult education, or should the needs of society play a determining role in the creation of educational programs?
- What implications do different theories of knowledge, or of the nature of man and society, have for the planning and operation of adult education programs?

The 1956 conference did not resolve these issues, but it produced three positive results:

- It uncovered some tool concepts that would prove useful in working through the strife of tongues and the maze of special interests and moved the emphasis toward areas of genuine agreement and disagreement.
- It revealed the importance of philosophizing as a necessary and continuing ingredient of all policy formulation and program determination.
- It furnished an example of the pains and tribulations that men from many disciplines and from many special vantage points in adult education encounter as they venture seriously and thoughtfully to seek common ground in their chosen field (Sillars, 1958, p. 5).

Clearly, the conference stimulated continuing discussion of the philosophical issues in adult education, as evidenced by numerous articles in the periodical literature and in at least four major books by authors Benne and Chin (1968); Bergevin (1967); Darkenwald and Merriam (1982); and Elias and Merriam (1980). It probably also influenced the publication of one book on philosophy for adult learners (Buford, 1980) and one book on the use of philosophical approaches to the improvement of practice in continuing education (Apps, 1985).

CONTRIBUTIONS FROM ADULT EDUCATION

Most scholars in the field of adult education itself have addressed the problem of learning by trying to adapt theories about child learning to the *differences in degree* among adults (Bruner, 1959; Kempfer, 1955; Kidd, 1959; Verner and Booth, 1964). For the most part, Howard McClusky followed this line, but began to map out directions for the development of a "differential psychology of the adult potential" in which the concepts of margin (the power available to a person over and beyond that required to handle his or her load), commitment, time perception, critical periods, and self-concept are central.

Cyril O. Houle began a line of investigations in the 1950s at the University of Chicago that has been extended by Allen Tough at the Ontario Institute and for Studies in Education and that has yielded better understanding about the process of adult learning. Their approach was a study through in-depth interviews of a small sample of adults who were identified as continuing learners.

Houle's study of 22 subjects was designed to discover primarily why adults engage in continuing education, but it also helped explain how they learn. Through an involved process of the analysis of the characteristics uncovered in the interviews, he found that his subjects could fit into three different categories. As Houle (1961) points out, "These are not pure types; the best way to represent them pictorially would be by three circles which overlap at their edges. But the central emphasis of each subgroup is clearly discernible" (p. 16). The criterion for classifying the individuals into subgroups was the major conception they held about the purposes and values of continuing education for themselves. The three types outlined by Houle's study are:

1. The *goal-oriented learners* use education for accomplishing fairly clear-cut objectives. These individuals usually did not make any real start on their continuing education until their mid-twenties and after—sometimes much later.

   The continuing education of goal-oriented learners occurs in episodes, each of which begins with the realization of a need or the identification of an interest. There is no even, steady, continuous flow to the learning of such people, though it is an ever-recurring characteristic of their lives. Nor do they restrict their activities to any one institution or method of learning. The need or interest appears and they satisfy it by taking a course, joining a group, reading a book, or going on a trip (Houle, 1961, p. 181).

2. The *activity-oriented* learners take part because they find in the circumstances of the learning a meaning that has no necessary connection, and often no connection at all, with the content or the announced purpose of the activity. These individuals also begin their sustained participation in adult education at the point when their problems or needs become sufficiently pressing.

   All of the activity-oriented people interviewed in this study were course-takers and group-joiners. They might stay within a single institution or they might go to a number of different places, but it was social contact that they sought and their selection of any activity was essentially based on the amount and kinds of human relationships it would yield (Houle, 1961, pp. 23–24).

3. The *learning-oriented* learners seek knowledge for its own sake. Unlike the other types, most learning-oriented adults have been engrossed in learning as long as they can remember. What they do has a continuity, a flow, and a spread that establishes the basic nature of their participation in continuing education. For the most part, they are avid readers and have been since childhood; they join groups and classes and organizations for educational reasons; they select the serious programs on television and radio; they make a production out of travel, being sure to prepare adequately to appreciate what they see; and they choose jobs and make other decisions in life in terms of the potential for growth that they offer (Houle, 1961, pp. 24–25).

Allen Tough's investigation was concerned not only with what and why adults learn, but how they learn and what help they obtain for learning. Tough (1979) found that adult learning is a highly pervasive activity:

> Almost everyone undertakes at least one or two major learning efforts a year, and some individuals undertake as many as 15 or 20. . . . It is common for a man or woman to spend 700 hours a year at learning projects. . . . About 70 percent of all learning projects are planned by the learner himself, who seeks help and subject matter from a variety of acquaintances, experts, and printed resources.
>
> (p. 1)

Tough (1979) found that his subjects organized their learning efforts around "projects . . . defined as a series of related episodes, adding up to at least seven hours. In each episode more than half of the person's total motivation is to gain and retain certain fairly clear knowledge and skill, or to produce some other lasting change in himself" (p. 6).

He found that in some projects the episodes may be related to the desired knowledge and skill. For example, the learner may want to learn more about India. In one episode he or she reads about the people of India; in another episode the learner discusses the current economic and political situation with an Indian graduate student; in a third, he or she watches a television program describing the life of an Indian child. The episodes can also be related by the use to which the knowledge and skill will be put. For instance, one person might engage in a project consisting of a number of learning experiences to improve parenting skills; another project might consist of episodes aimed at obtaining the knowledge and skills necessary for building a boat.

Tough was interested in determining what motivated adults to begin a learning project; and overwhelmingly found that his subjects anticipated several desired outcomes and benefits. Some of the benefits are immediate: satisfying a curiosity, enjoying the content itself, enjoying practicing the skill, delighting in the activity of learning; others are long-run: producing something, imparting knowledge or skill to others, understanding what will happen in some future situation. Clearly, pleasure and self-esteem were critical elements in the motivation of Tough's subjects.

Tough concluded that adult learners proceed through several phases in the process of engaging in a learning project, and speculated that helping them gain increased competence in dealing with each phase might be one of the most effective ways of improving their learning effectiveness.

The first phase is deciding to begin. Tough identified 26 possible steps the learner might take during this phase, including setting an action goal, assessing interests, seeking information regarding certain opportunities, choosing the most appropriate knowledge and skill, establishing a desired level or amount, and estimating the cost and benefits.

The second phase is choosing the planner, which may be the learner, an object (e.g., programmed text, workbook, tape recording), an individual learning consultant (e.g., instructor, counselor, resource person), or a group. Competence in choosing a planner and proactively using the planner in a collaborative rather than dependent manner were found to be crucial in this phase.

Finally, the learner engages in learning episodes sketched out in the planning process. The critical elements here are the variety and richness of the resources, their availability, and the learner's skill in making use of them.

Tough (1979) emerged from his study with this challenging vision regarding future possibilities in adult learning:

> The last 20 years have produced some important new additions to the content of adult learning projects. Through group and individual methods, many adults now set out to increase their self-insight, their awareness and sensitivity with other persons and their interpersonal competence. They learn to "listen to themselves," to free their bodies and their conversations from certain restrictions and tensions, to take a risk, to be open and congruent. Attempting to learn this sort of knowledge and skill seemed incredible to most people 20 years ago. Great changes in our conception of what people can and should set out to learn have been created by T-groups, the human potential movement, humanistic psychology, and transpersonal psychology.

> Perhaps the next 20 years will produce several important
> additions to what we try to learn. In 1990, when people look back to
> our conception of what adults can learn, will they be amused by
> how narrow it is?
>
> (pp. 43–44)

Tough's prediction in the final paragraph has been borne out. Since he made
it, a rising volume of research on adult learning has been reported. Most of
this research builds on, reinforces, and refines the research of Tough's "last
20 years," especially in regard to the developmental stages of the adult years.
Predictions are that the major new discoveries in the next decade will be
related to the physiology and chemistry of learning, with special implications
for the acceleration of learning and the efficiency of information processing.

THE ROOTS OF ANDRAGOGY: AN INTEGRATIVE CONCEPT

Attempts to bring the isolated concepts, insights, and research findings
regarding adult learning together into an integrated framework began as early
as 1949, with the publication of Harry Overstreet's *The Mature Mind*. Other
related publications followed, including *Informal Adult Education* (Knowles,
1950), *An Overview of Adult Education Research* (Bruner, 1959), *How
Adults Learn* (Kidd, 1973), J. R. Gibb's chapter titled "Learning Theory in
Adult Education" in the *Handbook of Adult Education* in the United States in
1960, and *Teaching and Learning in Adult Education* (Miller, 1964).
However, these turned out to be more descriptive listings of concepts and
principles than comprehensive, coherent, and integrated theoretical
frameworks. What was needed was an integrative and differentiating concept.

Such a concept had been evolving in Europe for some time—the concept of
an integrated framework of adult learning for which the label *andragogy* had
been coined to differentiate it from the theory of youth learning called
pedagogy. Dusan Savicevic, a Yugoslavian adult educator, first introduced
the concept and label into the American culture in 1967, and Knowles wrote
the article "Androgogy, Not Pedagogy" in *Adult Leadership* in April 1968.
(Note the misspelling, which was ultimately corrected through
correspondence with the publishers of Merriam–Webster dictionaries.) Since
this label has now become widely adopted in the literature, it may be
worthwhile to trace the history of its use.

A Dutch adult educator, Ger van Enckevort, has made an exhaustive study
of the origins and use of the term *andragogy*. A summary of his findings
follows (van Enckevort, 1971). The term (*andragogik*) was first coined, so

far as he could discover, by a German grammar school teacher, Alexander Kapp, in 1833. Kapp used the word in a description of the educational theory of the Greek philosopher Plato, although Plato never used the term himself. A few years later the better-known German philosopher Johan Friedrich Herbart acknowledged the term by strongly opposing its use. Van Enckevort observes that "the great philosopher had more influence than the simple teacher, and so the word was forgotten and disappeared for nearly a hundred years."

Van Enckevort found the term used again in 1921 by the German social scientist Eugen Rosenstock, who taught at the Academy of Labor in Frankfort. In a report to the Academy in 1921 he expressed the opinion that adult education required special teachers, special methods, and a special philosophy. "It is not enough to translate the insights of education theory [or pedagogy] to the situation of adults . . . the teachers should be professionals who could cooperate with the pupils; only such a teacher can be, in contrast to a *pedagogue*, an *andragogue*." Incidentally, Rosenstock believed that he invented the term until 1962, when he was informed of its earlier use by Kapp and Herbart. Van Enckevort reports that Rosenstock used the term on a number of occasions, and that it was picked up by some of his colleagues, but that it did not receive general recognition.

The Dutch scholar next finds the term used by a Swiss psychiatrist, Heinrich Hanselmann, in a book published in 1951, *Andragogy: Nature, Possibilities and Boundaries of Adult Education*, which dealt with the nonmedical treatment or re-education of adults. Only six years later, in 1957, a German teacher, Franz Poggeler, published a book entitled *Introduction to Andragogy: Basic Issues in Adult Education*. About this time, other Europeans began using the term. In 1956, M. Ogrizovic published a dissertation in Yugoslavia on *penological andragogy*, and in 1959 a book entitled *Problems of Andragogy*. Soon, other leading Yugoslavian adult educators, including Samolovcev, Filipovic, and Savicevic, began speaking and writing about andragogy, and faculties of andragogy offering doctorates in adult education were established at the universities of Zagreb and Belgrade in Yugoslavia and at the universities of Budapest and Debrecen in Hungary.

In the Netherlands, Professor T. T. ten Have began to use the term andragogy in his lectures in 1954. In 1959 he published the outline for a science of andragogy. Since 1966 the University of Amsterdam has had a doctorate for andragogues, and in 1970 a department of pedagogical and andragogical sciences was established in the faculty of social sciences. Current Dutch literature distinguishes between andragogy, andragogics, and andragology. *Andragogy* is any intentional and professionally guided activity that aims at a change in adult persons; *andragogics* is the background of methodological and ideological systems that govern the actual process of andragogy; and *andragology* is the scientific study of both andragogy and andragogics.

Andragogy was increasingly used by adult educators in France (Bertrand Schwartz), England (J. A. Simpson), Venezuela (Felix Adam), and Canada (a Bachelor of Andragogy degree program was established at Concordia University in Montreal in 1973).

Several major expositions of the theory of andragogy and its implications for practice appeared in the United States (e.g., Godbey, 1978; Ingalls and Arceri, 1972; Knowles, 1970, 1973, 1975, 1984b); a number of journal articles have been published reporting on applications of the andragogical framework to human resource development, social work education, religious education, undergraduate and graduate education, management training, and other spheres; and an increasing volume of research on hypotheses derived from andragogical theory are being reported. There is growing evidence, too, that the use of andragogical theory is making a difference in the way programs of adult education are being organized and operated, in the way teachers of adults are being trained, and in the way adults are being helped to learn. There is even evidence that concepts of andragogy are beginning to make an impact on the theory and practice of elementary, secondary, and collegiate education. *Andragogy in Action* (Knowles, 1984b) provides case descriptions of a variety of programs based on the andragogical model.

AN ANDRAGOGICAL THEORY OF ADULT LEARNING

Efforts to formulate a theory that considers what we know from experience and research about the unique characteristics of adult learners have been underway for more than five decades. An early attempt, *Informal Adult Education* (Knowles, 1950), organized ideas around the notion that adults learn best in informal, comfortable, flexible, nonthreatening settings. Then, in the mid-1960s a Yugoslavian adult educator attending a summer workshop at Boston University exposed participants to the term *andragogy*, and it seemed to be a more adequate organizing concept. It meant the art and science of helping adults learn, and was ostensibly the antithesis of the pedagogical model. (In fact, the subtitle of Knowles's 1970 edition of *The Modern Practice of Adult Education* was *Andragogy versus Pedagogy.*) Accordingly, an explanation of the meaning of pedagogy is required to fully elaborate on the meaning of andragogy.

First there was pedagogy

Pedagogy is derived from the Greek words *paid*, meaning "child" (the same stem from which "pediatrics" comes) and *agogus*, meaning "leader of." Thus, pedagogy literally means the art and science of teaching children. The pedagogical model of education is a set of beliefs. As viewed by many traditional teachers, it is an ideology based on assumptions about teaching and learning that evolved between the seventh and twelfth centuries in the monastic and cathedral schools of Europe out of their experience in teaching basic skills to young boys. As secular schools organized in later centuries, and public schools in the nineteenth century, the pedagogical model was the only existing educational model. Thus, the entire educational enterprise of US schools, including higher education, was frozen into this model. Systematic efforts to establish adult education programs in the US, initiated after World War I, also used this model because it was the only model teachers had. As a result, until fairly recently, adults have by and large been taught as if they were children.

The pedagogical model assigns to the teacher full responsibility for making all decisions about what will be learned, how it will be learned, when it will be learned, and if it has been learned. It is teacher-directed education, leaving to the learner only the submissive role of following a teacher's instructions. Thus, it is based on these assumptions about learners:

1. *The need to know*. Learners only need to know that they must learn what the teacher teaches if they want to pass and get promoted; they do not need to know how what they learn will apply to their lives.
2. *The learner's self-concept*. The teacher's concept of the learner is that of a dependent personality; therefore, the learner's self-concept eventually becomes that of a dependent personality.

    As individuals mature, their need and capacity to be self-directing, to use their experience in learning, to identify their own readiness to learn, and to organize their learning around life problems increases steadily from infancy to preadolescence, and then increases rapidly during adolescence (see Bower and Hollister, 1967; Bruner, 1960; Cross, 1981; Erikson, 1950, 1959, 1964; Getzels and Jackson, 1962; Iscoe and Stevenson, 1960; Smith, 1982; White, 1959).

    In Figure 3.1 this rate of natural maturation is represented as a decrease in dependency (as represented by the solid line). Thus, pedagogical assumptions are realistic—and pedagogy is practiced appropriately, due to the high degree of dependency during the first year. Yet, the assumptions become decreasingly appropriate in the second, third, fourth, and subsequent years (as represented by the area with the

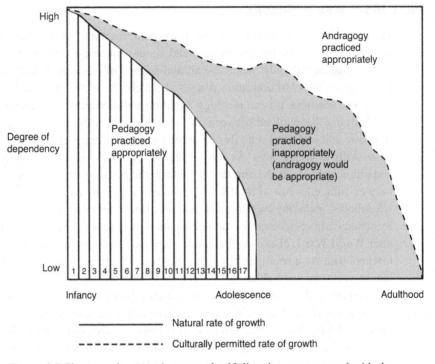

High

Andragogy
practiced
appropriately

Degree of
dependency

Pedagogy
practiced
appropriately

Pedagogy
practiced
inappropriately
(andragogy would
be appropriate)

Low   1 2 3 4 5 6 7 8 9 10 11 12 13 14 15 16 17

Infancy   Adolescence   Adulthood

———————————— Natural rate of growth

– – – – – – – – – –· Culturally permitted rate of growth

Figure 3.1 The natural maturation toward self-direction as compared with the
culturally permitted rate of growth of self-direction

vertical lines). Seemingly, US culture (home, school, religious
institutions, youth agencies, governmental systems) assumes, and
therefore permits, a growth rate that is much slower (as represented by
the broken line). Accordingly, pedagogy is practiced increasingly
inappropriately (as represented by the shaded area between the solid and
broken lines). The problem is that the culture does not nurture the
development of the abilities required for self-direction, while the
increasing need for self-direction continues to develop organically. The
result is a growing gap between the need and the ability to be self-
directing; which can produce tension, resistance, resentment, and often
rebellion in the individual.

3. *The role of experience.* The learner's experience is of little worth as a
resource for learning; the experience that counts is that of the teacher,
the textbook writer, and the audiovisual aids producer. Therefore,
transmittal techniques (e.g., lectures, assigned readings, etc.) are the
backbone of pedagogical methodology.

4. *Readiness to learn.* Learners become ready to learn what the teacher tells
them they must learn if they want to pass and get promoted.

5. *Orientation to learning.* Learners have a subject-centered orientation to learning; they see learning as acquiring subject-matter content. Therefore, learning experiences are organized according to the logic of the subject-matter content.
6. *Motivation.* Learners are motivated to learn by external motivators (e.g., grades, the teacher's approval or disapproval, parental pressures).

And then came andragogy

Before describing the andragogical assumptions about learners and learning, it is helpful to look at what is meant by "adult." There are at least four viable definitions of *adult*. First, the biological definition: biologically, we become adults when we reach the age at which we can reproduce (i.e., in early adolescence). Second, the legal definition: legally, we become adults when we reach the age at which the law says we can vote, get a driver's license, marry without consent, and the like. Third, the social definition: socially, we become adults when we start performing adult roles, such as the role of full-time worker, spouse, parent, voting citizen, and the like. Finally, the psychological definition: psychologically, we become adults when we arrive at a self-concept of being responsible for our own lives, of being self-directing. With regard to learning, it is the psychological definition that is most crucial. But it seems that the process of gaining a self-concept, of self-directedness, starts early in life and grows cumulatively as we biologically mature, start performing adult-like roles, and take increasing responsibility for making our own decisions. So, we become adults by degree as we move through childhood and adolescence, and the rate of increase by degree is probably accelerated if we live in homes, study in schools, and participate in youth organizations that foster our taking increasing responsibilities. But most of us probably do not have full-fledged self-concepts and self-directedness until we leave school or college, get a full-time job, marry, and start a family.

The andragogical model

The *andragogical model* is based on several assumptions that are different from those of the pedagogical model:

1. *The need to know.* Adults need to know why they need to learn something before undertaking to learn it. Tough (1979) found that when adults undertake to learn something on their own, they will invest considerable energy in probing into the benefits they will gain from learning it and the negative consequences of not learning it.

Consequently, one of the new aphorisms in adult education is that the first task of the facilitator of learning is to help the learners become aware of the *need to know*. At the very least, facilitators can make an intellectual case for the value of the learning in improving the effectiveness of the learners' performance or the quality of their lives. Even more potent tools for raising the level of awareness of the need to know are real or simulated experiences in which the learners discover for themselves the gaps between where they are now and where they want to be. Personnel appraisal systems, job rotation, exposure to role models, and diagnostic performance assessments are examples of such tools. Paulo Freire, the great Brazilian adult educator, developed an elaborate process for what he calls the *consciousness-raising* of peasants in developing countries in his *Pedagogy of the Oppressed* (1970).

2. *The learners' self-concept.* Adults have a self-concept of being responsible for their own decisions, for their own lives. Once they have arrived at that self-concept, they develop a deep psychological need to be seen by others and treated by others as being capable of self-direction. They resent and resist situations in which they feel others are imposing their wills on them. This presents a serious problem in adult education: The minute adults walk into an activity labeled "education," "training," or anything synonymous, they hark back to their conditioning in their previous school experience, put on their dunce hats of dependency, fold their arms, sit back, and say "teach me." This assumption of required dependency and the facilitator's subsequent treatment of adult students as children creates a conflict within them between their intellectual model—learner equals dependent—and the deeper, perhaps subconscious, psychological need to be self-directing. And the typical method of dealing with psychological conflict is to try to flee from the situation causing it, which probably accounts in part for the high dropout rate in much voluntary adult education. As adult educators become aware of this problem, they make efforts to create learning experiences in which adults are helped to make the transition from dependent to self-directing learners. *Self-Directed Learning: A Guide for Learners and Teachers* (Knowles, 1975) is a collection of such experiences.

3. *The role of the learners' experiences.* Adults come into an educational activity with both a greater volume and a different quality of experience from that of youths. By virtue of simply having lived longer, they have accumulated more experience than they had as youths. But they have also had a different kind of experience. This difference in quantity and quality of experience has several consequences for adult education.

It assures that in any group of adults there will be a wider range of individual differences than is the case with a group of youths. Any group of adults will be more heterogeneous in terms of background, learning style, motivation, needs, interests, and goals than is true of a group of youths. Hence, greater emphasis in adult education is placed on individualization of teaching and learning strategies.

It also means that for many kinds of learning, the richest resources for learning reside in the adult learners themselves. Hence, the emphasis in adult education is on experiential techniques—techniques that tap into the experience of the learners, such as group discussions, simulation exercises, problem-solving activities, case methods, and laboratory methods instead of transmittal techniques. Also, greater emphasis is placed on peer-helping activities.

But the fact of greater experience also has some potentially negative effects. As we accumulate experience, we tend to develop mental habits, biases, and presuppositions that tend to cause us to close our minds to new ideas, fresh perceptions, and alternative ways of thinking. Accordingly, adult educators try to discover ways to help adults examine their habits and biases and open their minds to new approaches. Sensitivity training, values clarification, meditation, and dogmatism scales are among the techniques that are used to tackle this problem.

There is another, more subtle reason for emphasizing the experience of the learners; it has to do with each learner's self-identity. Young children derive their self-identity largely from external definers—who their parents, brothers, sisters, and extended families are; where they live; and what churches and schools they attend. As they mature, they increasingly define themselves in terms of the experiences they have had. To children, experience is something that happens to them; to adults, experience is who they are. The implication of this fact for adult education is that in any situation in which the participants' experiences are ignored or devalued, adults will perceive this as rejecting not only their experience, but rejecting themselves as persons.

4. *Readiness to learn.* Adults become ready to learn those things they need to know and be able to do in order to cope effectively with their real-life situations. An especially rich source of *readiness to learn* is the developmental tasks associated with moving from one developmental stage to the next. The critical implication of this assumption is the importance of timing learning experiences to coincide with those developmental tasks. For example, a sophomore girl in high school is not ready to learn about infant nutrition or marital relations, but let her get engaged after graduation and she will be very ready.

Bench workers are not ready for a course in supervisory training until they have mastered doing the work they will supervise and have decided that they are ready for more responsibility.

It is not necessary to sit by passively and wait for readiness to develop naturally, however. There are ways to induce readiness through exposure to models of superior performance, career counseling, simulation exercises, and other techniques.

5. *Orientation to learning.* In contrast to children's and youths' subject-centered orientation to learning (at least in school), adults are life-centered (or task-centered or problem-centered) in their orientation to learning. Adults are motivated to learn to the extent that they perceive that learning will help them perform tasks or deal with problems they confront in their life situations. Furthermore, they learn new knowledge, understandings, skills, values, and attitudes most effectively when they are presented in the context of application to real-life situations.

This point is so critical that reinforcement is required.

For many years, educators sought to reduce illiteracy in the USA by teaching courses in reading, writing, and arithmetic; and the record was terribly disappointing. The dropout rate was high, motivation to study was low, and achievement scores were poor. When researchers started to discover what was wrong, they quickly found that the words presented in the standard vocabulary lists in the reading and writing courses were not the words the students used in their life situations and that the mathematical problems presented in their arithmetic courses were not the problems they had to be able to solve when they went to the store, the bank, or the shop. As a result, new curricula organized around life situations and the acquisition of coping skills (e.g., coping with the world of work, of local government and community services, of health, of the family, of consuming) were constructed. Many of the problems encountered in the traditional courses disappeared or were greatly reduced.

A second example is from university extension courses. For many years, it was the practice of universities to offer late afternoon or evening courses for adults that were exactly the same courses taught to teenagers in the day. Then in the 1950s, the evening programs changed. A course titled "Composition I" in the day program became "Writing Better Business Letters" in the evening program; "Composition II" became "Writing for Pleasure and Profit"; and "Composition III" became "Improving Your Professional Communications." And it wasn't just the titles that changed; the way the courses were taught also changed. While students in "Composition I" still memorized rules of grammar, students in "Writing Better Business Letters" immediately began writing business letters and then extracted principles of grammatical writing from an analysis of what they had written.

6. *Motivation.* Adults are responsive to some external motivators (better jobs, promotions, higher salaries, and the like), but the most potent motivators are internal pressures (the desire for increased job satisfaction, self-esteem, quality of life, and the like). Tough (1979) found in his research that all normal adults are motivated to keep growing and developing, but this motivation is frequently blocked by such barriers as negative self-concept as a student, inaccessibility of opportunities or resources, time constraints, and programs that violate principles of adult learning.

It is important to note that the number of assumptions has grown from four to six over the years. Originally, andragogy presented four assumptions (shown here as numbers 2–5; Knowles, 1975, 1978, 1980b). Assumption number 6, motivation to learn, was added in 1984 (Knowles, 1984a), and assumption number 1, the need to know, in more recent years (Knowles, 1989b, 1990).

Putting the pedagogical and andragogical models in perspective

So far, the treatment of these two models may suggest that they are antithetical, that pedagogy is bad and andragogy is good, and that pedagogy is for children and andragogy is for adults. This is pretty much the way the models were presented in the first edition of *The Modern Practice of Adult Education: Andragogy versus Pedagogy* (Knowles, 1970). But during the next decade, a number of teachers in elementary and secondary schools and in colleges reported that they were experimenting with applying the andragogical model, and that children and youths seemed to learn better in many circumstances when some features of the andragogical model were applied. So, in the revised edition of *The Modern Practice of Adult Education* (1980), the subtitle was changed to *From Pedagogy to Andragogy*. Also, a number of trainers and teachers of adults described situations in which they found that the andragogical model did not work.

Therefore, putting the two models into perspective requires making a distinction between an ideology and a system of alternative assumptions. It seems that the pedagogical model has taken on many of the characteristics of *ideology*, which is defined as a systematic body of beliefs that requires loyalty and conformity by its adherents. Consequently, teachers often feel pressure from the educational system to adhere to the pedagogical mode.

For example, the best motivator of performance, teachers are told, is competition for grades; therefore, grades must be on a curve of normal distribution—only so many "A"s are allowed and there must be some failures. The pedagogical ideology is typically sanctified by the shibboleth *academic standards*, which is that giving "A"s violates academic standards.

What this means in practice is that we educators now have the responsibility to check out which assumptions are realistic in a given situation. If a pedagogical assumption is realistic for a particular learner in regard to a particular learning goal, then a pedagogical strategy is appropriate, at least as a starting point. Examples of this occur when learners are indeed dependent, such as when entering into a totally strange content area, when they have in fact had no previous experience with a content area, when they do not understand the relevance of a content area to their life tasks or problems, when they do need to accumulate a given body of subject matter in order to accomplish a required performance, and when they feel no internal need to learn that content. But there is one big difference between how an ideological pedagog and an andragog would go from here. The pedagog, perceiving the pedagogical assumptions to be the only realistic assumptions, will insist that the learners remain dependent on the teacher. On the other hand, the andragog, perceiving that movement toward the andragogical assumptions is a desirable goal, will do everything possible to help the learners take increasing responsibility for their own learning.

Even dyed-in-the-wool pedagogical instructors have reported that their teaching became more effective when they adapted some of the andragogical concepts to the pedagogical model. Some ways they do this are by providing a climate in which the learners feel more respected, trusted, unthreatened, and cared about; by exposing them to the need to know before instructing them; by giving them some responsibility in choosing methods and resources; and by involving them in sharing responsibility for evaluating their learning.

Chapter 4 explores the implications for applying these assumptions to planning and conducting programs of adult education and human resources development.

SUMMARY

Despite the fact that educating adults has been a concern for centuries, there has been relatively little research in the area of adult learning until recently. Only after World War I did a growing body of assumptions about the unique characteristics of adult learners emerge. Within the study of adult learning, there are two streams of inquiry, *scientific* and *artistic*, that are distinguishable. Initiated by Thorndike, the scientific stream uses rigorous investigation to discover new information. In contrast, the artistic stream, launched by Lindeman's *The Meaning of Adult Education*, uses intuition and analysis of experience to discover new information. A pioneering theorist, Lindeman laid the foundation for a systematic theory of adult education and identified key assumptions about adult learners. These include the following concepts. Adults are motivated to learn as they experience needs and interests that learning will satisfy; adults' orientation to learning is life-centered; experience is the richest resource for adults' learning; adults have a deep need to be self-directing; and individual differences among people increase with age.

Subsequent to the 1926 publication of *The Meaning of Adult Education*, interest in the field became evident and other related articles began appearing in the *Journal of Adult Education*. By 1940, most of the elements required for a conceptualization of adult learning had been discovered. However, these fragmented elements were not yet incorporated into an integrated framework. During the 1950s, the social sciences seized on adult learning and more intensive research began. These social science disciplines include clinical psychology, developmental psychology, sociology and social psychology, and philosophy. Noted clinical psychologists such as Freud, Jung, Erikson, Maslow, and Rogers made significant contributions to the study of adult learning. Freud identified the influence of the subconscious on behavior; Jung introduced the idea that human consciousness possesses four functions: sensation, thought, emotion, and intuition; Erikson provided the Eight Ages of Man; Maslow emphasized the importance of safety; and Rogers conceptualized a student-centered approach to education based on five *basic hypotheses*. Developmental psychologists provided knowledge of characteristics associated with age (i.e., physical capabilities, mental abilities, interests, attitudes, values, creativity, and lifestyles), whereas sociology and social psychology provided knowledge about group and social system behavior, including factors that facilitate or inhibit learning.

The label and concept of andragogy greatly enhanced the efforts to create a conceptual framework of adult learning. Although the term was first used in 1833, Americans were not introduced to it until 1967. Since then, a number of journal articles have reported on applications of the andragogical frameworks to social work education, religious education, undergraduate and graduate education, management training, and other spheres; and there is an increasing volume of research on hypotheses derived from the andragogical model.

A distinction between the concepts of pedagogy and andragogy is required to fully grasp the concept of andragogy. The pedagogical model, designed for teaching children, assigns to the teacher full responsibility for all decision making about the learning content, method, timing, and evaluation. Learners play a submissive role in the educational dynamics. In contrast, the andragogical model focuses on the education of adults and is based on the following precepts: adults need to know why they need to learn something; adults maintain the concept of responsibility for their own decisions, their own lives; adults enter the educational activity with a greater volume and more varied experiences than do children; adults have a readiness to learn those things that they need to know in order to cope effectively with real-life situations; adults are life-centered in their orientation to learning; and adults are more responsive to internal motivators than external motivators.

The pedagogical model is an ideological model that excludes the andragogical assumptions. The andragogical model is a system of assumptions that includes the pedagogical assumptions. The andragogical model is not an ideology; it is a system of alternative sets of assumptions, a transactional model that speaks to those characteristics of the learning situation.

REFLECTION QUESTIONS

3.1 From your own experience, think of a situation that clearly illustrates pedagogy and one for andragogy.

3.2 What is the underlying perspective that Carl Rogers brings to the understanding of adult learning?

3.3 Reflect on one of Lindeman's five key assumptions about adult learners.

3.4 How has clinical psychology contributed to andragogy?

3.5 How has adult education contributed to andragogy?

3.6 For each of the six andragogy model assumptions, report on a personal experience that highlights and supports that assumption.

3.7 How does the andragogical model fit with your own learning style?

THE ANDRAGOGICAL PROCESS MODEL FOR LEARNING

4

INTRODUCTION

The andragogical model is a *process* model, in contrast to the *content* models employed by most traditional educators. The difference is this: in traditional education the *instructor* (teacher or trainer or curriculum committee) decides in advance what knowledge or skill needs to be transmitted, arranges this body of content into logical units, selects the most efficient means for transmitting this content (lectures, readings, laboratory exercises, films, tapes, etc.), and then develops a plan for presenting these content units in some sort of sequence. This is a content model (or design). The andragogical *instructor* (teacher, facilitator, consultant, change agent) prepares in advance a set of procedures for involving the learners and other relevant parties in a process involving these elements: (1) preparing the learner; (2) establishing a climate conducive to learning; (3) creating a mechanism for mutual planning; (4) diagnosing the needs for learning; (5) formulating program objectives (which is content) that will satisfy these needs; (6) designing a pattern of learning experiences; (7) conducting these learning experiences with suitable techniques and materials; and (8) evaluating the learning outcomes and rediagnosing learning needs. This is a *process* model. The difference is not that one deals with content and the other does not; the difference is that the content model is concerned with transmitting information and skills, whereas the process model is concerned with providing procedures and resources for helping learners acquire information and skills. A comparison of these two models and their underlying assumptions is presented in Table 4.1 in which the content model is conceived as being pedagogical and the process model as being andragogical.

Table 4.1 Process elements of andragogy

Process elements		
Element	Pedagogical approach	Andragogical approach
1. Preparing learners	Minimal	Provide information
		Prepare for participation
		Help develop realistic expectations
		Begin thinking about content
2. Climate	Authority-oriented	Relaxed, trusting
	Formal	Mutually respectful
	Competitive	Informal, warm
		Collaborative, supportive
		Openness and authenticity
		Humanness
3. Planning	By instructor	Mechanism for mutual planning by learners and facilitator
4. Diagnosis of needs	By instructor	By mutual assessment
5. Setting of objectives	By instructor	By mutual negotiation
6. Designing learning plans	Logic of subject matter	Sequenced by readiness
	Content units	Problem units
7. Learning activities	Transmittal techniques	Experiential techniques (inquiry)
8. Evaluation	By instructor	Mutual re-diagnosis of needs
		Mutual measurement of program

PREPARING THE LEARNER

It was not until 1995 (Knowles, 1995) that it became apparent that the preparation of the learner step needed to be added as a separate step to the process model. Previously the process model had consisted of only seven steps, all of which will be discussed in this chapter. It became apparent that an important aspect of program design flowed from the adult educational models that assumed a high degree of responsibility for learning to be taken by the learner. Especially in the andragogical and learning projects models, the entire systems are built around the concept of self-directed learning. Even so, the adults we work with have by and large not learned to be self-directing inquirers. They have been conditioned to be dependent on teachers to teach them. And so, they often experience a form of culture-shock when first exposed to adult educational programs that require them to participate in the planning.

For this reason, programs for new entrants increasingly include a preparatory learning-how-to-learn activity in the design. This learning-how-to-learn activity may range from an hour to a day in length, depending on the length and intensity of the total program, and consists of the following elements:

1. A brief explanation of the difference between proactive and reactive learning.
2. A short experience in identifying the resources of the participants (who knows what, or who, has had experience doing what) and establishing collaborative, I–Thou (rather than It–It) relationships with one another as human beings. For this exercise, groups of four or five participants are recommended.
3. A mini-project in using the skills of proactive learning, such as reading a book proactively or using a supervisor proactively.

It has been our experience that even a brief experiential encounter with the concepts and skills of self-directed learning helps adults feel more secure in entering into an adult learning program. For a manual on how to help people become self-directed learners, see Knowles (1975), Brookfield (1986), Daloz (1986), Long et al. (1988), Moore and Willis (1989), Robertson (1988), Rountree (1986), and Smith (1988).

ESTABLISHING A CLIMATE CONDUCIVE TO LEARNING

Just as we have witnessed a growing concern for the quality of our environment for living, so there has been increasing concern among educators for the quality of environments for learning. From the ecological psychologists we have begun to obtain valuable information about the effects of the physical properties of environment on learning. The social psychologists have taught us much about the effects of the human environment—especially the quality of interpersonal relations. And from the industrial psychologists have come many useful insights about the effects of the organizational environment—the structure, policies, procedures, and spirit of the institution in which learning takes place.

The physical environment requires provision for animal comforts (temperature, ventilation, easy access to refreshments and rest rooms, comfortable chairs, adequate light, good acoustics, etc.) to avoid blocks to learning. More subtle physical features may make even more of an impact. Ecological psychologists are finding, for example, that color directly influences mood; bright colors tend to induce cheerful, optimistic moods, and dark or dull colors induce the opposite.

If you are saying, "But what can I, a mere educator, do about the color of my institution?" let me share an experience from several years ago. The setting was a class of about 50 students in a large classroom in the basement of a university building. The windows were small and transmitted very little light, so we had to have the yellow ceiling lights on all the time. The walls were painted dusty institutional beige, and two walls were ringed with black chalkboards. During the third meeting of the class, I became conscious of the fact that this class wasn't clicking the way most classes do, and I shared my feeling of discouragement with the students. It took them no time at all to diagnose the problem as being the dolorous environment of our meetings.

One of our learning/teaching teams agreed to experiment with our environment at the next meeting. They went to a discount store and bought brightly colored construction paper and a variety of other materials and objects, the total cost of which was very low. The purchases were turned into collages for the walls, mobiles for the ceiling and simulated flagstones for the floor. What a happier mood characterized our fourth class meeting!

Ecological psychologists also suggest that the size and layout of physical space affects learning quality. In planning the Kellogg Centers for Continuing Education, great emphasis was placed on providing small discussion-group-sized rooms in close proximity to larger general-session-sized rooms. All of them are provided with round, oval, or hexagon-shaped tables to encourage interaction among the learners (Alford, 1968; Knowles, 1980b, pp. 163–165). This concern for environmental facilitation of interaction among the learners is supported by the behaviorists' concept of immediacy of feedback, the importance placed on the learner having an active role is supported by Dewey, and the utilization of the constructive forces in groups is supported by field theorists and humanistic psychologists. (See, especially, Alford, 1968; Bany and Johnson, 1964; Bergevin and McKinley, 1965; Jaques, 1984; Leypoldt, 1967; Mouton and Blake, 1984; Zander, 1982.)

Another aspect of the environment that all theorists agree is crucial to effective learning is the richness and accessibility of resources—both material and human. Provision of a basic learning resource center with computers, books, pamphlets, manuals, reprints, journals, and audiovisual aids and devices is a minimal requirement. In no dimension of education have there been more explosive developments in recent times than in educational technology. (See Clark, 2012; Rossi and Biddle, 1966.)

The important thing is not just that these resources are available, but that learners use them proactively rather than reactively—although mechanistic and organismic theorists would likely disagree on this.

Regarding the human and interpersonal climate, there are useful concepts from many theories. Behaviorists, although not very concerned with psychological climate, would acknowledge that it may reinforce desired behaviors, especially in motivation and transfer or maintenance of learning. An institutional climate in which self-improvement is highly approved (and even better, concretely rewarded) is likely to increase motivation to engage in learning activities. And a climate that approves and rewards new behaviors will encourage the maintenance of these behaviors, especially if it allows frequent practice of these new behaviors. This is why supervisors who learn Theory Y behaviors in an outside human relations laboratory so frequently revert to Theory X behaviors after returning to a Theory X environment.

Cognitive theorists stress the importance of a psychological climate of orderliness, clearly defined goals, careful explanation of expectations and opportunities, openness of the system to inspection and questioning, and honest and objective feedback. The cognitive theorists who emphasize learning by discovery also favor a climate that encourages experimentation (hypothesis testing) and is tolerant of mistakes provided something is learned from them.

Personality theorists, especially those who are clinically oriented, emphasize the importance of a climate in which individual and cultural differences are respected, in which anxiety levels are appropriately controlled (enough to motivate but not so much as to block), in which achievement motivations are encouraged for those who respond to them, and affiliation motivations are encouraged for those who respond to them, and in which feelings are considered to be as relevant to learning as ideas and skills. They prescribe a *mentally healthful* climate. (See, especially, Waetjen and Leeper, 1966.)

Humanistic psychologists suggest that we create psychological climates experienced by the individuals in them as safe, caring, accepting, trusting, respectful, and understanding. The field theorists among them especially emphasize collaboration rather than competitiveness, encouragement of group loyalties, supportive interpersonal relations, and a norm of interactive participation. The andragog would include these characteristics under the heading, "An Atmosphere of Adultness," but would give added emphasis to the conditions of mutuality and informality in the climate.

The notion of an organizational climate involves several sets of ideas. One set has to do with the policy framework undergirding the human resource development (HRD) program. In some organizations, personnel development is relegated to peripheral status in the policy framework (therefore, there is not much reinforcement of motivation to engage in it). But contemporary organization theorists (Argyris, Bennis, Blake, Drucker, Likert, Lippitt, MacGregor, Odiorne, and Schein) assign it a central role in the achievement of organizational goals, and this is the trend among at least the largest organizations. (See Craig and Bittel, 1967, pp. 493–506; Knowles, 1980b, pp. 274–294; Swanson and Holton, 2009.)

Another set of ideas regarding organizational climate has to do with management philosophy. As discussed earlier in this chapter, a Theory X management philosophy provides an organizational climate that almost dictates mechanistic models of training, and a Theory Y philosophy requires an organismic (and probably humanistic) model of HRD.

A third aspect of organizational climate, closely related to the second and possibly a part of it, is the structure of the organization. A number of studies have shown that in hierarchically structured organizations there is less motivation for self-improvement and more blocks to learning (such as high anxiety) than in organizations more functionally structured such as by interlinked work groups or by project task forces. (See Marrow et al., 1968; Katz and Kahn, 1966; Likert, 1961, 1967.) The rapid growth of quality circles in recent years is another manifestation of this trend.

Organizational climate is also affected by financial policies. At the most primary level, the sheer amount of financial resources made available to HRD influences attitudes toward personnel development all the way down the line. When employees see that their organization values HRD highly enough to support it liberally, they are likely to value it—and vice versa. And if in times of austerity it is the first budget to be reduced, it will come to be seen as a peripheral activity. Perhaps the ultimate signal that an organization has a deep commitment to human resources development is when the HRD budget is handled as a capital investment (like a new building), rather than as an operating cost. (See Cascio and Boudreau, 2007; Carnevale, 1983; Eurich, 1985; Swanson, 2001.)

Finally, a most crucial determinant of climate is the reward system. All learning and teaching theorists would jump on the Stimulus–Reward (S–R) theorists' bandwagon in acknowledging that those behaviors (including engaging in education) that are rewarded are likely to be maintained. Accordingly, in those organizations in which participation in the HRD program is given obvious weight in wage and salary increases, promotion, and other job emoluments, the climate will certainly be more conducive to learning than in organizations in which the attitude is that learning should be its own reward.

In the andragogical model presented here, climate setting is probably the most crucial element in the whole process of HRD. If the climate is not really conducive to learning, if it doesn't convey that an organization values human beings as its most valuable asset and their development its most productive investment, then all the other elements in the process are jeopardized. There is not much likelihood of having a first-rate program of educational activities in an environment that is not supportive of education.

This emphasis on organizational climate has critical implications for the role of the human resource developer, for it implies that of the three roles Nadler and Nadler (1970, pp. 174–246) assign to him or her, by far the most critical is the role of consultant, within which the most critical subroles are those of advocate, stimulator, and change agent. If the human resources developer sees himself or herself essentially as a teacher and administrator, managing the logistics of learning experiences for collections of individuals, then he or she will have little influence on the quality of the climate of the organization. Only if the human resource developer defines the client as the total organization, and his or her mission as the improvement of its quality as an environment for the growth and development of people, will he or she be able to affect its climate. This means that the human resource developer must perceive management to be a prime target in his or her student body, and all the line supervisors as part of his or her faculty. In this conceptualization, training is not a staff function; it is a line function. The job of the human resource developer is to help everybody be a better educator.

The theories most relevant to this set of functions are those of systems analysis (Baughart, 1969; Bushnell and Rappaport, 1972; Davis, 1966; Handy and Hussain, 1969; Hare, 1967; Hartley, 1968; Kaufman, 1972; Leibowitz et al., 1986; Optner, 1965; Schuttenberg, 1972); and change theory, consultation, and intervention theory (Arends and Arends, 1977; Argyris, 1962, 1970; Bennis, 1966; Bennis et al., 1968; Blake and Mouton, 1964, 1976; Eiben and Milliren, 1976; Goodlad, 1975; Greiner, 1971; Hornstein et al., 1971; Lippitt, 1969, 1978; London, 1988; Martorana and Kuhns, 1975; Nadler et al., 1986; Swanson and Holton, 2009; Tedeschi, 1972; Tough, 1982; Watson, 1967; Zurcher, 1977).

CREATING A MECHANISM FOR MUTUAL PLANNING

One aspect of educational practice that most sharply differentiates the pedagogical from the andragogical, the mechanistic from the organismic view, and moving from the *teaching* to the *facilitating of learning* perspective includes the role of the learner in planning. Responsibility for planning traditionally has been assigned almost exclusively to an authority figure (teacher, programmer, trainer). But this practice is so glaringly in conflict with the adult's need to be self-directing that it is a cardinal principle of andragogy (and, in fact, all humanistic and adult education theory). A mechanism should be provided for involving all the parties concerned in the educational enterprise in its planning. One of the basic findings of applied behavioral science research is that people tend to feel committed to a decision or activity in direct proportion to their participation in or influence on its planning and decision making. The reverse is even more relevant, which is that people tend to feel uncommitted to any decision or activity they feel is being imposed on them without their having a chance to influence it.

It is for this reason that the potent HRD programs almost always have planning committees (or councils or task forces) for every level of activity: one for organization-wide programs, one for each departmental- or other functional-group program, and one for each learning experience. There are guidelines for selecting and utilizing these planning groups that will help to assure their being helpful and effective rather than the ineffectual nuisances that stereotypic committees so often are. (See Houle, 1960, 1989; Knowles, 1980b, pp. 72–78; Shaw, 1969; Trecker, 1970.)

Merely having mechanisms for mutual planning will not suffice. Members of the planning group must be treated in good faith, with real delegation of responsibility and real influence in decision making, or the process will backfire. Avoid playing the kind of game that Skinner (1968) cites from Rousseau's *Émile*:

> Let [the student] believe that he is always in control though it is always you [the teacher] who really controls. There is no subjugation so perfect as that which keeps the appearance of freedom, for in that way one captures volition itself. The poor baby, knowing nothing, able to do nothing, having learned nothing, is he not at your mercy? Can you not arrange everything in the world which surrounds him? Can you not influence him as you wish? His work, his play, his pleasures, his pains, are not all these in your

hands and without his knowing it? Doubtless he ought to do only
what he wants; but he ought to want to do only what you want
him to do; he ought not to take a step which you have not predicted;
he ought not to open his mouth without your knowing what he
will say.

(p. 260)

DIAGNOSING THE NEEDS FOR LEARNING: CONSTRUCTING A MODEL

Constructing a model of desired behavior, performance, or competencies is
an effective vehicle for determining learning needs. There are three sources
of data for building such a model: the individual, the organization, and the
society.

To the cognitive, humanistic, and adult education (andragogical) theorists,
the individual learner's own perception of what he or she wants to become,
what he or she wants to be able to achieve, and at what level he or she wants
to perform is the starting point in building a model of competencies; to the
behaviorists, such subjective data are irrelevant. Incidentally, andragogs
prefer competencies—requisite abilities or qualities—whereas the
behaviorists prefer behavior—manner of conducting oneself—or
performance. It is not assumed that the learner necessarily starts out
contributing his or her perceptions to the model; he or she may not know the
requisite abilities of a new situation. The human resources developer has
some responsibility for exposing the learner to role models he or she can
observe, or providing information from external sources, so that the learner
can begin to develop a realistic model for him- or herself.

Organizational perceptions of desired performance are obtained through
systems analyses, performance analyses (Mager, 1972; Swanson, 2007),
and analyses of such internal documents as job descriptions, safety reports,
productivity records, supervisors' reports, personnel appraisals, and cost-
effectiveness studies.

Societal perceptions of desired performance or competencies are obtained
from reports by experts in professional and technical journals, research
reports, periodical literature, and books and monographs.

The model that is then used in the diagnostic process is ideally one that
represents an amalgamation of the perceptions of desired competencies from
all these sources, but in case of conflicting perceptions my practice is to
negotiate with the conflicting sources—usually the organization and the

individual. I make no bones about the fact that there are *givens* in every situation, such as minimal organizational requirements, and that we have to accept and live with them.

Commercial firms can be hired to develop competency models. A more common and less expensive method is through the use of task forces composed of representatives of the individuals, the organization, and society. An elaborate model of the competencies for performing the role of human resource developer, developed by a combination of the above strategies, can be obtained from the American Society for Training and Development in Washington, DC.

In our own experience, the excellence of the model is not the most critical factor in the contribution that competency-based education makes to the effectiveness of the learning. The most critical factor is what it does to the mindset of the learner. When learners understand how the acquisition of certain knowledge or skills will add to their ability to perform better in life, they enter into even didactic instructional situations with a clearer sense of purpose and see what they learn as more personal. It converts course-takers and seminar participants into competency developers. (For references on competency-based education, see Bette, 1975; Blank, 1982; Brethower and Smalley, 1998; Grant et al., 1979; Totshen, 1977.)

ASSESSING DISCREPANCIES

A *learning need* can be defined as the discrepancy or gap between the competencies specified in the model and their present level of development by the learners.

According to andragogy, the critical element in the assessment of the gaps is the learners' own perception of the discrepancy between where they are now and where they want and need to be. So the assessment is essentially a self-assessment, with the human resource developer providing the learners with the tools and procedures for obtaining data and making responsible judgments about their level of development of the competencies. Humanistic psychologists would urge the human resource developer to provide a safe, supportive, nonthreatening atmosphere for what could be an ego-deflating experience. Behaviorists have developed a variety of feedback-yielding tools and procedures that can be adapted to the self-assessment process.

Examples of programs that incorporate the most advanced concepts and technologies of model-building and discrepancy-assessment in industry are the ROCOM Intensive Coronary Multimedia Learning System (ROCOM, 1971), the General Electric Corporation Career Development Program (Storey, 1972), and the Westinghouse Electric Company's Executive Forum. In higher education, outstanding examples are Alverno College in Milwaukee, Holland College on Prince Edward Island, the McMaster University Schools of Nursing and Medicine in Hamilton, Ontario, and the University of Georgia School of Social Work. Other sources of information about tools and procedures for diagnosing needs for learning are "Hospital Continuing Education Project" (1970, pp. 7–34); Ingalls and Arceri (1972, pp. 20–34); Knowles (1980b, pp. 82–119, 1984b); and Tough (1979, pp. 64–75).

FORMULATING PROGRAM OBJECTIVES

At this point we hit one of the raging controversies among theorists. Behaviorists insist that objectives are meaningless unless they describe terminal behaviors in very precise, measurable, and observable terms. Gagné (1965), for example, defines an objective as:

> a verbal statement that communicates reliably to any individual (who knows the words of the statement as concepts) the set of circumstances that identifies a class of human performances.

The kind of statement required appears to be one having the following components:

1. A verb denoting observable action (*draw, identify, recognize, compute*, and many others qualify; *know, graph, see*, and others do not).
2. A description of the class of stimuli being responded to (for example, "Given the printed statement ab + ac = a (b + c)").
3. A word or phrase denoting the object used for action by the performer, unless this is implied by the verb (for example, if the verb is "draw," this phrase might be "with a ruling pen"; if it is "state," the word might simply be "orally").
4. A description of the class of correct responses (for example, "a right triangle," or "the sum," or "the name of the rule" (p. 243)).

Mager (1962, p. 53) gives some practical guidelines for defining objectives:

1. A statement of instructional objectives is a collection of words or symbols describing one of your educational intents.

2. An objective will communicate your intent to the degree you have described what the learner will be DOING when demonstrating his achievement and how you will know when he is doing it.
3. To describe terminal behavior (what the learner will be DOING):

   a. Identify and name the overall behavior act.
   b. Define the important conditions under which the behavior is to occur (givens and/or restrictions and limitations).
   c. Define the criterion of acceptable performance.

4. Write a separate statement for each objective; the more statements you have, the better chance you have of making clear your intent.
5. If you give each learner a copy of your objectives, you may not have to do much else.

Moving up the scale from the behaviorists, Taba (1962, pp. 200–205)—with a more cognitive orientation—gives "principles to guide the formulation of objectives":

1. A statement of objectives should describe both the kind of behavior expected and the content or the context to which that behavior applies.
2. Complex objectives need to be stated analytically and specifically enough so that there is no doubt as to the kind of behavior expected, or what the behavior applies to.
3. Objectives should also be so formulated that there are clear distinctions among learning experiences required to attain different behaviors.
4. Objectives are developmental, representing roads to travel rather than terminal points. (Note that at this point Taba departs sharply from the behaviorists.)
5. Objectives should be realistic and should include only what can be translated into curriculum and classroom experience.
   The scope of objectives should be broad enough to encompass all types of outcomes for which the school [program] is responsible.

In elaboration on her last point, Taba (1962, pp. 211–228) develops a classification of objectives by types of behavior:

• Knowledge (facts, ideas, concepts).
• Reflective thinking (interpretation of data, application of facts and principles, logical reasoning).
• Values and attitudes.
• Sensitivities and feelings.
• Skills.

Building on the thinking of Tyler (1950), as did Taba, Houle (1972, pp. 139–312) identifies these attributes of objectives:

- An objective is essentially rational, being an attempt to impose a logical pattern on some of the activities of life.
- An objective is practical.
- Objectives lie at the end of actions designed to lead to them.
- Objectives are usually pluralistic and require the use of judgment to provide a proper balance in their accomplishment.
- Objectives are hierarchical.
- Objectives are discriminative.
- Objectives change during the learning process.

Houle goes on to give guidelines for stating objectives. Educational objectives may be stated in terms of the desired accomplishments of the learner. Educational objectives may also be stated in terms of the principles of action that are likely to achieve desired changes in the learner. The understanding and acceptance of educational objectives will usually be advanced if they are developed cooperatively. An objective should be stated clearly enough to indicate to all rational minds exactly what is intended. In many teaching and learning situations, but particularly in those sponsored by institutions, objectives can be stated not only in terms of the outcomes of education but also in terms of changes in the design components that will presumably make those outcomes better (facilitative objectives) (Houle, 1972, pp. 147–149).

Theorists who see learning as a process of inquiry expressly, and sometimes rather vehemently, reject the idea that there should be preset or prescribed objectives at all.

Educators have long been accustomed to ask at this point in a curricular discussion, "What is the intended outcome?" The question arises from the dogma that curricula should be devised, controlled, and evaluated in the light of *objectives* taken as the leading principles. Consideration of the practical character of curriculum and instruction convinces me that this dogma is unsound; I do not intend or expect one outcome or one cluster of outcomes but any one of several, a plurality. Recognition of the several outcomes stems from consideration not of possible outcomes, but of the materials under treatment: pluralities of theory, their relations to the matter they try in their various ways to subsume, their relations to one another (Schwab, 1971, p. 540).

In his analysis of how adults actually engage in independent learning projects, Tough (1979) found that goals tended to emerge organically as part of the process of inquiry, with various degrees of clarity and preciseness, and to be continuously changing, subdividing, and spawning offspring.

Maslow, with his conception of self-actualization as the ultimate aim of learning, also sees goal formation as a highly dynamic process occurring through the interaction of the learner with his experience.

As might be expected, such a position has certain implications for helping us to understand why conventional education in the United States falls so far short of its goals. We shall stress only one point here—namely that education makes little effort to teach the individual to examine reality directly and freshly. Rather, it gives the person a complete set of prefabricated spectacles with which to look at the world in every aspect (e.g., what to believe, what to like, what to approve of, what to feel guilty about). Rarely is each person's individuality made much of, rarely is he or she encouraged to be bold enough to see reality in his or her own style, or to be iconoclastic or different (Maslow, 1970, p. 223).

Other theorists focus primarily on developing the skills of self-directed inquiry, holding that all other substantive learning objectives flow from the process of accomplishing this one (Allender, 1972, pp. 230–238).

Perhaps these differences in viewpoint on objectives are partly reconcilable by assigning the more terminal-behavior-oriented procedures to training and the more inquiry-process-oriented procedures to education, much the way we handle teaching models in Table 7.3. Even then, according to andragogical theory, the learner is likely to resist unless he or she freely chooses them as being relevant to his or her self-diagnosed needs. Among the most helpful treatments of the process of formulating objectives in adult education are Brookfield (1986, pp. 209–220); "Hospital Continuing Education Project" (1970, pp. 35–46); Houle (1972, pp. 136–150, 200–212); Ingalls and Arceri (1972, pp. 35–42); Knowles (1980b, pp. 120–126), and Merriam et al. (2007).

DESIGNING A PATTERN OF LEARNING EXPERIENCES

To the behaviorists, program design is essentially a matter of arranging contingencies of reinforcement so as to produce and maintain the prescribed behaviors. To cognitive and inquiry theorists, it is a matter of arranging a sequence of problems that flow according to organic stages of development, and providing appropriate resources for the solving of these problems by the learner (Bruner, 1966, pp. 71–112; Suchman, 1972, pp. 147–159). To the third-force psychologists, it is a matter of providing supportive environments (usually relatively unstructured groups) in which the participants (learners and trainers together) can help one another grow in existentially determined directions (Rogers, 1969).

Adult education theorists have tended to build design models into which aspects of all these approaches can be fitted. The three most recent are by Knowles, Tough, and Houle (in order of publication). The andragogical design model involves choosing problem areas that have been identified by the learners through self-diagnostic procedures and selecting appropriate formats (individual, group, and mass activities) for learning, designing units of experiential learning utilizing indicated methods and materials, and arranging them in sequence according to the learners' readiness and aesthetic principles (Ingalls and Arceri, 1972, pp. 43–49; Knowles, 1980b, pp. 127–154).

Tough (1979) employs the concept of a learning project consisting of a series of related episodes as his basic framework for program design. A program would consist of a number of simultaneous individual and group learning projects; each project having been collaboratively planned by learners and selected helpers and carried out at the learners' initiative. The learners could use the whole gamut of human resources (experts, teachers, colleagues, fellow students, people in the community) and material resources (literature, programmed instruction devices and software, audiovisual media) almost without regard for the theoretical orientation underlying them. Even the most didactic teacher or linear teaching machine program will be used proactively rather than reactively by a self-directed learner.

Houle (1972) has developed a fundamental system of educational design, which was described in outline in Chapter 3 and is recapitulated in graphic form in Table 7.4.

OPERATING THE PROGRAM

This element of the program development process is concerned focally with the human resources developer's role as administrator, and learning/teaching theories have very little to say about this role. Nadler and Nadler (1970, pp. 202–231) describe the functions associated with this role, and ideas about how to carry them out andragogically are developed by Ingalls and Arceri (1972, pp. 54–62), Knowles (1980b, pp. 155–197), and Laird et al. (2003).

The centrally crucial factor in program operation seems to be the quality of faculty resources. The current staffing sources for HRD contain numerous subject-matter experts who know how to teach only in the traditional pedagogical fashion. This is the way they were taught or were taught to teach. You can't rely very much on simple selection procedures to provide you with good teachers. Most often you have to train them yourself, through both pre-service and in-service educational programs. The single most critical aspect of the role of program administrator is to function as a developer of human resources development personnel (see Knowles, 1980b, pp. 159–162).

EVALUATING THE PROGRAM

Here is the area of greatest controversy and weakest technology in all of education, especially in adult education and training (Swanson and Holton, 1999). As Hilgard and Bower (1966) point out regarding educational technology in general,

> It has been found enormously difficult to apply laboratory-derived principles of learning to the improvement of efficiency in tasks with clear and relatively simple objectives. We may infer that it will be even more difficult to apply laboratory-derived principles of learning to the improvement of efficient learning in tasks with more complex objectives.
>
> (p. 542)

This observation applies doubly to evaluation, the primary purpose of which is to improve teaching and learning—not, as is so often misunderstood, to justify what we are doing. One implication of Hilgard and Bower's statement is that, difficult as it may be to evaluate training, it is doubly difficult to evaluate education.

Donald Kirkpatrick's (Craig and Bittel, 1976, pp. 18–1 to 18–27; Kirkpatrick, 1971, pp. 88–103) conceptualization of the evaluation process is fairly congruent with andragogical principles. He conceives of evaluation as four levels, all of which are required for an effective assessment of a program.

The first level is reaction evaluation, getting data about how the participants are responding to a program as it takes place—what they like most and least and what positive and negative feelings they have. These data can be obtained through end-of-meeting reaction forms, interviews, or group discussions. It is usually desirable to feed back data from one session at the beginning of the next session, so that indicated program modifications can be negotiated.

The second level is learning evaluation, which involves getting data about the principles, facts, and techniques that were acquired by the participants. This step should include both pretests and posttests, so that specific gains resulting from the learning experiences can be measured. Performance tests are indicated (such as operating a machine, interviewing, speaking, listening, reading, writing, etc.) for skill learning. Either standardized or tailor-made information-recall tests or problem-solving exercises can be used to gauge knowledge. Such devices as attitudinal scales, role-playing or other simulations, or critical-incident cases may yield helpful progress in attitude-learning.

The third level is behavior evaluation, requiring data such as observers' reports about actual changes in what the learner does after the training as compared with what the learner did before. Sources of this kind of data include productivity or time-and-motion studies; observation scales for use by supervisors, colleagues, and subordinates; self-rating scales; diaries; interview schedules; questionnaires; and so on.

The fourth level is results evaluation, data for which are usually contained in the routine records of an organization—including effects on turnover, costs, efficiency, frequency of accidents or grievances, frequency of tardiness or absences, quality control rejections, and the like.

The main difficulty in evaluation, as in research, is in controlling the variables sufficiently to be able to demonstrate that it was the training that was mainly responsible for any changes that occurred. For this reason, Kirkpatrick recommends using control groups whenever possible. More recent works on program evaluation have tended to continue and deepen this emphasis on results (Brinkerhoff, 1987; Harris and Bell, 1986; Rae, 1986; Swanson and Holton, 1999).

All learning and teaching theorists acknowledge the importance of evaluation. Behaviorists maintain that evaluation is built into their very process—when a learner makes an error in a frame of a teaching machine program, it shows up immediately and corrective action is taken; and if a program doesn't produce the prescribed behavior, it is modified until it does. They insist that evaluation is intrinsic to their process—not something that happens at a different time from learning. To some degree, Kirkpatrick's reaction evaluation employs this principle.

Cognitive theorists stress the importance of the learner's ability to retrieve and apply information to new problems as the key to evaluation, which is what learning evaluation is essentially about. Field theorists and humanistic psychologists emphasize the translation of learning into behavior back home or in the field (the humanists, of course, stressing self-actualizing behavior), which is the purpose of behavior evaluation. Organization theorists point out that unless desirable results can be demonstrated, management will withhold support from training—which is the essence of results evaluation.

Here is the addition of a fifth dimension—one that springs directly from the fundamental conception of adult education as continuing education: re-diagnosis of learning needs. If every learning experience is to lead to further learning, as continuing education implies, then every evaluation process should include some provision for helping the learners re-examine their models of desired competencies and reassess the discrepancies between the model and their newly developed levels of competencies. Thus, repetition of the diagnostic phase becomes an integral part of the evaluation phase.

What has been said above describes the state of the art in program evaluation until relatively recently. But starting around 1980, the leading theorists and practitioners in the field of program evaluation began making an almost 180-degree turn in their very way of thinking about evaluation. During the preceding 40 years, there had been a growing emphasis on quantitative methods of evaluation. The norm was set that if evaluation didn't have numbers and statistics attached to it, it wasn't respectable. In the late 1970s, evaluators began having second thoughts about what they were learning from their quantitative evaluations that was making so much difference in what was happening in programs. They began to realize that there is a difference between measurement and evaluation.

Evaluation, they began to report in the literature, requires getting inside the skulls of the participants—and inside the social systems in which they are performing—and finding out what is happening in their way of thinking, feeling, and doing. This is qualitative evaluation. It requires using such methods as participant observation, in-depth interviews, case studies, diaries, and other ways of getting "human" data. By getting the whole picture of "real-life" effects of a program first, they were then able to determine what quantitative data were needed to correlate real outcomes with program operations. So now the state of the art involves both quantitative and qualitative data, but with the qualitative coming first. The results have been astounding. So much more useful information is being obtained from this combination. The best current sources of information about this new development are Cronbach (1980), Guba and Lincoln (1981), and Patton (1980, 1981, 1982). This turn of events becomes even more convincing when one realizes that all of these people made their first reputations as leaders of the quantitative evaluation movement.

CONTRACT LEARNING: A WAY TO PUT IT ALL TOGETHER

Without question, Knowles notes that the single most potent tool in his more than half-century of experience with adult education is contract learning. It has solved more problems than any other invention. It solves the problem of the wide range of backgrounds, education, experience, interests, motivations, and abilities that characterize most adult groups by providing a way for individuals (and subgroups) to tailor-make their own learning plans. It solves the problem of getting the learner to have a sense of ownership of the objectives he or she will pursue. It solves the problem of identifying a wide variety of resources so that different learners can go to different resources for learning the same things. It solves the problem of providing each learner with a visible structure for systemizing his or her learning. Finally, it solves the problem of providing a systematic procedure for involving the learner responsibly in evaluating the learning outcomes.

Learning contracts can be used in all academic courses and in the in-service education programs in educational institutions, industry, and the professions. Learning contracts are being used by a number of continuing professional development programs in medicine, nursing, dentistry, engineering, social work, and the ministry.

THE EVOLVING MEANING OF HUMAN RESOURCE DEVELOPMENT

Human resource development is more than just a higher sounding name for what we have always done. It is not just a synonym for training or in-service education or management development, or even broader workforce development. If it were only this, one or more of the traditional learning theories would serve.

Human resource development can be visualized as something deeper and more comprehensive than any of these concepts. This book will hopefully stimulate others to sharpen the vision. A vision that includes McGregor's and Likert's (and others') conception of all organizations as human enterprises in their most vital essence. It includes the conception of systems theorists and organization development theorists of an organization as a dynamic arrangement of interacting subsystems of people, processes, equipment, materials, and ideas. It includes the conception of modern economic theorists that the input of human capital is an even more critical determinant of organizational output than material capital. It also includes the nuclear physicists' conception of an energy system that is infinitely amplifiable through the releasing of energy rather than the control of energy. It envisions the role of the human resources developer as being more crucial than any other role in determining which organizations will be alive 20 years from now and which will be extinct.

A drastically new role evolving for the human resource developer will emerge as we begin to conceptualize an organization as a system of learning resources. The role of human resource developers then becomes that of manager of these systems—quite a different role from that of the past, as manager of the logistics of operating training programs of courses, workshops, seminars, and other scheduled activities.

In this new role they have to ask a very different set of questions from the questions they have traditionally asked. The first question they have to ask is, "What are all of the resources in our system that are potentially available for the growth and development of people?" A typical organization will come up with a list like this:

1. Scheduled instructional activities.
2. All line supervisors and managers.
3. Materials and media, including packaged programs, computer programs, and the like.
4. Content specialists, who often use their content specialty for work, but not for education.
5. Other individuals with special resources, including retired employees.
6. Community resources, including educational institutions and commercial providers.
7. Professional associations.

The second question the human resource developers will then have to ask is, "How can we make more effective use of these resources for the systematic and continuous development of our people?" And some of the answers they might come up with might look like this:

1. Scheduled instructional activities could be redesigned so as to be more congruent with principles of adult learning. The resource people conducting them could be given special training on how to treat learners as adults.
2. The line supervisors and managers could be exposed to the idea that their role is not just to supervise work, but to develop their people as well. Substantial blocks of time could be built into the supervisory training and management development programs dealing with the

principles of adult learning and the skills of facilitating learning. The human resources developers and their staff could be available to the line officers as consultants in performing their role as facilitators of learning.

3. The materials and media could be selected according to their congruence with the theory of learning appropriate to the situations in which they will be used. They can be made more accessible to all the people in the system than is often the case now.

4. Information about the remaining resources—content specialists, other individuals, community resources, and professional associations—can be collected and put into a data bank, which can serve as a clearinghouse or educational brokering center (see Heifernan et al., 1976).

5. Learning contracts—developed as an integral part of the supervisory process—can provide the means for helping individuals make use of all these resources in a systematic program of continuous self-development.

As systems of learning resources evolve, the human resource developers must increasingly radiate a professional confidence. It will no longer suffice to be a good learning specialist, a good administrator, and a good consultant. They will have to know more than learning specialists, administrators, and consultants know. They will have to know a new theory of human resource development and possess a new set of skills in applying that theory to their systems. How much more rewarding this role will be!

REFLECTION QUESTIONS

4.1 Discuss the implications of dealing with the learning process first and then content, versus dealing with content and then the learning process.

4.2 Report on a personal experience where the climate was not conducive to learning. Cite ideas from the chapter that speak directly to the situation.

4.3 Why is the idea of program/learning objectives so controversial?

4.4 Discuss the purpose and process of program evaluation and then comment on the primary evidence that you think (1) would satisfy the learner, (2) the facilitator, and (3) the agency financially underwriting the program.

4.5 What are your initial understandings of adult learning in the context of human resource development?

ANDRAGOGY IN PRACTICE

EXPANDING THE USEFULNESS OF THE ANDRAGOGICAL MODEL

5

INTRODUCTION TO ANDRAGOGICAL ASSUMPTIONS

Various authors present andragogy in different ways. Accordingly, it has often been difficult to determine precisely the number of core assumptions of andragogy. This difficulty stems from the fact that the number of andragogical principles has grown from four to six over the years as Knowles (1989b) refined his thinking. In addition, many authors continue to use the earliest list as the core citation for andragogical assumptions, despite the list being updated twice since then (Knowles, 1980b). Thus, the addition of assumptions and the discrepancy in the number cited in the literature has led to some confusion.

Table 5.1 shows the six principles (or assumptions) of the current model, as well as the ones cited in Knowles's previous works. As the table indicates, andragogy was originally presented with four assumptions, numbers 2–5 (Knowles, 1980b, 1978, 1975). These first four assumptions are similar to Lindeman's four assumptions about adult education, though there is no evidence that Knowles obtained his early formulation of andragogy directly from Lindeman (Knowles et al., 1998; Stewart, 1987). Assumption number 6, motivation to learn, was added in 1984 (Knowles, 1984a) and assumption number 1, the need to know, was added in more recent years (Knowles, 1990, 1989b, 1987). Today there are six core assumptions or principles of andragogy (Knowles et al., 1998).

AN INDIVIDUAL-TRANSACTIONAL FRAMEWORK

Some of the sharpest criticism of andragogy has come from theorists operating from a critical philosophical perspective. Grace (1996), for example, criticizes andragogy for focusing solely on the individual and not

Table 5.1 Changes in core andragogical principles

	The Adult Learner, 5th ed. (Knowles, Holton and Swanson, 1998)	Adult Learner, 4th ed. (Knowles, 1990)	Making of an Adult Educator (Knowles, 1989b)	Adult Learner, 3rd ed. (Knowles, 1984a)	Andragogy in Action (Knowles, 1984b)	Modern Practice of Adult Education, 2nd ed. (Knowles, 1980b)	Adult Learner, 2nd ed. (Knowles, 1978b)
Need to know	Y	Y	Y	Y	N	N	N
Learner self-concept (self-directed)	Y	Y	Y	Y	Y	Y	Y
Learner's experience	Y	Y	Y	Y	Y	Y	Y
Readiness to learn (life tasks)	Y	Y	Y	Y	Y	Y	Y
Orientation to learning (problem-centered)	Y	Y	Y	Y	Y	Y	Y
Motivation to learn (internal)	Y	Y	Y	N	Y	N	N

operating from a critical social agenda or debating the relationship of adult education to society. Cross (1981) concluded that "whether andragogy can serve as the foundation for a unifying theory of adult education remains to be seen" (p. 227). Others have pushed for adult learning theory to reach beyond the teaching/learning transaction to encompass some elements of desired outcomes. Most prominent of these include perspective transformation (Mezirow, 1991) and a critical paradigm of self-directed learning (Brookfield, 1984b, 1987). Pratt (1993) also criticizes andragogy for not adopting a critical paradigm of adult learning. He concludes: "Clearly andragogy is saturated with the ideals of individualism and entrepreneurial democracy. Societal change may be a by-product of individual change, but it is not the primary goal of andragogy" (p. 21).

Andragogy's critics are correct in saying that andragogy does not explicitly and exclusively embrace outcomes such as social change and critical theory, but they are incorrect in thinking that it should. Knowles (1989b, 1990) and others clearly identify andragogy as being rooted in humanistic and pragmatic philosophy (Darkenwald and Merriam, 1982; Grace, 1996; Merriam and Brockett, 1997). The humanistic perspective, reflected by the influence of Maslow and Rogers, is primarily concerned with the self-actualization of the individual (see Knowles, 1989b). The pragmatic philosophy, reflected in the influence of Dewey and Lindeman, valued knowledge gained from experience rather than from formal authority (Merriam and Brockett, 1997).

It is easy to see from its philosophical roots that andragogy is an individual-transactional model of adult learning (Brookfield, 1986). The philosophies of pragmatism, behaviorism, humanism, and constructivism focus most of their assumptions on two dimensions: the learner and the learning transaction. Critical theory, however, is much more concerned with the outcomes of learning—namely social change (Merriam and Brockett, 1997). Knowles (1990) implicitly acknowledged this tension when he wrote of the philosophical debates between 1926 and 1948 with "one side holding that this goal [for adult education] should be the improvement of individuals, and the other holding that it should be the improvement of society" (p. 44).

Our view is that andragogy was never intended to be a theory of the discipline of adult education as it is defined by the critical theorists, or any of its sub-fields for that matter. Attempts to embed the specific goals and purposes of any sub-field into the andragogical model of adult learning are conceptually and philosophically flawed. Adult learning occurs in many settings for many different reasons. Andragogy is a transactional model of *adult learning* that is designed to transcend specific applications and situations. *Adult education* is one of many fields of application in which adult learning occurs. Others include human resource development, higher education, or any other arena in which adult learning occurs.

Furthermore, adult education is a very diverse discipline with little agreement as to its definition. For example, many definitions of adult education would incorporate human resource development (HRD) as a sub-field, but few definitions of HRD label it as such. Each sub-field engaged in adult learning has its own philosophical foundations regarding the role of education in society and the desired outcomes from educational activities for adults (Darkenwald and Merriam, 1982; Merriam and Brockett, 1997). For example, in HRD critical theory is only one of several theoretical frames. Unfortunately, andragogy has been critiqued mostly through the critical philosophical lens; which is only one sub-field interested in a particular type of adult learning.

The debates about the ends and purposes of adult learning events are important and vital, but they should be separated from debates about models of the adult learning *process*. There are real issues that each arena of adult education must debate and carefully consider. Our point is that those issues are not, and were never intended to be, part of andragogy. For example, scholars might debate whether organizational HRD should be approached from a critical theory or a performance perspective—but that is *not* a debate about andragogy. Debates about ends and purposes are more relevant to *why* adult learning events or programs are conducted (i.e., their desired outcomes) than to *how* the adult learning transaction occurs, which is the more central concern of andragogy. Andragogy may not be a defining theory of *any* sub-field of adult education.

It is important to note that andragogy does not *prohibit* combining it with other theories that speak to goals and purposes. Andragogy can be embedded within many different sets of goals and purposes, each of which may affect the learning process differently. For example, in adult learning for the purpose of social change (critical theory) an andragogical approach to adult learning is possible. Similarly, in adult learning for performance improvement in an organization (performance/human capital theory) an andragogical approach is possible.

To the extent that critical theory has become the predominant paradigm among adult education researchers, prior criticisms of andragogy point to missing elements that keep it from being a defining theory of the *discipline of adult education*, not of *adult learning* (Davenport and Davenport, 1985; Grace, 1996; Hartree, 1984). Merriam and Brockett (1997) note that "adult education can be distinguished from adult learning and indeed it is important to do so when trying to arrive at a comprehensive understanding of adult education" (p. 5). Knowles may have invited this confusion with his statements in early works that andragogy might provide a unifying theory for adult education or for all of education (Knowles, 1973, 1978); a stance that he softened over time (Knowles, 1989b).

A DYNAMIC VIEW OF ANDRAGOGY

That andragogy does not speak to all possible goals and purposes of learning is not a weakness but a strength, because andragogy can then transcend arenas of application. Ironically, by focusing andragogy more narrowly on its original intent, it may become stronger and more versatile, though incomplete as a full description of adult learning in all situations. We recognize that critical theorists would likely disagree because they have a particular world view that emphasizes adult education for a certain purpose. As Podeschi (1987) points out, the debate about andragogy has been confounded by conflicting philosophical views about adult education. It is unfortunate that andragogy has not been as heavily critiqued and researched from other philosophical perspectives; as it may well be more appropriate when viewed through other philosophical lenses.

There are other theories that are similarly neutral to goals and purposes. Consider, for instance, Kurt Lewin's three-stage theory of change (unfreezing–movement–refreezing) that has long stood as one cornerstone of organization development theory. His theory also does not debate the ends or means of any particular type of change, but rather focuses simply on the change process. We could criticize Lewin's theory because it does not embrace the goals of re-engineering or of egalitarian corporate structures, for example; but it would be violating the boundaries of the theory. One critical component of any theory-building effort is to define the boundaries of the theory (Dubin, 1969). Much of the criticism of andragogy has come from attempts to make it become more than it was intended to be, particularly within the adult education scholarly community. Such efforts violated the boundaries of the theory, and resulted in confusion and frustration.

Knowles's (1980b) conception of *adult education* was broad. His definition of an adult educator was "one who has responsibility for helping adults to learn" (p. 26). He also noted that there were at least three meanings of the term *adult education*. One meaning was a broad one to describe the *process* of adult learning. A more technical meaning, he suggested, was of adult education as an *organized set of activities* to accomplish a set of educational objectives. Finally, a third meaning was a combination of the two into a *movement or a field of social practice.* In his examples, he listed everyone in what would today be called adult education, human resource development, community development, higher education, extension, library educators, and more. It seems clear that he intended for andragogy to be applicable to *all* adult learning environments.

INTEGRATED SYSTEM OR FLEXIBLE ASSUMPTIONS?

In early works, andragogy was presented as an integrated set of assumptions. However, through years of experimentation it now seems that the power of andragogy lies in its potential for more flexible application. The assumptions became viewed by some practitioners as a recipe, implying that all adult educators should facilitate the same in all situations (Brookfield, 1986; Feur and Gerber, 1988; Pratt, 1993). There is clear evidence that they were intended to be viewed as flexible assumptions to be altered depending on the situation. For example, Knowles (1979) stated early on:

> My intention, therefore, was to present an alternative set of assumptions to those that had been traditionally made by teachers of children, so that others would have another choice. I saw them as assumptions to be tested (not to be presumed), so that if a pedagogical assumption was the realistic condition in a given situation then pedagogical strategies would be appropriate. For example, if I were now, at age 66, to undertake to learn a body of totally strange content (for example, the higher mathematics of nuclear physics), I would be a totally dependent learner. I would have very little previous experience to build on, I probably would have a low degree of readiness to learn it, and I don't know what developmental task I would be preparing for. The assumptions of pedagogy would be realistic in this situation, and pedagogical strategies would be appropriate.
>
> I would like to make one caveat to this proposition, though: an ideological pedagog would want to keep me dependent on a teacher, whereas a true andragog would want to do everything possible to provide me with whatever foundational content I would need and then encourage me to take increasing initiative in the process of further inquiry.
>
> (pp. 52–53)

Knowles (1984b) reiterated this point in the conclusion to his casebook examining 36 applications of andragogy. He noted that he had spent two decades experimenting with andragogy and had reached certain conclusions. Among them were:

1. The andragogical model is a system of elements that can be adopted or adapted in whole or in part. It is not an ideology that must be applied totally and without modification. In fact, an essential feature of andragogy is flexibility.
2. The appropriate starting point and strategies for applying the andragogical model depend on the situation.

(p. 418)

More recently, Knowles (1989b) stated in his autobiography:

> So I accept (and glory in) the criticism that I am a philosophical eclectic or situationalist who applies his philosophical beliefs differentially to different situations. I see myself as being free from any single ideological dogma, and so I don't fit neatly into any of the categories philosophers often want to box people in.

(p. 112)

He further stated that "what this means in practice is that we educators now have the responsibility to check out which assumptions are realistic in a given situation" (Knowles, 1990, p. 64).

It seems clear that Knowles always knew, and then confirmed through use, that andragogy could be utilized in many different ways and would have to be adapted to fit individual situations. Unfortunately, he never offered a systematic framework of factors that should be considered when determining which assumptions are realistic in order to adapt andragogy to the situation. As a result, the andragogical assumptions about adults have been criticized for appearing to claim to fit all situations or persons (Davenport, 1987; Davenport and Davenport, 1985; Day and Baskett, 1982; Elias, 1979; Hartree, 1984; Tennant, 1986). Although a more careful read of Knowles's work shows he did not believe this; andragogy is none the less open to this criticism because it fails to explicitly account for the differences. Because of the conceptual uncertainty, Merriam and Caffarella (1999) go so far as to say that "andragogy now appears to be situation-specific and not unique to adults" (p. 20).

Several researchers have offered alternative contingency models in an effort to account for the variations in adult learning situations (Grow, 1991; Pratt, 1988; Cross, 1981). Pratt (1988) proposed a useful model of how an adult's life situation not only affects that person's readiness to learn, but also his or her readiness for andragogical-type learning experiences. He recognized that most learning experiences are highly situational, and that a learner may exhibit very different behaviors in different learning situations. For example, it is entirely likely that a learner may be highly confident and self-directed in one realm of learning, but very dependent and unsure in another. This is operationalized by identifying two core dimensions within which adults vary in each learning situation: *direction* and *support*. These and other related responses attack the same problem: the need for a contingency framework that avoids a *one-size-fits-all* approach and offers more clear guidance to adult educators. It seems clear that this is one area in which andragogy has been weakest, though experienced users learned to make modifications as needed. The need here is to clarify andragogy by more explicitly taking into account key factors that affect the application of andragogical principles. Thus, a more complete andragogical model of practice should attune users to key factors that affect its use in practice.

THE ANDRAGOGY IN PRACTICE MODEL

Andragogy in practice, the framework depicted in Figure 5.1, is an enhanced conceptual framework to more systematically apply andragogy across multiple domains of adult learning practice. The three dimensions of Andragogy in practice, shown as rings in the figure, are:

(1) goals and purposes for learning,
(2) individual and situation differences, and
(3) andragogy: core adult learning principles.

This approach conceptually integrates the added learning influences with the core adult learning principles. The three rings of the model interact and offer a three-dimensional process for understanding adult learning situations. The result is a model that recognizes the lack of homogeneity among learners and learning situations, and illustrates that the learning transaction is a multifaceted activity. This approach is entirely consistent with most of the program development literature in adult education that in some manner incorporates contextual analysis as a step in developing programs (e.g., Boone, 1985; Houle, 1972; Knox, 1986). The following sections describe each of the three dimensions in the model.

Goals and purposes for learning

Goals and purposes for learning, the outer ring of the model, are portrayed as developmental outcomes. The goals and purposes of adult learning serve to shape and mold the learning experience. In this model, goals for adult

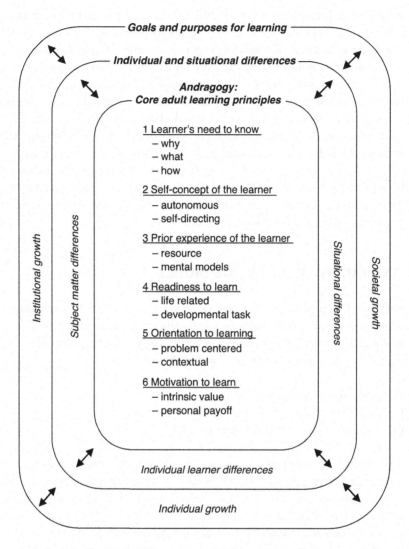

Figure 5.1 Andragogy in practice model
Source: From Knowles et al. (1998)

learning events may fit into three general categories: *individual, institutional,* or *societal* growth. Knowles (1970, 1980b) used these three categories to describe the missions of adult education, although he did not directly link them to the andragogical assumptions. Beder (1989) also used a similar approach to describe the purposes of adult education as facilitating change in society and supporting and maintaining good social order—*societal*;

promoting productivity—*institutional*; and enhancing personal growth—*individual*.

Merriam and Brockett (1997) discuss seven content-purpose typologies (Bryson, 1936; Grattan, 1955; Liveright, 1968; Darkenwald and Merriam, 1982; Apps, 1985; Rachal, 1988; Beder, 1989), using Bryson's (1936) five-part typology (liberal, occupational, relational, remedial, and political) and noted that the purposes for adult learning have changed little since then. Bryson's (1936) typology would also fit into Knowles's three-part typology with *liberal, relational,* and *remedial* fitting into the *individual* category, *occupational* fitting into the institutional category, and *political* fitting into the *societal* category. Thus, Knowles's three-category typology can be seen as also encompassing all of the categories found in other major typologies of purposes for adult learning.

That so many researchers have attempted to create typologies for adult learning outcomes reinforces our position that the goals and purposes are conceptually separate from the core andragogical assumptions. As was seen in the early discussion about criticisms of the andragogical model, it is easy to attempt to imbue the core principles with value-based or philosophical dimensions of the goals and purposes. Andragogy has almost always been found lacking when examined from that perspective. That is, attempts to take a transactional model of adult learning and make it bigger have failed.

We are not suggesting that goals and purposes of the learning program do not affect the learning transaction. To the contrary, it is vitally important that they be analyzed alongside the core principles as they may influence how the core principles fit a given situation. It is unrealistic to think that the core principles of andragogy will always fit the same in learning programs offered for different goals and purposes. However, keeping them conceptually distinct and analyzing them separately allows andragogy to accommodate multiple perspectives on learning outcomes. Also, only then can the interactions between the goals, philosophies, and contexts with the adult learning transaction be fully identified and correctly defined.

It is for that reason that Knowles (1984b, 1990) talked extensively about adapting the use of andragogy to fit the purpose of the learning event. Consider adult literacy programs as an example. Such programs may be conducted by an adult education center to help individuals improve life skills (an individual goal); by a corporation to improve job and organizational performance (an institutional goal); or by some other entity seeking to help a disadvantaged group of citizens improve their socio-economic position (a societal goal). Although the goal differs in each of these situations, the actual learning program and immediate learning outcomes (e.g., improved literacy) may be quite similar or even identical. Therefore, andragogy is equally applicable to each scenario because andragogy focuses on the learning transaction, as opposed to the overall goal for which the program is offered.

However, the goal will also likely affect the learning process. For example, when offered for societal improvement purposes, extra emphasis may be placed on developing self-directedness among the learners. When offered for work-related performance improvement, extra emphasis might be placed on relating the content to work situations. However, these changes are *not* a direct result of applying the andragogical model, but of the context in which andragogy is utilized. This illustrates the strength of andragogy: it is a set of core adult learning principles that can be applied to all adult learning situations.

Individual growth

The traditional view among most scholars and practitioners of adult learning is to think exclusively of individual growth. Representative researchers in this group might include some mentioned earlier, such as Mezirow (1991) and Brookfield (1987, 1984a). Others advocate an individual development approach to workplace adult learning programs (Bierema, 1996; Dirkx, 1996). At first glance, andragogy would appear to best fit with individual development goals because of its focus on the individual learner.

Institutional growth

Adult learning is equally powerful in developing better institutions as well as individuals. Human resource development, for example, embraces organizational performance as one of its core goals, which andragogy does not explicitly embrace either (Brethower and Smalley, 1998; Swanson and Arnold, 1996). From this view of HRD, the ultimate goal of learning activities is to improve the institution sponsoring the learning activity. Thus, control of the goals and purposes is shared between the organization and the individual. The adult learning transaction in an HRD setting still fits nicely within the andragogical framework; although the different goals require adjustments to be made in how the andragogical assumptions are applied.

Societal growth

Societal goals and purposes that can be associated with the learning experience can be illustrated through Freire's work (1970). This Brazilian educator saw the goals and purposes of adult education as societal transformation and contended that education is a consciousness-raising process. From his view, the aim of education is to help participants put knowledge into practice and that the outcome of education is societal transformation. Freire believed in humans' ability to re-create a social world and establish a dynamic society, and that the major aim of education is to help people put knowledge into action. Doing so, according to Freire, would enable people to change the world—to humanize it. Freire is clearly concerned with creating a better world and the development and liberation of people. As such, the goals and purposes within this learning context are oriented to societal as well as individual improvement. Once again, though, the actual adult learning transactions fit within the andragogical framework with a few modifications.

This perspective acknowledges that learning occurs for a variety of reasons, has outcomes beyond the individual level, and is frequently sponsored by or embedded in organizational or societal contexts (Boone, 1985; Brookfield, 1986; Knowles, 1980b). Andragogy is an individual learning framework, but individual learning may occur for the purpose of advancing individual, institutional or societal growth.

Individual and situational differences

Individual and situational differences, the middle ring of the andragogy in practice model, are portrayed as variables. We continue to learn more about the differences that impact adult learning and that act as filters that shape the practice of andragogy. These variables are grouped into the categories of *subject-matter differences, situational differences*, and *individual learner differences*.

Subject-matter differences

Different subject matter may require different learning strategies. For example, individuals may be less likely to learn complex technical subject matter in a self-directed manner. Or, as Knowles stated in the earlier quote, introducing unfamiliar content to a learner will require a different teaching/learning strategy. Simply, not all subject matter can be taught or learned in the same way.

Situational differences

The situational effects category captures any unique factors that could arise in a particular learning situation and incorporates several sets of influences. At the micro-level, different local situations may dictate different teaching/learning strategies. For example, learners in remote locations may be forced to be more self-directed, or perhaps less so. Alternatively, learning in large groups may mean that learning activities are less tailored to particular life circumstances.

At a broader level, this group of factors connects andragogy with the socio-cultural influences now accepted as a core part of each learning situation. This is one area of past criticism that seems particularly appropriate. Jarvis (1987a) sees all adult learning as occurring within a social context through life experiences. In his model, the social context may include social influences prior to the learning event that affect the learning experience, as well as the social milieu within which the actual learning occurs. Thus, situational influences prior to the learning event could include anything from cultural influences to learning history. Similarly, situational influences during learning can be seen as including the full range of social, cultural, and situation-specific factors that may alter the learning transaction.

Individual differences

In the last two decades there has been a surge of interest in linking the adult education literature with psychology to advance understanding of how individual differences affect adult learning, analyzing psychological theories from an adult learning perspective and arguing for psychology as a foundation discipline of adult education (Tennant, 1997). Interestingly, a group of educational psychologists have argued for building a bridge between educational psychology and adult learning, calling for the creation of a new sub-field of adult educational psychology (Smith and Pourchot, 1998).

This may be the area in which our understanding of adult learning has advanced the most since Knowles first introduced andragogy. A number of researchers have expounded on a host of individual differences affecting the learning process (e.g., Dirkx and Prenger, 1997; Kidd, 1978; Merriam and Cafferella, 1999). This increased emphasis on linking adult learning and psychological research is indicative of an increasing focus on how individual differences affect adult learning. From this perspective, there is no reason to expect that all adults behave the same. Rather our understanding of individual differences should help to shape and tailor the andragogical approach to fit the uniqueness of the learners. It is somewhat ironic that

Table 5.2 Individual learner differences

___

Cognitive

1. General mental abilities	Hierarchical abilities (fluid, crystallized, and spatial)
2. Primary mental abilities	Products Operations Content
3. Cognitive controls	Field dependence/independence Field articulation Cognitive tempo Focal attention Category width Cognitive complexity/simplicity Strong vs. weak automatization
4. Cognitive styles: information gathering	Visual/haptic Visualizer/verbalizer Leveling/sharpening
5. Cognitive styles: information organizing	Serialist/holist Conceptual style
6. Learning styles	Hill's cognitive style mapping Kolb's learning styles Dunn and Dunn learning styles Grasha–Reichman learning styles Gregorc learning styles

Personality

7. Personality: attentional and engagement styles	Anxiety Tolerance for unrealistic expectations Ambiguity tolerance Frustration tolerance
8. Personality: expectancy and incentive styles	Locus of control Introversion/extraversion Achievement motivation Risk taking vs. cautiousness

Prior knowledge

9. Prior knowledge	Prior knowledge and achievement Structural knowledge

___

Source: Based on data from Jonassen and Grabowski (1993).

andragogy first emerged as an effort to focus on the uniqueness between adults and other learners. Now, we know that andragogy must be further tailored to fit the uniqueness among adults.

It is beyond the scope of this chapter to delineate all the individual differences that may affect learning. However, one typology of individual differences that affect learning which incorporates three broad categories of individual differences includes: *cognitive* (including cognitive abilities, controls, and styles), *personality*, and *prior knowledge* (Jonassen and Grabowski, 1993). Table 5.2 shows a list of individual differences that may have an impact on learning.

Although there remains much uncertainty in the research, the key point is clear—individuals vary in their approaches, strategies, and preferences during learning activities. Few learning professionals would disagree. At one level, merely being sensitive to those differences should significantly improve learning. Even better, the more that is understood about the exact nature of the differences, the more specific learning theorists can be about the exact nature of adaptations that should be made.

Another area of individual differences in which our understanding is expanding rapidly is adult development. Adult development theories are generally divided into three types: physical changes; cognitive or intellectual development; and personality and lifespan role development (Merriam and Cafferella, 1999; Tennant, 1995). Cognitive development theory's primary contributions are twofold. First, they help to explain some differences in the way adults learn at different points in their lives. Second, they help to explain why the core learning principles are exhibited in different ways at different points in life. Lifespan role development theory's primary contribution is to help explain when adults are most ready for learning, most need learning, and when they may be most motivated to learn.

An understanding of individual differences helps make andragogy more effective in practice. Effective adult learning professionals use their understanding of individual differences to tailor adult learning experiences in several ways. First, they tailor the manner in which they apply the core principles to fit adult learners' cognitive abilities and learning style preferences. Second, they know which of the core principles are most salient to a specific group of learners. For example, if learners do not have strong cognitive controls, they may not initially emphasize self-directed learning. Third, they expand the goals of learning experiences. For example, one goal might be to expand learners' cognitive controls and styles to enhance future learning ability. This flexible approach explains why andragogy is applied in so many different ways (Knowles, 1984b).

APPLYING THE ANDRAGOGY IN PRACTICE FRAMEWORK

The andragogy in practice framework is an expanded conceptualization of andragogy that incorporates domains of factors that will influence the application of core andragogical principles. We turn now to an example to illustrate how to use the andragogy in practice model.

As a general note, we have observed interesting differences in the way people apply the model and therefore explain it. Those familiar with the six core principles of andragogy tend to want to conceptually begin in the middle of the model, working outward to adjust the six principles to fit the individual and situational differences as well as differences due to the goals and purposes. For them, the outer two rings act as *filters* through which the core principles are examined to make adjustments. Those unfamiliar with the six principles seem to prefer to start with the outer ring and work inward. For these individuals, it makes more sense to analyze the goals and purposes first, then the individual and situational differences, and finally to adjust their application of the core principles to fit the full context.

Both perspectives have merit, depending on the application. We suggest a three-part process for analyzing adult learners with the andragogy in practice model:

1. The core principles of andragogy provide a sound foundation for planning adult learning experiences. Without any other information, they reflect a sound approach to effective adult learning.
2. Analysis should be conducted to understand (a) the particular adult learners and their individual characteristics, (b) the characteristics of the subject matter, and (c) the characteristics of the particular situation in which adult learning is being used. Adjustments necessary to the core principles should be anticipated.
3. The goals and purposes for which the adult learning is conducted provide a frame that shapes the learning experience. They should be clearly identified and possible effects on adult learning explicated.

This framework should be used in advance to conduct what we call *andragogical learner analysis*. As part of needs assessment for program development, andragogical learner analysis uses the andragogy in practice model to determine the extent to which andragogical principles fit a particular situation. Figure 5.2 is a worksheet created for this purpose. The six core assumptions are listed in the left-hand column and comprise the rows in the matrix. Each of the two outer rings and the six groups of factors

Andragogical principle	Applies to these learners?	Expected influence of					
		Individual and situational differences			Goals and purposes for learning		
		Subject matter	Individual learner	Situational	Individual	Institutional	Societal
1. Adults need to know why they need to learn something before learning it.							
2. The self-concept of adults is heavily dependent upon a move toward self-direction.							
3. Prior experiences of the learner provide a rich resource for learning.							
4. Adults typically become ready to learn when they experience a need to cope with a life situation or perform a task.							
5. Adults' orientation to learning is life-centered; education is a process of developing increased competency levels to achieve their full potential.							
6. The motivation for adult learners is internal rather than external.							

Figure 5.2 Worksheet for andragogical learner analysis

contained within the andragogy in practice model is shown in the other six columns. Thus, each cell of the matrix represents the potential effect of one of the factors on a core assumption.

The analyst using the andragogical lens should first assess the extent to which the andragogical assumptions fit the learners at that point in time and check the appropriate cells in column 2. Then, he or she must determine the extent to which each of the six groups of factors would impact on each of the six core assumptions. That impact might be to make it more important, less important, not present in the learner group, and so on. Deviations and potential changes should be noted in the appropriate cell of the matrix. When used for this purpose, it is probably best to start with the outer ring and work inward. On the other hand, if one does not have much of an opportunity to analyze the learners in advance, then it may be more appropriate to begin the program with the core principles as a guide, and make adjustments as the other elements of the model become known.

CASE EXAMPLE 1

ADULT BASIC EDUCATION PROGRAM

Case example 1 shows an andragogical learner analysis for a classic adult basic education case. In this case, the learners are disadvantaged citizens who lack the basic literacy skills to obtain well-paying jobs. They have been struggling in life, holding minimum-wage or close to minimum-wage jobs because of low reading and math skills. They are enrolled in a workplace literacy program to improve their literacy skills in the hopes that they can obtain better jobs to improve their individual lives. The goal of the program is clearly an individual life-improvement goal, although the funding agency's goal is a community development goal.

The andragogical learner analysis shows that learners generally fit the core assumptions of the andragogical model (see Figure 5.3). However, assumption number 2, self-directedness of the learners, is the weakest because the learners have a history of not being successful in similar learning situations and often lack confidence as learners when it comes to reading and math. Fortunately, they have exhibited successful learning in other parts of their lives so the potential for self-directedness exists, but they will need strong support initially. Their motivation is high because they are trapped in low-wage jobs and are anxious to improve their lives; but their prior experiences with this type of learning could be a significant barrier to learning if self-directed learning is thrust upon them too quickly.

Andragogical principle	Applies to these learners?	Expected influence of					
		Individual and situational differences			Goals and purposes for learning		
		Subject matter	Individual learner	Situational	Individual	Institutional	Societal
1. Adults need to know why they need to learn something before learning it.	✍	Some basic subject matter may not seem relevant to life needs.			Participants need to build better basic skills to raise their standard of living through better jobs.		The workplace literacy program is designed to help reduce the number of disadvantaged workers in the community.
2. The self-concept of adults is heavily dependent upon a move toward self-direction.	✍	Unfamiliar subject matter.	Low confidence in self-directed learning capability; will need high support initially.				
3. Prior experiences of the learner provide a rich resource for learning.	✍	Prior experience may be a barrier to learning because they have not been successful learners in traditional education.					
4. Adults typically become ready to learn when they experience a need to cope with a life situation or perform a task.	✍			Most participants are struggling with finding jobs that pay a decent wage due to their poor skills.			
5. Adults' orientation to learning is life-centered; education is a process of developing increased competency levels to achieve their full potential.	✍	Will need to make basic subjects highly life relevant.					
6. The motivation for adult learners is internal rather than external.	✍			High motivation to learn due to economic difficulties.			

Figure 5.3 Andragogical learner analysis: case 1

However, they are judged to be highly pragmatic learners; assumption number 5 (life-centered orientation to learning) is expected to be particularly important in that the learning will have to be highly contextualized in work and life situations. Thus, the instructors have chosen not to use traditional General Educational Development (GED)-type learning and instead will use work-based experiential learning techniques to keep motivation high.

CASE EXAMPLE 2

MANAGEMENT DEVELOPMENT PROGRAM

In case example 2, a municipal government has developed a new management development program to help change the organization to a high-performance workplace. It was developed based on best practices and thinking in performance improvement leadership. Figure 5.4 shows the andragogical learner analysis form completed for this scenario.

An analysis of the learners indicates that they generally fit the core assumptions of the andragogical model (check marks in column 2). This presents several problems because the program cannot be conducted in a completely andragogical approach (comments that follow are noted in the appropriate cell in Figure 5.4). First, the ultimate goal of the program is to enhance organizational performance. Thus, learners will not have as much choice about the content of the learning (goal factor). It was determined that considerable effort will have to be devoted to convincing the learners of the *need to know* because some may not perceive they need the program. Second, most of the learners are experienced managers who consider themselves to be reasonably accomplished at their jobs. However, the program will challenge learners' mental models of management development as it presents a new approach to managing in the public sector. Thus, their prior experience could actually be a barrier to learning (individual difference factor). Next, it was determined that few of them had engaged in self-directed learning with regard to management issues. This fact, coupled with the unfamiliarity of the material, will make self-directed learning unlikely, at least in the early stages of the program. Further complicating the design is that there is likely to be little formal payoff, because public sector employment systems do not allow for performance or skill-based pay increases (a situational factor). Much of the *payoff* will be intrinsic, and learners will have to be convinced of the value. Finally, the subject matter itself will shape the learning. The approach

Andragogical principle	Applies to these learners?	Expected influence of					
		Individual and situational differences			Goals and purposes for learning		
		Subject matter	Individual learner	Situational	Individual	Institutional	Societal
1. Adults need to know why they need to learn something before learning it.	✎					Learners may not perceive they need program so must work harder here.	
2. The self-concept of adults is heavily dependent upon a move toward self-direction.	✎			Few have engaged in self-directed learning on management issues.			
3. Prior experiences of the learner provide a rich resource for learning.	✎	Prior experiences may be a barrier to learning because new program is very different.					
4. Adults typically become ready to learn when they experience a need to cope with a life situation or perform a task.	✎	Will have to convince learners of the value of the new learning.				Need for program is not immediately apparent in their everyday jobs.	
5. Adults' orientation to learning is life-centered; education is a process of developing increased competency levels to achieve their full potential.	✎	New material may be complex and unfamiliar; learners may feel threatened.					
6. The motivation for adult learners is internal rather than external.	✎			No formal rewards in public sector for participating so will have to depend on internal motive.			

Figure 5.4 Andragogical learner analysis: case 2

being taught relies on a complex integration of theories and would be unfamiliar to these managers. Thus, some portions of the program may be more didactic than others (subject-matter factor).

This example illustrates how andragogy becomes more powerful by explicitly accommodating contingencies present in most adult learning situations. It is difficult to explicate the precise mechanisms by which the factors in the outer ring will influence application of the core assumptions, due to the complex ways in which they interact. But andragogical learner analysis based on the andragogy in practice framework provides practitioners with a structured framework within which to consider key ways in which andragogy will have to be adapted.

SUMMARY

This chapter provides a clarified conceptualization of the andragogical model of adult learning that more closely parallels the way andragogy is applied in practice. We believe it is closer to the original intent. The *andragogy in practice* model expands andragogy's utility by (1) conceptually separating the goals and purposes of learning from the core andragogical principles of the learning transaction so that the interactions and adaptations can be more clearly defined; and (2) explicitly accounting for individual, situational, and subject-matter differences in the learning situation.

This is not an attempt to reignite previous debates about andragogy or to suggest that andragogy should be the single defining model of adult learning. Rather, we tend to agree with Merriam and Cafferella (1999), who said: "We see andragogy as an enduring model for understanding certain aspects of adult learning. It does not give us the total picture, nor is it a panacea for fixing adult learning practices. Rather, it constitutes one piece of the rich mosaic of adult learning" (p. 278). Knowles's original work is entirely consistent with this expanded view. To the extent that andragogy is the right model of adult learning in a given situation, the andragogy in practice framework should improve its application.

As some critics have pointed out, andragogy has not been well tested empirically (Grace, 1996; Pratt, 1993). However, the reality is that none of the prominent theories or models of adult learning have been well tested empirically (Caffarella, 1993; Clark, 1993; Hiemstra, 1993; Merriam and Caffarella, 1999). All, including andragogy, are in need of more research. Knowles (1989b) himself acknowledged in his autobiography that he no longer viewed andragogy as a complete theory: "I prefer to think of it as a model of assumptions about adult learning or a conceptual framework that serves as a basis for emerging theory" (p. 112).

It is important that andragogy be evaluated from multiple perspectives. However, such research should not ask questions about andragogy that are outside its intended transactional frame. Further research is needed to more explicitly define how the andragogical principles will be affected as different factors change. We see this as a further attempt to clarify how andragogy can be a more realistic, and therefore useful, approach to adult learning.

REFLECTION QUESTIONS

5.1 Discuss the ideas of adult learning and adult education and the implication of the differences.

5.2 Do you see andragogy's focus on the learning transaction versus the goals and content of adult learning as a strength or a weakness? Discuss your position.

5.3 Discuss the utility of the andragogy in practice figure from a practitioner perspective.

5.4 In defending this extension of andragogy into practice, what would be your main supporting arguments?

5.5 Discuss the case example 1 by simply changing two of the specific influences (two of the cells) that could radically impact on the learning approach to be taken.

5.6 Discuss the case example 2 by simply changing two of the specific influences (two of the cells) that could radically impact on the learning approach to be taken.

PART 2

THE BACKDROP OF LEARNING AND TEACHING THEORIES

THEORIES OF
LEARNING

6

INTRODUCTION

Traditionally, we have known more about how animals learn than about how children learn; and we know much more about how children learn than about how adults learn. Perhaps this is because the study of learning was taken over early by experimental psychologists whose standards require the control of variables. And it is obvious that the conditions under which animals learn are more controllable than those under which children learn; and the conditions under which children learn are much more controllable than those under which adults learn. As a result, many of the "scientific" theories of learning have been derived from the study of learning by animals and children.

PROPOSERS AND INTERPRETERS

In general, there are two types of literature about learning theory: that produced by proposers of theories (who tend to be single-minded), and that produced by interpreters of theories (who tend to be reconciliatory). Admittedly, the distinction between proposers and interpreters is not absolute. For instance, some theorists, such as Pressey, Estes, Lorge, Gagné, Hilgard, and Huhlen, have made contributions of both sorts.

Table 6.1 presents a historic list of the major early proposers and interpreters in the literature of learning theory. To keep the list reasonably short, we have defined "major" as those who have made the greatest impact on the thinking of others. Those making contributions of both sorts have been placed in the column representing their major work. To provide a sense of historical development, the theorists are listed more or less in the order of appearance in the evolving body of literature.

Table 6.1 Propounders and interpreters of learning theory

Propounders	Interpreters
Ebbinghaus (1885)	
Thorndike (1898)	
Angell (1896)	
Dewey (1896)	
Pavlov (1902)	
Woodworth (1906)	
Watson (1907)	
Judd (1908)	
Freud (1911)	
Kohler (1917)	
Tolman (1917)	Swanson (1996)
Wertheimer (1923)	
Koffka (1924)	Kilpatrick (1925)
Pressey (1926)	
Guthrie (1930)	Rugg (1928)
Skinner (1931)	Hilgard (1931)
Hall (1932)	
McGeoch (1932)	
Lewin (1933)	
Piaget (1935)	
Miller (1935)	
Spence (1936)	
Mowrer (1938)	
Katona (1940)	Bode (1940)
Maslow (1941)	Melton (1941)
Festinger (1942)	Cronbach (1943)
Rogers (1942)	Brunner (1943)
Estes (1944)	Lorge (1944)
Krech (1948)	
McClelland (1948)	
Sheffield (1949)	
Underwood (1949)	
Dollard (1950)	Schaie (1953)

Table 6.1 continued

Propounders	Interpreters
Tyler (1950)	Garry (1953)
	Koch (1954)
	McKeachie (1954)
	Birren (1954)
Bloom (1956)	Getzels (1956)
Bruner (1956)	Bugelski (1956)
Erikson (1959)	Kuhlen (1957)
Crowder (1959)	Kidd (1959)
Lumsdaine (1959)	Botwinick (1960)
Combs and Snygg (1959)	Miller (1960)
Ausubel (1960)	Glaser (1962)
Glaser (1962)	Flavell (1963)
Gagné (1963)	
	Hill (1963)
	Gage (1963)
	McDonald (1964)
Jourard (1964)	Goldstein (1965)
Suchman (1964)	Reese and Overton (1970)
Crutchfield (1969)	Goble (1971)
Freire (1970)	
Knowles (1970)	Holton (1998)
Tough (1971)	
Houle (1972)	
Dave (1973)	
Loevinger (1976)	
Cross (1976)	
Botwinick (1977)	Howe (1977)
Gross (1977)	Knox (1977)
Srinivasan (1977)	
Cropley (1980)	Chickering (1981)
Mezirow (1981)	Darkenwald (1982)
Smith (1982)	Merriam (1982)
Wlodkowski (1985)	Brookfield (1986)
Daloz (1986)	

The proliferation of proposers has presented a major challenge to the interpreters in their quest to bring some sort of order to learning theories. Researchers have exerted considerable effort in their attempts to structure the knowledge. However, no single, unified classification emerged from their early efforts. For instance, Hilgard and Bower identify 11 categories of theories, McDonald identifies 6, and Gage names 3. Hilgard and Bower's (1966) 11 categories are:

- Connectionism (Thorndike)
- Classical conditioning (Pavlov)
- Contiguous conditioning (Guthrie)
- Operant conditioning (Skinner)
- Systematic behavior theory (Hull)
- Purposive behaviorism (Tolman)
- Gestalt theory (Koffka and Kahler)
- Psychodynamics (Freud)
- Functionalism
- Mathematical learning theory
- Information processing models.

McDonald (1964, pp. 1–26) breaks the theories down into six categories in his analysis:

- Recapitulation (Hull)
- Connectionism (Thorndike)
- Pragmatism (Dewey)
- Gestalt and field theory (Ogden, Hartman, Lewin)
- Dynamic psychology (Freud)
- Functionalism (Judd).

Gage (1972, p. 19) identifies three families of learning theories: (1) conditioning; (2) modeling; and (3) cognitive. Kingsley and Garry (1957, p. 83) provide two sets: (1) association or stimulus–response (Thorndike, Guthrie, and Hull) and (2) field theories (Lewin, Tolman, and the Gestalt psychologists). Taba (1962, p. 80) agrees with the two-family set, but uses different labels: (1) associationist or behaviorist theories; and (2) organismic, gestalt, and field theories.

These exhibits profile some of the debate in arranging the disparate categories of theories into a definitive pattern.

Learning theories primarily fall into two major families: behaviorist/connectionist theories and cognitive/gestalt theories, but not all theories fit clearly into these two families. The behaviorist theories include such diverse theories as those of Thorndike, Pavlov, Guthrie, Skinner, and Hull. The cognitive theories include at least those of Tolman and the classical gestalt psychologists. The theories of functionalism, psychodynamics, and the probabilistic theories of the model builders do not completely and clearly fit. The distinctions between the two families of theories are not based only on differences within learning theories; there are other specific issues upon which theories within one family may differ (Hilgard and Bower, 1966, p. 8).

Obviously, the interpreters continue to struggle in organizing the field of learning theories in a really fundamental way. In 1970, two developmental psychologists, Hayne W. Reese and Willis F. Overton, presented a way to conceptualize the theories in terms of broader models: the mechanistic or elemental model and the organismic or holistic model.

CONCEPTS OF ELEMENTS AND WHOLES

"Any theory presupposes a more general model according to which the theoretical concepts are formulated" (Reese and Overton, 1970, p. 117). The most general models are the world views that constitute basic models of the essential characteristics of humankind and ultimately the nature of learning.

Two systems that have been pervasive in both the physical and the social sciences are the *elemental* world view (the basic metaphor of which is the machine) and the *holistic* world view (the basic metaphor of which is the organism—the living, organized system presented to experience in multiple forms). Please refer to Table 6.2 for further clarification.

The elemental model represents the universe as a system composed of discrete pieces. These pieces—elementary particles in motion—and their relations form the basic reality to which all other more complex phenomena are ultimately reducible. When forces are applied in the operation of the system, a chain-like sequence of events results. Since these forces are the

Table 6.2 World views or metaphysical systems

Elemental model	*Holistic model*
Represents the universe as a machine composed of discrete pieces operating in a spatio-temporal field: reactive and adaptive model of man.	Represents the world as a unitary, interactive, developing organism: active and adaptive model of man.

only efficient or immediate causes of the events in principle, complete prediction is possible, and susceptible to quantification (Reese and Overton, 1970, p. 131).

The holistic model represents the universe as a unitary, interactive, developing organism. It perceives the essence of substance to be activity, rather than the elementary particle. From such a point of view, one element can never be like another. As a consequence, it is the diversity that constitutes the unity (Reese and Overton, 1970, p. 133).

The whole is therefore organic rather than mechanical in nature. "The nature of the whole, rather than being the sum of its parts, is presupposed by the parts and the whole constitutes the condition of the meaning and existence of the parts" (Reese and Overton, 1970, p. 133). Thus, the possibility of a predictive and quantifiable universe is precluded. When applied to the sphere of epistemology and psychology, this world view results in an inherently and spontaneously active organism model of humans. It sees people as an active organism rather than a reactive organism, as a source of acts rather than as a collection of acts initiated by external forces. It also represents individuals as an organized entity, a configuration of parts which gain their meaning, their function, from the whole in which they are imbedded. From this point of view, the concepts of psychological structure and function, or means and ends, become central rather than derived. Inquiry is directed toward the discovery of principles of organization, toward the explanation of the nature and relation of parts and wholes, structures and functions, rather than toward the derivation of these from elementary processes.

The individual who accepts this model will tend to emphasize the significance of processes over products and qualitative change over quantitative change. In addition, he/she will tend to emphasize the significance of the role of experience in facilitating or inhibiting the course of development, rather than the effect of training as the source of development (Reese and Overton, 1970, pp. 133–134).

With this and the preceding set of concepts as a frame of reference, what follows is a brief examination of the theories about learning derived from the study of learning in animals and children.

Theories based on an elemental model

While John B. Watson (1878–1958) is considered the father of behaviorism, Edward L. Thorndike (1874–1949) conducted the first systematic investigation in the US of the phenomenon we call learning. It was a study of learning in animals, which was first reported in his *Animal Intelligence* in 1898.

Thorndike perceived inexperienced learners to be empty organisms who more or less responded to stimuli randomly and automatically. A specific response is connected to a specific stimulus when it is rewarded. In this situation, the stimulus, S, is entirely under the control of the experimenter (or teacher), and in large measure so is the response, R; for all the experimenter has to do to connect the particular R to a particular S is to reward the R when the organism happens to make it. This association between sense impressions and impulses to action came to be known as a bond or a connection. Thus, Thorndike's learning theory has sometimes been called bond psychology or connectionism, and was the original stimulus–response (or S–R) psychology of learning.

Thorndike developed three laws that he believed governed the learning of animals and human beings:

1.   The law of readiness (the circumstances under which a learner tends to be satisfied or annoyed, to welcome or to reject).
2.   The law of exercise (the strengthening of connections with practice).
3.   The law of effect (the strengthening or weakening of a connection as a result of its consequences).

In the course of his long and productive life, and with help from many collaborators, both friendly and critical, Thorndike's learning theory became greatly refined and elaborated. It provided the foundation of the behaviorist theories of learning.

While Thorndike conducted his work on connections in the US, the Russian physiologist Ivan Pavlov (1849–1936) conducted his experiments which resulted in the concept of conditioned reflexes. Hilgard and Bower (1966) describe his classical experiment:

> When meat powder is placed in a dog's mouth, salivation takes place; the food is the unconditioned stimulus, and salivation is the unconditioned reflex. Then some arbitrary stimulus, such as a light, is combined with the presentation of the food. Eventually, after repetition and if time relationships are right, the light will evoke salivation independent of the food; the light is the conditioned stimulus and the response to it is the conditioned reflex.
>
> (p. 48)

Pavlov's work resulted in a system that has been termed classical conditioning. This is to distinguish it from later developments in instrumental conditioning and operant conditioning. In his learning theory, he developed several concepts and accompanying techniques that have since been incorporated into the behaviorist thinking. These concepts are reinforcement, extinction, generalization, and differentiation. In reinforcement, a conditioned reflex becomes fixed by providing the conditioned stimulus and following it repeatedly with the unconditioned stimulus and response at appropriate time intervals. Extinction occurs when reinforcement is discontinued and the conditioned stimulus is presented alone, unaccompanied by the unconditioned stimulus. The conditioned response gradually diminishes and disappears. It becomes "extinct." In generalization, a conditioned reflex evoked to one stimulus can also be elicited by other stimuli, not necessarily similar to the first. A fourth basic concept Pavlov developed was differentiation. In differentiation, the initial generalization is overcome by the method of contrasts in which one of a pair of stimuli is regularly reinforced and the other is not; in the end, the conditioned reflex occurs only to the positive (reinforced) stimulus and not to the negative (non-reinforced) stimulus.

The behaviorists have a common conviction that a science of psychology must be based on a study of that which is overtly observable: physical stimuli, the muscular movements and glandular secretions which they arouse, and the environmental products that ensue. The behaviorists have differed among themselves as to what may be inferred in addition to what is measured, but they all exclude self-observation (Hilgard and Bower, 1966, p. 75).

Watson placed emphasis on kinesthetic stimuli as the integrators of animal learning; and, applying this concept to human beings, conjectured that thought was merely implicit speech—that sensitive-enough instruments would detect tongue movements or other movements accompanying thinking.

Edward R. Guthrie (1886–1959) built on the works of Thorndike, Pavlov, and Watson; and added the principle of contiguity of cue and response. He stated his only law of learning, "from which all else about learning is made comprehensible," as follows: "A combination of stimuli which has accompanied a movement will on its recurrence tend to be followed by that movement" (Hilgard and Bower, 1966, p. 77). In his later work, Guthrie placed increasing emphasis on the part played by the learner in selecting the physical stimuli to which it would respond; hence, the attention or scanning behavior that goes on before association takes place became important.

Guthrie's learning theory was further clarified and formalized by his students, Voeks and Sheffield; but the next major advance in behaviorist psychology was the result of the work of B. F. Skinner and his associates. It is from their work that the educational technology of programmed instruction and teaching machines so popular in the 1960s were derived. Skinner's ideas are summarized in Chapter 3.

Another development in behaviorist psychology occurring during the middle decades of the twentieth century was the construction of Clark L. Hull's systematic behavior theory, and its elaboration by Miller, Mowrer, Spence, and others. Hull's contribution is a conceptual descendant of Thorndike's theory. He adopted reinforcement as an essential characteristic of learning. Hull constructed an elaborate mathematico-deductive theory revolving around the central notion that there are intervening variables in the organism that influence what response will occur following the onset of a stimulus. He developed 16 postulates regarding the nature and operation of these variables, and stated them in such precise terms that they were readily subjected to quantitative testing. Hilgard and Bower's (1966) assessment of the effect of Hull's work follows:

> It must be acknowledged that Hull's system, for its time, was the best there was—not necessarily the one nearest to psychological reality, not necessarily the one whose generalizations were the most likely to endure—but the one worked out in the greatest detail, with the most conscientious effort to be quantitative throughout and at all points closely in touch with empirical tests. . . . Its primary contribution may turn out to lie not in its substance at all, but rather in the ideal it set for a genuinely systematic and quantitative psychological system far different from the schools which so long plagued psychology.
>
> (p. 187)

Undoubtedly, Hull's work also stimulated the rash of mathematical models of learning that were developed after 1950 by Estes, Burke, Bush, Mosteller, and others. It should be pointed out that these are not themselves learning theories, but mathematical representations of substantive theories.

Theories based on a holistic model

John Dewey, in 1896, launched the first direct protest against the elemental model of the associationists. Although his work falls into the category of educational philosophy rather than learning theory, his emphasis on the role of interest and effort and on the child's motivation to solve his or her own problems became the starting point for a line of theorizing that has been given the label functionalism. Translated into schoolroom practices, functionalism provided the conceptual basis for progressive education, which as Hilgard and Bower (1966) state, "at its best was an embodiment of the ideal of growth toward independence and self-control through interaction with an environment suited to the child's developmental level" (p. 299).

The spirit of experimentalism fostered by functionalism is reflected in the work of such learning theorists as Woodworth, Carr, McGeogh, Melton, Robinson, and Underwood. The essence of functionalism is summarized by Hilgard and Bower (1966, pp. 302–304):

1. The functionalist is tolerant but critical.
2. The functionalist prefers continuities over discontinuities or typologies.
3. The functionalist is an experimentalist.
4. The functionalist is biased toward associationism and environmentalism.

The most complete break with behaviorism occurred at the end of the first quarter of the twentieth century with the importation of the notion of insight learning in the gestalt theories of the Germans Wertheimer, Koffka, and Kohler. These theorists took issue with the proposition that all learning consisted of the simple connection of responses to stimuli; insisting that experience is always structured, that we react not just to a mass of separate details, but to a complex pattern of stimuli. We also need to perceive stimuli in organized wholes, not in disconnected parts. The learner tends to organize his or her perceptual field according to four laws:

1. *The law of proximity.* The parts of a stimulus pattern that are close together or near each other tend to be perceived in groups; therefore, the proximity of the parts in time and space affects the learner's organization of the field.
2. *The law of similarity and familiarity.* Objects similar in form, shape, color, or size tend to be grouped in perception; familiarity with an object facilitates the establishment of a figure–ground pattern. (Related to this law is the gestaltists' view of memory as the persistence of traces in the brain that allows a carryover from previous to present experiences. They view these traces not as static, but as modified by a continual process of integration and organization.)
3. *The law of closure.* Learners try to achieve a satisfying endstate of equilibrium; incomplete shapes, missing parts, and gaps in information

are filled in by the perceiver. [Kingsley and Garry (1957) observe that "closure is to Gestalt psychology what reward is to association theory" (p. 109).]

4. *The law of continuation.* Organization in perception tends to occur in such a manner that a straight line appears to continue as a straight line, a part circle as a circle, and a three-sided square as a complete square.

Gestalt psychology is classified by most interpreters as within the family of field theories, which are theories that propose that the total pattern or field of forces, stimuli, or events determine learning.

Kurt Lewin (1890–1947) developed what he referred to specifically as a field theory. Using the topological concepts of geometry, Lewin conceptualized each individual as existing in a life-space in which many forces are operating. The life-space includes features of the environment to which the individual reacts: such as material objects encountered and manipulated; people met; and private thoughts, tensions, goals, and fantasies. Behavior is the product of the interplay of these forces, the direction, and relative strength of which can be portrayed by the geometry of vectors. Learning occurs as a result of a change in cognitive structures produced by changes in two types of forces: (1) change in the structure of the cognitive field itself; or (2) change in the internal needs or motivation of the individual. Because of its emphasis on the immediate field of forces, field theory places more emphasis on motivation than on any of the preceding theories. Lewin felt that success was a more potent motivating force than reward, and gave attention to the concepts of ego involvement and level of aspiration as forces affecting success. He saw change in the relative attractiveness of one goal over another, which he called valence, as another variable affecting motivation. Since some of the strongest forces affecting an individual's psychological field are other people, Lewin became greatly interested in group and institutional dynamics; and as you will see later, it is in this dimension of education that his strongest influence has been felt.

Developments in the field-theory approach have appeared under several labels: phenomenological psychology, perceptual psychology, humanistic psychology, and third-force psychology. Since the bulk of the work with this approach has been with adults, major attention to it will be reserved for a later section. Since phenomenologists are concerned with the study of the progressive development of the mind, or as our contemporaries would insist, the person, they see humans as organisms forever seeking greater personal adequacy. The urge for self-actualization is the driving force motivating all human behavior.

Two phenomenologists, Arthur Combs and Donald Snygg, have focused on the learning of children and the role of their educators, and their findings have important implications for learning theories. The flavor of Combs and Snygg's learning theory can be caught from statements from Pittenger and Gooding (1971):

A person behaves in terms of what is real to him or her and what is related to his or her self at the moment of action. (p. 130)

Learning is a process of discovering one's personal relationship to and with people, things, and ideas. This process results in and from a differentiation of the phenomenal field of the individual. (p. 136)

Further differentiation of the phenomenological field occurs as an individual recognizes some inadequacy of a present organization. When a change is needed to maintain or enhance the phenomenal self, it is made by the individual as the right and proper thing to do. The role of the teacher is to facilitate the process. (p. 144)

Given a healthy organism, positive environmental influences, and a nonrestrictive set of percepts of self, there appears to be no foreseeable end to the perceptions possible for the individual. (pp. 150–151)

Transfer is a matter of taking current differentiations and using them as first approximations in the relationship of self to new situations. (p. 157)

Learning is permanent to the extent that it generates problems that may be shared by others and to the degree that continued sharing itself is enhancing. (p. 165)

In a sense, Edward C. Tolman (1886–1959) represents a bridge between the elemental and the holistic models. His system was behavioristic in that he rejected introspection as a method for psychological science; but it was molar rather than molecular behaviorism—an act of behavior has distinctive properties all of its own, to be identified and described irrespective of the muscular, glandular, or neural processes that underlie it. But, most importantly, he saw behavior as purposive, being regulated in accordance with objectively determined ends. Purpose is, of course, an organismic concept. Tolman rejected the idea that learning is the association of particular responses to particular stimuli. In contrast to the associationists, who believed that it is the response or sequence of responses resulting in reward that is learned, Tolman believed it is the route to the goal that is learned. He believed that organisms, at their respective levels of ability, are capable of recognizing and learning the relationships between signs and desired goals; in short, they perceive the significance of the signs (Kingsley and Garry, 1957, p. 115). Tolman called his theory purposive behaviorism.

CHILD LEARNING

Two other later psychologists, Jean Piaget and Jerome Bruner, have had great impact on thinking about learning, although they are not literally learning theorists. Their focus is on cognition and the theory of instruction. Piaget has conceptualized the process of the development of cognition and thought in evolutionary stages. According to Piaget, the behavior of the human organism starts with the organization of sensory-motor reactions, and becomes more intelligent as coordination between the reactions to objects becomes progressively more interrelated and complex. Thinking becomes possible after language develops, and with it a new mental organization. This development involves the following evolutionary periods (Piaget, 1970, pp. 30–33):

1. *The formation of the symbolic or semiotic function* (ages 2 to 7 or 8). The individual is able to represent objects or events that are not at the moment perceptible by evoking them through the agency of symbols or differentiated signs.
2. *The formation of concrete mental operations* (ages 7 or 8 to 11 or 12). Characteristic of this stage are the linking and dissociation of classes; the sources of classification; the linking of relations; correspondences, and so on.
3. *The formation of conceptual thought or formal operations* (ages 11 or 12 through adolescence). "This period is characterized by the conquest of a new mode of reasoning, one that is no longer limited exclusively to dealing with objects or directly representable realities, but also employs 'hypotheses.'"

Some reservations have been expressed about the rigid age scale and minimization of individual differences in Piaget's schema; but his conception of evolutionary stages adds a dimension that is not generally given much attention in the established learning theories.

Jerome Bruner has also been interested in the process of intellectual growth, and his benchmarks were described in Chapter 2. His main interest, however, has been in the structuring and sequencing of knowledge and translating this into a theory of instruction. However, Bruner does have a basic theory about the act of learning, which he views as involving three almost simultaneous processes: (1) acquisition of new information, which is often information that runs counter to or is a replacement of what the person has previously known but which, at the very least, is a refinement of previous knowledge; (2) transformation, or the process of manipulating knowledge to make it fit new tasks; and (3) evaluation, or checking whether the way the person manipulated information is adequate to the task (Bruner, 1960, pp. 48–49). We shall return to this theory of instruction in a later chapter.

The main criticism of Piaget, Bruner, and other cognitive theorists by other adherents to the holistic model is that they are unbalanced in their overemphasis on cognitive skills at the expense of emotional development; that they are preoccupied with the aggressive, agentic, and autonomous motives to the exclusion of the homonymous, libidinal, and communal motives; and that they concern themselves with concept attainment to the exclusion of concept formation or invention (Jones, 1968, p. 97).

In the years following Piaget's pronouncements, new avenues opened in such learning-related fields of inquiry as:

- neurophysiology (M. Boucouvalas, K. H. Pribrain, G. A. Miller, J. E. Delefresnaye, H. E. Harlow, D. P. Kimble, W. G. Walter, D. E. Wooldridge, J. Z. Young);
- mathematical modeling (R. C. Atkinson, R. R. Bush, W. K. Estes, R. D. Luce, E. Restle);
- information processing and cybernetics (H. Borko, E. A. Feigenbaum, B. E. Green, W. R. Reitman, K. M. Sayre, M. Yovitts, J. Singh, K. O. Smith);
- creativity (J. P. Guilford, R. P. Crawford, J. E. Drevdahl, A. Meadow, S. J. Parnes, J. W. Getzels, P. W. Jackson); and
- ecological psychology (R. G. Barker, P. V. Gump, H. E. Wright, E. P. Willems, H. L. Raush).

SUMMARY

Learning theory literature falls into two general types: that produced by proposers and that produced by interpreters. Many proposers of theories have made a concerted effort to impose order on the system of learning theory. Among these are Hilgard and Bower, McDonald, and Gage. It was Reese and Overton, however, who successfully conceptualized the theories within a larger construct—the concept of models of development. Reese and Overton postulated that "any theory presupposes a more general model according to which the theoretical concepts are formulated." Building on this premise, they developed the *elemental model* and the *holistic models* of individuals. Among the theories based on the elemental model are Thorndike's connectionism, Pavlov's classical conditioning, and Watson's behaviorism. Other theories within this category were those developed by Guthrie, which resulted both in the principle of contiguity of cue and response and an emphasis on the importance of attention behavior. It was Guthrie's work that spawned additional research by Voeks, Sheffield, Skinner, and Hull's systematic behavior theory. Behaviorism was uniquely American, and mirrored the philosophy of the turn-of-the century notion that all people could achieve great accomplishments given the opportunity (stimulus), individual initiative (response), and fair treatment (rewards).

Paralleling this effort were the holistic models. It was Dewey's work that initiated a line of theorizing called functionalism. Tolman, however, bridged the gap between cognitive and behavioral psychologies with a theory that he called purposive behaviorism. Gestalt theories, classified by most interpreters as within the family of field theories, paralleled behaviorism. The notable field theories in which Lewin was intensely interested—group and institutional dynamics—greatly influenced this educational dimension. Recent developments in the field-theoretical approach have appeared under the labels of phenomenological psychology, perceptual psychology, humanistic psychology, and cognitive psychology.

REFLECTION QUESTIONS

6.1 Speculate as to why so many learning theories have been created.

6.2 What is the value of thinking of wholes and parts as they relate to learning?

6.3 What are some of the important points derived from elemental model learning theories?

6.4 What are some of the important points derived from holistic model learning theories?

THEORIES OF
7 TEACHING

INTRODUCTION

Theories of learning are typically only useful to adult learning practitioners when they are applied to the facilitation of learning—a function assigned usually in our society to a person designated as teacher or trainer.

A distinction must be made between theories of learning and theories of teaching. Theories of learning deal with the ways in which people learn, whereas theories of teaching deal with the ways in which one person influences others to learn (Gage, 1972, p. 56).

Presumably, the learning theory subscribed to by a teacher will influence his or her teaching theory.

Early on, Hilgard resisted this fragmentation of learning theory. He identified 20 principles he believed to be universally acceptable from three different families of theories: *Stimulus–Response (S–R) theory*, *cognitive theory*, and *motivation and personality theory*. These principles are summarized in Table 7.1.

Hilgard's conviction in his belief that his 20 principles would be "in large part acceptable to all parties" was grounded in his limited verification process. The "parties" with whom he checked out these principles were control-oriented theorists. In spite of their differences about the internal mechanics of learning, these theorists are fairly close in their conceptualization of the role of the teacher.

Table 7.1 Summary of Hilgard's principles

Principles emphasized in S–R theory

1. The learner should be an active, rather than a passive, listener or viewer.

2. Frequency of repetition is still important in acquiring skill and for retention through overlearning.

3. Reinforcement is important; that is, repetition is desirable and correct responses should be rewarded.

4. Generalization and discrimination suggest the importance of practice in varied contexts, so that learning will become (or remain) appropriate to a wider (or more restricted) range of stimuli.

5. Novelty in behavior can be enhanced through imitation of models, through cueing, through shaping, and is not inconsistent with a liberalized S–R approach.

6. Drive is important in learning, but all personal–social motives do not conform to the drive-reduction principles based on food-deprivation experiments.

7. Conflicts and frustrations arise inevitably in the process of learning difficult discriminations and in social situations in which irrelevant motives may be aroused. Hence we must recognize and provide for their resolution or accommodation.

Principles emphasized in cognitive theory

1. The perceptual features of the problems given the learner are important conditions of learning figure–ground relations, directional signs, sequence, organic interrelatedness. Hence a learning problem should be so structured and presented that the essential features are open to the inspection of the learner.

2. The organization of knowledge should be an essential concern of the teacher or educational planner so that the direction from simple to complex is not from arbitrary, meaningless parts to meaningful wholes, but instead from simplified wholes to more complex wholes.

3. Learning is culturally relative, and both the wider culture and the subculture to which the learner belongs may affect his or her learning.

4. Cognitive feedback confirms correct knowledge and corrects faulty learning. The learner tries something provisionally and then accepts or rejects what he or she does on the basis of its consequences. This is, of course, the cognitive equivalent of reinforcement in S–R theory, but cognitive theory tends to place more emphasis upon a kind of hypothesis testing through feedback.

5. Goal-setting by the learner is important as motivation for learning and personal successes and failures determine how individuals set future goals.

6. Divergent thinking, which leads to inventive problem solving or the creation of novel and valued products, is to be nurtured along with convergent thinking, which leads to logically correct answers.

Table 7.1 continued

Principles from motivation and personality theory

1. The learner's abilities are important, and motivation and provisions have to be made for slower and more rapid learners, as well as for those with specialized abilities.

2. Postnatal development may be as important as hereditary and congenital determiners of ability and interest. Hence, the learner must be understood in terms of the influences that have shaped his or her development.

3. Learning is culturally relative, and both the wider culture and the subculture to which the learner belongs may affect learning.

4. Anxiety level of the individual learner may determine the beneficial or detrimental effects of certain kinds of encouragements to learn.

5. The same objective situation may tap appropriate motives for one learner and not for another; as, for example, in the contrast between those motivated by affiliation and those motivated by achievement.

6. The organization of motives and values within the individual is relevant. Some long-range goals affect short-range activities. Thus college students of equal ability may do better in courses perceived as relevant to their majors than in those perceived as irrelevant.

7. The group atmosphere of learning (competition vs. cooperation, authoritarianism vs. democracy, individual isolation vs. group identification) will affect satisfaction in learning as well as the products of learning.

Source: Hilgard and Bower (1966, pp. 562–564).

TEACHING CONCEPTS BASED ON ANIMAL AND CHILD LEARNING THEORIES

Let's examine the concepts of a variety of theories about the nature of teaching and the role of the teacher. First, we'll look at the members of Hilgard's jury. These include Thorndike, Guthrie, Skinner, Hull, Tolman, and Gagné.

Thorndike

Thorndike essentially saw teaching as the control of learning by the management of reward. The teacher and learner must know the characteristics of a good performance in order that practice may be appropriately arranged.

Errors must be diagnosed so that they will not be repeated. The teacher is not primarily concerned with the internal states of the organism, but with structuring the situation so that rewards will operate to strengthen desired responses. The learner should be interested, problem-oriented, and attentive. However, the best way to obtain these conditions is to manipulate the learning situation so that the learner accepts the problem posed because of the rewards involved. Attention is maintained and appropriate S–R connections are strengthened through the precise application of rewards toward the goals set by the teacher. A teacher's role is to cause appropriate S–R bonds to be built up in the learner's behavior repertoire (Hilgard and Bower, 1966, pp. 22–23; Pittenger and Gooding, 1971, pp. 82–83).

Guthrie

Guthrie's suggestions for teaching are summarized as follows:

1. If you wish to encourage a particular kind of behavior or discourage another, discover the cues leading to the behavior in question. In the one case, arrange the situation so that the desired behavior occurs when those cues are present; in the other case, arrange it so that the undesired behavior does not occur in the presence of the cues. This is all that is involved in the skillful use of reward and punishment. A student does not learn what was in a lecture or a book. He or she learns only what the lecture or book caused him or her to do.
2. Use as many stimulus supports for desired behavior as possible, because any ordinary behavior is a complex of movements to a complex of stimuli. The more stimuli there are associated with the desired behavior, the less likely that distracting stimuli and competing behavior will upset the desirable behavior (Hilgard and Bower, 1966, pp. 86–87).

Skinner

From Skinner's (1968) vantage point, "Teaching is simply the arrangement of contingencies of reinforcement" (p. 5). Subsequent statements in *The Technology of Teaching* throw further light on his position:

Some promising advances have recently been made in the field of learning. Special techniques have been designed to arrange what are called contingencies of reinforcement—the relations which prevail between behavior on the one hand and the consequences of behavior on the other—with the result that a much more effective control of behavior has been achieved.

(p. 9)

Comparable results have been obtained with pigeons, rats, dogs, monkeys, human children and psychotic subjects. In spite of great phylogenic differences, all these organisms show amazingly similar properties of the learning process. It could be emphasized that this has been achieved by analyzing the effects of reinforcement with considerable precision. Only in this way can the behavior of the individual organism be brought under such precise control.

(p. 14)

The human organism does, of course, learn without being taught. It is a good thing that this is so, and it would no doubt be a good thing if more could be learned in that way. . . . But discovery is no solution to the problems of education. A culture is no stronger than its capacity to transmit itself. It must impart an accumulation of skills, knowledge, and social and ethical practices to its new members. The institution of education is designed to serve this purpose. . . . It is dangerous to suggest to the student that it is beneath his dignity to learn what others already know, that there is something ignoble (and even destructive of "rational powers") in memorizing facts, codes, formulae, or passages from literary works, and that to be admired he must think in original ways. It is equally dangerous to forego teaching important facts and principles in order to give the student a chance to discover them for himself.

(p. 110)

Hull

Hull was primarily concerned with the development of a systematic behavior theory that would improve the laboratory study of learning, and so he gave little attention to its implications for teaching. In assessing the significance of his work for education, Kingsley and Garry (1957) point out:

Systematic order and arrangement would characterize the classroom patterned after Hull's theory. The development of habits and skills would proceed from the simple to the complex with a clear understanding of the stimuli and responses to be associated. The program would have to be dynamic and stimulating in view of the central position that reinforcement holds, inasmuch as aroused drives which can be reduced by satisfying outcomes are an essential condition of learning. . . . Practice would be presented for the purpose of building the desired habits and maintaining them, but would not proceed to the point at which the increase in inhibition from repeating the same response would make the child reluctant to respond.

(pp. 104–105)

Tolman

Tolman was also principally concerned with the laboratory study of learning, and Kingsley and Garry (1957) point out that "the fact that Tolman accepts different forms of learning makes it more difficult to infer how an educational program which followed his theory literally would operate." But the teacher's task would be concerned primarily with "the fact that Tolman accepts different forms of learning makes it more difficult to infer how an educational program which followed his theory literally would operate" (pp. 119–120).

The gestalt psychologists saw the teacher's task as being essentially to help the individual see significant relationships and to manage instruction in order to organize his or her experiences into functional patterns. Through verbal explanations, showing pictures, putting words on chalkboards, presenting reading matter, and many other teaching activities, the teacher provides stimulating situations.

For this reason, careful lesson planning with due regard for suitable arrangement and orderly presentation is essential for good teaching. Practices conducive to the establishment of appropriate relations and organization include starting with the familiar, basing each step on those already taken, putting together facts that belong together, grouping items according to their natural connections, placing subtopics under the topic to which they belong, using illustrations based on the learner's experience, giving major emphasis to essentials, centering supporting details around the main points, and avoiding irrelevant details (Kingsley and Garry, 1957, pp. 111–112). Furthermore, all the divisions and topics of each subject must be integrated, and all the various subjects of a course or program must be related to one another.

Gagné

Robert Gagné in *The Conditions of Learning* (1965) agrees with these learning theorists that teaching means the arranging of conditions that are external to the learner (p. 26), but he disagrees that learning is a phenomenon that can be explained by simple theories. He believes that there are eight distinct types of learning, each with its own set of required conditions. These are summarized in Table 7.2.

Gagné (1965) further believes that the most important class of conditions that distinguishes one form of learning from another is its prerequisites, since the types are in hierarchical order, as follows:

- Problem-solving (type 8) requires as prerequisites
- Principles (type 7), which require as prerequisites
- Concepts (type 6), which require as prerequisites
- Multiple discriminations (type 5), which require as prerequisites
- Verbal associations (type 4) or other chains (type 3), which require as prerequisites
- Stimulus–response connections (type 2). (p. 60)

Gagné specifies eight component functions of the instructional situation that represent the ways in which the learner's environment acts on him or her and that must be managed by the teacher:

1. *Presenting the stimulus*. Every type of learning requires a stimulus, and usually these stimuli must be located within the learning environment, outside the learner. If a chain is being learned, an external cue must be provided for each link, even though these may become unnecessary later. If multiple discrimination is to be accomplished, the stimuli to be discriminated must be displayed so that correct connections can become differentiated from incorrect ones. If concepts are being learned, a suitable variety of objects or events representing a class must be displayed. If principles are being acquired, the stimulus objects to which they are expected to apply must somehow be represented to the student. And if problem solving is undertaken, the "problem situation" must similarly be represented in many different ways by objects already in the learner's environment, or by means of pictures, printed books, or oral communication.

2. *Directing attention and other learner activities*. Environmental components also act on the learner by directing attention to certain stimuli or aspects of stimulus objects and events. In very young children, vivid or suddenly changing stimulation may be used for this purpose. Very soon these can be supplanted by oral commands, and later still by printed directions such as "Notice the number of electrons in the outer ring," or "Look at the graph in Figure 23." As implied by the statements "Remember how a line is defined," or "Complete the following sentence," activities other than attention may also be directed by such instructions. These activities are not themselves learning. They are

Table 7.2 Gagné's eight distinctive types of learning

Type 1	*Signal learning.* The individual learns to make a general, diffuse response to a signal. This is the classical conditioned response of Pavlov.
Type 2	*Stimulus–response learning.* The learner acquires a precise response to a discriminated stimulus. What is learned is a connection (Thorndike) or a discriminated operant (Skinner), sometimes called an instrumental response (Kimble).
Type 3	*Chaining.* What is acquired is a chain of two or more stimulus–response connections. The conditions for such learning have been described by Skinner and others.
Type 4	*Verbal association.* The learning of chains that are verbal. Basically, the conditions resemble those for other (motor) chains. However, the presence of language in the human being makes this a special type because internal links may be selected from the individual's previously learned repertoire of language.
Type 5	*Multiple discrimination.* The individual learns to make different identifying responses to as many different stimuli, which may resemble each other in physical appearance to a greater or lesser degree.
Type 6	*Concept learning.* The learner acquires a capability to make a common response to a class of stimuli that may differ from each other widely in physical appearance. He or she is able to make a response that identifies an entire class of objects or events.
Type 7	*Principle learning.* In simplest terms, a principle is a chain of two or more concepts. It functions to control behavior in the manner suggested by a verbalized rule of the form "If A, then B," which, of course, may also be learned as Type 4.
Type 8	*Problem solving.* A kind of learning that requires the internal events usually called thinking. Two or more previously acquired principles are somehow combined to produce a new capability that can be shown to depend on a "higher-order" principle.

Source: Gagné (1965, pp. 58–59).

simply actions that must be taken by the learner in order to create the proper conditions for learning. Verbal directions that have these purposes can be presented either orally or in printed form.

3. *Providing a model for terminal performance.* The importance of the function of informing the learner about the general nature of the performance to be acquired has been emphasized previously on

several occasions. There is no single way to do this, and many different components of the instructional situation may be employed. Most commonly, the "model" of performance to be expected following learning is conveyed by oral or printed communication.

4. *Furnishing external prompts.* In learning chains, as well as multiple discriminations, cues may be provided in the instructional situation to establish a proper sequence of connections or to increase the distinctiveness of stimuli. As learning proceeds, these extra cues may be made to "vanish" when they are no longer needed. Stimuli that function as extra cues may take a variety of forms. For example, they may be pictorial, as when a sequence is depicted in a diagram reading from left to right. Or they may be auditory, as in emphasizing the differences in sound of such French words as *rue* and *rouge*. Verbal stimuli are often employed for both of these purposes, as well as for the purpose of furnishing distinctive *coding links* in verbal chains. For example, when learning color coding for resistors, the word penny is used to link "brown" and "one"; the word nothingness is used to link "black" and "zero."

5. *Guiding the direction of thinking.* When principles are being learned, and particularly when learning takes the form of problem solving, instructions from the learner's environment may guide the direction of recalled internal connections (thoughts). As described previously, such guidance is presumed to increase the efficiency of learning by reducing the occurrence of irrelevant *hypotheses*. Generally, instructions having this function of *hinting* and *suggesting* take the form of oral or printed prose statements.

6. *Inducing transfer of knowledge.* Transferring learned concepts and principles to novel situations may be accomplished in a number of ways. Discussion is one of the most convenient. Obviously, this is a special kind of interaction between the learner and his or her environment, and it is not possible to specify exactly what form of discussion will be taken at any given moment by stimulation from the environment. The process is usually initiated, however, by verbally stated questions of the *problem-solving* variety. An important alternative method is to more or less directly place the individual within a problem situation, without the use of words to describe it. A science demonstration may be used to serve this function. Also, videos can be used with considerable effectiveness to initiate problem-solving discussion by "getting the students into the situation" in a highly realistic manner.

7. *Assessing learning attainments.* The environment of the learner also acts to assess the extent to which the individual has attained a specific learning objective or sub-objective. It does this by deliberately placing

the learner in representative problem situations that concretely reflect the capability the individual is expected to have learned. Most frequently, this is done by asking questions. Although it is conceivable for the learner to formulate for himself or herself the questions to be asked, this is difficult for even the experienced adult learner. Preferably, the questions must come from an independent source, to ensure that they will be uninfluenced by the learner's wishes, but will accurately represent the objective.

8. *Providing feedback.* Feedback concerning the correctness of the learner's responses is closely related to assessment of learning outcomes. The questions that are asked of the learner, followed by his or her answers, must in turn be followed by information that lets the learner know whether he or she is right or wrong. Sometimes, this feedback from the learner's environment is very simple to arrange: a foreign word pronounced by the student may sound like one heard on a tape, or the color of a chemical solution may indicate the presence of an element being sought. At other times, it may be considerably more complex; as, for example, when the adequacy of a constructed prose paragraph describing an observed event is assessed, and the results are fed back to the learner.

These eight functions represent the ways in which the learner's environment acts on the individual. These are the external conditions of learning that, when combined with certain prerequisite capabilities within the learner, bring about the desired change in performance. Obviously, there are many ways to establish these conditions in the learning environment; and many combinations of objects, devices, and verbal communications may be employed in doing so. Probably the most important consideration for the design of the learning environment, however, is not that several alternative ways of accomplishing the same function are usually available. Rather, the important point is that for a given function certain means of interacting with the learner are quite ineffective. Accordingly, the characteristics of various media of instruction in performing these functions need to be considered carefully in making a choice (Gagné, 1965, pp. 268–271).

The learning theorists described above are the ones Hilgard believed would agree with his 20 principles (with the exception of the motivation and personality theorists, whom Hilgard didn't identify, so we can't check with them directly). Obviously these theorists are unanimous in seeing teaching as the management of procedures that will assure specified behavioral changes as prescribed learning products. The role of the teacher, therefore, is that of a behavior shaper. Stated this baldly, it smacks of what contemporary critics of education see as a God-playing role (Bereiter, 1972, p. 25; Illich, 1970, p. 30).

TEACHING CONCEPTS BASED ON ADULT LEARNING THEORIES

When we look at the concepts of teaching of those theorists who derived their theories of learning primarily from studies of adults, it is obvious that they are very different from those discussed in the previous section.

Rogers

Carl Rogers (1969) makes one of the sharpest breaks in his lead statement:

> Teaching, in my estimation, is a vastly over-rated function. Having made such a statement, I scurry to the dictionary to see if I really mean what I say. Teaching means "to instruct." Personally I am not much interested in instructing another in what he should know or think. "To impart knowledge or skill." My reaction is, why not be more efficient, using a book or programmed learning? "To make to know." Here my hackles rise. I have no wish to make anyone know something. "To show, guide, direct." As I see it, too many people have been shown, guided, directed. So I come to the conclusion that I do mean what I said. Teaching is, for me, a relatively unimportant and vastly overvalued activity.
>
> (p. 103)

Rogers (1969) goes on to explain that in his view teaching and the imparting of knowledge make sense in an unchanging environment, which is why it has been an unquestioned function for centuries. "But if there is one truth about modern man, it is that he lives in an environment which is continually changing," and, therefore, the aim of education must be the facilitation of learning (pp. 104–105). He defines the role of the teacher as that of a facilitator of learning. The critical element in performing this role is the personal relationship between the facilitator and the learner, which in turn is dependent on the facilitator's possessing three attitudinal qualities: (1) realness or genuineness; (2) non-possessive caring, prizing, trust, and respect; and (3) empathic understanding and sensitive and accurate listening (pp. 106–206). Rogers provides the following guidelines for a facilitator of learning (pp. 164–166):

1. The facilitator has much to do with setting the initial mood or climate of the group or class experience. If the facilitator's own basic philosophy is one of trust in the group and in the individuals who compose the group, then this point of view will be communicated in many subtle ways.

2. The facilitator helps to elicit and clarify the purposes of the individuals in the class as well as the more general purposes of the group. If he or she is not fearful of accepting contradictory purposes and conflicting aims, and is able to permit the individuals a sense of freedom in stating what they would like to do, then the facilitator is helping to create a climate for learning.

3. The facilitator relies on the desire of each student to implement those purposes that have meaning for him or her as the motivational force behind significant learning. Even if the desire of the student is to be guided and led by someone else, the facilitator can accept such a need and motive and can either serve as a guide when this is desired or can provide some other means, such as a set course of study, for the student whose major desire is to be dependent. And, for the majority of students, the facilitator can help to use a particular individual's own drives and purposes as the moving force behind his or her learning.

4. The facilitator endeavors to organize and make easily available the widest possible range of resources for learning. He or she strives to make available writings, materials, psychological aids, persons, equipment, trips, audiovisual aids—every conceivable resource that his or her students may wish to use for their own enhancement and for the fulfillment of their own purposes.

5. The facilitator regards himself or herself as a flexible resource to be used by the group. The facilitator does not downgrade himself or herself as a resource. He or she is available as a counselor, lecturer, and advisor, a person with experience in the field. The facilitator wishes to be used by individual students and by the group in ways that seem most meaningful to them insofar as he or she can be comfortable in operating in the ways they wish.

6. In responding to expressions in the classroom group, the facilitator accepts both intellectual content and the emotionalized attitudes, endeavoring to give each aspect the approximate degree of emphasis that it has for the individual or the group. Insofar as the facilitator can be genuine in doing so, he or she accepts rationalizations and intellectualizing, as well as deep and real personal feelings.

7. As the acceptant classroom climate becomes established, the facilitator is increasingly able to become a participant learner, a member of the group, expressing his or her views as those of one individual only.

8. The facilitator takes the initiative in sharing his or her feelings as well as thoughts with the group—in ways that do not demand or impose but represent simply the personal sharing that students may take or leave. Thus, the facilitator is free to express his or her own feelings in giving feedback to students, in reacting to them as individuals, and in sharing personal satisfactions or disappointments. In such expressions it is the facilitator's *owned* attitudes that are shared, not judgments of evaluations of others.

9. Throughout the classroom experience, the facilitator remains alert to the expressions indicative of deep or strong feelings. These may be feelings of conflict, pain, and the like, which exist primarily within the individual. Here, the facilitator endeavors to understand these from the person's point of view and to communicate his or her empathic understanding. On the other hand, the feelings may be those of anger, scorn, affection, rivalry, and the like—interpersonal attitudes among members of the group. Again, the facilitator is alert to these feelings, and by his or her acceptance of such tensions or bonds he or she helps to bring them into the open for constructive understanding and use by the group.

10. In this functioning as a facilitator of learning, the leader endeavors to recognize and accept his or her own limitations. The facilitator realizes that he or she can grant freedom to students only to the extent that he or she is comfortable in giving such freedom. The facilitator can be understanding only to the extent that he or she actually desires to enter the inner world of students. The facilitator can share himself or herself only to the extent that he or she is reasonably comfortable in taking that risk. The facilitator can participate as a member of the group only when the facilitator actually feels that he or she and the students have an equality as learners. The facilitator can exhibit trust of the students' desire to learn only insofar as he or she feels that trust. There will be many times when the facilitator's attitudes are not facilitative of learning. He or she will feel suspicious of the students, or will find it impossible to accept attitudes that differ strongly from his or her own, or will be unable to understand some of the students' feelings that are markedly different from his or her own, or feel strongly judgmental and evaluative. When the facilitator experiences non-facilitative attitudes, he or she will endeavor to get close to them, to be clearly aware of them, and to state them just as they are within him- or herself. Once the facilitator has expressed these angers, these judgments, these mistrusts, these doubts of others and doubts of self as something coming from within him- or herself, not as objective facts in outward reality, he or she will find the air cleared for a significant interchange with his or her

students. Such an interchange can go a long way toward resolving the very attitudes that he or she has been experiencing, and thus make it possible to be more of a facilitator of learning.

Although Maslow does not spell out his conception of the role of teacher, he would no doubt subscribe to Rogers's guidelines, with perhaps a bit more emphasis on the teacher's responsibility for providing safety. Several followers of Rogers and Maslow have experimented with translating their theories into classroom behavior. George Brown, for example, describes the development of confluent education ("the term for the integration or flowing together of the affective and cognitive elements in individual and group learning") in the Ford Esalen Project in Affective Education in California in the late 1960s in his *Human Teaching for Human Learning* (1971). Elizabeth Drews (1966) describes an experiment to test a new program designed to foster self-initiated learning and self-actualization in ninth-graders in Michigan in which the teachers defined their roles as facilitators of learning.

Watson

Flowing in the same stream of thought, Goodwin Watson (1960–61) provides the following summary of "what is known about learning," which is easily read as "guidelines for the facilitation of learning":

1. Behavior which is rewarded—from the learner's point of view—is more likely to recur.
2. Sheer repetition without reward is a poor way to learn.
3. Threat and punishment have variable effects upon learning, but they can and do commonly produce avoidance behavior in which the reward is the diminution of punishment possibilities.
4. How *ready* we are to learn something new is contingent upon the confluence of diverse—and changing—factors, some of which include:

    a. Adequate existing experience to permit the new to be learned or we can learn only in relation to what we already know.
    b. Adequate significance and relevance for the learner to engage in learning activity or we learn only what is appropriate to our purposes.
    c. Freedom from discouragement, the expectation of failure, or threats to physical, emotional, or intellectual well-being.

5. Whatever is to be learned will remain unlearnable if we believe that we cannot learn it or if we perceive it as irrelevant or if the learning situation is perceived as threatening.

6. Novelty (per 4 and 5 above) is generally rewarding.
7. We learn best that which we participate in selecting and planning ourselves.
8. Genuine participation as compared with feigned participation intended to avoid punishment intensifies motivation, flexibility, and rate of learning.
9. An autocratic atmosphere (produced by a dominating teacher who controls direction via intricate punishments) produces in learners apathetic conformity, various—and frequently devious—kinds of defiance, scapegoating (venting hostility generated by the repressive atmosphere on colleagues), or escape. An autocratic atmosphere also produces increasing dependence upon the authority, with consequent obsequiousness, anxiety, shyness, and acquiescence.
10. *Closed*, authoritarian environments (such as are characteristic of most conventional schools and classrooms) condemn most learners to continuing criticism, sarcasm, discouragement, and failure so that self-confidence, aspiration (for anything but escape), and a healthy self-concept are destroyed.
11. The best time to learn anything is when whatever is to be learned is immediately useful to us.
12. An *open*, non-authoritarian atmosphere can, then, be seen as conductive to learner initiative and creativity; encouraging the learning of attitudes of self-confidence, originality, self-reliance, enterprise, and independence. All of which is equivalent to learning how to learn.

Houle

Houle (1972, pp. 32–39) has proposed a *fundamental system* of educational design that rests on seven assumptions:

1. Any episode of learning occurs in a specific situation and is profoundly influenced by that fact.
2. The analysis or planning of educational activities must be based on the realities of human experience and on their constant change.
3. Education is a practical art (like architecture) that draws on many theoretical disciplines in the humanities and the social and biological sciences.
4. Education is a cooperative rather than an operative art *fundamental system*.
5. The planning or analysis of an educational activity is usually undertaken in terms of some period that the mind abstracts for analytical purposes from the complicated reality.

6. The planning or analysis of an educational activity may be undertaken by an educator, a learner, an independent analyst, or some combination of the three.

7. Any design of education can best be understood as a complex system of interacting elements, not as a sequence of events.

Houle (1972, pp. 48–56) then identifies the following components in his fundamental system, which it is the task of the educator to manage:

1. A possible educational activity is identified.
2. A decision is made to proceed.
3. Objectives are identified and refined.
4. A suitable format is designed.

   a. Learning resources are selected.
   b. A leader or group of leaders is chosen.
   c. Methods are selected and used.
   d. A time schedule is made.
   e. A sequence of events is devised.
   f. Social reinforcement of learning is provided.
   g. The nature of each individual learner is taken into account.
   h. Roles and relationships are made clear.
   i. Criteria for evaluating progress are identified.
   j. The design is made clear to all concerned.

5. The format is fitted into larger patterns of life.

   a. Learners are guided into or out of the activity both at the beginning and subsequently.
   b. Lifestyles are modified to allow time and resources for the new activity.
   c. Financing is arranged.
   d. The activity is interpreted to related publics.

6. The program is carried out.
7. The results of the activity are measured and appraised.
8. The situation is examined in terms of the possibility of a new educational activity.

Tough

Tough's studies were concerned with the self-initiated learning projects of adults. He has focused on the *helping role* of the teacher or other resource person. His investigations have produced the following "fairly consistent composite picture of the ideal helper":

> One cluster of characteristics might be summarized by saying that the ideal helper is warm and loving. The individual accepts and cares about the learner and about the learner's project or problem, and takes it seriously. The helper is willing to spend time helping and showing approval, support, encouragement, and friendship. He or she regards the learner as an equal. As a result of these characteristics, the learner feels free to approach this ideal helper, and can talk freely and easily with him or her in a warm and relaxed atmosphere.

A second cluster of characteristics involves the helper's perceptions of the person's capacity as a self-planner. The ideal helper has confidence in the learner's ability to make appropriate plans and arrangements for this learning. The helper has a high regard for the learner's skill as a self-planner, and does not want to take the decision-making control away from him or her.

Third, the ideal helper views personal interaction with the learner as a dialogue, a true encounter in which he or she listens as well as talks. Help will be tailored to the needs, goals, and requests of this unique learner. The helper listens, accepts, understands, responds, and helps. These perceptions of the interaction are in sharp contrast to those of *helpers* who want to control, command, manipulate, persuade, influence, and change the learner. Such helpers seem to view communication as "an inexhaustible monologue, addressed to everyone and no one in the form of 'mass communication'. . . . Such a helper perceives the learner as an object, and expects to do something to that object. He is not primarily interested in the other person as a person, and in his needs, wishes, and welfare" (Tough, 1979).

Another cluster of internal characteristics involves the helper's reasons for helping. Perhaps the helper helps because of his or her affection and concern for the learner; or perhaps the helper may, in an open and positive way, expect to gain as much as he or she gives. Other sorts of motivation are feelings of pleasure for knowing he or she was helpful, and satisfaction from seeing progress or from the learner's gratitude.

Finally, the ideal helper is probably an open and growing person, not a closed, negative, static, defensive, fearful, or suspicious sort of person. The helper him- or herself is frequently a learner, and seeks growth and new experiences. He or she probably tends to be spontaneous and authentic, and to feel free to behave as a unique person rather than in some stereotyped way (Tough, 1979, pp. 195–197).

These characteristics fit well into an integrated conception of the role of the andragogical teacher. An operational set of principles for that conception of the andragogical teacher is shown in Table 7.3.

Table 7.3 The role of the teacher

Conditions of learning	Principles of teaching
The learners feel a need to learn.	1. The teacher exposes students to new possibilities of self-fulfillment. 2. The teacher helps each student clarify his own aspirations for improved behavior. 3. The teacher helps each student diagnose the gap between his aspiration and his present level of performance. 4. The teacher helps the students identify the life problems they experience because of the gaps in their personal equipment.
The learning environment is characterized by physical comfort, mutual trust and respect, mutual helpfulness, freedom of expression, and acceptance of differences.	5. The teacher provides physical conditions that are comfortable (as to seating, smoking, temperature, ventilation, lighting, decoration) and conducive to interaction (preferably, no person sitting behind another person). 6. The teacher accepts each student as a person of worth and respects his feelings and ideas. 7. The teacher seeks to build relationships of mutual trust and helpfulness among the students by encouraging cooperative activities and refraining from inducing competitiveness and judgmentalness. 8. The teacher exposes his own feelings and contributes his resources as a co-learner in the spirit of mutual inquiry.
The learners perceive the goals of a learning experience to be their goals.	9. The teacher involves the students in a mutual process of formulating learning objectives in which the needs of the students, of the institution, of the teacher, of the subject matter, and of the society are taken into account.
The learners accept a share of the responsibility for planning and operating a learning experience, and therefore have a feeling of	10. The teacher shares his thinking about options available in the designing of learning experiences and the selection of materials and methods and involves the students in deciding among these options jointly.

Table 7.3 continued

Conditions of learning	Principles of teaching
commitment toward it. The learners participate actively in the learning process.	11. The teacher helps the students to organize themselves (project groups, learning–teaching teams, independent study, etc.) to share responsibility in the process of mutual inquiry.
The learning process is related to and makes use of the experience of the learners.	12. The teacher helps the students exploit their own experiences as resources for learning through the use of such techniques as discussion, role-playing, case method, etc.
	13. The teacher gears the presentation of his own resources to the levels of experience of his particular students.
	14. The teacher helps the students to apply new learning to their experience, and thus to make the learning more meaningful and integrated.
The learners have a sense of progress toward their goals.	15. The teacher involves the students in developing mutually acceptable criteria and methods for measuring progress toward the learning objectives.
	16. The teacher helps the students develop and apply procedures for self-evaluation according to these criteria.

TEACHING CONCEPTS FROM THEORIES OF TEACHING

Some teaching theories, especially the mechanistic models, have evolved directly from learning theories. Others have evolved from analyses of teacher behavior and its consequences and from experimenting with manipulation of the variables in the teaching/learning situation. The previous section presented teaching theories derived from learning theories; this section discusses concepts derived from theories of teaching.

Dewey's concepts

Perhaps the system of ideas about effective teaching propounded by John Dewey during the first half of the twentieth century has had the greatest impact in the field. Dewey (1938, pp. 5–6) contrasted his basic principles with those of traditional education:

To imposition from above is opposed expression and cultivation
of individuality; to external discipline is opposed free activity;
to learning from texts and teacher, learning through experience;
to acquisition of isolated skills and techniques by drill, is opposed
acquisition of them as means of attaining ends which make direct
vital appeal; to preparation for a more or less remote future is
opposed making the most of the opportunities of present life; to
static aims and materials is opposed acquaintance with a changing
world.

Dewey's system is organized around several key concepts. The central
concept is *experience*. In Dewey's system, experience is always the starting
point of an educational process; it is never the result. All genuine education
comes about through experience (1938, p. 13). The central challenge of an
education based on experience is to select the kinds of present experiences
that live fruitfully and creatively in subsequent experiences (pp. 16–17).

A second key concept is *democracy*:

> The question I would raise concerns why we prefer democratic and
> humane arrangements to those which are autocratic and harsh. . . .
> Can we find any reason that does not ultimately come down to the
> belief that democratic social arrangements promote a better quality
> of human experience, one which is more widely accessible and
> enjoyed, than do nondemocratic and antidemocratic forms of social
> life?
>
> (pp. 24–25)

Another key concept is *continuity*:

> The principle of continuity of experience means that every
> experience both takes up something from those which have gone
> before and modifies in some way the quality of those which come
> after. . . .Growth, or growing and developing, not only physically but
> intellectually and morally, is one exemplification of the principle of
> continuity.
>
> (pp. 27–28)

A primary responsibility of educators is that they not only be aware
of the general principle of the shaping of actual experience by
environing conditions; but that they also recognize in the concrete
what surroundings are conducive to having experiences that lead

to growth. Above all, they should know how to utilize the surroundings, both physical and social, that exist so as to extract from them all that they have to contribute to building up experiences that are worth while.

(p. 35)

Another key concept is *interaction*:

The word "interaction" expresses the second chief principle for interpreting an experience in its educational function and force. It assigns equal rights to both factors in experience—objective and internal conditions. Any normal experience is an interplay of these two sets of conditions. Taken together, or in their interaction, they form what we call a situation. The trouble with traditional education was not that it emphasized the external conditions that enter into the control of the experiences, but that it paid so little attention to the internal factors which also decide what kind of experience is had [the powers and purposes of those taught].

(pp. 38–44)

It is not the subject per se that is educative or that is conducive to growth. There is no subject that is in and of itself, or without regard to the stage of growth attained by the learner, [an end] such that inherent educational value may be attributed to it. Failure to take into account adaptation to the needs and capacities of individuals was the source of the idea that certain subjects and certain methods are intrinsically cultural or intrinsically good for mental discipline. . . . In a certain sense every experience should do something to prepare a person for later experiences of a deeper and more expansive quality. That is the very meaning of growth, continuity, reconstruction of experience.

(pp. 46–47)

The educator is responsible for a knowledge of individuals and for a knowledge of subject matter that will enable activities to be selected which lend themselves to social organization, an organization in which all individuals have an opportunity to contribute something, and in which the activities in which all participate are the chief carrier of control. . . . The principle that development of experience comes about through interaction means that education is essentially a social process. . . . The teacher loses the position of external boss or dictator but takes on that of leader of group activities.

(pp. 61–66)

Many of Dewey's ideas were distorted, misinterpreted, and exaggerated during the heyday of the progressive school movement a few generations ago; which is why it is important to quote him directly. In light of contemporary thinking about teaching, though, don't these ideas seem fresh and useful?

Teaching through inquiry

A second set of concepts about teaching with roots both in Dewey's ideas—especially his formulation of scientific thinking—and in those of the cognitive theorists is referred to as the discovery method, the inquiry method, self-directed learning, and problem-solving learning.

Jerome Bruner, perhaps the most notable proponent of this approach to teaching, offers the cognitive theorists' perspective of inquiry teaching and learning (1960, 1966). In an extensive series of essays, he identifies three roles of teachers as communicators of knowledge, models who inspire, and symbols of *education*.

Bruner (1966, pp. 40–41) contends that a theory of instruction or inquiry teaching must meet the following four criteria:

1. A theory of instruction should specify the experiences that most effectively implant in the individual a predisposition toward learning.
2. A theory of instruction must specify the ways in which a body of knowledge should be structured so that it can be most readily grasped by the learner.
3. A theory of instruction should specify the most effective sequences in which to present the materials to be learned.
4. A theory of instruction should specify the nature and pacing of rewards and punishments in the process of learning and teaching.

Any attempts to determine whether a theory of instruction meets Bruner's four criteria should include considerations of the following types of questions:

Are there materials that will increase a student's desire to learn? If so, what are they?
How can I, as a teacher, enhance the students' will to learn? What can be done to make students eager to learn the material?
What is the most effective method of presentation for this material? Is an interactive or representative presentation best suited for this material? Bruner (1966) identifies modes of presentation in a hierarchical system

involving an enactive mode, iconic mode, and symbolic mode (pp. 10–14). The first level, the *enactive mode*, requires action on the part of the learner; the second level, the *iconic mode*, refers to the process of mentally organizing material; and the third level, the *symbolic mode*, involves use of symbols such as language.

Are the learning materials, tools, and even material appropriate for the level of the students?

What is the optimal presentation sequence? Is the holistic approach most effective, or should the teacher teach the foundations of the material and then supply the details?

What and when are rewards to be administered? How will the instruction handle students' successes and errors?

Bruner predicates his system on the will to learn, a trait he believes to exist in all people. The will to learn is an intrinsic motive, one that finds both its source and its reward in its own exercise. The will to learn becomes a *problem* only under specialized circumstances such as those of a school, where a curriculum is set, students confined, and a path fixed. The problem exists not so much in learning itself, but in the fact that what the school imposes often fails to enlist the natural energies that sustain spontaneous learning—curiosity, a desire for competence, aspiration to emulate a model, and a deep-sensed commitment to the web of social reciprocity (the human need to respond to others and to operate jointly with them toward an objective) (1966, pp. 125–127).

Bruner (1960) further distinguishes teaching in the expository mode and teaching in the hypothetical mode:

> In the former, the decisions concerning the mode and pace and style of exposition are principally determined by the teacher as expositor; the student is the listener. . . . In the hypothetical mode, the teacher and the student are in a more cooperative position. . . . The student is not a bench-bound listener, but takes a part in the formulation and at times may play the principal role in it.
>
> (p. 126)

The hypothetical mode leads to students engaging in acts of discovery, a process that Bruner sees as having four benefits: (1) increasing intellectual powers; (2) shifting from extrinsic to intrinsic rewards; (3) learning the heuristics of discovering; and (4) making material more readily accessible in memory. This mode is more congruent with and more likely to nurture the will to learn.

Bruner conveys the operational aspects of discovery teaching by describing it in action in case studies of actual courses. But Postman and Weingartner (1969) provide the following list of behaviors observable in teachers using the inquiry method:

> The teacher rarely tells students what he thinks they ought to know. He believes that telling, when used as a basic teaching strategy, deprives students of the excitement of doing their own finding and of the opportunity for increasing their power as learners.
>
> His basic mode of discourse with students is questioning. While he uses both convergent and divergent questions, he regards the latter as the more important tool. He emphatically does not view questions as a means of seducing students into parroting the text or syllabus; rather, he sees questions as instruments to open engaged minds to unsuspected possibilities.
>
> Generally, he does not accept a single statement as an answer to a question. In fact, he has a persisting aversion to anyone, any syllabus, any text that offers The Right Answer. Not because answers and solutions are unwelcome—indeed, he is trying to help students be more efficient problem solvers—but because he knows how often The Right Answer serves only to terminate further thought. He knows the power of pluralizing. He does not ask for the reason, but for the reasons. Not for the cause, but the causes. Never the meaning, what are the meanings? He knows, too, the power of contingent thinking. He is the most *It depends* learner in his class.
>
> He encourages student/student interaction as opposed to student/teacher interaction. And generally he avoids acting as a mediator or judge of the quality of ideas expressed. If each person could have with him at all times a full roster of authorities, perhaps it would not be necessary for individuals to make independent judgments. But so long as this is not possible, the individual must learn to depend on himself as a thinker. The inquiry teacher is interested in students developing their own criteria or standards for judging the quality, precision, and relevance of ideas. He permits such development to occur by minimizing his role as arbiter of what is acceptable and what is not.
>
> He rarely summarizes the positions taken by students on the learnings that occur. He recognizes that the act of summary, of *closure*, tends to have the effect of ending further thought. Because he regards learning as a process, not a terminal event, his *summaries* are apt to be stated as hypotheses, tendencies, and directions. He assumes that no one ever learns once and for all how to write, or

how to read, or what were the causes of the Civil War. Rather, he assumes that one is always in the process of acquiring skills, assimilating new information, formulating or refining generalizations. Thus, he is always cautious about defining the limits of learning, about saying, "This is what you will learn between now and the Christmas holidays," or even (especially), "This is what you will learn in the ninth grade." The only significant terminal behavior he recognizes is death, and he suspects that those who talk of learning as some kind of "terminal point" are either compulsive travelers or have simply not observed children closely enough. Moreover, he recognizes that learning does not occur with the same intensity in any two people, and he regards verbal attempts to disregard this fact as a semantic fiction. If a student has arrived at a particular conclusion, then little is gained by the teacher's restating it. If the student has not arrived at a conclusion, then it is presumptuous and dishonest for the teacher to contend that he has. (Any teacher who tells you precisely what his students learned during any lesson, unit, or semester quite literally does not know what he is talking about.)

His lessons develop from the responses of students and not from a previously determined *logical* structure. The only kind of lesson plan, or syllabus, that makes sense to him is one that tries to predict, account for, and deal with the authentic responses of learners to a particular problem: the kinds of questions they will ask, the obstacles they will face, their attitudes, the possible solutions they will offer, and soon. Thus, he is rarely frustrated or inconvenienced by *wrong answers*, false starts, irrelevant directions. These are the stuff of which his best lessons and opportunities are made. In short, the *content* of his lessons are the responses of his students. Since he is concerned with the processes of thought rather than the end results of thought (The Answer!), he does not feel compelled to *cover ground* (there's the traveler again), or to ensure that his students embrace a particular doctrine, or to exclude a student's idea because it is not germane. (Not germane to what? Obviously, it is germane to the student's thinking about the problem.) He is engaged in exploring the way students think, not what they should think (before the Christmas holidays). That is why he spends more of his time listening to students than talking to or at them.

Generally, each of his lessons poses a problem for students. Almost all of his questions, proposed activities, and assignments are aimed at having his students clarify a problem, make observations relevant to the solution of the problem, and make generalizations based on their observations. His goal is to engage students in those activities that produce knowledge: defining, questioning, observing, classifying, generalizing, verifying, and applying. As we have said, all knowledge is a result of these activities. Whatever we think we *know* about astronomy, sociology, chemistry, biology, linguistics, and the like was discovered or invented by someone who was more or less an expert in using inductive methods of inquiry. Thus, our inquiry, or *inductive*, teacher is largely interested in helping his students to become more proficient as users of these methods. He measures his success in terms of behavioral changes in students: the frequency with which they ask questions; the increase in the relevance and cogency of their questions; the frequency and conviction of their challenges to assertions made by other students or teachers or textbooks; the relevance and clarity of the standards on which they base their challenges; their willingness to suspend judgments when they have insufficient data; their willingness to modify or otherwise change their position when data warrant such change; the increase in their tolerance for diverse answers; their ability to apply generalizations, attitudes, and information to novel situations.

These behaviors and attitudes amount to a definition of a different role for the teacher from that which he has traditionally assumed. The inquiry environment, like any other school environment, is a series of human encounters, the nature of which is largely determined by the teacher. Teacher is placed in quotation marks here to call attention to the fact that most of the word's conventional meanings are inimical to inquiry methods. It is not uncommon, for example, to hear "teachers" make statements such as, "Oh, I taught them that, but they didn't learn it." There is no utterance made in the Teachers' Room more extraordinary than this. From our point of view, it is on the same level as a salesman's remarking, "I sold it to him, but he didn't buy it," which is to say, it makes no sense. It seems to mean that "teaching" is what a "teacher" does which, in turn, may or may not bear any relationship to what those being "taught" do.

(Postman and Weingartner, 1969, pp. 34–37)

Suchman (1972) has described vividly the success of the Inquiry Training Project at the University of Illinois in developing inquiry skills in elementary schoolchildren. As a result of this experience, he feels confident in the feasibility of *an inquiry-centered curriculum* in which the children would find themselves launched into areas of study by first being confronted by concrete problem-focused episodes for which they would attempt to build explanatory systems. Part of their data gathering might well be in the question-asking mode and certainly along the way time would have to be spent in building inquiry skills through critiques and other such procedures. Yet there would also be room for helping the children enlarge their conceptual systems through more teacher-directed means.

(p. 158)

Crutchfield (1972, pp. 192–195) counts four sets of skills involved in productive thinking, his synonym for problem-solving or inquiry learning:

1. Skills of problem discovery and formulation.
2. Skills in organizing and processing problem information.
3. Skills in idea generation.
4. Skills in the evaluation of ideas.

The notion that the development of skills of inquiry should be a primary goal of youth education is the cornerstone of the concept of education as a lifelong process. This makes it especially significant that the Governing Board of the UNESCO Institute for Education in Hamburg, Germany decided in March 1972 to focus on research and experimental projects in an exploratory study, *The Concept of Lifelong Education and its Implications for School Curriculum.*

Teaching through modeling

Albert Bandura, at Stanford University, has developed the most elaborate system of thought on imitation, identification, or modeling as concepts of teaching. Labeling the system social learning, Bandura regards reinforcement theories of instrumental conditioning, such as Skinner's, as able to account for the control of previously learned matching responses, but unable to account for the way new response patterns are acquired through observation and imitation.

In teaching by modeling, the teacher behaves in ways that he or she wants the learner to imitate. The teacher's basic technique is role-modeling. Bandura and Walters (1963) identified three kinds of effects from exposing the learner to a model: (1) a modeling effect, whereby the learner acquires new kinds of response patterns; (2) an inhibitory or disinhibitory effect, whereby the learner decreases or increases the frequency, latency, or intensity of previously acquired responses; and (3) an eliciting effect, whereby the learner merely receives from the model a cue for releasing a response that is neither new nor inhibited. For example, the modeling effect occurs when the teacher him- or herself shows learners how to listen empathically to one another by listening empathically to them. The inhibiting or disinhibiting effect occurs when the teacher lets the learners know, through modeling, that it is or is not approved behavior to express their feelings openly. Thus, the teacher inhibits or disinhibits an old response. The eliciting effect occurs when, through modeling, the teacher teaches the art of giving and receiving feedback by inviting the learners to constructively criticize his or her own performance. Accordingly, the teacher is providing a cue eliciting a response neither new nor inhibited.

Gage (1972) remarks that "learning through imitation seems to be especially appropriate for tasks that have little cognitive structure" (p. 47). This observation seems to be borne out by the fact that social learning has been applied principally to behavioral modification in therapeutic settings to correct deviant or antisocial behavior, but its application to such positive educational purposes as the development of attitudes, beliefs, and performance skills has also been demonstrated (Bandura, 1969, pp. 599–624). No doubt every teacher employs modeling as one of many techniques, whether consciously or unconsciously. The teacher's potency as a model will be influenced by such characteristics as age, sex, socio-economic status, social power, ethnic background, and intellectual and vocational status.

Although social learning has been employed chiefly to achieve behavioral changes through external management of reinforcement contingencies, in recent years there has been a growing interest in self-control processes in which individuals regulate their own behavior by arranging appropriate contingencies for themselves. These self-directed endeavors comprise a variety of strategies, about which Bandura (1969, pp. 254–257) makes the following observations:

> The selection of well-defined objectives, both intermediate and ultimate, is an essential aspect of any self-directed program of change. The goals that individuals choose for themselves must be specified in sufficiently detailed behavioral terms to provide adequate guidance for the actions that must be taken daily to attain desired outcomes.
>
> To further increase goal commitment, participants are asked to make contractual agreements to practice self-controlling behaviors in their daily activities. . . . Under conditions where individuals voluntarily commit themselves to given courses of action,

subsequent tendencies to deviate are likely to be counteracted by negative self-evaluations. Through this mechanism, and anticipated social reactions of others, contractual commitments reinforce adherence to corrective practices.

Satisfactions derived from evident changes help to sustain successful endeavors, therefore, utilized objective records of behavioral changes as an additional source of reinforcement for their self-controlling behavior.

Since behavior is extensively under external stimulus control, persons can regulate the frequency with which they engage in certain activities by altering stimulus conditions under which the behavior customarily occurs. Overeating, for example, will arise more often when appetizing foods are prominently displayed in frequented places in the household than if they are stored out of sight and made less accessible.

Behavior that provides immediate positive reinforcement, such as eating, smoking, and drinking, tends to be performed in diverse situations and at varied times. Therefore, another important aspect of self-managed change involves progressive narrowing of stimulus control over behavior. Continuing with the obesity illustration, individuals are encouraged gradually to delimit the circumstances under which they eat until eventually their eating behavior is brought under control of a specific set of stimulus conditions. This outcome is achieved by having the clients commit themselves to a graduated program in which they refrain from eating in non-dining settings, between regular mealtimes, and while engaging in other activities such as watching television, reading, or listening to the radio.

The foregoing procedures are primarily aimed at instituting self-controlling behavior, but unless positive consequences are also arranged the well-intentioned practices are likely to be short-lived. . . . Self-control measures usually produce immediate unpleasant effects while the personal benefits are considerably delayed. Self-reinforcing operations are, therefore, employed to provide immediate support for self-controlling behavior until the benefits that eventually accrue take over the reinforcing function.

As a final feature of self-directed change programs, increases in desired behavior and reductions in undesired behavior are attempted gradually. In this way the incidence of experienced discomforts is kept low, and steady progress toward the eventual goal can be achieved.

PERSPECTIVE TRANSFORMATION AND CRITICAL REFLECTIVITY

A recent new thrust in theorizing about the purpose of teaching/learning is the notion that it is not sufficient for adult education programs to satisfy the identified learning needs of individuals, organizations, and society. Rather, they should seek to help adult learners transform their very way of thinking about themselves and their world—what Mezirow (1991) calls "perspective transformation." Brookfield (1986) proposes that this can be achieved through the development of competence in *critical reflectivity*. He states his case in these words:

> It will be the case, then, that the most significant personal learning adults undertake cannot be specified in advance in terms of objectives to be obtained or behaviors (of whatever kind) to be performed. Thus, significant personal learning might be defined as that learning in which adults come to reflect on their self-images, change their self-concepts, question their previously internalized norms (behavioral and moral), and reinterpret their current and past behaviors from a new perspective. . . .
>
> Significant personal learning entails fundamental change in learners and leads them to redefine and reinterpret their personal, social, and occupational world. In the process, adults may come to explore affective, cognitive, and psychomotor domains that they previously had not perceived as relevant to themselves.
>
> (pp. 213–214)

Brookfield (1986) points out that the addition of this *analytic component* to the role of the facilitator of learning requires that the facilitators and practitioners prompt learners to consider alternative perspectives on their personal, political, work, and social lives. Hence, effective facilitation means that learners will be challenged to examine their previously held values, beliefs, and behaviors and will be confronted with ones that they may not want to consider. Such challenges and confrontations need not be done in an adversarial, combative, or threatening manner; indeed, the most effective facilitator is one who can encourage adults to consider rationally and carefully perspectives and interpretations of the world that diverge from those they already hold, without making these adults feel they are being cajoled or threatened. This experience may produce anxiety, but such anxiety should be accepted as a normal component of learning and not something to be avoided at all costs for fear that learners will leave the group. There are forms of fulfillment that are quite unlike those produced by a wholly joyful encounter with a new form of knowledge or a new skill area. It is this dimension of increased insight through critical reflection on current assumptions and past beliefs and behaviors that is sometimes ignored in treatments of adult learning (pp. 285–286).

CHANGE THEORY

Another system of thought that has great implications for educational practice has to do with influencing the educative quality of total environments. Concepts and strategies in this system are drawn from field theory, systems theory, organizational development and consultation theories, and ecological psychology.

The systems theorists have provided conceptual frameworks for analyzing organizations of all types as complex social systems with interacting subsystems (Cleland, 1969; Kast and Rosenzweig, 1970; Knowles, 1980b; Parsons, 1951; Seiler, 1967; Von Bertalanffy, 1968; Zadeh, 1969). Knowles (1980b, pp. 66–68) presents an interpretation of some of the applications of their work for human resources development in one of his earlier works:

> One of the misconceptions in our cultural heritage is the notion that organizations exist purely to get things done. This is only one of their purposes; it is their work purpose. But every organization is also a social system that serves as an instrumentality for helping people meet human needs and achieve human goals. In fact, this is the primary purpose for which people take part in organizations—to meet their needs and achieve their goals—and when an organization does not serve this purpose for them they tend to withdraw from it. So organizations also have a human purpose.
>
> Adult education is a means available to organizations for furthering both purposes. Their work purpose is furthered to the extent that they use adult education to develop the competencies of their personnel to do the work required to accomplish the goals of the organizations. Their human purpose is furthered to the extent that they use adult education to help their personnel develop the competencies that will enable them to work up the ladder of Maslow's hierarchy of needs for survival through safety, affection, and esteem to self-actualization.
>
> As if by some law of reciprocity, therefore, organization provides an environment for adult education. In the spirit of Marshall McLuhan's *The Medium is the Message*, the quality of learning that takes place in an organization is affected by the kind of organization

it is. This is to say that an organization is not simply an instrumentality for providing organized learning activities to adults; it also provides an environment that either facilitates or inhibits learning.

For example, if a young executive is being taught in his corporations' management development program to involve his subordinates in decision making within his department, but his own superiors never involve him in making decisions, which management practice is he likely to adopt? Or if an adult church member is being taught to "love thy neighbor," but the total church life is characterized by discrimination, jealousy, and intolerance, which value is more likely to be learned? Or if an adult student in a course on "The Meaning of Democratic Behavior" is taught that the clearest point of differentiation between democracy and other forms of government is the citizen's sharing in the process of public policy formulation, but the teacher has never given him a chance to share responsibility for conducting the course and the institution has never asked his advice on what courses should be offered, what is he likely to learn about the meaning of democracy?

No educational institution teaches just through its courses, workshops, and institutes; no corporation teaches just through its in-service education programs; and no voluntary organization teaches just through its meetings and study groups. They all teach by everything they do, and often they teach opposite lessons in their organizational operation from what they teach in their educational program.

This line of reasoning has led modern adult-education theorists to place increasing emphasis on the importance of building an educative environment in all institutions and organizations that undertake to help people learn. What are the characteristics of an educative environment? They are essentially the manifestations of the conditions of learning . . . . But they can probably be boiled down to four basic characteristics: (1) respect for personality; (2) participation in decision making; (3) freedom of expression and availability of information; and (4) mutuality of responsibility in defining goals, planning and conducting activities, and evaluating.

In effect, an educative environment—at least in a democratic culture—is one that exemplifies democratic values, that practices a democratic philosophy.

A *democratic philosophy* is characterized by a concern for the development of persons, a deep conviction as to the worth of every individual, and faith that people will make the right decisions for themselves if given the necessary information and support. It gives precedence to the growth of people over the accomplishment of things when these two values are in conflict. It emphasizes the release of human potential over the control of human behavior. In a truly democratic organization there is a spirit of mutual trust, an openness of communications, a general attitude of helpfulness and cooperation, and a willingness to accept responsibility; in contrast to paternalism, regimentation, restriction of information, suspicion, and enforced dependency on authority.

When applied to the organization of adult education, a democratic philosophy means that the learning activities will be based on the real needs and interests of the participants; that the policies will be determined by a group that is a representative of all participants; and that there will be a maximum of participation by all members of the organization in sharing responsibility for making and carrying out decisions. The intimate relationship between democratic philosophy and adult education is eloquently expressed in these words of Eduard Lindeman:

> One of the chief distinctions between conventional and adult education is to be found in the learning process itself. None but the humble become good teachers of adults. In an adult class the student's experience counts for as much as the teacher's knowledge. Both are exchangeable at par. Indeed, in some of the best adult classes it is sometimes difficult to discover who is learning most, the teacher or the students. This two-way learning is also reflected in the management of adult-education enterprises. Shared learning is duplicated by shared authority. In conventional education the pupils adapt themselves to the curriculum offered, but in adult education the pupils aid in formulating the curricula. . . . Under democratic conditions authority is of the group. This is not an easy lesson to learn, but until it is learned democracy cannot succeed.
>
> (Gessner, 1956, p. 166)

For an organization to foster adult learning to the fullest possible degree it must go even further than merely practicing a democratic philosophy. It will stimulate individual self-renewal to the extent that it consciously engages in continuous self-renewal for itself. Just as a teacher's most potent tool is the example of his or her own behavior, so an organization's most effective instrument of influence is its own behavior.

This proposition is based on the premise that an organization tends to serve as a role model for those it influences. So if its purpose is to encourage its personnel, members, or constituents to engage in a process of continuous change and growth, it is likely to succeed to the extent that it models the role of organizational change and growth. This proposition suggests, therefore, that an organization must be innovative as well as democratic if it is to provide an environment conducive to learning. [Table 7.4] provides some illustrative characteristics that seem to distinguish innovative from static organizations. The insights come from recent research on this fascinating subject. The right-hand column might well serve as a beginning checklist of desirable organizational goals in the dimensions of structure, atmosphere, management philosophy, decision making, and communication.

(Knowles, 1980b, pp. 66–68)

An increasing number of systems theory applicators are developing sophisticated procedures and tools to assess organizational health, diagnose needs for change, feed data back into the system for continued renewal, and use the data for precision in planning (Baughart, 1969; Bushnell and Rappaport, 1972; Davis, 1966; Handy and Hussain, 1969; Hare, 1967; Hartley, 1968; Kaufman, 1972; Rudwick, 1969; Schuttenberg, 1972).

The change theorists, building largely on the field-theoretical concepts of Kurt Lewin, have been concerned with the planning of change, the choice and use of strategies of change, organizational development, the role of the consultant and change agent, management of conflict, intervention theory, resistance to change, human relations training and the ethics of change agentry (Argyris, 1962, 1970; Bennis, 1966; Bennis et al., 1968; Blake and Mouton, 1964; Eiben and Milliren, 1976; Greiner, 1971; Lewin, 1951; Lippitt, 1969; Schein, 1969; Watson, 1967; Zurcher, 1977).

SUMMARY

Theories of learning differ from theories of teaching. Various researchers have studied the topics of learning and teaching theories and the teaching/learning interaction. Consequently, a variety of theories exist about the nature of teaching and the teacher's role. Gage recognizes the distinction between the two theoretical frameworks, and asserts that learning theories address methods of learning, whereas teaching theories address the methods employed to influence learning. Understandably, there is a strong correlation

Table 7.4 Some characteristics of static versus innovative organizations

Dimensions	Characteristics	
	Static organizations	*Innovative organizations*
Structure	Rigid—much energy given to maintaining permanent departments, committees; reverence for tradition, constitution and by-laws. Hierarchical—adherence to chain of command. Roles defined narrowly. Property-bound.	Flexible—much use of temporary task forces; easy shifting of departmental lines; readiness to change constitution; depart from tradition. Multiple linkages based on functional collaboration. Roles defined broadly. Property-mobile.
Atmosphere	Task-centered, impersonal. Cold, formal, reserved. Suspicious.	People-centered, caring. Warm, informal, intimate. Trusting.
Management	Function of management is to control personnel through coercive power.	Function of management is to release the energy of personnel; power is used supportively.
Philosophy and attitudes	Cautious—low risk-taking. Attitude toward errors: to be avoided. Emphasis on personnel selection. Self-sufficiency—closed system regarding sharing resources. Emphasis on conserving resources. Low tolerance for ambiguity.	Experimental—high risk-taking. Attitude toward errors: to be learned from. Emphasis on personnel development. Interdependency—open system regarding sharing resources. Emphasis on developing and using resources. High tolerance for ambiguity.
Decision making and policy making	High participation at top, low at bottom. Clear distinction between policy making and execution. Decision making by legal mechanisms. Decisions treated as final.	Relevant participation by all those affected. Collaborative policy making and policy execution. Decision making by problem solving. Decisions treated as hypotheses to be tested.
Communication	Flow restricted. One-way—downward. Feelings repressed or hidden.	Open flow—easy access. Multidirectional—up, down, sideways. Feelings expressed.

between learning and teaching theories: the learning theory(ies) adopted by the teacher affect the teaching theory(ies) employed. Both learning theories and teaching theories have played a prominent role in the research efforts, providing both principles of teaching and teaching concepts.

Hilgard's contribution is the identification of a schema of 20 learning principles from S–R, cognitive, and motivation and personality theories. He used prominent theorists with similar notions about the roles of teachers to validate his premise. These included Thorndike, Guthrie, Skinner, Hull, Tolman, and Gagné, each an important contributor to the field.

Other theorists, including Rogers and Maslow, have focused on studies of adults in their research efforts. Their findings differ vastly from researchers who focused on animals and children. For instance, Rogers emphasizes the concepts of environment and facilitation in his explication of teaching—a sentiment with which Maslow would undoubtedly agree. The only exception is that Maslow would place an even greater emphasis on the teacher's responsibility for providing safety. Watson, Houle, and Tough have also provided insight in this area of study.

Of the concepts derived from theories of teaching, Dewey's are perhaps the most influential. His work resulted in the development of a system established on the concepts of experience, democracy, continuity, and interaction. It is Dewey's conceptualization of scientific thinking, in conjunction with those of cognitive theorists, that spawned the discovery or inquiry method. Other contributors in this area include Bruner, Suchman, and Crutchfield.

Identification or modeling as concepts of teaching, the most elaborate system of thought or imitation, was developed by Bandura. In this system, role-modeling is the teacher's fundamental technique. Gage, analyzing the usefulness of the technique, states, "learning through imitation seems to be especially appropriate for tasks that have little cognitive structure."

Continued research efforts have resulted in new systems of thought. The value of teaching/learning as a tool to invoke critical thinking on the part of adults is an emerging concept: Mezirow calls this perspective transformation, and Brookfield calls it critical reflectivity. Another system of thought, drawing from field theory, systems theory, organizational development and consultation theories, and ecological psychology, encompasses the ramifications of influencing the educative quality of total environments.

REFLECTION QUESTIONS

7.1 What is the wisdom behind Hilgard's 20 principles of teaching?

7.2 What ideas from Guthrie and Skinner (both behaviorists) make the most sense to you and why?

7.3 Using Robert Gagné's types of learning (Table 7.2), classify your own learning when reading this chapter versus applying what you have learned when instructing.

7.4 Summarize Carl Rogers's view of the teacher/learner relationship.

7.5 Summarize John Dewey's contribution to understanding the learning process.

7.6 How do you see teaching through *inquiry* and teaching through *modeling* as being useful?

7.7 Describe a transformational learning experience that you or someone you know has gone through.

ADULT LEARNING WITHIN HUMAN RESOURCE DEVELOPMENT

8

INTRODUCTION

The disciplines of human resource development (HRD) and adult education (AE) both view the process of adult learning as being central to their theory and practice. Even so, the purposes of HRD and AE differ, and their perspective on adult learning differs. The core difference is related to control of the goals and purposes for which adult learning is employed—organizational versus individual control. This chapter looks closely at HRD, the role of adult learning within HRD, and the issue of control.

HUMAN RESOURCE DEVELOPMENT GOALS

HRD professionals are in general agreement as to their goals. Most take the position that HRD should focus on increasing the performance requirements of its host organizations through the development of the organization's workforce (ASTD-USDL, 1990; Bassi, 2014; Knowles, 1990; McLagan, 1989; Swanson, 2007; Swanson and Holton, 2009).

Others believe HRD should focus on individual development and personal fulfillment without using organizational performance as the measure of worth (Dirkx, 1996). Yet, it is the increase in performance resulting from HRD that justifies its existence. From either perspective, the question of contribution always comes into play. Holton (1998b) provides a very useful taxonomy of *performance outcomes* and *performance drivers* that accommodates the gap between those focused on the organization first and then the individual versus those focused on the individual first and then the organization. He informs HRD professionals to pay attention to both performance outcomes and performance drivers. Thus, organization *performance*, such as high-quality services delivered to external customers, can be logically connected to performance drivers, such as learning and process improvement (see Chapter 17 for a more complete explanation).

When practiced within productive organizations, HRD should strive to contribute directly to the host organization's goals. The host organization is a purposeful system that must attain effective and efficient survival goals. Consequently, it is the responsibility of HRD to focus on those goals as well as individual employee goals.

HRD can be thought of as a subsystem that functions within the larger organizational system. An *organization* is defined as a productive enterprise having a mission and goals (Holton, 1998b). Additionally, an organization is a system, with definable inputs, processes, outputs, parts, and purposes (Rummler and Brache, 1995; Brache, 2002). Contemporary HRD literature talks consistently of linking HRD to the strategic goals of the organization (see, for example, Gill, 1995). If HRD is to be respected and useful in organizations, it must position itself as a strategic partner and achieve the same level of importance as traditional core organizational processes, such as finance, production, and marketing (Torraco and Swanson, 1995). To gain an understanding of the purpose of the HRD subsystem, the goals of the larger system in which it operates should be considered.

Of the scarce resources that organizations must procure and allocate, perhaps none is more important to the success of the firm than human resources (Edvinsson and Malone, 1997). A major expenditure for most organizations is tied directly to workers, including wages, benefits, and HRD (Becker, 1993; Noe, 2012). And although human resources are unique in that people have feelings, make plans, support families, and develop communities, they are in some ways similar to other resources, in that firms expect a return on the money invested in their employees (Cascio, 1987; Swanson, 2001). Unless workers contribute to the profitability and viability of an organization, it would make economic sense to invest the money elsewhere. Even in nonprofit organizations, employees must contribute meaningfully to organizational goals that are essential to survival, even though those goals are not stated in dollars of profit.

The purpose of reviewing this basic reality of organizational survival is not to paint an unfeeling picture of the workplace in which people are merely cogs in a mechanistic machine. There are numerous examples of companies that meet their organizational goals that are also among the most progressive in terms of employee treatment and relations (Levering and Moskowitz, 1994). Nowhere has it been shown that organizational success should be in direct conflict with employee happiness and well-being.

Performance is defined as *the organizational system outputs that have value to the customer in the form of productivity attributable to the organization, work process, and/or individual contributor levels.* Using this definition, performance is the means by which organizations measure their goals. Performance can be measured in many ways: rate of return, cycle time, and quality of output are three such possibilities. Additionally, it is important to make the distinction between levels of performance. Performance takes place and can be measured at the organizational, process, and individual levels.

If HRD is to be aligned with the goals and strategies of the organization, and performance is the primary means by which the goals and strategies of organizations are realized, then it follows that HRD should be first and foremost concerned with maintaining and/or improving performance at the organizational, process, and individual levels. If HRD is to be a value-added activity of the firm (instead of a line item of cost that is to be controlled and minimized), then HRD practitioners must be concerned about performance and how it enables organizations to achieve their goals.

HUMAN RESOURCE DEVELOPMENT AND PERFORMANCE IMPROVEMENT

How can HRD improve performance? There are many possibilities at the individual, process, and organizational levels. Figure 8.1 is a matrix of performance levels and variables that can aid in the diagnosis of performance problems (Swanson, 2007, p. 52). Within each cell are enabling questions that permit diagnosis of performance, but each cell can also serve as a conceptual framework for classifying performance interventions.

As an example, the mission/goal variable at the organizational level asks whether the organization's mission and goals fit various internal and external realities. If they do not, then most likely performance is being impeded. Assume that an organization's mission and goals do not fit the reality of its culture and this is resulting in suboptimized performance. HRD could attempt to solve this performance problem through structured intervention in a couple of ways, depending on the outcomes of detailed analysis. A process could be put in place to formulate mission and goals that accommodate the organizational culture. On the other hand, a cultural change process could be implemented to modify the culture so that it is better aligned with the mission and goals of the organization. This example and the performance diagnosis matrix show that numerous impediments to performance, and consequently numerous challenges and opportunities for HRD to improve performance, exist.

PERFORMANCE VARIABLES	PERFORMANCE LEVELS		
	Organizational level	Process level	Individual level
Mission/goal	Does the organization's mission/goal fit the reality of the economic, political, and cultural forces?	Do the process goals enable the organization to meet organizational and individual missions/goals?	Are the professional and personal missions/goals of individuals congruent with the organization's?
System design	Does the organizational system provide structure and policies supporting the desired performance?	Are processes designed in such a way to work as a system?	Do individuals face obstacles that impede their job performance?
Capacity	Does the organization have the leadership, capital, and infrastructure to achieve its mission/goals?	Does the process have the capacity to perform(quantity, quality, and timeliness)?	Does the individual have the mental, physical, and emotional capacity to perform?
Motivation	Do the policies, culture, and reward systems support the desired performance?	Does the process provide the information and human factors required to maintain it?	Does the individual want to perform no matter what?
Expertise	Does the organization establish and maintain selection and training policies and resources?	Does the process of developing expertise meet the changing demands of changing processes?	Does the individual have the knowledge, skills, and experience to perform?

Figure 8.1 Performance diagnosis matrix of enabling questions

When business and industry leaders talk about the high values of core competence to the life of their companies, they are talking primarily about knowledge and expertise that fits within and between the 15 cells in the performance diagnosis matrix. This learning can also be categorized as public knowledge, industry-specific knowledge, or firm-specific knowledge that is critical to sustaining organizational performance (Leonard-Barton, 1995, p. 21).

Notice that *adult learning* plays an important role in most, if not all, of the matrix cells. Just getting to the point of doing the work in each diagnostic cell of the organizational system requires much to be learned in order to understand and operate within and between these cells. For example, if HRD is to change culture, then certainly the principles and practices of adult learning will play an important role as employees develop and learn new norms. Most process improvement strategies embrace some form of self-directed teams that examine their work processes and learn better ways to perform them. Building leadership capacity is a learning process. In organizations where innovation is a key performance driver, learning becomes central to survival (Senge, 1990; Watkins and Marsick, 1993). It is not difficult to see that there are potential needs for adult learning within every cell of the performance diagnosis matrix.

One important strategic role for HRD is to build the organization's strategic capability—the knowledge and expertise required to figure out the present and to develop rational scenarios of the future and ways to connect them (Torraco and Swanson, 1995). Adult learning, from this perspective, is critical in order to maintain the performance of an existing system and to improve on that system. Increasingly, it is an organization's intellectual capital that leads to sustained competitive advantage (Edvinsson and Malone, 1997; Stewart, 1997). Adult learning becomes a powerful organizational improvement strategy when it is embedded in a holistic performance improvement system framework.

HUMAN RESOURCE DEVELOPMENT AND ADULT LEARNING

The issue of control—organizational versus individual—is useful in exploring the role of adult learning in HRD. Cervero and Wilson help in their book, *Planning Responsibly for Adult Education: A Guide to Negotiating Power and Interests* (1994), by noting that the adult education literature has been "focused on technical, 'how to' skills, while presupposing some ideally neutral staging area in which these skills will be exercised, and have remained surprisingly silent on the troublesome issues of 'what for' and 'for whom.'" They go on to speak more forcefully: "Which people get to decide the purpose, content, and format of the program? Is it always the people with the most power? Is it the adults who will participate in the program, the leadership of the institution sponsoring the program, or the planners themselves?" (Cervero and Wilson, 1994, p. xii).

So what is the relationship between HRD and adult learning? Swanson (1996) defines HRD as a process of developing and unleashing human expertise through organizational development and personnel training and development for the purpose of improving performance at the organization, work process, and individual levels. McLagan (1989) offers an earlier definition of HRD along similar lines: the integrated use of training and development, organizational development and career development to improve individual, group, and organizational effectiveness. In both definitions, it is apparent that the outcome of HRD is *performance improvement*. It should be equally apparent that *learning*—knowledge and expertise—is a core component of HRD but not the whole of HRD.

HRD is broader than training or adult learning. There are HRD interventions that involve much more than training or learning activities, and some can have no planned educational component. This aspect of HRD falls in the *unleashing* element of the definition. For example, HRD might be involved in improving a business process intended to result in a newly engineered business process and minor work method modifications that are transparent to the worker. They could require no formal learning effort to implement. If training were required, it would be a relatively small part of the entire intervention. One could attempt to argue that the HRD work to improve the process involves acts of learning and is therefore adult learning. The rebuttal is that the desired outcome is to improve the process rather than the learning in individuals working in the business process.

These remarks should not be construed as an argument that the discipline of AE is a subset of HRD. It is not. Although adult learning takes place in both HRD and AE and both are deeply committed to adult learning, HRD and AE are discrete disciplines. Their area of intersection occurs within adult learning. When adult learning outcomes and learning process decisions about individuals are bounded by rules and requirements of the organization, adult learning is HRD. When the adult learning outcomes and learning process rules and requirements are located in the individual, it is AE. The core difference is in the idea of control. If the organization retains the authority to approve or disapprove learning interventions, the control is with the organization, and therefore it is HRD. To the point that control is overtly and formally shared, the learning process is both AE and HRD (Swanson and Arnold, 1996). For example, Robinson and Stern (1997) offer vivid illustrations of two essential elements that foster corporate creativity and encourage employees to control their learning journey. They speak of *self-initiated activity,* which is an activity performed by an individual who is not asked to do it; and *unofficial activity,* which is an activity performed by an individual over a period of time in which he or she continues to work on his learning journey without direct official recognition and/or support, and the benefits organizations gain by allowing both of these activities to take place among workers.

Thus, some HRD processes and interventions do not focus on adult learning. By the same token, AE does not always take place in the context of organizations for the purpose of performance improvement. The outcome of AE can be personal growth, general knowledge, or even amusement.

For HRD, adult learning focuses on development interventions that have two attributes: first, the context is organizational; and second, the desired outcome is learning—knowledge and expertise—that will impact the performance goals of the host organization.

Facilitating adult learning in performance-oriented organizations often creates a tension between the assumptions underlying andragogical practice and the organization's performance requirements. For many, best AE practices allow maximum individual control and appeal directly to the needs most meaningful to the individual (Hiemstra and Sisco, 1990). When the individual's needs are consistent with the organization's needs, there is no tension. When the individual's needs and goals are not congruent with the organization's performance requirements, and the organization is providing the required learning experience, a tension exists and inevitably results in some degree of organizational control.

For this reason, learning professionals in HRD must balance practices that lead to the most effective adult learning with those that will lead to performance outcomes. When learning is required, performance will be compromised if effective adult learning principles are not incorporated. However, learning will also be compromised without an emphasis on performance principles because the learning opportunities will likely be discontinued if performance outcomes are not achieved.

Effective HRD professionals have the ability to find the optimum balance in each situation. Fortunately, the majority of learning situations present no problem. In many cases, the best interests of the employee and the organization can be met at the same time. This is especially true in organizations that link employee career advancement to performance so that employees' lives are enhanced as the organization's performance improves.

However, there are other instances where adult learning principles cannot be wholly implemented. Consider organizational change, for example. Can a large organization in a survival mode allow individuals the freedom to choose whether they want to learn a new way to run the organization? Hardly. Can an organization continue to invest in learning programs for its employees that do not lead to performance improvement over the long run? No.

In summary, HRD has a great concern to create more humane organizations. However, by definition, HRD must ensure that the organization's performance improvement needs are met. At certain points, this is likely to lead to some adaptation and compromise of the core andragogical principles. Effective application of adult learning principles in HRD requires practitioners to become comfortable with, and even embrace, the tension between adult learning and performance principles.

THE PREMISE OF ADULTS CONTROLLING THEIR OWN LEARNING

One of the most popular ideas in AE is that individuals want to have control over their learning based on their personal goals and that learning will increase as a result. The idea is that better outcomes result when the learner retains control throughout the learning phases. There is controversy related to this idea of how much control individual learners want and can handle.

During the 1980s there was considerable discussion about embracing self-directed learning as a unifying theory and goal for the discipline of AE. Even one of the leading proponents, Stephen Brookfield (1988), acknowledged that self-directed learning is far more complex than first proposed; and that the push in AE to embrace self-directed learning was motivated in part by the discipline's search for an identity and unifying theory.

The point of this discussion is not to enter the AE debate about self-directed learning. It must be recognized that the core assumptions of andragogy do not raise learner self-directedness to the same high level as has been proposed by many AE theorists and practitioners. Andragogy suggests that adults have a *self-concept* of being responsible for their own lives and expect others to treat them as being capable of self-direction (see Chapter 3). AE suggests that the purpose of learning should be to develop self-directed learning capacity in adults (Brookfield, 1986). The self-concept principle in adult learning theory has consistently been confused with the democratic humanism goals of AE that all adults become self-directing. The first is a *characteristic of adults*, the latter a *purpose for learning*. This should not be interpreted to say that the AE goals are wrong, but rather that the core learning principle of independent self-concept must be considered separately from the goals and purposes of AE. It is the latter that has falsely made HRD look inconsistent with adult learning principles. HRD practice is generally in harmony with the andragogical notion of independent *self-concept*, but clearly does not share the goals and purposes of AE.

Because HRD focuses on performance outcomes, the significance of learner control is viewed as secondary by most professionals in HRD. The AE reaction to the performance focus rests with the concern that the feelings and worth of human beings as individuals are ignored by too much emphasis on bottom-line results. There is evidence that learning, or enhancing the capacity to learn, is a valuable outcome in and of itself and that sponsoring organizations logically benefit (Robinson and Stern, 1997). Thus, the line is sometimes falsely drawn between those who view HRD as tied to business goals and focused on the bottom line and those who would like to take a more humanistic stance in the matter. In fact, HRD shares concerns for a humanistic workplace, has adult learning as one of its core components, but also embraces organizational performance theory. The gap is not as wide as some would portray it to be.

THE PHASES OF THE ADULT LEARNING PLANNING PROCESS

Adult learning is defined as the process of adults gaining knowledge and expertise. Additionally, the ideas that (1) learners universally want to have control over their learning process, and (2) learning increases as a result comes from AE. Adult learning theory takes a more situational stance on shared control.

Just what are the issues surrounding this core idea of learners controlling their own learning process? A contradiction exists between the AE ideal of individuals taking control of their learning and the reality of adult limitations in taking control of their own decision making. The following sections discuss the practical issues facing HRD as it relates to adults directing their own learning at the needs, creation, implementation, and evaluation planning phases.

Figure 8.2 provides the framework for this discussion. It shows the four phases of the adult learning planning process and an outer ring of theory. The four phases are:

Need. Determine what learning is needed so as to achieve goals.
Create. Create a strategy and resources to achieve the learning goal(s).
Implement. Implement the learning strategy and use the learning resources.
Evaluate. Assess the attainment of the learning goal and the process of
reaching it.

These four phases serve as the categories or lenses used to search for what is known about learners controlling their own learning process.

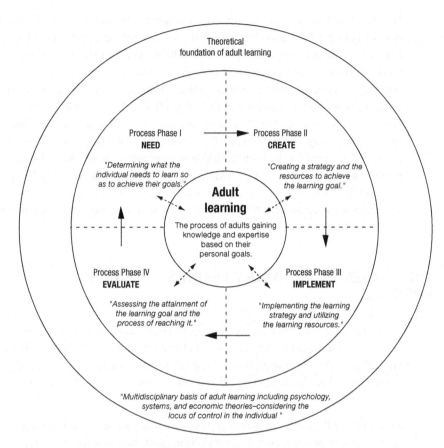

Figure 8.2 Adult learners controlling their own learning process
Source: © Richard A. Swanson, St. Paul, MN 1996

ADULTS DETERMINE THEIR OWN LEARNING NEEDS

"Who needs what, as defined by whom?" is a wonderful way to sum up the issues of needs assessment in relation to the issue of control. At the *need* phase, adults who exhibit control will fully determine the learning needs required to achieve their personal goal(s). The idea of control at the need determination phase can better be examined through the perspective of four types of learning:

Type of learning	Locus of control
Unintended learning	No control
Self-directed learning	Learner controlled
Mediated learning	Shared control between learner and external authority
Authority-directed learning	Authority controlled (organization or individual)

Even though there are limitations to learner control, Penland (1979) found that the top four reasons why adults chose to learn on their own were all related to wanting to retain control of the learning process. In this vein, the determination of learning *needs*, the up-front commitment to learning, is the phase with the greatest amount of attention in the literature.

The determination of the learning needs perspective in the AE literature is primarily reactive in nature rather than strategic or even tactical. Learning professionals are portrayed as reacting to the needs expressed by adult learners. The control resides with the learner, and the learning professional responds to those felt needs. This assumes that the learner (1) is fully aware of his or her needs, (2) can accurately assess the specific learning required, (3) is motivated enough to engage in any learning required, and (4) is motivated enough to engage in any learning needed, even if threatening. Brookfield (1986) reacts to this notion:

> To take learners' definitions of need as always determining appropriate practice is to cast the facilitator as a technician within the consumer mode. It is to remove from the facilitator all professional judgment and to turn him or her into a *knee-jerk* satisfier of consumer needs. Education becomes one giant department store in which facilitators are providers of whatever learners (consumers) believe will make them happy.
>
> (p. 97)

The extension of this idea into HRD is to conduct a learning/training *wants* analysis among employees and to call it a training *needs* analysis. Employees are surveyed as to what training they would like to have and then the training options gaining the most votes are used as a basis for the course offerings. Recent developments in conducting these low-level surveys through computers and electronic data-gathering systems have provided an air of sophistication to this incomplete and/or incompetent practice. Surveys of this nature can be one important element in a sound needs analysis process, but not the process itself.

The fundamental flaw with this approach is that there is no substantial attention given to individuals, work process, or the organization. It does nothing well. This popular vote strategy requires almost no professional expertise on the part of those running the process, and allows them to hide behind the cloak of democracy. On the positive side, the fundamental strength of this approach is that it provides the opportunity to participate, even if at a minimum level. Given such opportunity, objections are minimized and motivation is increased even when unpopular alternatives are put forward.

The reality is that this approach is not effective for improving performance (Swanson, 1996). Employee *wants* are only sometimes related to real performance improvement *needs*. Frequently, this is not due to employee ignorance, but simply to the fact that they do not have the expertise, information, or time to properly analyze their needs. Their wants are their best guess, but are not accurate. Performance improvement often requires joint planning and, occasionally, an external analyst. Although this may create some tension initially as control is shifted to the organization, adults frequently become quite comfortable with it when they realize that giving up some control will ultimately enable them to do their jobs better and thus gain another form of control.

ADULTS CREATE AND IMPLEMENT THEIR OWN LEARNING

The second phase of the adult learning planning process is *creating* a strategy and the resources to achieve the learning goal. The third phase is *implementing* the learning strategy and using the learning resources.

Rosenblum and Darkenwald (1983) concluded from their experimental research that high motivation could lead to high satisfaction and achievement *without* participant planning involvement. If this was the case, one interpretation could be that involvement at the *need* phase is critical for the purpose of motivation and that similar learner involvement in the other phases is not as important. This could also be the reason why there is so little planning literature related to the *create* and *implement* phases other than in-process instructional techniques for engaging the learner. Without the issue of control, it is easy to see that these techniques at the *create* and *implement* phases use the core assumptions of andragogy while avoiding the fundamental question of control.

The relevant AE literature focused on learner control of the creation and implementation planning phase is scant. Most inferences must be made from related studies and from the *mediated learning*—the shared control between the learner and an external authority (usually the instructor).

For example, the effect of adult learners' self-concepts and their opinions about the content at the time they are directly engaged in the learning process has been studied. The classic Spelman and Levy (1966) study related to adults' self-concept of powerlessness and the distorting impact it had on their learning. In this study, heavy smokers learned as much general medical knowledge as non-smokers, but learned significantly less about the relation to lung cancer than non-smokers. Smokers, feeling relatively powerless in the context of their smoking addiction and its consequences, ended up learning less about lung cancer. The liberating knowledge was ineffectual.

In a more hopeful vein, part of Tolman's (1959) theory of purposive behaviorism explains *expectancies* in context of experience. Tolman suggests that adults learn where the goal is and how to get to it. Thus, it is reasonable to think that there is a melding of purposes between the organization and the individual contributor and that the means (creation and implementation) of achieving those purposes becomes relatively easy.

It could be that self-directed learning decisions at the *create* and *implement* phases result in high motivation, minimum growth, and high satisfaction. Thus, a counter-theory to self-directed learning is that pursuing the opinions of adults to create and implement learning leads to low-risk decisions–comfort rather than growth. The control dilemma concerns HRD professionals as they struggle to meet organizational goals, determine the content and method of programs, and seek to fully engage learners.

Brookfield (1988) sheds light on this dilemma: "For a facilitator to completely ignore learners' needs and expressions of preference is arrogant and unrealistic. But it is just as misguided for a facilitator to completely repress his or her own ideas concerning worthwhile curricula or effective methods and to allow learners complete control over these" (p. 97). When it comes to the *create* and *implement* phases of planning learning theory and practice, the shared control between the external authority or instructor and the learner is the primary focus rather than learner self-direction. Within this model, professional educators engage learners and potential learners in the *create* phase so as to establish motivation and community and to promote validity of the experience and materials. At the *implementation* phase, shared control can take a variety of forms, including formative evaluation, team learning, and peer instruction.

ADULTS EVALUATE THEIR OWN LEARNING

The fourth phase of the adult learning planning process is *evaluation*, which is defined as "a systematic collection of evidence to determine if desired changes are taking place" (Swanson, 1996, p. 26). Before discussing adult learners controlling the *evaluation* of their own learning, it is critical to separate learning that they have controlled up to this phase from learning that has been controlled by others up to this point.

Assuming the learner has retained and executed control to this stage, the learner should be asking the evaluation question, "What systematic collection of evidence needs to be carried out to determine whether my desired changes took place?" The follow-up question is, "Based on the evidence collected, to what degree did the desired changes take place?" The questions are focused on learning outcomes or summative evaluation, not the process of working toward the learning outcomes or formative evaluation.

The learning evaluation literature is careful about noting direct measures of outcomes versus proxy, or related, measures. For example, a direct measure of a desired knowledge and/or expertise learning outcome would require instruments to directly measure the change. An indirect measure of knowledge might be to ask oneself or participants if they thought they learned a lot or whether they were satisfied with their learning. Indirect measures have highly questionable validity. Research has shown that participant self-ratings of learning are not related to actual learning (Alliger and Janak, 1989; Alliger et al., 1997; Dixon, 1991). Although self-ratings are generally reliable (consistent), they are generally not trusted as being accurate (valid). Furthermore, participant ratings can be easily inflated by influential techniques by the instructor (Swanson and Fentress, 1975).

Thus, if adult learners rely on proxy measures—*self-assessment* of anticipated outcomes—they will most likely make false conclusions based on invalid data. Worse yet, if the learning professional, serving as a resource to the adult learning process, relies on learner perceptions and feelings about desired changes having taken place (even more indirect measures), the problem is compounded. Examples of such highly questionable evaluation practices relying on secondary sources of perception data are reported in the literature (see Cervero and Wilson, 1994, pp. 60–61, 86–87, 111–113).

The adult learner, wanting to retain control over the evaluation process while gaining valid data, will, in most instances, have to reach outside his or her internal reference to gain rational evaluation data. Obtaining direct measures of learning—knowledge and expertise—from formal tests or expert judges would be the most likely alternative. In many avocational realms of personal development, interest groups provide external measures of skill through competitive judging (for example, car shows, stamp shows, dance competitions, etc.). At a less threatening level, experts serving as mentors can provide similar evaluation.

The humanistic side of the evaluation literature has had a resistance to summative, outcome evaluation. The *formative evaluation* view is that evaluation should be diagnostic and have the purpose of improving learning, rather than simply determining if the desired changes took place. Formative evaluation is seen as feedback and feed-forward between the various phases of learning. Again, the purpose of formative evaluation is to be a part of the learning process, not to assess the drive toward organization performance and the demands for adult competence in the workplace. Furthermore, it is controlled by the organization, not the individual. HRD functions in an organizational world, and demands results and the assessing of results. Management or work teams will likely be full partners in the *evaluation* phase of learning outcomes rather than the individual learners.

In summary, adult learning theory provides sound advice to HRD at each phase of the planning process:

Phase	Sound practice
Need	Engage learners in this phase to gain higher motivation.
	Do not expect self-reported needs to be accurate for either the individual or the organization.
Create	Engage learners in this phase to gain higher validity in the selected learning strategies.
Implement	Engage learners in this phase to better mediate the actual learning.
Evaluate	Engage learners in this phase to gain higher self-reflection and integration of the knowledge and expertise being sought.

SUMMARY

Exploring the gaps between research and practice is a primary role for the reflective practitioner in HRD (Swanson and Holton, 1997). The call to action is to implement best-known practices *and* to conduct more research related to the methods to assess valid learning needs, create and implement valid strategies for achieving learning goals, and conduct valid assessment of learning. This effort should be directed at organization needs as well as those of individual performers.

The idea that the goal of HRD is or should be performance improvement is by no means universally accepted by practitioners or researchers in the field. Some hold that fostering learning or the capacity to learn is a valuable outcome in and of itself and assume that sponsoring organizations will logically benefit. Thus, the line is sometimes drawn between those who view HRD as tied to business goals and focused on performance and those who would like to take a more humanistic stance in the matter. This dichotomy can be termed the *performance-versus-learning debate* as a matter of convenience (see Swanson, 1995; Watkins and Marsick, 1995).

This debate, like many others, is fueled by an often-misconstrued delineation of the opposing sides. Upon closer examination, the two sides may have more in common than first proposed. On the one hand, those who adhere to the performance orientation of HRD do not do so in an attempt to deny the dignity and worth of employees. Neither do they deny that learning is a necessary component of performance. The goal of performance-focused HRD is simply to ensure that the HRD process within organizations contributes to the goals of the organizational system within which it operates. This does not necessarily imply an authoritarian management style. Some might argue that to *ignore* performance issues is itself inhumane and inconsiderate of the workforce. Although organizational performance does not guarantee job security, poor organizational performance puts jobs at serious risk. On the other hand, those on the learning side of the debate are not so naive as to think that organizational goals and performance are irrelevant to HRD. Quite the contrary, they *are* seen as core, but that learning is not always directly tied to the bottom line of an organization.

From the HRD perspective, adult learning, when practiced within productive organizations, should strive to contribute directly to the advancement of the host organization's goals. The host organization is a purposeful system that must pursue effective and efficient survival goals. Consequently, it is the responsibility of HRD to focus on organizational goals as well as individual goals.

REFLECTION QUESTIONS

8.1 Discuss how both disciplines of adult education and human resource development connect to adult learning.

8.2 From your experience, how does learning connect with performance? Speak to performance at various levels (individual, work process, and organization).

8.3 What is your general position related to the idea of adult learners controlling their own learning?

8.4 Discuss the relative ease and difficulty of adults controlling the various learning phases:

a. need,
b. create,
c. implement, and
d. evaluate.

PART 3

ADVANCEMENTS IN ADULT LEARNING

NEW PERSPECTIVES
ON ANDRAGOGY

9

INTRODUCTION

This chapter discusses new perspectives on andragogy that have emerged from research and theory in a variety of disciplines. The chapter is organized by the core andragogical principles and examines new thinking that refines and elaborates on each principle. These core principles are (1) the learner's need to know, (2) self-directed learning (SDL), (3) prior experiences of the learner, (4) readiness to learn, (5) orientation to learning and problem solving, and (6) motivation to learn.

THE LEARNER'S NEED TO KNOW

The core principle that adults *need to know* why before they engage in learning has led to the now generally accepted premise that adults should be engaged in a collaborative planning process for their learning. Indeed, one of the distinguishing characteristics of many adult learning programs is the shared control of program planning and facilitation. Even in learning situations in which the learning content is prescribed, sharing control over the learning strategies is believed to make learning more effective. Engaging adults as collaborative partners for learning satisfies their *need to know* as well as appeals to their self-concept as independent learners.

Because mutual planning is so widely accepted and generally found to be effective by most practitioners, few researchers have been motivated to test this assumption. Training researchers have conducted research related to this premise that suggests three dimensions to the need to know: the need to know *how* learning will be conducted, *what* learning will occur, and *why* learning is important.

How learning is conducted

Tannenbaum and colleagues (1991) studied a group of new employees to examine the extent to which training fulfillment predicted post-training attitudes. *Training fulfillment* was defined as the extent to which training met or fulfilled the group's expectations and desires. The study focused mostly on how the training was conducted and was somewhat consistent with adult learning principles. The study showed that training fulfillment was related to post-training organizational commitment, academic self-efficacy, physical self-efficacy, and motivation to use the training. The positive results were strongest for commitment and motivation to use training. These findings clearly point to the importance of understanding trainees' expectations and desires through needs assessment and mutual planning.

What learning will occur

Hicks and Klimoski (1987) studied a group of managers attending training on performance appraisals. The group that received a more realistic preview of what topics would be covered and the expected outcomes and were given a choice about whether to attend the training were more likely to believe the workshop was appropriate for them. The group also believed they were better able to profit from the workshop, showed more commitment to their decision to attend the training, and were more satisfied with the learning. Students with a high degree of choice were also more motivated to learn and learned more.

Baldwin et al. (1991) directly tested the proposition that trainee involvement in planning about learning would enhance the learning process. Their findings reinforce the importance of choice about learning. Trainees who had a choice about attending training, and received their choice, had higher pre-training motivation and learning. The worst results were found for those who were offered a choice but did not get it.

Why learning is important

Clark et al. (1993) explored a third dimension of a learner's need to know in their study of 15 training groups across 12 different organizations representing a wide variety of organizational types and training topics. Their findings showed that job and career utility were significant predictors of training motivation. Furthermore, when employees had the chance to provide input into the training decision, they were more likely to perceive job and career utility.

Reber and Wallin's (1984) work took this a step further. They investigated the effect of trainees receiving knowledge of results from previous trainees' successful application of training. Trainees with knowledge of results achieved post-training goals, while others did not.

Implications

These studies all focused on adult learning in one setting (organizational training), so some caution is appropriate in generalizing about *all* adult learning situations. None the less, these are strong studies that directly support this andragogical assumption. The message to adult learning professionals is that the common prescription to involve adults in mutual planning and as learning partners is a sound one. However, the exact means by which this effect works cannot be determined from this research. That is, engaging adults in planning the learning process could enable people to decide not to participate in low-value learning, or could actually change their attitudes toward the learning. Regardless, the research seems to point to three areas in which adults need information and involvement before learning: the how, the what, and the why of learning.

SELF-DIRECTED LEARNING

Perhaps no aspect of andragogy has received so much attention and debate as the premise that adults are self-directed learners. That adults can and do engage in SDL is now a foregone conclusion in adult learning research. Questions remain as to whether SDL is a characteristic of adult learners, and whether it should be a goal of adult educators to help all adult learners become self-directed. Much of the confusion surrounding the SDL assumption stems from conceptual confusion about the meaning of SDL.

There are two conceptions of SDL prevalent in the literature (Brookfield, 1986; Candy, 1991). First, SDL is seen as self-teaching, whereby learners are capable of taking control of the mechanics and techniques of teaching themselves in a particular subject. For example, a person who completes an independent study course would clearly engage in self-teaching. Second, SDL is conceived of as personal autonomy, which Candy (1991) calls autodidaxy. Autonomy means taking control of the goals and purposes of learning and assuming ownership of learning. This leads to an internal change of consciousness in which the learner sees knowledge as contextual and freely questions what is learned.

These two dimensions of SDL are relatively independent, although they may overlap. A person may have a high degree of personal autonomy but choose to learn in a highly teacher-directed instructional setting because of convenience, speed, or learning style. For example, a person may decide to learn more about personal financial planning, and after weighing different strategies, decide that attending courses at a university is his or her preferred approach. In fact, many adults decide that traditional instruction is the best approach when they know little about a subject. Choosing traditional instruction over self-teaching does not mean a person has given up ownership or control just because he or she chooses to access learning in this manner. Conversely, just because an adult engages in self-teaching does not mean that the person is autonomous. Continuing the earlier example, the student in the independent study course may have little ownership if the supervising teacher sets all the requirements. Thus, the presence or absence of activities associated with self-teaching is not an accurate indicator of personal autonomy. For most learning professionals, the most important dimension of SDL is building personal autonomy.

The assumption that all adults have full capacity for self-teaching and personal autonomy in every learning situation is generally not accepted. Any particular learner in a particular learning situation is likely to exhibit different capabilities and preferences. Grow (1991) suggested that SDL is situational and that the *teacher's* job is to match styles with the student. Grow proposed four stages, and corresponding teaching styles, as presented in Table 9.1.

It is important to note that mismatches can occur in either direction. That is, too much self-directedness can be as big a problem as too little, depending on the learner. For example, a learner who is experienced with the subject matter and has strong learning skills will likely be frustrated in highly controlled learning situations. Conversely, a learner who is inexperienced with the subject and has poorly developed SDL skills will likely be intimidated, at least initially, in highly SDL situations. Because learners in any given learning situation are likely to vary widely as to what stage they are in, the teacher has to structure the learning situation to accommodate all stages.

It is also important to note that the reason a learner is in a particular stage may be related to self-teaching skills, or personal autonomy, or both. Suppose a learner exhibits Stage 1 behaviors. That person could be highly autonomous but does not know how to learn particular material. Or, the person could have strong self-teaching skills but little autonomy. Or, the person could be highly autonomous and a good self-teacher but simply chooses not to learn individually.

Table 9.1 Grow's stages in learning autonomy

Stage	Student	Teacher	Examples
Stage 1	Dependent	Authority, coach	Coaching with immediate feedback, drill. Informational lecture. Overcoming deficiencies and resistance.
Stage 2	Interested	Motivator, guide	Inspiring lecture plus guided discussion. Goal-setting and learning strategies.
Stage 3	Involved	Facilitator	Discussion facilitated by teacher who participates as equal. Seminar. Group projects.
Stage 4	Self-directed	Consultant, delegator	Internship, dissertation, individual work or self-directed study group.

Garrison (1997) more formally captured this multidimensional view of SDL. He proposed a comprehensive model of SDL based on three core components: (1) self-management (control); (2) motivation (entering and task); and (3) self-monitoring (responsibility). According to Garrison, AE has traditionally focused on the first component, the control of learning, and has paid less attention to the learning processes. He suggests that equal attention should be focused on motivation issues, including the motivation to engage in SDL and to complete SDL tasks. Garrison's third component, self-monitoring, is the cognitive learning processes as well as metacognitive skills a person needs to engage in SDL. Adult learning professionals need to pay attention to all three components.

A related stream of research comes from psychology and the concept referred to as "locus of control" (Rotter, 1966, 1990). *Locus of control* occurs when

> people attribute the cause or control of events to themselves or to an external environment. Those who ascribe control of events to themselves are said to have internal locus of control and are referred to as *internals*. People who attribute control to outside forces are said to have an external locus of control and are termed *externals*.
>
> (Spector, 1982)

Internals perceive greater control and actually seek situations in which control is possible (Kabanoff and O'Brien, 1980). When it comes to successfully performing a task that requires luck or skill, *externals* are more likely to choose luck and *internals* choose skill (Kahle, 1980). There appears to be a relationship between locus of control and experience. Phares (1976) notes that internals exert greater control of their environment, exhibit better learning, seek new information more actively, and seem more concerned with information than with social demands of situations. Externals tend to be more nervous than internals (Archer, 1979). Thus, internals do not need as much help when it comes to learning, and externals, even after given help, tend not to take control.

"Locus of control is considered an important personality variable in organizational research and theory" (Spector, 1982, p. 493). As such, it is believed to be a stable trait, not easily changed. Thus, research suggests that freeing those who have not taken charge of their learning in the past to now take charge of their learning must be tempered by realities of the limits of the individual's personality. Some individuals will naturally prefer and seek more independence (internals), whereas others will prefer and may seek more direction (externals).

As a practical matter, the contingency model of self-directedness seems most appropriate for facilitators of adult learning because it more closely matches the reality of most learning situations. There are many factors that individuals weigh in choosing whether to behave in a self-directed way at a particular point. These may include:

- Learning style.
- Previous experience with the subject matter.
- Social orientation.
- Efficiency.
- Previous learning socialization.
- Locus of control.

That an adult learner may choose not to be self-directed, for whatever reason, does not invalidate the core principle that adults, and adults in the United States in particular, have a self-concept of being independent. In fact, it is having the freedom to choose their learning strategy that is critical. It is the sense of personal autonomy, not self-teaching, that seems to be most important for adults. The biggest problems arise when adult learners want to have more independence in their learning but are denied that opportunity.

Some adult educators insist that the goal of all learning should be to increase personal autonomy in a learner. We agree that there are many learning situations in which this is true, but we must also be careful to avoid imposing a set of goals and purposes on each learning event. Although it can be argued that any learning has the effect of building autonomy in a person, there may be learning events in which there is not a core aim to build autonomy in a learner. For example, a cardiopulmonary resuscitation (CPR) class taught by a hospital may help people to be more self-sufficient but may not enhance SDL ability. Grow's (1991) model does not necessarily presume a goal of building self-directedness.

PRIOR EXPERIENCES OF THE LEARNER

The role of the adult learner's experience has become an increasingly important area of focus, particularly in the professional development arena. Chapter 3 noted four means by which adults' experiences impact learning. These are:

1. Create a wider range of individual differences.
2. Provide a rich resource for learning.
3. Create biases that can inhibit or shape new learning.
4. Provide grounding for adults' self-identity.

Traditionally, adult learning professionals have focused on items 1, 2, and 4 by emphasizing experiential learning techniques. However, much of the recent emphasis has been on item 3, focusing on how an adult's experience serves to shape or inhibit new learning. Several lines of research are connected to this central premise that adults' experiences play a major role in shaping their learning. Although they are largely separate streams of research, and none is specifically anchored in the andragogical model, collectively they reinforce this core principle. The remainder of this section summarizes these different lines of research.

Chris Argyris (1982) and Donald Schon (1987) have written extensively about the difficulties and importance of overcoming the natural tendency to resist new learning that challenges existing mental schema from prior experience. Argyris labels learning as either single-loop or double-loop learning. *Single-loop learning* is learning that fits prior experiences and existing values, which enables the learner to respond in an automatic way. *Double-loop learning* is learning that does not fit the learner's prior experiences or schema. Generally it requires learners to change their mental schema in a fundamental way.

Similarly, Schon (1987) talks about "knowing-in-action" and "reflection-in-action." *Knowing-in-action* is the somewhat automatic responses based on a person's existing mental schema that enable him or her to perform efficiently in daily actions. *Reflection-in-action* is the process of reflecting while performing to discover when existing schema are no longer appropriate, and changing those schema when appropriate. The most effective practitioners, and learners, are those who are good at reflection-in-action and double-loop learning.

Three streams of closely related cognitive psychological research help explain how prior experience influences learning: schema theory, information processing, and memory research (Jonassen and Grabowski, 1993). *Schema* are the cognitive structures that are built as learning and experiences accumulate and are packaged in memory. Merriam and Cafarella (1991) point out that all people carry around a set of schemata that reflect their experiences and, in turn, become a basis for assimilating new information. Rummelhart and Norman (1978) proposed three different modes of learning in relation to schema: *accretion, tuning,* and *restructuring.* Accretion is typically equated with learning of facts and involves little change in schema. Tuning involves a slow and incremental change to a person's schemata. Restructuring involves the creation of new schema and is the hardest learning for most adults.

Schema theory is closely related to mental models. Senge (1990), building on schema theory and Argyris's work, identifies "mental models" as one of the five core characteristics of the learning organization. The learning organization, a relatively new strategy that many organizations embrace, is defined by Marquardt (1996) as an "organization that learns powerfully and collectively and is continually transforming itself to better collect, manage, and use knowledge for corporate success" (p. 19). It is a complex strategy that positions learning as a core asset of the organization to cope with the rapid pace of change in a global economy.

Senge (1990) defines *mental models* as "deeply held internal images of how the world works, images that limit us to familiar ways of thinking and acting" (p. 174). In other words, mental models are the cognitive structures that arise from an individual's experiences. They enable employees to function efficiently on a day-to-day basis. However, they also impede change because many people resist changes that do not fit their mental model, particularly if change involves restructuring long or deeply held schema. To become more effective learners, adults have to identify their mental models, test them, and then learn how to change them. In Argyris's terms, they have to become better double-loop learners, which Schon would label as *reflection-in-action.* The result can be powerful improvement in individual and organizational learning, and perhaps performance, if employees understand that their mental models are assumptions, not facts, that filter their view of the world and events.

Information-processing theory suggests that prior knowledge acts as a filter to learning through attentional processes. That is, learners are likely to pay more attention to learning that fits with prior knowledge schema and, conversely, less attention to learning that does not fit.

The predominant model of human memory divides memory into three components: sensory, short term, and long term (Huber, 1993). Experience affects sensory memory through the process of attention and selecting what information to process. Selection depends in part on what information is already stored in long-term memory from prior learning and experience.

For long-term memory, prior experience has a major effect on how information is retained and stored. Ormrod (1990) offers the following principles of long-term memory storage:

1. Some pieces of information are selected and others are excluded.
2. Underlying meanings are more likely to be stored than verbatim input.
3. Existing knowledge about the world is used to understand new information.
4. Some existing knowledge may be added to the new information, so what is learned may be more than, or different from, the information actually learned.

These cognitive processes explain in part the emergence of constructivism as a new perspective on learning (Duffy and Jonassen, 1992). Although controversial, especially in its more radical versions, constructivism is emerging as a useful perspective for some adult learning situations (Wiswell and Ward, 1997). Constructivism stresses that all knowledge is context bound, and that individuals make personal meaning of their learning experiences. Thus, learning cannot be separated from the context in which it is used. Constructivists also stress the cumulative nature of learning. That means that new information must be related to other existing information in order for learners to retain and use it. For adults, experience might be conceptualized as a giant funnel of previous knowledge, and new information that enters the top of the funnel cascades downward and eventually falls out unless it "sticks" to some element of prior knowledge.

Constructivists advocate a different approach to learning. Savery and Duffy (1996) suggest eight constructivist instructional principles:

1. Anchor all learning activities to a larger task or problem.
2. Support the learner in developing ownership for the overall problem or task.

3. Design an authentic task.
4. Design the task and the learning environment to reflect the complexity of the environment in which learners should be able to function at the end of learning.
5. Give the learner ownership of the process used to develop a situation.
6. Design the learning environment to support and challenge the learner's thinking.
7. Encourage testing ideas against alternative views and alternative contexts.
8. Provide opportunity for and support reflection on both the content learned and the learning process.

The parallels between moderate views of constructivism and andragogy are rather striking. Both stress ownership of the learning process by learners, experiential learning, and problem-solving approaches to learning. However, andragogy and the more extreme views of constructivism are not compatible.

Traditional instructional design theory is also evolving to emphasize the importance of mental models (Merrill, 1992). Although at sharp odds with many aspects of constructivism, this is one area of clear agreement. Tessmer and Richey (1997) point out that there has been a rediscovery of contextual analysis in instructional design. Although it has always been a part of instructional systems design models, it has been neglected over the years. Traditional front-end environmental analysis emphasized the importance of analyzing elements in the external environment that might affect learning but largely ignored learner characteristics. *Systemic training design* extends environmental analysis to include learner characteristics such as attitudes and accumulated knowledge from prior experiences (Richey, 1995). One of the core directions for change in instructional design is a commitment to the belief that mental structures do exist and shape the way people learn (Kember and Murphy, 1995). Tessmer and Richey (1997) propose a general model of contextual factors that influence learning, one level of which is the orienting context. The orienting context consists of all the prelearning factors that affect the learning event. The elements of a person's background and experiences are among the critical factors they say shape learning.

In summary, there is growing recognition from multiple disciplines that adults' experiences have a very important impact on the learning process. Adult learning leaders have long capitalized on adult learners' experiences as a resource for learning; but they have not adequately recognized its role as a gatekeeper for learning. On the one hand, experience can aid in learning new knowledge if the new knowledge is presented in such a way that it can be related to existing knowledge and mental models. On the other hand, those same mental models can become giant barriers to new learning when the new learning challenges them.

Thus, the unlearning process becomes as important as the learning process when new learning significantly challenges existing schema. Kurt Lewin (1951) recognized this when he talked about the first stage of change being the "unfreezing" stage (the other two being change and refreezing). From this perspective, individuals cannot be expected to change unless attention is first paid to unfreezing them from their existing beliefs and perspectives. Said differently, people will not engage in double-loop learning until they are unfrozen from existing mental models. Kolb (1984) points out that learning is a continuous process grounded in experience, which means that all learning can be seen as relearning. This is particularly true for adults who have such a large reservoir of experiences.

READINESS TO LEARN

Adults generally become ready to learn when their life situation creates a need to know. It then follows that the more adult learning professionals can anticipate and understand adults' life situations and readiness for learning, the more effective they can be. The challenge has been to develop models to explain typical variability in adults' readiness to learn.

Pratt (1988) proposed a useful model of how adults' life situations not only affect their readiness to learn but also their readiness for andragogical-type learning experiences. He recognizes that most learning experiences are highly situational, and that a learner may exhibit very different behaviors in different learning situations. For example, it is entirely likely that a learner may be highly confident and self-directed in one realm of learning but very dependent and unsure in another.

Pratt illustrated this by identifying two core dimensions within which adults vary in each learning situation: *direction* and *support*. Pratt's model recognizes that learners may have fundamentally different needs for assistance from an adult learning professional. Some may need direction in the mechanics or logistics of learning, whereas others need emotional support. Learning professionals who notice learners who do not seem ready for learning in an andragogical manner must understand within which dimension the need exists.

Direction refers to the learner's need for assistance from other persons in the learning process and is a function of an adult's competence in the subject matter and general need for dependence. Adults who have high competence in the subject matter and low general need for *dependence* will be much more independent as learners than those who have little competence and prefer dependency. Even adults who have low general dependence may need direction in the early stages of learning new subject matter in which they have little competence.

Support refers to the affective encouragement the learner needs from others. It is also the product of two factors: the learner's *commitment* to the learning process and the learner's *confidence* about his or her learning ability. Thus, learners who are very highly committed and confident will need less support. Conversely, those who have low commitment and low confidence will need more support.

Pratt proposes a four-quadrant model (see Figure 9.1) to reflect combinations of high and low direction or support. Learners in quadrants 1 and 2 need a more highly teacher-directed approach to learning, whereas those in quadrants 3 and 4 are more capable of self-direction. It is important to note, however, that learners in quadrant 3 still need a high level of involvement with another person in the learning process, but for support, not direction.

Pratt's model, though untested, provides a conceptual explanation for some of the variability that adult learning facilitators encounter in any group of

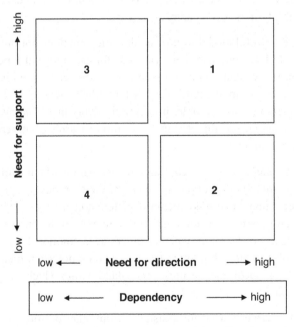

Figure 9.1 Pratt's model of high and low direction and support

Source: Pratt (1988).

adult learners. Assemble a group of adults for learning and you will likely find some who need a great deal of direction and emotional support (quadrant 1), some who need direction but not much support (quadrant 2), some who may act like they need direction by being in the group but who are really there to get support (quadrant 3), and finally, some who like a true andragogical approach (quadrant 4). To further complicate the picture, those same people may switch quadrants when learning different subject matter. By recognizing situational influences on adult learning behavior, Pratt helps explain why the core assumptions are not always a perfect fit, at least initially in learning situations. It seems reasonable to expect that learners in quadrants 1, 2, and 3 may move toward quadrant 4 as their competence and confidence grows. The challenges for adult learning leaders are to (1) recognize where individual learners are at the beginning of a learning experience, and (2) be attentive to changes in needs for direction and support during the learning experience.

ORIENTATION TO LEARNING AND PROBLEM SOLVING

Closely related to the role of prior experience in shaping learning is the role of current experiences in shaping the need to learn. We said earlier that adults generally prefer a problem-solving orientation to learning, rather than subject-centered learning. Furthermore, they learn best when new information is presented in a real-life context. As a result, the experiential approach to learning has become firmly rooted in adult learning practice.

David Kolb (1984) has been a leader in advancing the practice of experiential learning. He defines *learning* as "the process whereby knowledge is created through transformation of experience" (p. 38). For Kolb, learning is not so much the acquisition or transmission of content as the interaction between content and experience, whereby each transforms the other. The educator's job, he says, is not only to transmit or implant new ideas but also to modify old ones that may get in the way of new ones.

Kolb bases his model of experiential learning on Lewin's problem-solving model of action research, which is widely used in organization development (Cummings and Worley, 1997). He argues that it is very similar to Dewey's and Piaget's models as well. Kolb (1984) suggests that there are four steps in the experiential learning cycle (see Figure 9.2).

1. *Concrete experience.* Full involvement in new here-and-now experiences.

2. *Observation and reflection.* Reflection on and observation of the learners' experiences from many perspectives.
3. *Formation of abstract concepts and generalization.* Creation of concepts that integrate the learners' observations into logically sound theories.
4. *Testing implications of new concepts in new situations.* Using these theories to make decisions and solve problems.

Kolb goes on to suggest that these four modes combine to create four distinct learning styles (see Chapter 10 for more information on learning styles).

Kolb's (1984) model has made a major contribution to the experiential learning literature by (1) providing a theoretical basis for experiential learning research and (2) providing a practical model for experiential learning practice. The four steps in his model are an invaluable framework for designing learning experiences for adults. At a macrolevel programs and classes can be structured to include all four components, and at the microlevel these components can be included as units or lessons. Table 9.2 provides examples of learning strategies that may be useful in each step.

Research on Kolb's model has focused mostly on the learning styles he proposed. Unfortunately, research has done little to validate his theory, due in large part to methodological concerns about his instrument (Cornwell and Manfredo, 1994; Freedman and Stumpf, 1980; Kolb, 1981; Stumpf and Freedman, 1981).

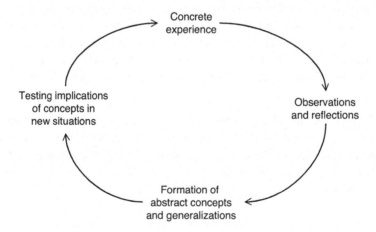

Figure 9.2 Kolb's experiential learning model

Table 9.2 Kolb's model with suggested learning strategies

Kolb's stage	Example learning/teaching strategy
Concrete experience	Simulation, case study, field trip, real experience, demonstrations
Observe and reflect	Discussion, small groups, buzz groups, designated observers
Abstract conceptualization	Sharing content
Active experimentation	Laboratory experiences, on-the-job experience, internships, practice sessions

Human resource development practitioners, while always valuing experience, increasingly emphasize experiential learning as a means to improve performance (Swanson, 2007; Swanson and Holton, 2009). Action reflection learning is one technique developed to focus on learners' experiences and integrate experience into the learning process (ARL Inquiry, 1996). Transfer-of-learning researchers also focus on experiential learning as a means to enhance transfer of learning into performance (Holton et al., 1997; Bates et al., 1997; Seyler, 1997) and to increase motivation to learn (Seyler et al., 1997). Structured on-the-job training (Jacobs and Jones, 1995) has emerged as a core method to more systematically capitalize on the value of experiential learning in organizations and as a tool to more effectively develop new employees through the use of experienced co-workers (Holton, 1996). Experiential learning approaches have the dual benefit of appealing to the adult learner's experience base as well as increasing the likelihood of performance change after training. It seems that many domains of adult learning would benefit in the same manner.

MOTIVATION TO LEARN

The andragogical model of adult learning makes some fundamentally different assumptions about what motivates adults to learn. Adults tend to be more motivated toward learning that helps them solve problems in their lives or results in internal payoffs. This does not mean that external payoffs (for example, salary increase) have no relevance, but rather that the internal need satisfaction is the more potent motivator.

Wlodowski (1985) provides a partial explanation for this difference. He suggests that adult motivation to learn is the sum of four factors:

1. *Success*. Adults want to be successful learners.
2. *Volition*. Adults want to feel a sense of choice in their learning.
3. *Value*. Adults want to learn something they value.
4. *Enjoyment*. Adults want to experience the learning as pleasurable.

The first principle of andragogy states that "adults need to know why they need to learn something before undertaking to learn it." Knowing why they need to learn something is the key to giving adults a sense of volition about their learning. Principle 6 states that the most potent motivators for adults are internal ones—for example, quality of life, satisfaction, and self-esteem. Said differently, the learning that adults value the most will be that which has personal value to them.

This position is also quite consistent with expectancy theory (Vroom, 1995), a classic theory of adult motivation in the workplace. Expectancy theory posits that an individual's motivation is the sum of three factors:

1. *Valence*. The value a person places on the outcome.
2. *Instrumentality*. The probability that the valued outcomes will be received given that certain outcomes have occurred.

Table 9.3 Characteristics and skills of motivating instructors

1. *Expertise*: the power of knowledge and preparation.
   - Knows something beneficial to adults.
   - Knows it well.
   - Is prepared to convey it through an instructional process.
2. *Empathy*: the power of understanding and consideration.
   - Has a realistic understanding of the learner's needs and expectations.
   - Has adapted instruction to the learner's level of experience and skill development.
   - Continuously considers learners' perspectives.
3. *Enthusiasm*: the power of commitment and animation.
   - Cares about and values what is being taught.
   - Expresses commitment with appropriate degrees of emotion, animation, and energy.
4. *Clarity*: the power of language and organization.
   - Can be understood and followed by most learners.
   - Provides for learners a way to comprehend what has been taught if it is not clear in the initial presentation.

Source: Wlodowski (1985).

3. *Expectancy*. The belief a person has that certain effort will lead to outcomes that get rewarded.

Put into learning terms, adult learners will be most motivated when they believe that they can learn the new material (expectancy), that the learning will help them with a problem or issue (instrumentality), and that it is important in their life (valence).

Wlodowski (1985) suggests a model of characteristics and skills for instructors who are good motivators of adults. They are grouped into four categories: *expertise, empathy, enthusiasm*, and *clarity* (see Table 9.3). Adult learning facilitators who develop these characteristics are likely to be highly motivating.

SUMMARY

That adults have a need to know prior to learning is now axiomatic for learning professionals. Research in organizational training suggests there are three aspects to the need to know: the need to know how the learning will be conducted, what will be learned, and why it will be valuable. Research indicates that the need to know affects motivation to learn, learning outcomes, and post-training motivation to use learning.

The concept of self-directedness has perhaps been the most debated aspect of andragogy. There are two prevalent and relatively independent dimensions of self-direction: self-teaching and personal autonomy. The assumption that all adults have full capacity or both dimensions in every possible learning situation is generally not accepted. Grow (1991), addressing this issue, postulates four stages and corresponding teaching styles:

Stage 1: dependent student/authority, coach/teacher.
Stage 2: interested student/motivator, guide/teacher.
Stage 3: involved student/facilitator, teacher.
Stage 4: self-directed student/consultant, delegator teacher.

The role of the adult learner's experience has become an increasingly important focus area as well. Much of the recent emphasis has revolved around the notion that experience creates biases that can greatly impact new learning. Prominent researchers in this area include Argyris, Schon, and Senge. Labeling learning as either single- or double-loop learning, Argyris writes about the difficulties and importance of overcoming the natural tendency to resist new learning that challenges existing mental schema resulting from prior experience. Schon concentrates on knowing-in-action and reflection-in-action, concluding that the most effective practitioners and learners are those who are successful at knowing-in-action and double-loop learning. Senge identifies mental models as one of the five core characteristics of learning organization. Other researchers, particularly cognitive psychologists, have conducted extensive research in this field, resulting in a generally held belief that adults' prior experiences can both help and hinder the learning process and outcome.

The level of readiness of an adult is closely associated to the need to know. Recognizing that most learning experiences are situational and that the behavior of the learner varies with the learning situation, Pratt proposes a model of how life situations affect both readiness to learn and readiness for andragogical-style learning experiences. He identifies direction and support as core dimensions of variance and proposes a four-quadrant model reflecting combinations of direction and/or support.

Closely related to the role of prior experience in shaping learning is the role of current experiences in shaping the orientation to learning. Adults seem to learn best when new information is present in a real-life context. As a result, the experiential approach to learning, most effectively advanced by Kolb, has become firmly rooted in adult learning practice. His four-stage model provides a theoretical basis and a practical model for experiential learning.

It is evident that adults are more motivated toward learning that helps them solve problems or results in internal payoffs. Wlodowski, in a theory closely related to Vroom's expectancy theory, explains the difference between adult and non-adult learners with four factors: success, volition, value, and enjoyment. Vroom uses three factors—valence, instrumentality, and expectancy—in his explanation.

Over the years, a variety of refinements to the core adult learning principles of the andragogical model have emerged. Some might view the refinements as weakening the model, but our view is that they strengthen it. Learning is a complex phenomenon that defies description by any one model. The challenge has been, and continues to be, to define what is most characteristic of adult learners, to establish core principles, and to define how to adapt those core principles to varying circumstances. The more researchers identify factors that moderate and mediate adult learning, the stronger the core principles become.

REFLECTION QUESTIONS

9.1 Report on a personal experience confirming the principle, *Learners need to know.*

9.2 Report on a personal experience confirming the principle, *Self-directed learning.*

9.3 Report on a personal experience confirming the principle, *Prior experience of the learner.*

9.4 Report on a personal experience confirming the principle, *Readiness to learn.*

9.5 Report on a personal experience confirming the principle, *Orientation to learning problem solving.*

9.6 Report on a personal experience confirming the principle, *Motivation to learn.*

BEYOND
10 ANDRAGOGY

INTRODUCTION

One aspect of the andragogical model that disturbs many people is that not all adults seem to fit the assumptions. Any facilitator of adult learning will tell you that adult learners are not as homogeneous as the andragogical model implies. Research has shown that there are many individual differences among learners that interact with the core adult learning principles to shape adults' learning behaviors. As noted earlier, the andragogical principles are powerful but incomplete descriptors of adults' learning behavior. Experienced adult learning professionals have learned that, like most models, the andragogical learning principles are tempered by an array of other factors that affect learning behavior. Knowles (1984b) reinforced this when examining lessons learned from andragogy in practice: "The andragogical model is a system of elements that can be adopted or adapted in whole or in part. It is not an ideology that must be applied totally and without modification. In fact, an essential feature of andragogy is flexibility" (p. 418).

This chapter introduces more new perspectives on adult learning that help explain and refine the core learning principles of andragogy. Included are introductions to the individual difference perspective of psychology, new thinking about learning how to learn, and developmental perspectives. These new understandings are important for developing effective andragogical adult learning in practice.

INDIVIDUAL DIFFERENCES IN ADULT LEARNERS

The major premise of research on individual difference is that instructors should adapt instruction to accommodate differences in individual abilities, styles, and preferences (Jonassen and Grabowski, 1993). By doing so, it is expected that learning outcomes will improve. Instructors are encouraged either to capitalize on learner strengths or to help learners develop a broader range of capabilities.

Researchers call this an *aptitude-by-treatment interaction,* which simply means that the treatment (instruction in this case) interacts with individual *aptitudes* abilities, which include styles and traits, in producing learning outcomes. Unfortunately, research has not provided consistent support for aptitude–treatment interactions, although it has shown many instances in which the interactions do occur (Jonassen and Grabowski, 1993; Snow, 1989). Methodological issues have limited researchers from generalizing about this premise. At the same time, most practitioners find high face validity in the notion that different learners require different instructional strategies based on their individual differences. It is the anecdotal evidence, case studies, and promising research studies that keep the individual differences hypotheses alive. The safe conclusion at this point is that individual differences do indeed affect learning, but researchers simply do not have the tools and methodologies to adequately measure or study them. In addition, learning may be so highly context specific, and the interactions so complex, that consistent relationships will never emerge, at least not with the degree of generalization we might desire.

Jonassen and Grabowski (1993) present a typology of individual differences that impact learning (see Table 10.1). Table 10.1 incorporates three broad categories of individual differences: *cognitive, personality,* and *prior knowledge.* There is no generally agreed-upon schema for categorizing individual differences, but this one is quite useful for adult learning purposes. Prior knowledge was considered in Chapter 5 in our discussion of experience. This section will be devoted primarily to the cognitive group of differences because they seem to have a large impact on adult learners.

Jonassen and Grabowski (1993) conceptually divide cognitive differences into four levels:

1. *Cognitive abilities.* Psychometric models of intelligence, including primary and secondary abilities (categories 1 and 2 in Table 10.1).
2. *Cognitive controls.* Patterns of thinking that control the ways individuals process and reason about information. These are the psychometric entities that regulate perception, and are direct descendants from cognitive abilities (category 3 in Table 10.1).
3. *Cognitive styles.* As defined by Messick (1984), they are "characteristic self-consistencies in information processing that develop in congenial

ways around underlying personality trends." They reflect ways in which learners process information to make sense of their world (categories 4 and 5 in Table 10.1).

4. *Learning styles.* General tendencies to *prefer* to process information in different ways. They are less specific than cognitive styles, and are usually assessed by self-reported preferences (category 6 in Table 10.1).

Level 4, learning styles, is the most visible level and can be thought of as the *outer level*, whereas cognitive abilities is the *inner level* and may be the least visible. Cognitive abilities influence cognitive controls, which influence cognitive styles, which in turn influence learning styles. As Table 10.1 shows, the list of characteristics that could be considered in each category is extensive. We will consider only selected ones that show promise for enhancing the core learning principles.

Cognitive abilities: new thinking about intelligence

Intelligence has traditionally been referred to in a unidimensional manner rooted in the psychological conception of intelligence as academic intelligence quotient (IQ). At one time, cross-sectional studies led to the conclusion that intelligence declined in the adult years. This was inconsistent with the general observation that adults did not seem to become "less smart" and, in fact, usually became quite a lot more successful and competent as they aged. This led researchers to question IQ as a universal measure of intelligence and to search for conceptions of intelligence that would help explain outcomes of adult life and adult learning. This section reviews thinking about alternate forms of intelligence, most of which tend to support the andragogical notions of adult learning.

One of the earlier attempts to explicate multiple intelligences was Horn and Cattell's theory of *fluid* and *crystallized* intelligence (Cattell, 1963; Horn and Cattell, 1966). Fluid intelligence is similar to the traditional notions of IQ, and refers to the ability to solve novel problems. It was believed to peak in teen years and remain stable in adult years, largely because it is most closely linked to physiological factors such as memory. Crystallized intelligence, on the other hand, is a function of experience and education, and increases in adult years. The presumption was that any loss in fluid abilities was compensated for by crystallized intelligence in stable environments. In fact, adults do show some loss of fluid abilities, particularly on speeded tasks; however, they become better at using the knowledge they have.

The research on the relationship between aging and adult intelligence is somewhat controversial. The pioneering work of Schaie (1994) and the

Table 10.1 Individual learner differences

Cognitive	1.	General mental abilities
		Hierarchical abilities (fluid, crystallized, and spatial)
	2.	Primary mental abilities
		Products
		Operations
		Content
	3.	Cognitive controls
		Field dependence/independence
		Field articulation
		Cognitive tempo
		Focal attention
		Category width
		Cognitive complexity/simplicity
		Strong vs. weak automatization
	4.	Cognitive styles: information gathering
		Visual/hepatic
		Visualizer/verbalizer
		Leveling/sharpening
	5.	Cognitive styles: information organizing
		Serialist/holist
		Conceptual style
	6.	Learning styles
		Hill's cognitive style mapping
		Kolb's learning styles
		Dunn and Dunn learning styles
		Grasha–Reichman learning styles
		Gregorc learning styles
Personality	7.	Personality: attentional and engagement styles
		Anxiety
		Tolerance for unrealistic expectations
		Ambiguity tolerance
		Frustration tolerance
	8.	Personality: expectancy and incentive styles
		Locus of control
		Introversion/extroversion
		Achievement motivation
		Risk taking vs. cautiousness
Prior knowledge	9.	Prior knowledge
		Prior knowledge and achievement
		Structural knowledge

Source: Based on data from Jonassen and Grabowski (1993).

Seattle Longitudinal Study suggests that earlier conclusions about decline in IQ may not be correct. In this study, Schaie and his colleagues followed a set of subjects since 1956 and used the Primary Mental Abilities Test to assess IQ. When the data on IQ is analyzed cross-sectionally, a decline in IQ with age is shown. When analyzed longitudinally, no decline is indicated. In fact, IQ shows a slight rise during middle age, and only declines below the 25-year-old level after reaching age 67. The conclusion from these studies is that there is no decline in fluid or crystallized intelligence until late in life.

Kaufman (1990) disputes these findings based on his analysis of data from the Wechsler Adult Intelligence Scale (WAIS and WAIS-R). He argues that the WAIS-R is the most valid assessment instrument for adult intelligence, particularly in clinical settings. Longitudinal analyses from WAIS-R data support Horn and Cattell's (1966) theory that fluid abilities decline substantially throughout life, starting as early as the late twenties, but that crystallized intelligence remains relatively stable until old age.

There are complex research methodology issues underlying these studies that are beyond the scope of this book but that also affect conclusions about adult intelligence. These two lines of research not only use different instruments but different research methods as well. The conclusions at this point are that (1) crystallized intelligence does *not* decline until old age but (2) fluid intelligence may. The implication of this research is that adult learning professionals must be alert to the possibility that adult learners, particularly older ones, may not respond as quickly to totally new material or situations. Adjustments may need to be made to allow additional time for learning. On the other hand, when learning depends on prior experience and education, no adjustments should be needed.

Others have also proposed models of multiple intelligences, but they have not been fully researched. Guilford (1967) also observed that IQ tests were inadequate for assessing adult intelligence and this led him to propose a three-factor structure of intellect. He suggested three types of mental abilities:

1. *Intellectual abilities.* Classified according to operation (cognition, memory, production, and evaluation).
2. *Intellect.* Classified according to content (verbal, numeric, behavioral).
3. *Intelligence.* Classified according to product (simple to complex).

Because the product is the result of the interaction between mental abilities and learning content, adults might develop better mental abilities in compensating for any loss of learning content.

Another perspective was offered by Gardner's (1983) theory of multiple intelligences. He suggests there are seven types of intelligence: linguistic, logical–mathematical, spatial, musical, bodily kinesthetic, understanding oneself, and understanding others. He suggests that a person might exhibit high intelligence in one or more of these, and low intelligence in others. Critics classify Gardner's multiple intelligences as *talents*, not intelligence.

Sternberg (1988) regards most theories of intelligence as incomplete. He argues for a broader view of intelligence that leads to educational systems that more fully promote lifelong learning and success (Sternberg, 1997). His theory outlines three components of intelligence:

1. *Meta-components.* "The executive processes used to plan, monitor, and evaluate problem solving."
2. *Performance components.* "The lower-order processes used to implement the commands of the meta-components."
3. *Knowledge-acquisition components.* "Processes used to learn how to solve problems in the first place." (p. 59)

Unlike Gardner, these three components are not independent, but rather work together to define intellect. And, as adults age, continued learning makes all three components stronger, allowing intellect to continue to increase, despite any age-related decline in memory or sensory capacity.

All theories of intellectual development point to the importance of adult experience. The recurring theme in all these conceptions is that adults grow as learners because of their life experiences. It is likely that experience enables adults to apply their learning more effectively as it strengthens their ability to manage learning processes. Conversely, as adults become better at applying their learning and managing their learning processes, they expect opportunities to do just that. In andragogical terms, they seek more control over their learning process. A multidimensional view of intelligence also reinforces the notion that there are certain learning situations in which adults may not be ready for a pure andragogical approach. If certain types of intelligence do decline as adults age (e.g., fluid intelligence) and they become increasingly reliant on experience to compensate, then learning totally new material unrelated to prior learning will be more challenging.

Cognitive controls

The cognitive control that has been the most extensively researched and has received the most attention in adult learning literature is *field dependence/ independence* (Joughin, 1992; Smith, 1982). It refers to "the degree to which the learner's perception or comprehension of information is affected by the surrounding perceptual or contextual field" (Jonassen and Grabowski, 1993, p. 87). Field dependents tend to see and rely on the cues in the environment to aid in understanding information, whereas field independents tend to learn independent of external cues.

There are many implications that arise from this difference that affect learning. Research-based findings (Jonassen and Grabowski, 1993) on learning and instruction include the following:

Field-dependent learners:
- Like group-oriented and collaborative learning.
- Prefer clear structure and organization of material.
- Attend to the social components of the environment.
- Respond well to external reinforcers.
- Prefer external guidance.

Field-independent learners:
- Like problem solving.
- Prefer situations in which they have to figure out the underlying organization of information (e.g., outlining).
- Like transferring knowledge to novel situations.
- Prefer independent, contract-oriented learning environments.
- Respond well to inquiry and discovery learning.

As Joughin (1992) suggests, field dependence/independence may have its greatest impact on self-directed learning for adults. At first glance, it would appear that field dependents would be more limited in their ability to develop strong self-directed learning skills. Indeed, the behaviors exhibited by field-independent types are most often those ascribed to more *mature* adult learners: independent, critical reflection, goal-oriented, self-organizing, and so forth (Even, 1982). Joughin (1992) suggests that the capacity for self-directed learning may be more limited in field-dependent types. He goes on to cite others (Chickering, 1977; Even, 1982; Mezoff, 1982) who suggest similar lines of thinking.

We tend to agree with Brookfield (1986) in urging caution about this conclusion. As discussed earlier, we must distinguish between the *behaviors* of self-teaching, with the internal cognitive process of feeling and acting with *autonomy*. It seems possible that a field-dependent person might exhibit self-directed behaviors that are quite different from those of a field-independent person. Brookfield goes on to suggest that field-dependent persons are more aware of context, which contributes to critical thinking and facilitation skills.

He cites his own research which showed that successful independent learners cited networks of learners as their most important resource. Field-dependent persons might be more likely to develop such networks.

Most measures of self-directedness assess behaviors, not internal feelings of autonomy. It seems clear that field independence/dependence could affect the *manner* in which self-directed learning is conducted. If learners are forced into a traditional mode of independent learning, field-independent persons may indeed excel. However, we suspect that if internal feelings of autonomy were assessed, both types could be shown to be effective self-directed learners. As Brookfield (1988), and Caffarella and O'Donnell (1988) note, research indicates that the field-independent type of self-directed learning is more typical of males, the middle class, and US culture. It seems possible, then, that field-dependent persons (as well as other cultures, gender, and socio-economic status) are likely to choose different styles of independent learning, probably using networks of people and seeking more assistance, but they still feel quite autonomous. Learning professionals will have to allow room for alternate styles to emerge and should avoid forcing all learners into a field-independent style of self-directed learning, which is the traditional definition.

Cognitive styles

The terms *learning style* and *cognitive style* are often erroneously used interchangeably. Cognitive styles are thought to be more stable traits and refer to a person's typical manner of acquiring and processing information (Messick, 1984). Learning style is a broader concept, embracing more than just cognitive functioning, and refers to more general preferences for types of learning situations. Some learning-style taxonomies include cognitive styles as one type of learning style (Flannery, 1993; Hickcox, 1995). Although not totally incorrect, we prefer to separate them.

Acquiring information

Learners tend to have characteristic ways in which they prefer to receive information. Traditionally, cognitive pyschologists have divided them into three categories: visual, verbal, and tactile or psychomotor (Jonassen and Grabowski, 1993; Wislock, 1993). Others, such as James and Galbraith (1985), expand the list to seven elements (or more): print, aural (listening), interactive, visual, haptic (touch), kinesthetic (movement), and smell. The implication of this work is that adult learning professionals should design learning experiences that accommodate multisensory preferences.

Processing information

One of the most common distinctions is made between *global* versus *analytical* (or *holist* versus *serial*) information processing. Global persons tend to take in the whole picture first, then the details. They focus on multiple elements of the subject at once and look for interconnections among elements. Analytical persons are completely different in that they prefer to process information in a step-by-step linear manner, focusing on one element of the subject at a time. These characteristics are closely related to the intuitive versus sensing scale of the Myers–Briggs Type Indicator.

The implication of this for learning professionals is that information must be presented in multiple approaches so that different learners can understand it. Swanson (see Chapter 13) proposes the *whole–part–whole* approach to learning in which learners are presented with the global picture, the parts of information, and the global perspective is repeated with application.

Learning styles

Learning styles refer to the broadest range of preferred modes and environments for learning. Though there is little uniformity in the way researchers define them, they tend to differ from cognitive style in two key ways: (1) learning styles include cognitive, affective, and psychomotor/ physiological dimensions; and (2) they include characteristics of instruction and instructional settings along with learning. James and Blank (1993) and Smith (1982) provide a useful summary of available instruments. Table 10.2 describes some representative learning-style theories and associated instruments.

Learning-style research has shown both great promise and great frustration. On the one hand, learning styles have great face validity for learning professionals. Most know intuitively that there are differences in styles among the adult learners with whom they work. By considering various dimensions of style differences, they are often able to improve learning situations and reach more learners.

On the other hand, all of the learning-style systems have suffered from limited research, questionable psychometric qualities of the instruments, and mixed research findings. Kolb's theory and accompanying instrument, the Learning Style Inventory (LSI), have come under particularly harsh critique (Kolb, 1981; Stumpf and Freedman, 1981; Reynolds, 1997), perhaps because it is one of the older and better documented theories. However, more recent work suggests that the constructs in Kolb's theory may be valid, but not measured correctly by the LSI (Cornwell and Manfredo, 1994).

Table 10.2 Representative learning-style systems

Researcher	Style dimensions	Instrument(s)
Cognitive learning-style systems		
Kolb (1984)	Two dimensions (perceptual and processing) proposed: concrete experience vs. abstract generalization, and active experimentation vs. reflective observation. Results in four styles: divergers, assimilators, convergers, and accommodators.	Learning Style Inventory (LSI) (1984)
McCarthy (1987) Gregorc (1984)	Two dimensions (perceptual and processing) proposed: abstract vs. concrete experience, and sequential vs. random ordering of information. Results in four styles, though ranges are allowed: concrete sequential, concrete random, abstract sequential, and abstract random.	4MAT system Gregorc Learning Style (1984)
Cognitive, affective, and physiological systems		
Dunn and Dunn (1974), Dunn et al. (1989)	Assesses 20 factors in four groups: environmental, sociological, emotional, and physical preferences.	Learning Style Inventory (1989) (for children) Productivity Environmental Preference Survey (1989) (for adults)
Canfield (1988)	Assesses 20 factors in four groups: conditions of learning, content of learning, mode of learning, and expectations of learning.	Canfield's Learning Style Inventory
Personality systems (with implications for learning)		
Briggs and Meyers (1977)	Assesses four scales: extraversion vs. introversion; intuition vs. sensing; thinking vs. feeling; and judging vs. perceiving.	Myers–Briggs Type Indicator (MBTI)
Costa and McRae (1992)	Assesses "big five" personality dimensions: neuroticism, extraversion, openness, agreeableness, conscientiousness. Emerging as a strong research-based approach to personality assessment.	NEO-PI-R

There can be little question that the research support for learning styles is mixed at best. One key reason is that there is no unifying theory or generally accepted approach to learning-style research and practice. Another flaw in most critiques is that they fail to separate the validity of learning-style theory and constructs from the measurement issues. A theory cannot be dismissed simply because we don't yet know how to measure it. Of course, neither can a theory be assumed valid until it can be measured and researched. For example, just because Kolb's LSI has not withstood rigorous instrument validation (Reynolds, 1997) does not mean that his theory is invalid. It could mean that we simply do not know how to measure the constructs yet.

This confusion has led some researchers to urge appropriate caution in using learning styles (Bonham, 1988; James and Blank, 1993). We agree with the cautions, but also urge caution in rejecting them, particularly when the phenomenon continues to be regularly observed by researchers and practitioners. We also agree with Merriam and Caffarella (1991) and Hiemstra and Sisco (1990) that learning-style instruments are best used at this point (1) to create awareness among learning leaders and learners that individuals have different preferences, (2) as starting points for learners to explore their preferences, and (3) as catalysts for discussion between leaders and learners about the best learning strategies.

Summary of individual differences perspectives

Research in individual differences has been instrumental in advancing understanding of individual differences in adult learning behaviors. As noted, there remains much uncertainty in the research, but the key point is clear: individuals vary in their approaches, strategies, and preferences during learning activities. Few learning professionals would disagree. At one level, merely being sensitive to those differences should significantly improve learning. Even better, the more that is understood about the exact nature of the differences, the more specific learning theorists can be about the exact nature of adaptations that should be made.

Understanding of individual differences helps make andragogy more effective in practice. Effective adult learning professionals use their understanding of individual differences to tailor adult learning experiences in several ways. First, they tailor the manner in which they apply the core principles to fit adult learners' cognitive abilities and learning-style preferences. Second, they use their understanding of individual differences to know which of the core principles are applicable to a specific group of learners. For example, if learners do not have strong cognitive controls, they may not initially emphasize self-directed learning. Third, effective adult learning professions use their understanding of individual differences to expand the goals of learning experiences. For example, one goal might be to expand learners' cognitive controls and styles to enhance future learning ability. This flexible approach explains why andragogy is applied in so many different ways (Knowles, 1984b).

LEARNING HOW TO LEARN

Much of the emphasis in individual difference research is on how learning professionals should alter their learning facilitation and leadership to make learning more meaningful to learners. A complementary response has been an emphasis on helping learners expand their learning abilities through *learning-how-to-learn* interventions. Although almost all the evidence is anecdotal, learning how to learn holds great promise for helping adults to expand their learning effectiveness.

Smith (1982) defines learning how to learn: "Learning how to learn involves possessing, or acquiring, the knowledge and skill to learn effectively in whatever learning situation one encounters" (p. 19). "We describe the person who has learned how to learn as capable of learning efficiently, for many purposes, in a variety of situations, no matter what the method" (p. 20).

Gibbons (1990) offers a useful model that helps clarify the range and scope of learning-how-to-learn research and practice. First, she suggests that learners need to be effective at learning in three *kinds of learning:*

1. *Natural learning.* Learning that occurs as the individual interacts spontaneously with the environment. Skills include learning from interaction with others, the environment, exploration, practice, and the teacher within.
2. *Formal learning.* Learning in which the content is chosen by others and presented to the learner. Skills include learning from instruction, assigned learning tasks, basic learning skills, and how to generalize from a learning activity.
3. *Personal learning.* Self-directed, intentional learning activities. Skills to be learned include learning to decide what to learn, how to manage the learning process, how to learn from experience, how to be an intentional learner, and how to take learning action.

The second dimension defines three *aspects of learning*:

1. *Reason.* The executive operation, more concerned with the management of thinking than the thinking itself. Closely related to meta-cognition or cognitive strategies (Weinstein and Mayer, 1986), a key element of reason's role in thinking is learning to improve one's ability in perceiving, analyzing, proposing, imagining, and reflecting.
2. *Emotion.* Responding with feeling, developing commitment, and acting with confidence. Key elements in this aspect are experiencing feelings, clarity, developing confidence, developing determination, and trusting intuition.
3. *Action.* Using learning to take meaningful action. Key elements include making decisions, taking initiative, practicing, solving problems, and influencing others.

Third, there are three *domains of learning* in which adults must be effective:

1. *Technical.* Instrumental learning to conduct the practical activities of work and life.
2. *Social.* Learning how to relate to others for mutual benefit.
3. *Developmental.* Learning how to develop oneself as a person and a learner.

Smith (1982) suggests that there are three interrelated components to learning how to learn that are useful to help learners become more effective: needs, learning styles, and training.

Needs

Learners have a variety of needs if they are to grow as learners. Smith (1982) divides them into four groups (see Figure 10.1). First, learners need a general understanding about learning and its importance to develop a positive attitude and motivation to learn. Second, they need basic skills such as reading, writing, math, and listening to be able to perform in learning situations. Third, they need to understand their personal strengths and weaknesses as learners, as well as their personal preferences for learning situations and environments. Fourth, they need the skills to perform in three learning processes: self-directed, collaborative, and institutional. Self-directed learning requires highly developed skills for planning, directing, and monitoring one's own learning. Collaborative learning requires strength in teamwork and interpersonal skills. Institutional learning requires basic study skills such as taking notes, writing, and test taking.

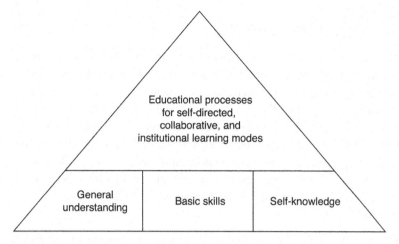

Figure 10.1 Learning-how-to-learn needs
Source: Smith (1982).

Learning styles

The core premise of learning style is that individual learner preferences will lead to learners being less effective in learning situations that require them to leave the comfort of their preferred learning strategies and styles. And, because it is completely unrealistic for a person to expect that all learning situations and leaders will accommodate their personal style, they will find themselves in many situations outside their comfort zone. Unless they develop a broader array of learning skills, they will struggle in those situations that don't fit their natural style. Furthermore, learning-how-to-learn theorists believe that learners do not have to be limited to only their natural strengths. That is, people can learn how to learn differently from ways they naturally prefer.

The array of skills and abilities grouped under the learning-how-to-learn label is diverse. Essentially, it involves learning how to function from an *opposite* style on every individual difference discussed so far. If you are a field-independent person, it means learning to learn in a field-dependent manner. If you have strong academic skills, but weak practical intelligence, it means developing practical intelligence. If you are a global learner, it means learning to learn more analytically, and so on.

Training

This third component refers to deliberate efforts to help learners develop the skills they lack. Such training might include workshops, coaching, self-study, and practice. Training topics might range from basic study skills taught in schools to learning-style workshops.

The promise of learning how to learn is becoming more important in a world economy that is increasingly dependent on knowledge and intellectual capital and faced with rapid change. For organizations, it has become increasingly important that employees be highly skilled learners so they can learn new technologies and adapt to changing market demands. For individuals, a person's job security is increasingly dependent on an ability to grow and learn, sometimes in rather radical ways. Adults today are often faced with demands to learn and relearn their jobs multiple times in a career. Those who do not have strong learning skills usually face layoffs.

It is for this reason that the American Society for Training has identified learning how to learn as one of the basic skills workers need (Carnevale et al., 1990). The US Department of Labor have included it in their SCANS model of skills workers need to develop to be competitive in today's workplace (Commission on the Skills of the American Workforce, 1990). As more states focus on enhanced workforce development systems, learning how to learn is likely to become more important.

DEVELOPMENTAL PERSPECTIVES ON ADULT LEARNING

Adults do not become adults in an instant—it is a developmental process. In addition, researchers now understand that development does not end when adulthood is reached, but rather continues to progress in a variety of ways. Adult development theories have a profound influence on thinking about adult learning because adults' learning behavior varies considerably due to developmental influences. What is not clear is exactly how it changes, largely because adult development theory is still mostly an array of untested models.

It is impossible to fully capture the considerable complexity of adult development theory in a chapter. Our purpose in this section is to discuss ways in which adult development theory suggests adult learning behavior might vary from the adult learning core principles. By necessity in an introductory book, our discussion of adult learning theories will be somewhat limited, focusing on a few representative models. Readers seeking a more complete discussion of adult development should consult Bee (1996), Tennant and Pogson (1995), Knox (1977), or Merriam and Caffarella (1991).

Tennant and Pogson (1995) explain why adult development matters:

> The identity of adult education as a field of study is largely
> premised on the identity of the adult. Much of the adult education
> literature, especially the literature on adult learning, makes reference
> to the distinct attributes of adults, and builds a rationale for practice
> based on these distinct attributes. . . . Because adult education
> necessarily involves some kind of intervention in the lives of
> participants, it is important for adult educators to recognize the
> nature and limits of this intervention, and to locate their intervention
> in some kind of lifespan framework.
>
> (p. 69)

Overview of adult development theories

Adult development theories are generally divided into three types: physical
changes, cognitive or intellectual development, and personality and lifespan
role development (Merriam and Caffarella, 1991; Tennant and Pogson,
1995). Cognitive development theory's primary contributions are twofold.
First, they help to explain some differences in the way adults learn at
different stages in their lives. Second, they help explain why the core
learning principles are exhibited in different ways at different stages of life.
Role development theory's primary contributions are to help explain when
adults are most ready for and most need learning and to explain when they
may be most motivated to learn.

Bee (1996) characterizes development theories as varying along two
dimensions. Some theories focus on *development*, and some focus on *change*
during adult life. *Development theories* imply a hierarchical ordering of
developmental sequences, with higher levels being better than lower levels.
They include a normative component, which suggests that adults should
progress to higher levels of development. Many of the cognitive development
theories fit into this category. Consider, for example, how your thinking and
perspectives on issues have matured during your life. As you have aged, you
have probably developed a more balanced perspective on life and begun to
recognize that there are many diverse and valid opinions. This change
represents a maturation and development process to what is generally
considered a preferred level of thinking.

Change theories

These theories are merely descriptive of typical changes experienced by
adults. There is no normative hierarchy intended, so one phase is no better

than another. The theories seek merely to describe typical or expected changes. Many of the lifespan role development theories fit into this category. Think about your life and the many changes you may have experienced that are typical of many adults—going to school, setting up a home, getting married, having children, experiencing the death of a parent, and so on. There is no developmental order implied here, simply a sequence of events.

The second dimension along which these theories vary is whether they include defined *stages*, or *no stages*. Stage theories imply fixed sequences of sequentially occurring stages over time. Stage theories are quite common, and are best represented by Levinson's (1978a) theory of adult development. Others offer no such fixed sequence of events. According to Bee (1996), Pearlin's (1980) theory of sources of adult distress over the lifespan is a good example.

We tend to agree with the prevailing thinking today that there is no one theory that is "best." Rather, adult development should be viewed as consisting of multiple pathways—multidimensional (Daloz, 1986; Merriam and Caffarella, 1991). This position is not intended to be an easy way out, but rather acknowledges the complexity of adult development. Adults develop along multiple dimensions simultaneously. The challenge for adult educators is to understand development well enough to recognize which dimensions are most relevant to a particular group of learners in a particular learning situation. That is our emphasis in this chapter.

Lifespan role development perspectives

The core contribution that lifespan development theories make to working with andragogical principles of adult learning is in clarifying and refining adult readiness to learn. The premise of all these theories is that there are certain predictable types of changes that occur throughout an adult's life. Life change is often an adult's primary driving force for learning. As the core principles of andragogy state, adults are most ready to learn when the learning meets an immediate life need, and are most motivated when it fills an internal need. Understanding the changes and transitions in adults' lives enables adult educators to:

- Anticipate learning needs that arise at various life points.
- Understand how life events facilitate or inhibit learning in a particular situation.
- Prepare adults for life changes.

- Capitalize on "teachable moments" (Havigurst, 1972) to accelerate learning.
- Plan learning experiences that are more meaningful.

Think about your own life course for a moment. How have the events of your life led you to or away from learning? How have your learning needs changed as you progressed through life? How have life events affected your motivation to engage in learning? How has learning changed your life course? I suspect that most readers will immediately feel the importance of lifespan development to adult learning.

Lifespan theories

Perhaps the best known of this group of theories are those describing the life course, and the best known of those was proposed by Levinson (1978a, 1978b, 1986) because it was popularized by Gail Sheehy's book *Passages* (1974). Levinson divides adult life into three eras: early adulthood (ages 17–45), middle adulthood (ages 40–60), and late adulthood (age 60+). Life then consists of alternating periods of stability and transition. Each era brings with it certain predictable tasks, and each transition between eras certain predictable challenges (see Table 10.3). It was Levinson's work that made midlife crisis a part of American culture. Although Levinson's model has drawn much criticism, primarily for its highly structured view of adult life, it has persisted as a core development theory.

Identity development

Another widely known and influential theory is Erikson's theory of identity development. Erikson proposed that an adult's identity develops through the resolution of eight crises or dilemmas (see Table 10.4).

If successfully resolved, each dilemma gives a person a certain strength. Erikson also believes that these dilemmas present themselves at certain predictable ages.

Ego development

Loevinger (1976) proposed a 10-stage model of ego development progressing from infancy to adulthood (see Table 10.5). Unlike Erikson or Levinson, Loevinger does not presume that adults progress through all stages. In fact, many get stuck in the middle stages. For adults, the developmental tasks are generally to move from a conformist stage to a more individualistic or autonomous stage. This theory has important implications for the

Table 10.3 Levinson's life task developmental model

Developmental period	Age group	Task
Early adult transition	17–22	Explore possibilities and make tentative commitments
Entering the adult world	22–29	Create first major life structure
Age 30 transition	29–33	Reassess life structure
Settling down	33–40	Create second life structure
Midlife transition	40–45	Ask "what have I done with my life?"
Entering middle adulthood	45–50	Create new life structure
Age 50 transition	50–55	Minor adjustments to middle life structure
Culmination of middle adulthood	55–60	Build second middle life structure
Late life transition	60–65	Prepare for retirement and old age
Late adulthood	65+	Create late life structure and deal with declines of old age

Table 10.4 Erikson's stages of identity development

Approximate age	Stage	Potential strength to be gained
0–1 years	Basic trust vs. mistrust	Hope
1–3 years	Autonomy vs. shame and doubt	Will
4–5 years	Initiative vs. guilt	Purpose
6–12 years	Industry vs. inferiority	Competence
13–18 years	Identity vs. role confusion	Fidelity
19–25 years	Intimacy vs. isolation	Love
25–65 years	Generativity vs. self-absorption and stagnation	Care
65+ years	Ego integrity vs. despair	Wisdom

Table 10.5 Loevinger's stages of ego development

Stage	Description
Presocial stage	Baby differentiates self from surroundings
Symbiotic stage	Baby retains symbiotic relationship with mother
Impulsive stage	Child asserts separate identity
Self-protective stage	Child learns self-control of impulses
Conformist state	Child or adult models behavior after the group
Self-aware stage	Self-awareness increases as does acceptance of individual differences
Conscientious stage	Person lives by individually created rules and ideals
Individualistic stage	Person focused on independence vs. dependence
Autonomous stage	Adults are fully independent and can cope with inner conflict

andragogical assumption of self-directedness, because the ego development stage may affect an adult's self-directedness.

Impact of lifespan theories

Regardless of whether one views the life course through Levinson's life stages, Erikson's developmental tasks, Loevinger's ego development, or some other lifespan perspective, the impact on learning is similar. First, all three researchers say that adult life is a series of stages and transitions, each of which pushes the adult into unfamiliar territory. Second, each transition to a new stage creates a motivation to learn. If adult learning professionals listen closely to the motivations of their learners, they will often hear some form of life transition pushing the adult to learn. By understanding the developmental lifespan, practitioners can be more attuned to adults' motivations to learn.

Cognitive development perspectives

Like lifespan developmental perspectives, cognitive development theories also help clarify and refine the andragogical principles. The core premise of cognitive development theories is that changes occur in a person's thinking process over time. These changes may affect adult learners by:

- Changing the way they interpret new information.
- Altering readiness for different learning experiences.
- Creating differing views and interpretations of material.
- Creating different degrees of meaningfulness for different people.
- Creating different developmental learning tasks.

Clearly, the more one knows about cognitive development, the more likely adult learning can be tailored to meet the needs of specific learners.

Consider how your personal views have changed during your adult life. Do you think about issues the same way you used to? Do you approach new information in the same manner? Do you find certain types of issues and learning more meaningful to you now than before? Most adults can chart progressions in their thinking that match at least some of the cognitive development theories.

The foundation of most adult cognitive development theories is the work of Piaget (Merriam and Caffarella, 1991). Piaget hypothesized that children move through four stages of thinking: *sensory motor*, *preoperational*, *concrete operational*, and *formal operations*. Formal operations, at which a person reaches the ability to reason hypothetically and abstractly, is considered the stage at which mature adult thought begins, though many adults never reach it. Because he was a child development specialist, Piaget's model implies that cognitive development stops upon reaching adulthood. Adult development theorists dispute that idea and have focused on various ways that cognitive development continues beyond *formal operations*. The following are some selected examples.

Dialectic thinking

Dialectic thinking is a level of thinking at which a person comes to see, understand, and accept alternate views and truths about the world, and the inherent contradictions in adult life. At this stage, the search for single truths and approaches to life is abandoned. A number of theorists have proposed dialectic thinking stages. Kramer (1989) and Riegel (1976) both suggested stage models of dialectic thinking that directly parallel the four stages of thought proposed by Piaget. In their view, dialectic thought develops along with formal operations and occurs in children at a low level. Others have looked at dialectical thinking as some type of extension to Piaget's four stages. Pascual-Leone (1983) proposed four stages of dialectic thought that occur after formal operations. Benack and Basseches (1989) also proposed four stages of post-formal thought that result in dialectic thinking.

Though the exact nature of its development is unclear, it does seem clear that dialectic thinking is an important developmental task for adults. Dialectic thinking enables adults to make peace with the complexity of life in which few truths exist and in which numerous contradictions and compromises are confronted daily. At some point, adults begin to realize that these are not wrong, but are inherent in life.

Other post-formal operations

Other theorists have recognized that thinking develops beyond formal operations, but propose different types of post-formal operations. For example, Arlin (1990) proposed a fifth stage of development, the problem-finding stage. Labouvie-Vief (1990) suggested that the hallmark of mature adult thought was the ability to make a commitment to a position or life course, despite recognizing the many different possibilities. That is, once one realizes the dialectic nature of life, a person must still make choices and commitments.

Relativistic thinking

Closely related to dialectic thinking is relativistic thinking. Perry (1970) proposed a nine-stage model of cognitive development based on his research with college students. These stages describe change from dualistic, right–wrong, black and white-type thinking to more complex relativistic thinking. Relativism indicates that knowledge is contextual, and there are few truths. In that sense, Perry's work is similar to dialectic thinking, but different in that he does not describe it as a post-formal operation.

Impact of cognitive development theories

Cognitive development theories are particularly useful in helping adult learning professionals understand why some adults struggle with highly complex issues that require dialectical or relativistic thinking. For example, some adult educators stress helping adults develop critical thinking skills (Brookfield, 1986). Critical thinking requires adults to be able to challenge assumptions that guide their lives, which also requires a higher level of cognitive development to recognize that there are multiple *correct* ways to live. Critical thinking may be a significant development step for a learner who has not reached that stage.

Implications from developmental theories

Although few of the theories about adult development have been thoroughly tested, they have persisted because most adults recognize intuitively that development continues throughout adult life. These theories provide the best framework available for understanding that development. A close examination of the development literature suggests these implications for adult learning:

- Adult learning is inextricably intertwined with adult development.
- Adult development occurs along multiple paths and multiple dimensions.
- Adult learning will vary primarily with stages of cognitive development.
- Motivation and readiness to learn will vary primarily according to stage of lifespan development.
- Adult learning facilitators must be attentive to learners' stage of development, and tailor learning experiences to fit that developmental stage.

SUMMARY

This chapter focused on the individual differences perspective of psychology, developmental perspectives, and lifespan development perspectives that enhance the core learning principles of andragogy. The individual differences perspective advocates that instructors adapt their teaching methodologies to accommodate differences in individual abilities, styles, and preferences. Theoretically, the result of such accommodation is increased learning outcomes. The research to support this contention is, however, mired in methodological problems. Thus, there is relatively little empirical evidence to support this premise. Yet, individual case studies, anecdotes, and current research efforts continue to sustain the individual differences perspectives.

Individual differences can be classified into broad categories of cognitive, personality, and prior knowledge. Cognitive differences can be further classified into the subcategories of cognitive abilities, cognitive controls, cognitive styles, and learning styles. There is an extensive list of characteristics that could be included in each category, but the individual differences that most directly impact adults' learning behavior described in the andragogical model are intelligence, field dependence/independence, learning style, locus of control, and prior knowledge.

Teaching learners how to learn serves as the complement to adjusting the instructional methodology. The fundamental precept in this response is that by broadening learning capabilities, learners can more readily adapt to a wide range of learning situations, thereby increasing the learning outcome. Learning how to learn has become increasingly important in the workplace. For employees to successfully obtain and retain their positions, they must be able to learn in a variety of learning environments. Employees are not often afforded the luxury of selecting their own learning situation and methodology and, consequently, must adapt or face the possibility of the loss of a job.

The developmental perspective of adult learning focuses on the progressive aspect of becoming an adult—it is not a status that is achieved instantaneously. Adult development theories are generally divided into three types: physical changes, cognitive or intellectual development, and personality and social role development. And, according to Bee, development theories vary only in two dimensions. The first of these dimensions involves development and change. Development theories imply a hierarchical ordering of developmental sequences, and change theories are descriptive of changes typically experienced by adults. The second variance revolves around the inclusion or exclusion of stages. Stage theories imply fixed, sequentially occurring stages.

Lifespan development theories clarify and refine adult learning principles by addressing the readiness to learn aspect of the learning event. Grounded in the premise that certain predictable types of changes occur in an adult's life, these changes often trigger a learning need.

REFLECTION QUESTIONS

10.1 Discuss the relative significance of cognitive, personality, and prior knowledge differences for adult learning.

10.2 As an adult educator, how would you use knowledge related to learning styles?

10.3 What is the difference between *learning and learning how to learn* and *learning*?

10.4 What is the utility of development theories when working as an adult educator?

10.5 As an adult learner, how do you see yourself evolving over the next decade?

11 INFORMATION TECHNOLOGY AND LEARNING

INTRODUCTION

The information in this chapter is likely to be dated by the time you read it. We apologize for that ahead of time. Our intention is that the core message of this chapter will be: *The incredible speed of advancements in information technology continues, and information technology provides alternatives for learning facilitators and adults themselves to guide learning.*

The goal of this chapter is to briefly paint a picture in time, recognizing that you are already hearing about and likely using the newest advancements in information technology. To accomplish this chapter goal, a profile of information technology and learning in the past, present, and future will be highlighted.

It would be interesting if each reader made a list of the top five to ten general information technology developments that have made fundamental changes in their lives. Doing this provides a reflective pause about the extent of the change we are all experiencing. Here is a sample list. Who wants to go back to their antecedents?

• Personal computer.
• Internet/email.
• Cell phone/smart phone portable computer connection.
• Computer-based digital information (Google, Wikipedia, YouTube).
• Computer shopping (Amazon et al.).
• Computer banking.
• Digital music and movies.

THE PAST

A little over a century ago, the big information technology developments impacting learning experiences were automatic teaching machines, television-delivered instruction, and xerography copied instructional materials.

Duplicating appropriate supporting instructional materials for learners was a chore. Stencil duplicator (mimeograph) and spirit duplicator (ditto) processes were part of an instructor's toolbox. These efforts often resulted in low composition and print quality instructional materials. While xerography was invented in 1938, it was not until 1960 that the first commercial xerography machine was on the market (McGraw-Hill, 2007). Xerography allowed instructors to take and combine duplicate original graphics (print, drawings, photos) on a single page and to quickly reproduce copies for learners.

Videotape technology evolved in the early 1950s and educational institutions began producing their own courses on videotapes for classroom broadcasting in the late 1960s. The early 2"-wide videotapes gave way to ever smaller and compact video recording and playback systems. Less costly and more mobile synchronized filmstrips and slideshows were also very popular.

The instructor mediated all aspects of the learning enterprise and any available information technology assists were simply a bonus (Clark, 2012). There was plenty of experimenting that foretold of things to come. Most notable was PLATO (Programmed Logic for Automatic Teaching Operations) that came out of the University of Illinois. PLATO, started in 1960, had a networked mainframe-terminal system that promised to revolutionize education. Control Data Corporation of Minneapolis, Minnesota, under the leadership of CEO William Norris, took over PLATO with his revolutionary vision for education and his company. When PLATO shut down in 2006 and the technology elapsed, Control Data Corporation and remnants of PLATO's early features ended up being refined and incorporated in new information technologies (see University of Illinois, 1960).

THE PRESENT

Some of the present state of information technologies impacting learning experiences include Internet-delivered information and training, digital books, free online learning, and the capacity for worldwide connection with experts. It is often difficult for instructors and learners to stay abreast of the varied mediums and their required techniques.

The core of present technology impacting learning is the personal computer in its various forms (desktop, laptop, pad, smart phone, etc.). Being comfortable with computer usage, variations in hardware, websites, and software is essential to maximizing the technology for learning purposes. Being able to deal with technology glitches creates a dividing line between those who like and those who dislike contemporary information technology.

Three ideas permeate the present state of information technology and its impact on learning: (1) learner controlled, (2) facilitator friendly, and (3) 24/7. All three are in perfect harmony with andragogy in practice. Never before has information and instruction been at the fingertips of learners as easily as it is today. The immensity of the information loaded on the World Wide Web is mind boggling. The good news is that it is available at the learner's command 24 hours a day for seven days a week. Facilitators can point learners to readily available valuable learning resources. The bad news is that the open access to those putting information on the Internet raises fundamental questions of quality, accuracy, and completeness of every entry. There is no regulatory body keeping the weirdos and liars out. Thus, learners need to know how to assess the credibility of information on the Internet. While there is no definitive guide, publisher McGraw-Hill (2014) offers the following points to consider when trying to judge the reliability of information found on the Internet:

- *Who is the author or sponsor of the page?* On the page you are citing, or on a page linked to it, that individual or organization should be identified, that individual's qualifications should be apparent, and other avenues of verification should be open to you. For a good example of a reliable source, see "Notes About This Document" for the hypertext version of *Pride and Prejudice* at http://www.pemberley.com/janeinfo/ pridprej.html. On the other hand, a page created by a person or an organization that does not provide this information is not a good source to cite.
- *Are there obvious reasons for bias?* If the page is presented by a tobacco company consortium, you should be suspicious of its reports on the addictiveness of nicotine. Is there any advertising? If the page is sponsored by Acme Track Shoes, you should be suspicious of its claims for Acme track shoes' performance.
- *Is contact information provided?* If the only identification available is something cryptic, such as "Society for Ferruginous Retorts," be suspicious of the page's reliability. If the page is sponsored by a reputable person or organization, there should be some other way to

verify that reputation, such as an email or postal address. (Note that a tilde [~] in the page's address usually indicates a personal home page and may require more searching to assess reliability.)

- *Is there a copyright symbol on the page?* If so, who holds the copyright?
- *Is this page a "zombie,"* or one considered "walking dead" because the person who posted it no longer maintains or updates it? Even though the information is "alive" in that it is still accessible, it is "dead" in that it could well be several years old!
- *What is the purpose of the page?* Why is this information being posted—as information, as a public service, as a news source, as a research tool for academics, as a personal axe to grind, or as a way to gain attention?
- *How well organized is the page?* Is the page easy to navigate? Is it complete? When was the page last updated? Is the information on it current? How credible are the links it provides?
- *Is the information on the page* primary *or* secondary*?* That is, is it a report of facts, such as a medical researcher's article counting cases of "mad cow" disease in England in 1997, thus making it primary information, or is it an Internet newsgroup discussion about "mad cow" disease, thus making it secondary information? The papers and reports you write for your college classes need to be based on primary information whenever possible. The further away from the primary sources your own sources are, the less reliable the information is.
- *Can you verify the information* on the web page some other way? For example, can you check the page's bibliography (if there is one) against your library's holdings or check the information against a source in the library?
- *If you are worried that the information may lack credibility, try starting with a source you know is reputable.* For example, if you have to do a project on the latest in cancer research, you can begin your search at major cancer research institutes, such as Mayo Clinic in Rochester, Minnesota.
- Finally, remember that *even though a page might not meet your standards as a citable source, it may help you generate good ideas* or point to other usable sources. Also, be sure not to stop your search at the first page you find—shop around and do some comparing so that you can have points of reference.

Digitizing books and libraries is a game changer. Digital books that can be downloaded on personal computer devices, obtained for free in some cases, or rented instead of being purchased are radically changing the book industry and library functions. Then there are open classrooms where world-class experts (mostly university sponsored) teach classes over the Internet to all who register. Simultaneously, a learner in Singapore can and does feel empowered to fire off an email question about a point from page 86 to an author located on the other side of the globe. For sure, the information and learning technology of the present day would have been incomprehensible just a few decades ago.

THE FUTURE

The future state of information technology on learning could see technology as the (1) lone facilitator of learning, (2) leading to the abolishment of traditional learning hierarchies, and (3) leading to self-directed expertise development and certification. These are quite radical, but not improbable ideas.

Information technology will likely allow a self-directed learner to do it all in terms of managing their targeted learning experience. This could be initially framed out by an organization or solely by the learner. Traditional learning hierarchies could go away as learners jump in where they want to and when they get stuck a computer-based diagnosis would direct them to the appropriate remediation, and then back to where the learner wanted to be. With such an information infrastructure and database, learners could self-enroll and progress through the development and verification of the knowledge requirements and expertise requirements (through high-fidelity simulations) of certifiable realm. The three ideas portray a radically different learning environment.

More systematic efforts at forecasting trends impacting adult learning have been reported. One extensive study of future key trends reports the following (Johnson et al., 2014):

• Growing ubiquity of social media.
• Integration of online, hybrid, and collaborative learning.
• Rise of data-driven learning and assessment.
• Shift from learners as consumers to learners as creators.
• Agile approaches to change.
• Evolution of online learning.
• Significant challenges impeding technology adoption.
• Low digital fluency of instructors.
• Relative lack of rewards for teaching.
• Competition from new models of education.
• Scaling teaching innovations.

- Expanding access.
- Keeping education relevant.
- Flipped classroom.
- Learning analytics.
- 3D printing.
- Games and gamification.
- Quantified self.
- Virtual assistants.

These pictures of the future will have varying meaning to each of you depending on your own information technology experience and views of adult learning.

SUMMARY

When it comes to change, the analogy of static and dynamic quality comes to mind. Pirsig (1991) believes that the wholesale front-end adoption of change is foolhardy and that total resistance to change is a ticket for total demise. Holding on to some old while adopting some new is his formula for quality and sustainability. Each educator has the challenge of moving with the times without losing a foundation of principles and practice. The utility of many information technologies is learning content and audience specific. Remaining still is not a rational option and making good choices requires rational thinking.

REFLECTION QUESTIONS

11.1 Name five information technology developments in your lifetime that have impacted your life.

11.2 Discuss one recent information technology and how it is impacting your own learning.

11.3 Speculate on the next advancement in information technology that will have a great impact on adult learning. Present a scenario of this advancement in action.

11.4 Identify and describe a potential loss or pitfall from a high investment in information technology in the context of learning.

12 NEUROSCIENCE AND ANDRAGOGY

INTRODUCTION

The advances being made through neuroscience research are revolutionizing our understanding of how people learn. Using modern imaging technologies, neuroscientists are now able to "look inside" the brain and explain in physiological terms what happens inside the brain as people learn.

A new interdisciplinary field is emerging called Mind Brain Education Science or MBE in short form (Tokuhama-Espinosa, 2011). This field is an integration of education, psychology, and neuroscience. This exciting new academic discipline is integrating the differing epistemologies of three previously disparate fields to reach new understandings about learning, including adult learning. "MBE science is the formal bridge linking the fields of neuroscience, psychology and education that has been missing for decades" (Tokuhama-Espinosa, 2011, p. 11). It is in the MBE spirit that we approach this chapter.

The purpose of this chapter is to review the support emerging from neuroscience research for andragogy. We will not attempt to provide a comprehensive overview of neuroscience research. Readers interested in a more in-depth understanding of neuroscience research are encouraged to explore references such as Glick (2011), Sousa (2011), and Tokuhama-Espinosa (2011). Instead, we will look at both meta-findings from brain research and findings that support each of andragogy's core assumptions about adult learning.

A PRIMER ON HOW THE BRAIN LEARNS

The human brain is an extremely complex organ that almost defies imagination. It is beyond the scope of this book to provide a complete description of the brain and all its components (see references noted above for more detail). Rather we will focus on those components of the brain that are central to the learning process.

Basic brain structure

There are four basic components to the brain (Sousa, 2011; Tokuhama-Espinosa, 2011). First is the *brain stem*. This is the oldest area of the brain and it controls all of the basic body functions such as heartbeat, respiration, digestion, etc.

Second is the *limbic system*, an area nestled above the brain stem and below the cerebrum. Four parts of the limbic system are important to learning (Sousa, 2011):

- The *thalamus*—all incoming sensory information except smell goes first to the thalamus from which it is directed to other parts of the brain for further processing.
- The *hypothalamus*—monitors all the internal functions of the body and releases hormones to regulate many body functions.
- The *hippocampus*—plays a major role in converting information from working memory to long-term storage.
- The *amygdala*—plays an important role in emotions, especially fear. Researchers believe that the amygdala encodes an emotional message with each memory.

Third is the *cerebrum* which is the largest area of the brain and is the part of the brain in which most cognitive processing and long-term memory occurs. The frontal lobes of the cerebrum, located just behind the forehead, are responsible for the *executive functions* of the brain. This is the control center for learning.

Fourth is the *cerebellum* which is located just below the cerebrum and is largely responsible for controlling movement.

Cellular structure

The brain is composed of a trillion cells of two known types: *neurons* and *glial cells* (Sousa, 2011). The neurons, representing about 10 percent of the total cells, are the functioning core of the brain and the nervous system. Each one has tens of thousands of branches emerging from its core, called *dendrites*. The dendrites receive and transmit electrical impulses along a long fiber called an *axon*. A layer called the *myelin sheath* surrounds and protects each axon.

Neurons have no direct contact with each other. Between each dendrite is a tiny gap (about a millionth of an inch) called a *synapse*. The synapses communicate with each other by releasing chemicals called *neurotransmitters* between the axons across the synapses. Some of these neurotransmitters central to learning include *acetylcholine, serotonin, dopamine* and *epinephrine*. In fact, learning occurs by changing the way synapses communicate with each other.

The growth of neurons is called *neurogenesis*. For a long time conventional wisdom has been that neurons are the only cell in the body that doesn't regenerate. Thus, the belief was that people were born with a fixed number of neurons and neurogenesis did not occur in adults. There is now increasing evidence that this is not true (Gross, 2000; Sousa, 2011; Tokuhama-Espinosa, 2011). This is an exciting finding both for educators and researchers working to cure neurological diseases such as Alzheimer's. While our understanding of adult neurogenesis is still in its infancy the prospects are good.

Cognitive processing

The brain is constantly scanning the environment and responding to stimuli. Each of us is bombarded with so many stimuli in a day that the brain has a well-developed system for filtering the stimuli to which it responds. Since learning is one type of stimulus, it is important to understand how information is processed so that real learning takes place.

Information first enters the brain through all our senses. The brain uses its *sensory register* (located in the thalamus which is part of the limbic system) to decide which stimuli to attend to and which to ignore (Sousa, 2011). The brain uses past experiences to determine the degree of importance of the data (more on this later).

The information then passes into *short-term memory* which is described as having two components: *immediate memory* and *working memory*. Think of these components as buffers in a computer, allowing information to accumulate temporarily before it is encoded into long-term memory.

According to Sousa (2011) there is a hierarchy of response to sensory data in short-term memory. The brain's main job is to help its owner survive. Thus, any sensory input that is perceived as a threat sends a rush of adrenaline to the brain and focuses the brain on those stimuli and blocks other stimuli.

Similarly, emotional data takes a high priority. When an individual responds emotionally, the complex rational processes are shut down and the limbic system takes over. This explains the experiences we have all had where our emotions overwhelm our reasoning ability. However, emotions can also enhance memory because we tend to remember emotional events (positive or negative) more readily.

The clear implication of this is that learners must feel physically safe and emotionally secure in the learning event before they will turn their attention to the cognitive processing (Sousa, 2011). As Sousa says, "How a person 'feels' abut a learning situation determines the amount of attention devoted to it. Emotions interact with reason to support or inhibit learning" (p. 48). As we shall see, this has enormous implications for andragogy and adult learning.

Working memory is the next stage of processing once information has passed through immediate memory. It is in this stage of memory that sensory input is combined with information from long-term memory. It is a type of "work table, a place of limited capacity, where we can build, take apart, or rework ideas for eventual storage somewhere else" (Sousa, 2011, p. 49).

The next stage of memory is long-term storage. Learners' brains make decisions about what information in working memory is to be transferred to long-term storage, and what is to be discarded. According to Sousa (2011, p. 52) two core questions are involved: "Does this make sense?" and "Does this have meaning?" As we shall see, this has significant implications for andragogy because the answer to these two questions is heavily dependent on the learner's past experiences.

META-FINDINGS FROM NEUROSCIENCE

Before exploring findings that support each of the core principles of andragogy, there are certain meta-findings that lay the foundation for andragogy.

Meta-finding 1: Adults can learn throughout life

Adult educators have long known that adults can learn throughout their lives, yet a myth has persisted that adults' learning capacity diminishes throughout life. Andragogy, on the other hand, is grounded in the belief that adults can continue to learn throughout life if learning experiences are facilitated in a manner conducive to adult learning.

Neuroscientists call this phenomenon *neuroplasticity*. Neuroscientists have shown definitively that the brain is capable of changing in the manner needed for learning throughout life (Royal Society, 2011; Grady, 2012). Thus, "it is never too late to learn" is indeed true (Goswami, 2008). With each new learning experience, the neurons in the brain can rearrange themselves. Called *neural networks* (Glick, 2011) these configurations of neurons are the physiological result of learning. Each learning experience results in new configurations that deepen understanding. It appears that the number of neural networks possible is limited only by the learner's reluctance to work at new learning. The brain itself is capable of creating new neural networks throughout life (Sousa, 2010) though memory changes do occur (Luo and Craik, 2008).

This is not a surprise to educators who work with adults. While we will show that certain conditions in the learning environment are more conducive to building new neural networks in adults, there is no biological basis for beliefs that adults diminish in their capacity for learning.

Meta-finding 2: Emotions play a critical role in learning

Andragogy has long been recognized as being particularly strong at creating positive emotions in adults during learning experiences because of the climate of "adultness" that is created. Adult educators have observed that when these conditions are present, adults are more motivated to learn and learn more easily.

Neuroscientists have now explained why this is true. It turns out that positive emotions during learning trigger the release of neurotransmitters which aid in information processing, while negative emotions also trigger the release of neurotransmitters but those which block new learning (e.g., fight or flight reactions). Emotions, then, are the "undercurrent of cognition" (Taylor, 2006, p. 81). Powerful positive emotions during a learning experience will aid in long-term memory whereas powerful negative emotions will block long-term memory (Glick, 2011).

- "Good" stress heightens attention and helps learning but "bad" stress detracts from learning by literally blocking the uptake of new information in the brain (Tokuhama-Espinosa, 2011, p. 132).
- Dopamine, which is released with happy experiences, has been shown to enhance information uptake (Tokuhama-Espinosa, 2011).
- During stressful learning, adrenaline is released which leads to the "fight or flight" reactions in the amygdala, focusing attention on the stress response rather than information uptake (Wolf, 2006).

Andragogy is known for creating a powerful positive affective state among adult learners. By catering to their "adultness" the learning experience is a positive, non-threatening event. Traditional learning approaches often remind adults of unpleasant school-based learning which can lead to stress responses. Approaches to learning that don't cater to their "adultness" are likely to generate negative emotions and stress, thereby blocking learning.

Thus, the power of andragogy to enhance adult learning can be seen from a neuroscientific perspective in part as an approach that stimulates the release of "good" neurotransmitters, and minimizes the release of "bad" neurotransmitters, thereby increasing cognitive uptake of learning. The affective focus of the andragogical approach turns out to be more than just a "feel-good" approach to learning. Rather it is supported by evidence from neuroscience that the positive affect it creates in adults should indeed increase learning.

Meta-finding 3: Learning occurs by connecting new knowledge to existing knowledge

Adult educators using andragogy have long understood the vital role that prior knowledge and experience plays in learning. Most have taken a constructivist approach to learning, understanding that adults make meaning of new learning using their prior knowledge and experience.

Neuroscientists have confirmed this. An essential part of learning occurs when the brain attempts to find a metaphorical "file cabinet" in which to store new information. The brain searches to connect and evaluate new learning using existing neural networks which are built on past experiences and learning. Learners use past experience embedded in neural networks to make sense of new information. Sometime this aids in learning, and sometime it is a barrier to learning. Regardless, the existing neural networks of experience will be a critical factor in determining what meaning is made of new information. Experienced teachers and facilitators know that you have to first meet learners "where they are" before you can move them to a different level of understanding or learning.

This also explains why transformative learning is so difficult for learners. Incremental changes in neural networks are far easier than constructing entirely new neural networks required by transformative learning. Transformative learning often challenges prior experience, a difficult process given what we now know from neuroscience.

NEUROSCIENCE SUPPORT FOR ANDRAGOGICAL PRINCIPLES

In this section we will look at support for the six andragogical principles from neuroscience. To be clear, no direct studies of andragogy have been conducted by neuroscientists. Nonetheless, we will suggest that many findings from neuroscience studies provide direct evidence of the efficacy of the andragogical principles.

Principle 1: The need to know

As discussed earlier, the frontal lobes of the brain are responsible for the executive functions of the brain:

> That means the frontal lobes help people think in ways that include setting goals, delaying gratification, recognizing future consequences from current actions, overriding or suppressing inappropriate responses, recalling memories that are not task based, synthesizing information, and making sense of emotions. This area of the brain is the mecca of problem solving, critical thinking, and creativity.
>
> (Glick, 2011, p. 7)

It is useful to think of the executive control center as the conductor of the orchestra (Caine and Caine, 2006).

Of particular significance to adult learning is the fact that this area of the brain doesn't mature until the second decade. This accounts for the weaker meta-cognitive skills found in younger learners. Adult learners, on the other hand, will tend to have much more highly developed executive control centers, with accompanying stronger meta-cognitive skills.

The andragogical approach to adult learning suggests that adults need to know the "who, what, why, and how" of the learning they undertake before they embark on the learning journey. From brain research it is not hard to see why. The "who, what, why, and how" of learning are all part of the executive control functions. If adults have well-developed executive control centers in the brain, then they are far more capable of controlling their own cognitive learning processes. It makes sense then that adults would want to engage in a meta-cognitive dialog about their learning before being receptive to new learning. In a sense, they "need to know" in order to prime their executive control centers.

Principle 2: The learner's self-concept

The maturing of the executive control functions in the adult brain also helps explain why self-directed learning is so fundamental to adult learning. Clearly, an adult with mature self-regulatory functions in the brain has a far greater capacity for self-directed learning than do younger persons.

In younger persons the frontal cortex is simply not as well developed and thus they are more dependent on teachers for meta-cognitive-type control and coaching. The adult, on the other hand, is more likely to have developed frontal cortex functions that enable them to self-regulate their learning. Especially if an adult has had positive experiences in the past regulating their own learning, they are likely to be more motivated to engage in self-directed learning.

Likewise, understanding the role of the executive control center helps explain why adults may also choose to use learning resources (even formal classroom instruction) for novel learning. With novel learning, adults are less likely to have developed the meta-cognitive skillset to regulate their own learning (Tokuhama-Espinosa, 2011). Experts, on the other hand, are able to process new information with greater speed because of their highly developed executive functions.

Thus, brain research would seem to point to most adults having greater potential for self-directed learning due to brain maturity. However, the efficacy of those control functions will depend on their experience with the type of new information they seek or process. It would also seem that the maturing executive functions of the brain interact with the adult's general life frame of self-directedness to create greater expectations of self-directed learning.

Principle 3: The role of experience

Perhaps no andragogical principle is so clearly supported from brain research as the role of experience in adult learning. Brain research indicates that new information entering the brain is processed using existing neural networks which are built from prior learning and experiences. Obviously adults have far more prior learning and experiences and thus have already formed extensive neural networks in the brain.

Brain research suggests that these neural networks can be either an aid or barrier to new learning. If a connection can be found between new information and existing neural networks, then new information is received and processed more readily. On the other hand, if new information can't be connected to existing networks, then learning is more difficult and may be resisted.

Furthermore, past experiences can be either negative or positive. If new information is connected to negative prior experiences, then the negative emotions encoded with those experiences are also recalled, further diminishing the chance of new information being positively received. If past experiences have positive emotions encoded with them then new information is more likely to be welcomed.

Past experiences and their associated neural networks are thus central to the person's decision-making process about whether to encode new information into long-term memory. The brain first searches for past experiences to which to connect new information. If a connection is made, then new learning is easier. That is not to suggest that the brain cannot form new neural networks and fundamentally restructure the encoded knowledge. It can, but that is the most difficult learning experience for an adult which accounts for the difficulty of higher order transformational learning.

Principle 4: Readiness to learn

Evidence suggests that the human brain is hard-wired to learn for survival. In fact, evidence from neuroscience now supports the long-standing Maslow's hierarchy of needs which says that first humans satisfy their physiological needs, then safety needs, then social needs, then esteem needs, and finally self-actualization needs (Tokuhama-Espinosa, 2011). It is not until lower level needs are satisfied that people seek to satisfy higher level needs.

Andragogy has long recognized that adults are most ready to learn when the learning meets a developmental need. Neuroscience tells us how this works. Recall that every day we are bombarded with stimuli from our environment. Using the executive functions in our frontal cortex, our brain makes decisions about which stimuli to process into memory and which to ignore. The same applies to learning. Nobody can learn all the knowledge and skills presented to them. Our developmental needs operate much like the filter of life experiences to help us sort out what learning is needed now and what can be deferred. So if new learning directly addresses an immediate developmental need, we pay close attention to it. If new learning is not relevant now, or not perceived to be needed in the future, adults will struggle to learn it.

Maslow's hierarchy of needs is but one useful way to look at developmental needs. Consider though its effect on learning. If an adult's developmental need is for job skills to feed a family, that's what they will be most ready to learn. If another adult's developmental need is for self-actualization because their other needs have been met, then they will be ready to learn a new hobby or job skills to earn a promotion. Each adult has different developmental needs which we know will help determine their readiness to learn what we teach.

Thus, "survival" takes on different meanings for different people. The key is that whatever the individual perceives is their need based on their developmental stage is what they will be most ready to learn. The brain's executive function is quite efficient in helping the brain focus its resources on learning that will have the greatest positive impact on a person's life.

Principle 5: Orientation to learning

Adults are problem-based learners. Andragogical facilitators know that adult learners are most motivated and receptive to learning when it helps them solve problems in their lives. It turns out that brain researchers have found the same to be true.

As Tokuhama-Espinosa says, "The human brain learns best when facts and skills are embedded in natural contexts of concrete examples, in which the learner understands the problems he or she faces, and recognizes how the facts or skills might play roles in solving that problem" (p. 218). From our earlier discussions, it is not hard to see why. Since the human brain learns by connecting new facts and skills to past experiences and knowledge, the brains of adults driven by the need to solve problems have natural "neural hooks" to which new knowledge can be connected.

Furthermore, problem-driven adults are highly motivated to pay attention to learning that solves their problems. That means that their executive control centers are highly tuned to pay attention to, learn, and use learning that solves their problems. And, if they are more highly motivated, then the learning process itself is easier as the learning-enhancing neurotransmitters are released.

Is it any wonder then that adults who don't *have to* learn like students in school are more motivated by problem-solving learning? Of course this principle applies in part to young learners as well. But younger learners lack the mature executive control centers to understand how learning will benefit them over the long term. Adults are more able to defer gratification and make good decisions about the learning that will most benefit them in their lives.

Principle 6: Motivation to learn

A particularly striking finding from brain research is that learning involves a chemical process in the brain via neurotransmitters. The findings confirm what many adult educators have long practiced—fear inhibits new learning while positive motivation enhances learning (Caine et al., 2009). Brain research tells us why: positive emotions evoke increased levels of neurotransmitters that enhance communication between neurons (Willis, 2010). The emotional context of learning is thus central to the learning process (Taylor and Lamoraux, 2008).

Neuroscience has focused more on extrinsic motivational factors to date than intrinsic motivation of adults (OECD, 2007). Nonetheless, neuroscience points to instructional strategies that foster an emotional connection to the learning as being most effective (Immordino-Yang and Faeth, 2010). The more the learning connects to the lives and interests of the learner, the more positive the emotional impact and thus learning is enhanced. Positive emotions also enhance the executive functions of the brain (Caine et al., 2009).

Thus, it stands to reason that learning that appeals to the intrinsic needs of learners will lead to greater positive affect, including motivation, and enhance learning. As noted, adults come to learning primarily motivated to solve their life problems (intrinsic motivation), not to achieve external rewards (extrinsic motivation). If facilitators can tap into adults' intrinsic motivation for learning, neuroscience tells us that the brain is more primed for learning due to the positive neurotransmitters produced by the positive affect.

SETTING THE CLIMATE FOR ADULT LEARNING

Andragogy is particularly known for setting a learning environment most conducive to adult learning. At its core, this environment is one that honors and respects the "adultness" of the learner. The eight-step program planning model in Chapter 4 is designed to set a climate that is most likely to enhance adult learning.

It is interesting to see brain researchers reach the same conclusion that adult learning specialists have recognized for many decades. As Tokuhama-Espinosa (2011) concludes, "Broadly defined, good learning environments in education are those that provide physical and mental security, respect, intellectual freedom, self-direction, paced challenges, feedback, and active learning experiences" (p. 220). These conclusions are built on the core knowledge that emotions play a critical role in brain processing. Learning environments that are disrespectful, anxiety-producing, or even unpleasant activate the limbic system emotional responses which inhibit learning. Positive, adult-oriented learning environments activate emotional responses which increase attention, aid in information processing, and facilitate lasting learning.

SUMMARY

This summary of key findings from neuroscience research is just an introduction to a fast-changing and fascinating field of study. Surely the future will bring even more intriguing findings as there is still much we don't know about the human brain. From what we do know it is becoming increasingly clear why andragogy has stood the test of time as core principles of adult learning.

MBE science offers bright promise for further understanding about andragogy and why it works so well with adults. It is exciting that neuroscientists are collaborating with educators and psychologists to connect educational theories (such as andragogy) with the physiological processes of the brain. Adult learning facilitators will be well served by paying close attention to new findings from neuroscience in the future.

REFLECTION QUESTIONS

12.1 How will you use findings from neuroscience research to improve your practice as an adult educator?

12.2 How do findings from neuroscience confirm or contradict your personal beliefs about adult learning?

12.3 Think of an adult learning situation that was *not* very successful. How does neuroscience help explain what went wrong?

12.4 Think of an adult learning situation that *was* very successful. How does neuroscience help explain why it was successful?

12.5 How does neuroscience help explain your personal learning strategies?

12.6 What other connections do you see between andragogy and neuroscience findings?

PART 4

PRACTICES IN ADULT LEARNING

This part of *The Adult Learner* focuses on insights and tools supporting adult learning practices. Six independent manuscripts written by various authors are presented as separate chapters. Each is preceded with reflections as to their connection to the andragogy in practice model that appeared first in Chapter 1 (see Figure 1.1). Each of these independent manuscripts highlights an aspect of adult learning and provides additional understanding of andragogy in practice. The six chapters (13–18) are:

Whole–Part–Whole Learning Model
Facilitating learning
Guidelines for using learning contracts
Core competency diagnostic and planning guide
Personal adult learning style inventory
Effective technology-based adult learning.

WHOLE–PART–WHOLE LEARNING MODEL

13

INTRODUCTION

The *Whole–Part–Whole Learning Model* represents a practical methodology for designing learning programs. The model honors general learning theory, the six *Core Adult Learning Principles*, and the *Subject Matter Differences* as presented in the more holistic *andragogy in practice* model. The whole–part–whole perspective is useful for the overall design of learning programs of any length—total courses as well as for short learning experiences. It is simple enough that it can be used by learners to design their own learning experiences, by subject matter experts not having a deep understanding of the learning process who want to develop learning experiences for others, and a practical tool for experienced educational professionals.

Human learning is one of the most complex subjects of the scientific and scholarly world. While it is easy to demonstrate how little we know about the human mind, we can, on the other hand, acknowledge the sheer volume of research and common sense available to us to better understand the learning phenomena. We are not ignorant about the learning process. In fact, we know quite a lot about how people learn.

The origins of the Whole–Part–Whole Learning Model go back to 1972 (Swanson and Law, 1993). At that time, the Johns-Manville Corporation contacted me to talk to the corporate training and education personnel about the psychology of learning. It became apparent that these people had a real need to improve their practice and that they wanted to be theoretically sound. They were not theoreticians, yet they had an appreciation for the practical potential of sound theory. Two elements from that early presentation remain as key elements of the Whole–Part–Whole Learning Model (WPW Learning Model). The first element was to separate the field of learning psychology into two camps—the behaviorist/connectionist camp and the gestalt/cognitive camp. The second element was to acknowledge the value of each camp and to integrate it through Tolman's concept of "purposive–behaviorism" (1959).

MODEL OVERVIEW

This WPW Learning Model goes beyond the present holistic, behavioristic, whole–part, and part–whole learning models. The WPW Learning Model purports that there is a natural whole–part–whole rhythm to learning. The basic WPW Learning Model is seen in Figure 13.1.

Whole	Part	Learning segments
		Segment #1
		Segment #2
		Segment #3
		Segment #4
		Segment #5

Figure 13.1 Basic Whole–Part–Whole Learning Model

Through the *first whole*, the model introduces new content to learners by forming in their minds the organizational framework required to effectively and efficiently absorb the forthcoming concepts into their cognitive capabilities. The supporting cognitive capabilities and component behaviors are then developed in the classical behavioristic style of instruction found in the "part," or several parts, aspect of the WPW Learning Model. After the learner has successfully achieved the performance criteria for the individual "parts" or components within the whole, the instructor links these parts together, thus forming the "second whole." The whole–part–whole learning experience provides the learner with the complete understanding of the content at various levels of performance and even allows for higher order cognitive development to the levels of improvement and invention (Swanson, 1991).

The WPW Learning Model can be considered systematic on several counts. One is that the model can be used all the way from program design to real-time instructional adjustments during a live presentation. The following review of the literature supports both the psychological foundations of whole–part–whole instruction and its systemic nature.

Beyond the superficial rhetoric of broad purpose and goals, most education and training thrives on the *parts*—the details of knowledge, expertise, and activity (Skinner, 1954, 1968). Even though this behaviorist perspective on learning has been under intellectual attack, the pragmatic requirements of education and training in our culture see to it that the *parts* and the mastery of the *parts* are as strong as ever. Without diminishing the behavioral stronghold on educational and training practices, it is the gestalt psychology concept that the whole is greater than the sum of the parts that is being more fully explored through this treatise. The approach is not to attack behaviorism. Behaviorism (the *parts*) is seen as a critical aspect of the WPW Learning Model. Instead, the focus is on the *first whole* and *second whole* that envelope the "parts."

THE FIRST WHOLE OF THE WHOLE–PART–WHOLE LEARNING MODEL

There are two main purposes of the *first whole*. One is to provide a mental scaffolding through advance organizers and schemata alignment to prepare learners for the new instruction they will receive. The other main purpose of the *first whole* is to provide motivation for the participant to want to learn by making the content meaningful and connecting it to the learner.

Advance organizers

The concept of an advance organizer was originally introduced by Ausubel (1968) as a technique for helping students learn and retrieve information by making it meaningful and familiar. This is accomplished by introducing the basic concepts of the new material, from which the students are able to organize the more specific information that will follow (Luiten et al., 1980).

The need for advance organizers comes from the psychological principle that previous knowledge and experiences form their own mental structures at a given level of development (Di Vesta, 1982). These individual structures are called schemata. "We have schemata for eating in restaurants, attending hockey games, and visiting our grandmothers. The knowledge associated with each of these activities is our schema for the activity" (Gage and Berliner, 1988, p. 293). The participant's orientations that encompass the previous consequences and their interpretations of experiences represent that person's current world view (Di Vesta, 1982).

Understanding that differences in individuals are present is important for an instructor. For example, an instructor giving a lecture on quality management in industry to 30 students is in the room with 30 different schemata, or mental structures, of what quality management in industry means. A unified concept in the classroom between the instructor and each of the students becomes an essential foundation for the instruction that follows.

A simple and powerful example of a unifying concept can be the editorial cartoon found in most daily newspapers. The effective editorial cartoon presents a clear concept to thousands of readers, each having their own personal schemata regarding that topic. Through the cartoon, readers have a common starting point from which to discuss the concepts with other readers, whether they agree with the original cartoon or not. Other examples of creating a unifying concept are video productions, literature (in the forms of essays, articles, or research), pictures, diagrams, and even music. All of these could be used in an instructional setting for the purpose of schemata alignment among students.

The act of creating a basic construct and/or framework for the learner at the beginning of instruction is a way to focus the learner and to introduce the content. These ideas are supported by Hilgard and Bower (1966) and Knowles (1988). The organization of knowledge should be an essential concern of the teacher or educational planner so that the direction from simple to complex is not from arbitrary, meaningless parts to meaningful wholes, but instead from simplified wholes to more complex wholes (Knowles, 1988).

Organization of knowledge in the beginning stages of instruction also serves the even larger purpose of memory retention and retrieval upon completion of instruction. "We have made it appear probable that association depends upon organization, because an association is the after-effect of an organized process. . . . Learning amounts to association, and association is the after-effect of organization" (Kohler, 1947, pp. 163–164).

Motivating the learner

Motivation on the part of the learner is an important aspect of the WPW Learning Model due to the fact that without learners valuing the new content that is being taught, there is little hope for retention or transfer to the workplace. However, many instructors leave student motivation in the hands of the students as their own responsibility. Support for the idea that motivation should be incorporated into a structured and systematic form of instruction came first from Lewin (1951). "Learning occurs as a result of change in cognitive structures produced by changes in two types of forces: (1) change in the structure of the cognitive field itself, or (2) change in the internal needs or motivation of the individual" (Knowles, 1988, p. 23).

The potential for change in the motivation of an individual is possible due to the fact that human behavior is goal oriented. One of the distinguishable characteristics of human behavior is its purposeful, goal-directed nature (Gage and Berliner, 1988). Lindeman (1926b), as cited by Knowles, gives a key assumption about adult learning that has been supported by later research. "Adults are motivated to learn as they experience needs and interests that learning will satisfy" (Knowles, 1988, p. 31).

Clearly, the opportunity to motivate the student comes from capitalizing on the learner's own internal desire for goal attainment and personal achievement. "Perseverance can be increased by increasing the expectation of reward and the bad consequences of failure" (Gage and Berliner, 1988, p. 334).

Motivation is also attained through clearly stated learning objectives at the beginning of instruction. Although much has been written about the value of clear, student-oriented terminal objectives for the purpose of evaluation, they also aid in motivation. Research done by Bandura in 1982 identifies the following two instructional motivational variables: "These two cognitive variables are self-efficacy (one's belief that one can execute a given behavior in a given setting) and outcome expectancies (one's belief that the given outcome will occur if one engages in the behavior)" (Latham, 1989, p. 265).

Clarifying instructional objectives for the instruction and the overall terminal objective meshes with the first component of motivation. By clarifying the purpose and rationale for instruction as it relates to the learner, then by detailing the how, what, and why of the instruction through clear objectives, the learner is fundamentally prepared for the instruction to follow.

To summarize, the importance of the *first whole* is found in the preparation of the learner for the instructional events to follow. This preparation will prove instrumental in the learners' recognition and recall on which the *second whole* is based (Kohler, 1947).

THE SECOND WHOLE OF THE WHOLE–PART–WHOLE LEARNING MODEL

While it is true of any system that each element within the system is critical to the success of the system, in the Whole–Part–Whole Learning Model, the *second whole* must be considered the major component. Based on gestalt psychology that the whole is greater than the sum of the parts, it is here, in the *second whole*, that we contend that complete understanding occurs.

The *second whole* links the individual *parts* back together to form the complete whole, for it is not only the mastery of each individual part of instruction that is important but also the relationship between those *parts* through the *second whole* that provides the learner with the complete understanding of the content.

Wolfgang Kohler, in his book *Gestalt Psychology* (1947), provides the basis for the *second whole* in his writings on association and recall. Kohler, using research done with animals, explains that because of the large amount of information that must be processed and stored, a simplification effect occurs. Simplification of large quantities of stimulus is narrowed down to only the outstanding features of the original stimuli. These outstanding features remain only as traces of the original stimulus. "Hence, only some effect of the first process (part) can remain when the process (part) itself has subsided. . . . All sound theories of memory, habit and so forth must contain hypothesis about memory traces as psychological facts" (Kohler, 1947, p. 149).

Knowing this about the cognitive capabilities of an individual, whole–part instruction becomes illogical. Ending instruction upon the completion of the final part leaves the learners with unorganized and vague traces of the preceding parts. The learners are also faced with the difficult task of organizing those parts into a whole on their own in order for the new knowledge to become useful. Kohler (1947) said of the organization of traces: "They must be organized in a way which resembles the organization of the original process. With this organization they take part in processes of recall" (p. 150).

The organization of the traces should be facilitated by the instructor, thus aiding the student in a comprehensive recall of the instructional material. Kohler (1947) speaks of the interrelationship between the organized traces (or parts): "When the members of a series are well associated, they prove to have characteristics which depend upon their position in the whole series— just as tones acquire certain characteristics when heard within a melody" (p. 158).

To summarize, the interrelationship between the *parts* of the content begins with the realization that only traces from the full amount of instructional material will remain upon completion of instruction. It is essential, therefore, for the instructor to go back and strengthen those traces by forming the instructional whole (for example, whole concept, whole definition). Upon the formation of the instructional whole, the *parts* of instruction take on new meaning *within* the whole just as the tones acquire certain characteristics within the melody.

After the formation of the cognitive whole, the instructor must pursue the transfer of this new knowledge from short-term memory/working memory into the long-term memory. Information that is rehearsed is encoded for storage in the long-term memory (Gage and Berliner, 1988). Instructors can support this rehearsal by incorporating active learning (Gage and Berliner, 1988) into the *second whole*. Active learning, in which learners take a participative role rather than a passive role, is incorporated in the *parts* instruction to aid in the mastery of the individual components. Furthermore, using active learning in the *second whole* will allow students to practice all of their skills in one continuous procedure. Production facilitates both learning and retention (Campbell, 1988; Perry and Downs, 1985).

Repetitive practice of the whole procedure not only aids in the transfer to long-term memory but it also provides the learner with a sense of comfort and eventually a relaxation with the procedure as a whole. Just as driving an automobile for the first time was a nervous collection of individual part performance, after a number of times behind the wheel, driving an automobile became a single procedure.

It is at this stage that the next step in the *second whole* may be pursued. The successful attempts by the learner on the complete procedure create in the learner a readiness for further understanding that until now was not available. According to Rosenshine (1986), further cognitive development can take place after automaticity, which he explains as follows: After substantial practice, students achieve an automatic stage where they are successful, and rapid, and no longer have to think through each step. The advantage of automaticity is that the students who reach it now can give their full attention to comprehension and application. The full attention that the learners are now able to give provides the instructor with the opportunity and the responsibility to develop the instructional whole further through the introduction of a higher level cognition that the learners are now ready for. The learner who has become successful at driving an automobile is now ready for further development with such topics as driving in poor weather, night driving, and the dangers of speeding. Previous to automaticity, this would not have been as effective. Instructors are ethically responsible for pursuing this further development of learning. For just as the driving instructor knows that operation of an automobile does not only occur on dry pavements during the daytime, successful practice in the classroom is not an automatic guarantee of success in the workplace.

A pattern will not often be repeated in precisely the environment in which it occurred when the association was formed. Now, quite apart from the cruder obstacles that have been considered above, even a slight change of the surrounding field may make a given pattern unable to cause recall of associated items. This is because the change introduces a new organization in which the experiences corresponding to that pattern are no longer present (Kohler, 1947).

Kohler (1947) argues that instructors should prepare the learners for the differing applications through the analysis, synthesis, and evaluation (see Bloom, 1956) procedures or at least to the troubleshooting stage of comprehension (see Swanson, 1991). By developing the learner to this point, the instructor has not only formed the complete content whole in the learner's mind but has also provided a deeper understanding of that content whole upon which the learner can keep adding to and refining as experiences dictate. The *second whole* provides the opportunity to delight both the instructor and the learner by moving from knowledge to wisdom. Dewey (1933) and others see this reflection as a major prerequisite to wisdom.

THE PARTS OF THE WHOLE–PART–WHOLE LEARNING MODEL

The parts component of the Whole–Part–Whole Learning Model relies on the standard systematic and behavioristic approach to instruction. Thousands of books and articles have been written regarding the effectiveness of this approach to teaching specific, structured material. To argue for what has already been established would be redundant. There are, however, some important points that should be addressed regarding this component of the WPW Learning Model. The first is that the learner must attain mastery of each *part* in order for the *second whole* to be effective. If the learner does not understand one of the *parts*, there cannot be the full understanding of the whole. Next, each *part* within the WPW Learning Model can (and should) be structured in a whole–part–whole fashion. Thus, within the larger whole–part–whole instructional program design, there are subset whole–part–whole unit designs being created. This provides the learner with the same benefits in the individual lesson that the larger program design provides.

SUMMARY

The Whole–Part–Whole Learning Model provides a systematic design framework for the instructor to follow. It lends itself to the practical work of designing education and training programs while holding on fiercely to learning theory and research. It provides a general whole–part–whole learning template. This learning template can be used at both the program design and lesson design levels. From a systems perspective, each of the program segments, whether they are classified as a part or a whole, can then constitute a subsystem. In curricular language, each program segment is a lesson. The initial lesson would therefore be focused on establishing the *first whole*. Succeeding lessons would then take on the logical *part(s)* and the concluding *second whole* functions. Each of the program lessons (or subsystems) is then designed to use the same whole–part–whole template (see Figure 13.2).

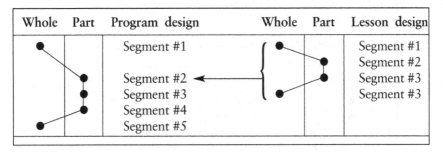

Whole	Part	Program design	Whole	Part	Lesson design
		Segment #1			Segment #1
					Segment #2
		Segment #2			Segment #3
		Segment #3			Segment #3
		Segment #4			
		Segment #5			

Figure 13.2 Whole–Part–Whole Learning Model applied to program and lesson design

The general program design of whole–part–whole lessons has been applied to the practical problem of differentiating between three types of training: management, motivational, and technical training. Through a series of structured observations of good training practices, general whole–part–whole program design templates were developed for these three types of training. Figure 13.3 illustrates the general program template of lessons.

It is interesting to note the unique roles of the *first whole* among the three types of training programs. Most technical training is focused on closed systems that are external to the learner. These learners typically understand and accept the fact that work systems get revised and/or replaced. In contrast, most management training is an attempt to alter the personal internal systems by which managers operate and which they often resist changing. Thus, dealing with program objectives and purpose becomes the critical role of the *first whole* for management training, while overviewing the new system is more typical of technical training. In motivational training (efforts at altering basic values and beliefs), the *first whole* addresses the critical need to accept the group and/or individuals. The templates and their proposed elements provide

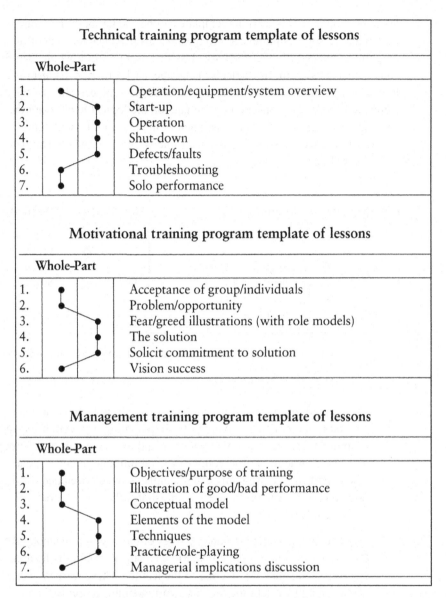

Figure 13.3 General program design templates using the Whole–Part–Whole Learning Model

a logical springboard for establishing the specific whole–part–whole lessons that make up a particular learning program.

As noted in the introduction, the Whole–Part–Whole Learning Model goes beyond the present holistic, behavioristic, whole–part, and part–whole learning models. The WPW Learning Model purports that there is a natural whole–part–whole rhythm to learning. The WPW Learning Model is an effort to acknowledge and use theory and best practices to design sound learning programs.

REFLECTION QUESTIONS

13.1 What is the essential thinking undergirding the Whole–Part–Whole Learning Model?

13.2 Why is the Whole–Part–Whole Learning Model particularly helpful in planning adult learning?

13.3 Based on personal experience, report on a learning experience that did not honor the Whole–Part–Whole Learning Model and discuss what changes would need to be made to make it conform.

13.4 Based on differing content and objectives, what are some of the variations in the Whole–Part–Whole Learning Model?

13.5 Discuss why some educators end up almost totally fixated on the "parts" while others are fixated on the "whole."

14 FACILITATING LEARNING

INTRODUCTION

Two major ideas are presented in this chapter—"From teacher to facilitator of learning" and "Releasing the energy of others." These are reports based on original writings by Malcolm Knowles. Both ideas require a basic reorientation by adult educators wanting to adopt them.

FROM TEACHER TO FACILITATOR OF LEARNING

Instructors of adults generally want to ensure efficient and effective learning. This focus often leads to concentration on what they are doing rather than what the learner is doing. Applying *core adult learning principles* 2, 3, and 4 from the *andragogy in practice* model directs the instructor to use the existing knowledge, experience, and motivation of learners to shape the learning experience. The principles include: self-concept of the learner, prior experience of the learner, and readiness to learn. When this shift to the learner occurs, the leader's role moves from that of a traditional teacher to a facilitator of learning. The facilitator role may appear to be more casual, but actually requires increased attentiveness to what is happening in individuals and groups of learners.

Most of us have been brought up to think of a teacher as one who is responsible ("accountable" is the current jargon) for what students should learn, how, when, and if they have learned. Instructors are supposed to transmit prescribed content, control the way students receive and use it, and then test if they have received it.

That is how most teachers perform. It is the only model of teaching many of us know. When invited to teach at George Williams College in Chicago shortly after World War II, that is how Knowles taught. Teachers can become pleased and proud of their performance as a pretty good transmitter—content well organized in a good logical outline; illustrating abstract concepts or principles with interesting examples, speaking clearly and dynamically; bringing forth frequent chuckles and inviting interruptions for questions of clarification along with lively discussions and practice exercises following lectures; and top this off with fair tests resulting in a good performance distribution curve.

Teachers can feel so good when their students did what they were told. Most students taking classes preparing for careers are conscientious and well behaved. They take notes, do homework, and are able to feed back on the final exam what they had been taught. When top students remember the very words from the instruction, teachers can feel psychically rewarded as being such a good transmitter of content and controller of students—being a really good teacher.

In retrospect, Knowles reports the following:

> I had started taking courses toward a master's degree in adult education at the University of Chicago a year earlier, and my first courses were with teachers who did just about the same things I was doing in my course. Toward the end of my course at George Williams College, I enrolled in a seminar in psychological counseling at the University of Chicago under Professor Arthur Shedlin, an associate of Carl Rogers. I was shocked by what happened at the first meeting. Some 15 students sat around the seminar table for 20 minutes making small talk. Finally, somebody asked if anyone knew where the teacher was. One of the people responded that his name was Art and that he had been designated by the Psychology Department to meet with us. Somebody else then asked if there was a course outline. Art responded, "You would like a course outline?" Silence for several minutes. Another student broke the silence by saying, "I'd like to know why everybody is here—what did you come to learn?" So we went around the table, stating our goals and expectations. When Art's turn came, he said, "I am hoping that you will help me become a better facilitator of learning."
>
> I won't attempt to reconstruct the ensuing events, but I can tell you that during the following week I read all the books Carl Rogers had written, located students who had taken the seminar and asked them what it was all about, and developed a plan for student inquiry teams, which I presented at the second meeting (which was adopted, with some modifications). I never read so many books and articles

and worked so hard in any course I had ever taken. I had never before experienced taking that degree of responsibility for my own learning, alone and with other students, as I did in that seminar. It was exhilarating. I began to sense what it means to get turned on to learning. I began to think about what it means to be a facilitator of learning rather than a teacher. Fortunately, my next seminar, with Cyril O. Houle, reinforced this line of inquiry.

After my completion of the seminar with Cyril Houle, George Williams College asked me to teach adult education methods again. That was the day I decided to switch from being a teacher to being a facilitator of learning. At the opening session I explained to the students that I wanted to experiment with a different approach to teaching, and described my own experience in being exposed to two role models—Shedlin and Houle—of the role of learning facilitator. I confessed that I was not secure about my ability to bring it off, since I had never done it before, that it would only work if they agreed to take a higher level of responsibility for their own learning, and that I wouldn't do it if they felt the risk was too high. They unanimously agreed to experiment with me.

I spent the rest of the first meeting having the students introduce themselves and identify their special interests and resources. I distributed a syllabus that listed the objectives the course was intended to help them accomplish and the content units (I called them "inquiry units"), with references to resource materials that would lead to the accomplishment of the objectives. I asked them which inquiry units they would take responsibility for during the week. In the second session I had them volunteer for the inquiry units they were especially interested in, and we formed "inquiry teams."

The inquiry teams met, with me as a roving consultant and resource person, for the next four weeks, and then the rest of the semester was spent with the teams putting on "show and tell" sessions. I had never seen such creative presentations and pride of accomplishment. By the end of that semester, I was a confirmed facilitator of learning.

THE TRANSFORMATION

When analyzing what had happened in his transformation, Knowles identified some fundamental changes. One's self-concept changes from teacher to facilitator of learning. He saw his role shifting from content transmitter to process manager and—only secondarily—to content resource.

A different system of psychic rewards takes place in the instructor/facilitator. Getting rewards from controlling students is replaced with getting rewards from releasing students. The releasing rewards are much more satisfying.

Additionally, facilitators find themselves performing a different set of functions that require a different set of skills. Instead of performing the function of content planner and transmitter, which requires primarily presentation skills, facilitators perform the function of process designer and manager, which require relationship building, needs assessment, involvement of students in planning, linking students to learning resources, and encouraging student initiative.

It is almost impossible to go back, once a person has made the transformation from teacher to facilitator.

RELEASING THE ENERGY OF OTHERS

Adult learning specialists are committed to helping adults learn. This zealousness often leads to too much focus on the instructor/facilitator maintaining control. Backing away can be hard, and acknowledging that "one way of gaining control is by giving up control" is not an easy lesson. This section discusses the process of letting go so as to release energy in others. Releasing the energy of others requires paying attention to the *andragogy in practice* model. Specifically the six *core adult learning principles* along with attention to *individual learner differences* and the *situational differences* present in any learning environment.

Knowles undertook a personal intellectual adventure that paid high dividends in terms of understanding the role of leadership and in selecting more effective leadership strategies. The adventure consisted of seeing what would happen if one conceptualized a social system (family, group, organization, agency, corporation, school, college, community, state, nation, or world) as a system of human energy.

All at once a set of questions very different from those typically asked by leaders come to mind: What is the sum total of the human energy available in the system? What proportion of this energy is now being used? Where is the unused energy located? Why is it not being tapped? What kinds of energy (physical, intellectual, psychic, moral, artistic, technical, social) are represented? What might be done to release this energy for accomplishing greater goals for the system and the individuals in it?

By virtue of simply asking these kinds of questions, you begin to think differently about the role of leadership. Clouded by the era of Frederick

Taylor's "scientific management," the role of leadership consisted primarily of controlling followers or subordinates. Effective leaders, from this view, were those who were able to get people to follow their orders. The consequence of this doctrine is, of course, that the output of the system was limited to the vision and ability of the leader. Realizing this provokes a rethinking of the leadership function. The alternative function of leadership is releasing the energy of the people in the system and managing the processes for giving that energy direction toward mutually beneficial goals. Perhaps a better way of saying this is that creative leadership releases the creative energy of the people being led.

Tests of this view of leadership have been done in two ways. First, by observing leaders of various sorts (teachers, business executives, educational administrators, and organizational and political leaders) through this frame of reference to identify characteristics that *releasing leaders* possess that *controlling leaders* don't have. Second, by re-examining the research literature on human behavior, organizational dynamics, and leadership to find out what support it contains for this way of viewing the concept of leadership. The result of this bifocal inquiry is in the form of the following propositions regarding the behavioral characteristics of creative leaders:

1. Creative leaders make a different set of assumptions (essentially positive) about human nature from the assumptions (essentially negative) made by controlling leaders. It has been my observation that creative leaders have faith in people, offer them challenging opportunities, and delegate responsibility to them. Two of the clearest presentations of these contrasting assumptions in the literature are reproduced in Table 14.1 by Douglas McGregor in the case of assumptions by managers and by Carl Rogers in the case of assumptions by educators.

   The validity of the positive set of assumptions is supported by research which indicates that when people perceive the locus of control to reside within themselves, they are more creative and productive (Lefcourt, 1976). The more they feel their unique potential is being used, the greater their achievement (Herzberg, 1966; Maslow, 1970).

2. Creative leaders accept as a law of human nature that people feel a commitment to a decision in proportion to the extent that they feel they have participated in making it. Creative leaders, therefore, involve their clients, workers, or students in every step of the planning process, assessing needs, formulating goals, designing lines of action, carrying out activities, and evaluating results (except, perhaps, in emergencies). The validity of this proposition is supported by locus of control studies (Lefcourt, 1976) and by research on organizational change (Bennis et al., 1968; Greiner, 1971; Lippitt, 1969; Martorana and Kuhns, 1975),

Table 14.1 A comparison of assumptions about human nature and behavior by leaders in management and education

Theory X assumptions about human nature (McGregor)* (Controlling)	Assumptions implicit in current education (Rogers)** (Controlling)
The average human being inherently dislikes work and will avoid it if he can.	The student cannot be trusted to pursue his own learning.
Because of this characteristically human dislike of work, most people must be coerced, controlled, threatened in the interest of organizational objectives.	Presentation equals learning. The aim of education is to accumulate brick upon brick of factual knowledge.
The average human being prefers to be directed, wishes to avoid responsibility, has relatively little ambition, wants security above all.	The truth is known. Creative citizens develop from passive learners. Evaluation is education and education is evaluation.
Theory Y assumptions about human nature (Releasing)	*Assumptions relevant to significant experiential learning (Releasing)*
The expenditure of physical and mental effort is as natural as play or rest.	Human beings have a natural potentiality for learning.
External control and threat of punishment are not the only means for bringing about effort toward organizational objectives. Man will exercise self-direction and self-control in the service of objectives to which he is committed.	Significant learning takes place when the subject matter is perceived by the student as relevant to his own purposes. Much significant learning is acquired through doing.
Commitment to objectives is a function of the rewards associated with their achievement.	Learning is facilitated by students' responsible participation in the learning process.
The average human being learns, under proper conditions, not only to accept but to seek responsibility.	Self-initiated learning involving the whole person—feelings as well as intellect—is the most pervasive and lasting.
A high capacity for imagination, ingenuity, and creativity in solving organizational problems is widely, not narrowly, distributed in the population.	Creativity in learning is best facilitated when self-criticism and self-evaluation are primary, and evaluation by others is of secondary importance.
Under the conditions of modern industrial life, the intellectual potential of the average human being is only partially utilized.	The most socially useful thing to learning in the modern world is the process of learning, a continuing openness to experience, an incorporation into oneself of the process of change.

Sources: *Adapted from McGregor (1960, pp. 33–34 and 47–48) in Knowles (1978, p. 102).
**Adapted from Rogers (1972, pp. 272–279) in Knowles (1978, p. 102).

administration (Baldridge et al., 1978; Dykes, 1968; Getzels et al., 1968; Likert, 1967; McGregor, 1967), decision making (Marrow et al., 1968; Millett, 1968; Simon, 1961), and organizational dynamics (Argyris, 1962; Etzioni, 1961; Schein and Bennis, 1965; Zander, 1977).

3. Creative leaders believe in and use the power of self-fulfilling prophecy. They understand that people tend to rise to the expectations of others. The creative coach conveys to his team that he knows they are capable of winning; the good supervisor's employees know that she has faith that they will do superior work; the good teacher's students are convinced that they are the best students in school. The classic study demonstrating this principle, Rosenthal and Jacobson's *Pygmalion in the Classroom* (1968), showed that the students of teachers who were told that they were superior students were superior students; whereas the students of teachers who were told that they were inferior students were inferior students. And, of course, there was no difference in the natural ability of the two groups of students. The relationship between positive self-concept and superior performance has been demonstrated in studies of students (Chickering, 1976; Felker, 1974; Rogers, 1969; Tough, 1979) and in general life achievement (Adams-Webber, 1979; Coan et al., 1974; Gale, 1974; Kelly, 1955; Loevinger, 1976; McClelland, 1975).

4. Creative leaders highly value individuality. They sense that people perform at a higher level when they are operating on the basis of their unique strengths, talents, interests, and goals than when they are trying to conform to some imposed stereotype. They are comfortable with a pluralistic culture and tend to be bored with one that is monolithic. As managers, they encourage a team arrangement in which each member works at what he or she does best and enjoys most; as teachers they strive to tailor the learning strategies to fit the individual learning styles, paces, starting points, needs, and interests of all the students. This proposition is widely supported in the research literature (Combs and Snygg, 1959; Csikszentmihalyi, 1975; Erikson, 1964; Goldstein and Blackman, 1978; Gowan et al., 1967; Kagan, 1967; Maslow, 1970; Messick et al., 1976; Moustakas, 1974; Tyler, 1978).

There is another dimension to this proposition—more of a philosophical note than a behavioral observation. It is that creative leaders probably have a different sense of the purpose of life from that of the controlling leaders. They see the purpose of all life activities—work, learning, recreation, civic participation, worship—as a way to enable each individual to achieve his or her full and unique potential. They seek to help each person become what Maslow (1970) calls a self-actualizing person, whereas the controlling leader's mission is to produce conforming persons.

5. Creative leaders stimulate and reward creativity. They understand that in a world of accelerating change, creativity is a basic requirement for the survival of individuals, organizations, and societies. They exemplify creativity in their own behavior and provide an environment that encourages and rewards innovation in others. They make it legitimate for people to experiment and to treat failures as opportunities to learn rather than as acts to be punished (Barron, 1963; Bennis, 1966; Cross, 1976; Davis and Scott, 1971; Gardner, 1963; Gowan et al., 1967; Herzberg, 1966; Ingalls, 1976; Kagan, 1967; Schon, 1971; Toffler, 1974; Zahn, 1966).

6. Creative leaders are committed to a process of continuous change and are skillful in managing change. They understand the difference between static and innovative organizations (as illustrated in Table 14.2) and aspire to make their organizations the latter. They are well grounded in the theory of change and skillful in selecting the most effective strategies for bringing about change (Arends and Arends, 1977; Baldridge and Deal, 1975; Bennis et al., 1968; Goodlad, 1975; Greiner, 1971; Hefferlin, 1969; Hornstein et al., 1971; Lippitt, 1978; Mangham, 1948; Martorana and Kuhns, 1975; Schein and Bennis, 1965; Tedeschi, 1972; Zurcher, 1977).

7. Creative leaders emphasize internal motivators over external motivators. They understand the distinction revealed in Herzberg et al.'s (1959) research between satisfiers (motivators), such as achievement, recognition, fulfilling work, responsibility, advancement, and growth; and dissatisfiers (hygienic factors), such as organizational policy and administration, supervision, working conditions, interpersonal relations, salary, status, job security, and personal life. They take steps to minimize the dissatisfiers but concentrate their energy on optimizing the satisfiers. This position is strongly supported by subsequent research (Levinson et al., 1963; Likert, 1967; Lippitt, 1969).

8. Creative leaders encourage people to be self-directing. They sense intuitively what researchers have been telling us for some time—that a universal characteristic of the maturation process is movement from a state of dependency toward states of increasing self-directedness (Baltes et al., 1984; Erikson, 1950, 1959, 1964; Goulet and Baltes, 1970; Gubrium and Buckholdt, 1977; Havighurst, 1972; Kagan and Moss, 1962; Loevinger, 1976; Rogers, 1961). They realize that because of previous conditioning as dependent learners in their school experience, adults need initial help in learning to be self-directing and will look to leaders for this kind of help (Kidd, 1973; Knowles, 1975, 1978, 1980b; Tough, 1967, 1979). And, to provide this kind of help, they have developed their skills as facilitators and consultants to a high level

Table 14.2 Some characteristics of static vs. innovative organizations

Dimensions	Characteristics	
	Static organizations	*Innovative organizations*
Structure	Rigid—much energy given to maintaining permanent departments, committees; reverance for tradition, constitution, and by-laws.	Flexible—much use of temporary task forces; easy shifting of departmental lines; readiness to change constitution, depart from tradition.
	Hierarchical—adherence to chain of command.	Multiple linkages based on functional collaboration.
	Roles defined narrowly.	Roles defined broadly.
	Property-bound.	Property-mobile.
Atmosphere	Task-centered, impersonal.	People-centered, caring.
	Cold, formal, reserved. Suspicious.	Warm, informal, intimate. Trusting.
Management, philosophy, and attitudes	Function of management is to control personnel through coercive power.	Function of management is to release the energy of personnel; power is used supportively.
	Cautious—low risk-taking.	Experimental—high risk-taking.
	Attitude toward errors: to be avoided.	Attitude toward errors: to be learned from.
	Emphasis on personnel selection.	Emphasis on personal development.
	Self-sufficiency—closed system regarding sharing resources.	Interdependency—open system regarding sharing resources.
	Low tolerance for ambiguity.	High tolerance for ambiguity.
Decision making and policy making	High participation at top, low at bottom.	Relevant participation by all those affected.
	Clear distinction between policy making and policy execution.	Collaborative policy making and policy execution.
	Decision making by legal mechanisms.	Decision making by problem solving.
	Decisions treated as final.	Decisions treated as hypotheses to be tested.
Communication	Restricted flow—constipated.	Open flow—easy access.
	One-way—downward.	Multidirectional—up, down, sideways.
	Feelings repressed or hidden.	Feelings expressed.

(Bell and Nadler, 1979; Blake and Mouton, 1976; Bullmer, 1975; Carkhuff, 1969; Combs et al., 1978; Laughary and Ripley, 1979; Lippitt and Lippitt, 1978; Pollack, 1976; Schein, 1969; Schlossberg et al., 1978).

SUMMARY

No doubt additional propositions and behavioral characteristics can be identified, but those listed above are the ones that stand out when both observing creative leaders and reviewing the literature. Wonderful things happen when these elements are put into practice. We have seen low-achieving students become high-achieving students when they discovered the excitement of self-directed learning under the influence of a creative teacher. We have seen bench workers in a factory increase their productivity and get a new sense of personal pride and fulfillment under a creative supervisor. We have seen an entire college faculty become creative facilitators of learning and content resource consultants through the stimulation of a creative administration. And we have observed instances in which the line managers of major corporations moved from controlling managers to releasing managers when their management development programs were geared to these propositions. How to optimize the release of the enormous pent-up energy in our human energy systems is a realistic and highly fruitful endeavor.

REFLECTION QUESTIONS

14.1 What are the barriers to succeeding as a facilitator?

14.2 Given there are times you need to be a teacher and other times a facilitator, what would you need to do to mentally prepare yourself for each role?

14.3 Discuss and contrast the concepts of controlling and releasing the energy of others.

14.4 Why is leadership important in releasing the energy of others?

14.5 What strikes you most when you compare and contrast static and innovative organizations?

15

GUIDELINES FOR USING LEARNING CONTRACTS

INTRODUCTION

Almost always there are alternative avenues to reaching a goal. The professional educator may be inclined to select what they believe to be the best way. This approach denies the variability in learners that is highlighted in the *andragogy in practice* model. Learning contracts are a way to engage learners to take charge of their learning and to communicate their plan to the facilitator. Using a learning contract makes the effort explicit and heads off potential undesirable extremes and misunderstandings. *Andragogy in practice* principles that particularly support the use of learning contracts include *orientation to learning* and *motivation to learn*.

WHY USE LEARNING CONTRACTS?

One of the most significant findings from research about adult learning (for example, Allen Tough's *The Adult's Learning Projects*, 1971, 1979) is that when adults go about learning something naturally (as contrasted with being taught something), they are highly self-directing. Evidence is beginning to accumulate, too, that what adults learn on their own initiative, they learn more deeply and permanently than what they learn by being taught.

Those kinds of learning that are engaged in for purely personal development can perhaps be planned and carried out completely by an individual on his or her own terms and with only a loose structure. But those kinds of learning that have as their purpose improving one's competence to perform in a job or in a profession must take into account the needs and expectations of organizations, professions, and society. Learning contracts provide a means for negotiating a reconciliation between these external needs and expectations and the learner's internal needs and interests.

Furthermore, in traditional education the learning activity is structured by the teacher and the institution. The learner is told what objectives to work toward, what resources to use and how and when to use them, and how accomplishment of the objectives will be evaluated. This imposed structure conflicts with the adult's deep psychological need to be self-directing and may induce resistance, apathy, or withdrawal. Learning contracts provide a vehicle for making the planning of learning experiences a mutual undertaking between a learner and his or her helper, mentor, teacher, and often, peers. By participating in the process of diagnosing his or her needs, formulating personal objectives, identifying resources, choosing strategies, and evaluating accomplishments, the learner develops a sense of ownership of (and commitment to) the plan.

Finally, in field-based learning particularly, there is a strong possibility that what is to be learned from the experience will be less clear to both the learner and the field supervisor than what work is to be done. There is a long tradition of field experience learners being exploited for the performance of menial tasks. The learning contract is a means for making the learning objectives of the field experience clear and explicit for both the learner and the field supervisor.

HOW DO YOU DEVELOP A LEARNING CONTRACT?

Step 1: Diagnose your learning needs

A learning need is the gap between where you are now and where you want to be in regard to a particular set of competencies.

You may already be aware of certain learning needs as a result of a personnel appraisal process or the long accumulation of evidence for yourself of the gaps between where you are now and where you would like to be.

If not (or even so), it might be worth your while to go through this process: First, construct a model of the competencies required to perform excellently the role (e.g., parent, teacher, civic leader, manager, consumer, professional worker, etc.) about which you are concerned. There may be a competency model already in existence that you can use as a thought-starter and checklist; many professions are developing such models. If not, you can build your own, with help from friends, colleagues, supervisors, and expert resource people. A competency can be thought of as the ability to do something at some level of proficiency; it is usually composed of some combination of knowledge, understanding, skill, attitude, and values. For example, "ability to ride a bicycle from my home to the store" is a competency that involves some knowledge of how a bicycle operates and the route to the store; an understanding of some of the dangers inherent in riding a bicycle; skill in mounting, pedaling, steering, and stopping a bicycle; an attitude of desire to ride a bicycle; and a valuing of the exercise it will yield. "Ability to ride a bicycle in a cross-country race" would be a higher level competency that would require greater knowledge, understanding, skill, and so on. It is useful to produce a competency model even if it is crude and subjective because of the clearer sense of direction it will give you.

Having constructed a competency model, your next task is to assess the gap between where you are now and where the model says you should be in regard to each competency. You can do this alone or with the help of people who have been observing your performance. The chances are that you will find that you have already developed some competencies to a level of excellence, so that you can concentrate on those you have not.

Step 2: Specify your learning objectives

You are now ready to start filling out the first column of the learning contract shown in Figure 15.1. Each of the learning needs diagnosed in Step 1 should be translated into a learning objective. Be sure that your objectives describe what you will *learn*, not what you will *do*. State them in terms that are most meaningful to you—content acquisition, terminal behaviors, or directions of growth.

Learning contract for:			
Name _____			
Activity _____			
Learning objectives	Learning resources and strategies	Evidence of accomplishment of objectives	Criteria and means for validating evidence

Figure 15.1 This is a typical learning contract

Step 3: Specify learning resources and strategies

When you have finished listing your objectives, move over to the second column of the contract in Figure 15.1, *Learning resources and strategies*, and describe how you propose to go about accomplishing each objective. Identify the resources (material and human) you plan to use in your field experience and the strategies (techniques, tools) you will employ in making use of them. For example, if in the *Learning objectives* column you wrote, "Improve my ability to organize my work efficiently so that I can accomplish 20 percent more work in a day," you might list the following in the *Learning resources and strategies* column:

1. Find books and articles in the library on how to organize my work and manage time.
2. Interview three executives on how they organize their work, then observe them for one day each, noting techniques they use.
3. Select the best techniques from each, plan a day's work, and have a colleague observe me for a day, giving me feedback.

Step 4: Specify evidence of accomplishment

After completing the second column, move over to the third column, *Evidence of accomplishment of objectives*, and describe what evidence you will collect to indicate the degree to which you have achieved each objective. Perhaps the following examples of evidence for different types of objectives will stimulate your thinking about what evidence you might accumulate (see Table 15.1).

Step 5: Specify how the evidence will be validated

After you have specified what evidence you will gather for each objective in column three, more over to column four, *Criteria and means for validating evidence*. For each objective, first specify by what criteria you propose the evidence will be judged. The criteria will vary according to the type of objective. For example, appropriate criteria for knowledge objectives might include comprehensiveness, depth, precision, clarity, authentication, usefulness, and scholarliness. For skill objectives, more appropriate criteria may be poise, speed, flexibility, gracefulness, precision, and imaginativeness. After you have specified the criteria, indicate the means you propose to use to have the evidence judged according to these criteria. For example, if you produce a paper or report, who will have read it and what are that person's qualifications? Will the person express his or her judgments by rating scales, descriptive reports, evaluative reports, or how? One of the

Table 15.1 Evidence of accomplishment of objectives

Type of objective	Examples of evidence
Knowledge	Reports of knowledge acquired, as in essays, examinations, oral presentations, audiovisual presentations, annotated bibliographies.
Understanding	Examples of utilizations of knowledge in solving problems, as in action projects, research projects with conclusions and recommendations, plans for curriculum change, etc.
Skills	Performance exercises, videotaped performances, etc., with ratings by observers.
Attitudes	Attitudinal rating scales; performance in real situations, role-playing, simulation games, critical incident cases, etc., with feedback from participants and/or observers.
Values	Value rating scales; performance in value clarification groups, critical incident cases, simulation exercises, etc., with feedback from participants and/or observers.

actions that help to differentiate "distinguished" from "adequate" performance in self-directed learning is the wisdom with which a learner selects his or her validators.

Step 6: Review your contract with consultants

After you have completed the first draft of your contract, you will find it useful to review it with two or three friends, supervisors, or other expert resource people to get their reactions and suggestions. Here are some questions you might have them ask about the contract to get optimal benefit from their help:

1. Are the learning objectives clear, understandable, and realistic; and do they describe what you propose to learn?
2. Can they think of other objectives you might consider?
3. Do the learning strategies and resources seem reasonable, appropriate, and efficient?
4. Can they think of other resources and strategies you might consider?
5. Does the evidence seem relevant to the various objectives, and would it convince them?

6. Can they suggest other evidence you might consider?
7. Are the criteria and means for validating the evidence clear, relevant, and convincing?
8. Can they think of other ways to validate the evidence that you might consider?

Step 7: Carry out the contract

You now simply do what the contract calls for. But keep in mind that as you work on it you may find that your notions about what you want to learn and how you want to learn it may change. So don't hesitate to revise your contract as you go along.

Step 8: Evaluate your learning

When you have completed your contract, you will want to get some assurance that you have in fact learned what you set out to learn. Perhaps the simplest way to do this is to ask the consultants you used in Step 6 to examine your evidence and validation data and give you their judgment about their adequacy.

SUMMARY

The idea of a learning contract seems simple. In fact, learning contracts are simple and they are effective. Simple as they are, it is important to honor the steps in creating a learning contract. Ignoring steps can result in miscommunication and disappointment.

REFLECTION QUESTIONS

15.1 What are the steps in creating a learning contract?

15.2 What learning contract step or steps do you think give learners the most difficulty?

15.3 Describe a personal learning situation where a learning contract would have been helpful and how it would have helped.

CORE COMPETENCY DIAGNOSTIC AND PLANNING GUIDE

16

INTRODUCTION

Mastering *andragogy in practice* at both the facilitator and administrator levels are learning journeys in themselves. Self-assessment and peer assessment provides important reflection as to the present state of affairs. The general question of asking how well expertise in facilitation and planning takes place can provoke some important unexpected responses. Yet, having focused questions that are connected to sound adult learning theory and practice provides greater direction for improvement. This is where the Core Competency Diagnostic and Planning Guide is most useful.

SELF-DIAGNOSTIC RATING SCALE COMPETENCIES

Name_____

Program_____

Indicate on the scale of 0 to 5 the level of each competency required for performing the particular role you plan to engage in by placing an "R" at the appropriate point. Then indicate your present level of development of each competency by placing a "P" at the appropriate point. For example, if you plan to make your career in teaching, you might rate required competencies as a learning facilitator as high and as a program developer and administrator as low or moderate; whereas, if you plan a career as a college administrator, you might rate the competencies as a learning facilitator as moderate and as a program developer and administrator as high. (Learners can add competencies of their own at the end of each section.)

AS A LEARNING FACILITATOR

A. *Conceptual and theoretical framework of adult learning*:

1. Ability to describe and apply modern concepts and research findings regarding the needs, interests, motivations, capacities, and developmental characteristics of adults as learners.

   0 1 2 3 4 5

2. Ability to describe the differences in assumptions about youths and adults as learners and the implications of these differences for teaching.

   0 1 2 3 4 5

3. Ability to assess the effects of forces impinging on learners from the larger environment (groups, organizations, cultures) and manipulate them constructively.

   0 1 2 3 4 5

4. Ability to describe the various theories of learning and assess their relevance to particular adult learning situations.

   0 1 2 3 4 5

5. Ability to conceptualize and explain the role of teacher as a facilitator and resource person for self-directed learners.

   0 1 2 3 4 5

B. *Designing and implementing learning experiences*:

1. Ability to describe the difference between a content plan and a process design.

   0 1 2 3 4 5

2. Ability to design learning experiences for accomplishing a variety of purposes that take into account individual differences among learners.

   0 1 2 3 4 5

3. Ability to engineer a physical and psychological climate of mutual respect, trust, openness, supportiveness, and safety.

   0 1 2 3 4 5

4. Ability to establish a warm, empathic, facilitative relationship with learners of all sorts.

   0 1 2 3 4 5

5. Ability to engage learners responsibly in self-diagnosis of needs for learning.

   0 1 2 3 4 5

6. Ability to engage learners in formulating objectives that are meaningful to them.

    0 1 2 3 4 5

7. Ability to involve learners in the planning, conducting, and evaluating of learning activities appropriately.

    0 1 2 3 4 5

C. *Helping learners become self-directing*:

1. Ability to explain the conceptual difference between didactic instruction and self-directed learning.

    0 1 2 3 4 5

2. Ability to design and conduct one-hour, three-hour, one-day, and three-day learning experiences to develop the skills of self-directed learning.

    0 1 2 3 4 5

3. Ability to model the role of self-directed learning in your own behavior.

    0 1 2 3 4 5

D. *Selecting methods, techniques, and materials*:

1. Ability to describe the range of methods or formats for organizing learning experiences.

    0 1 2 3 4 5

2. Ability to describe the range of techniques available for facilitating learning.

    0 1 2 3 4 5

3. Ability to identify the range of materials available as resources for learning.

    0 1 2 3 4 5

4. Ability to provide a rationale for selecting a particular method, technique, or material for achieving particular educational objectives.

    0 1 2 3 4 5

5. Ability to evaluate various methods, techniques, and materials as to their effectiveness in achieving particular educational outcomes.

    0 1 2 3 4 5

6. Ability to develop and manage procedures for the construction of models of competency.

    0 1 2 3 4 5

7. Ability to construct and use tools and procedures for assessing competency-development needs.

    0 1 2 3 4 5

8. Ability to use a wide variety of presentation   0 1 2 3 4 5
    methods effectively.

9. Ability to use a wide variety of experiential   0 1 2 3 4 5
    and simulation methods effectively.

10. Ability to use audience-participation methods   0 1 2 3 4 5
    effectively.

11. Ability to use group dynamics and small-group   0 1 2 3 4 5
    discussion techniques effectively.

12. Ability to invent new techniques to fit new   0 1 2 3 4 5
    situations.

13. Ability to evaluate learning outcomes and   0 1 2 3 4 5
    processes and select or construct appropriate
    instruments and procedures for this purpose.

14. Ability to confront new situations with   0 1 2 3 4 5
    confidence and a high tolerance for ambiguity.

AS A PROGRAM DEVELOPER

A. *Understanding the planning process*:

1. Ability to describe and implement the basic   0 1 2 3 4 5
    steps (e.g., climate setting, needs assessment,
    formulation of program objectives, program
    design, program execution, and evaluation)
    that undergird the planning process in adult
    education.

2. Ability to involve representatives of client   0 1 2 3 4 5
    systems appropriately in the planning
    process.

3. Ability to develop and use instruments and   0 1 2 3 4 5
    procedures for assessing the needs of
    individuals, organizations, and subpopulations
    in social systems.

4. Ability to use systems-analysis strategies in   0 1 2 3 4 5
    program planning.

B. *Designing and operating programs*:

1. Ability to construct a wide variety of program designs to meet the needs of various situations (basic skills training, developmental education, supervisory and management development, organizational development, etc.).   0   1   2   3   4   5

2. Ability to design programs with a creative variety of formats, activities, schedules, resources, and evaluative procedures.   0   1   2   3   4   5

3. Ability to use needs assessments, census data, organizational records, surveys, etc. in adapting programs to specific needs and clienteles.   0   1   2   3   4   5

4. Ability to use planning mechanisms, such as advisory councils, committees, task forces, etc., effectively.   0   1   2   3   4   5

5. Ability to develop and carry out a plan for program evaluation that will satisfy the requirements of institutional accountability and provide for program improvement.   0   1   2   3   4   5

AS AN ADMINISTRATOR

A. *Understanding organizational development and maintenance*:

1. Ability to describe and apply theories and research findings about organizational behavior, management, and renewal.   0   1   2   3   4   5

2. Ability to formulate a personal philosophy of administration and adapt it to various organizational situations.   0   1   2   3   4   5

3. Ability to formulate policies that clearly convey the definition of mission, social philosophy, educational commitment, etc. of an organization.   0   1   2   3   4   5

4. Ability to evaluate organizational effectiveness and guide its continuous self-renewal processes.   0   1   2   3   4   5

5. Ability to plan effectively with and through others, sharing responsibilities and decision making with them as appropriate. 0 1 2 3 4 5

6. Ability to select, supervise, and provide for in-service education of personnel. 0 1 2 3 4 5

7. Ability to evaluate staff performance. 0 1 2 3 4 5

8. Ability to analyze and interpret legislation affecting adult education. 0 1 2 3 4 5

9. Ability to describe financial policies and practices in the field of adult education and to use them as guidelines for setting your own policies and practices. 0 1 2 3 4 5

10. Ability to perform the role of change agent vis-à-vis organizations and communities utilizing educational processes. 0 1 2 3 4 5

B. *Understanding program administration*:

1. Ability to design and operate programs within the framework of a limited budget. 0 1 2 3 4 5

2. Ability to make and monitor financial plans and procedures. 0 1 2 3 4 5

3. Ability to interpret modern approaches to adult education and training to policy makers convincingly. 0 1 2 3 4 5

4. Ability to design and use promotion, publicity, and public relations strategies appropriately and effectively. 0 1 2 3 4 5

5. Ability to prepare grant proposals and identify potential funding sources for them. 0 1 2 3 4 5

6. Ability to make use of consultants appropriately. 0 1 2 3 4 5

7. Ability and willingness to experiment with programmatic innovations and assess their results objectively. 0 1 2 3 4 5

REFLECTION QUESTIONS

16.1 Taking the self-diagnostic, what is your greatest strength and how could you use this to your advantage?

16.2 Taking the self-diagnostic, what is your greatest weakness and how could you go about improving your competence in this realm?

16.3 Describe a hypothetical situation where this guide could improve an adult learning experience.

17

PERSONAL ADULT LEARNING STYLE INVENTORY

INTRODUCTION

The theory of andragogy was developed long before the notion of learning styles became popular. In fact, the *andragogy in practice* model illustrates phenomena of adult learning styles and the *orientation to learning* principle highlights this dimension. When individuals become conscious of their learning style and facilitators become aware of the styles of their learners, learning motivation and effectiveness increases. This instrument has particular utility for professionals to assess their understanding of learning styles.

This inventory is for anyone involved in organizing and administering adult learning activities. You might be a trainer, teacher, group facilitator, administrator, educator, or anyone who works with adults in teaching/learning relationships. Your responses to this inventory will give you some insight into your general orientation to adult learning, program development, learning methods, and program administration.

Self-assessments are not easy for anyone to make accurately. How we would like to be seen by others comes in conflict with how we really behave. Our vision of ourselves is likely to be somewhat optimistic. Please be as candid as possible in your responses so that you can obtain a better understanding of your own style.

Note: Permission is granted to use this inventory without limitation.

Directions: Thirty pairs of items are listed on the next few pages. The statements comprising each pair are labeled A and B. After reading each pair and considering your own approach, decide on the extent to which you agree with *each* statement. Place your response on the scale in the center of the page by circling *one* of the choices.

This inventory is designed to be used in a variety of settings; therefore, the words *facilitator* and *trainer* may be used interchangeably, as well as *learning* and *training*. Both words are included in the inventory and denoted with a slashmark ("/").

Use the following key:

A	=	I agree fully with statement A
A>B	=	I agree more with statement A than B
NANB	=	I do not agree with either statement A or B
B>A	=	I agree more with statement B than A
B	=	I agree fully with statement B

Go to the *Personal Adult Learning Style inventory* . . .

PERSONAL ADULT LEARNING STYLE INVENTORY

A	A	A>B	NANB	B>A	B	B
1 There are a number of important differences between youths and adults as learners that can affect the learning process.	A	A>B	NANB	B>A	B	For the most part adults and youths do not differ greatly in terms of the learning process.
2 Effective learning/training design puts equal weight on content and process plans.	A	A>B	NANB	B>A	B	Effective learning/training design is concerned with content first and process second.
3 Effective facilitators/trainers model self-directed learning in their own behavior, both within and outside the learning session.	A	A>B	NANB	B>A	B	Effective facilitators/trainers show learners that they, the facilitators/trainers, are content experts, with the knowledge and skills to be "in the driver's seat."
4 Effective learning/training is based on sound methods for involving learners in assessing their own learning needs.	A	A>B	NANB	B>A	B	Effective learning/training rests on the trainer's use of standard, valid methods for assessing learners' needs.
5 Client system representatives must be involved in the planning of learning/training programs.	A	A>B	NANB	B>A	B	It is the program developer's responsibility to provide clients with clear and detailed plans.
6 Program administrators must plan, work, and share decision making with client system members.	A	A>B	NANB	B>A	B	Program administrators must have full responsibility and be held accountable for their plans and decisions.
7 The role of the facilitator/trainer is best seen as that of a facilitator and resource person for self-directed learners.	A	A>B	NANB	B>A	B	The role of the facilitator/trainer is to provide the most current and accurate information possible for learners.
8 Effective learning designs take into account individual differences among learners.	A	A>B	NANB	B>A	B	Effective learning designs are those that apply broadly to most or all learners.

PERSONAL ADULT LEARNING STYLE INVENTORY

#	Statement A	A	A>B	NANB	B>A	B	Statement B
9	Effective facilitators/trainers are able to create a variety of learning experiences for helping trainees develop self-directed learning skills.	A	A>B	NANB	B>A	B	Effective facilitators/trainers concentrate on preparing learning/training sessions that effectively convey specific content.
10	Successful learning/training designs incorporate a variety of experiential learning methods.	A	A>B	NANB	B>A	B	Successful learning/training designs are grounded in carefully developed formal presentations.
11	Client system members should be involved in developing needs assessment instruments and procedures that provide the data for program planning.	A	A>B	NANB	B>A	B	Learning/training program developers are responsible for designing and using sound needs assessment instruments and procedures to generate valid data for program planning.
12	Program administrators must involve their clients in defining, modifying, and applying financial policies and practices related to learning/training programs.	A	A>B	NANB	B>A	B	Program administrators must be able to explain clearly to their clients their financial policies and practices related to learning/training programs.
13	Effective facilitators/trainers must take into account recent research findings concerning the unique characteristics of adults as learners.	A	A>B	NANB	B>A	B	Effective facilitators/trainers must use the respected, traditional learning theories as they apply to *all* learners.
14	Effective learning requires a physical and psychological climate of mutual respect, trust, openness, supportiveness, and security.	A	A>B	NANB	B>A	B	Effective learning depends on learners recognizing and relying on the expert knowledge and skills of the trainer.
15	It is important to help learners understand the differences between didactic instruction and self-directed learning.	A	A>B	NANB	B>A	B	Learners should concentrate on the content of learning/training rather than the method or methods of instruction.

#	Statement A	A	A>B	NANB	B>A	B	Statement B
16	Effective facilitators/trainers are able to get learners involved in the learning/ training.	A	A>B	NANB	B>A	B	Effective facilitators/trainers are able to get, focus, and maintain the learners' attention.
17	Client system representatives need to be involved in revising and adapting learning/training programs, based on continuing needs assessment.	A	A>B	NANB	B>A	B	Learning/training program developers must develop and use ongoing needs assessment data, to revise and adapt programs to better meet client needs.
18	Program administrators must involve organizational decision makers in interpreting and applying modern approaches to adult education and learning/training.	A	A>B	NANB	B>A	B	Program administrators must be able to explain clearly and convincingly modern approaches to adult education and learning/training to organizational policy makers.
19	Effective learning requires the facilitator/ trainer to assess and control the effects that factors such as groups, organizations, and cultures have on learners.	A	A>B	NANB	B>A	B	Effective learning requires the facilitator/ trainer to isolate learners from the possible effects of outside factors such as groups, organizations, or cultures.
20	Effective learning/training design engages the learners in a responsible self-diagnosis of their learning needs.	A	A>B	NANB	B>A	B	Effective learning/training can take place only after experts have diagnosed the real learning needs of learners.
21	Effective facilitators/trainers involve learners in planning, implementing, and evaluating their own learning activities.	A	A>B	NANB	B>A	B	Effective facilitators/trainers accept responsibility for the planning, implementation, and evaluation of the learning activities they direct.
22	Use of group dynamics principles and small-group discussion techniques is critical for effective learning.	A	A>B	NANB	B>A	B	Effective learning centers on the one-to-one relationship between the facilitator/trainer and the learner.
23	Program developers must help design and use program planning mechanisms such as client system advisory committees, task forces, and others.	A	A>B	NANB	B>A	B	Effective program planning is the result of the program developer's efforts to interpret and to use the client system data they collect.

PERSONAL ADULT LEARNING STYLE INVENTORY

#	Statement A	A	A>B	NANB	B>A	B	Statement B
24	Program administrators must collaborate with organizational members to experiment with program innovations, jointly assessing outcomes and effectiveness.	A	A>B	NANB	B>A	B	Program administrators must take the initiative to experiment with program innovations and assess their outcomes and effectiveness.
25	In preparing a learning/training activity, the facilitator/trainer should review those theories of learning relevant for particular adult learning situations.	A	A>B	NANB	B>A	B	In preparing a learning/training activity, the facilitator/trainer should rely on certain basic assumptions about the learning process that have been proven to be generally true.
26	Effective learning/training engages learners in formulating objectives that are meaningful to them.	A	A>B	NANB	B>A	B	Effective learning/training requires that the facilitator/trainer clearly defines the goals that learners are expected to attain.
27	Effective facilitators/trainers begin the learning process by engaging adult learners in self-diagnosis of their own learning needs.	A	A>B	NANB	B>A	B	Effective facilitators/trainers start by making a careful diagnosis of participant learning needs.
28	Learners must be involved in planning and developing evaluation instruments and procedures and in carrying out the evaluation of learning processes and outcomes.	A	A>B	NANB	B>A	B	Facilitators/trainers are responsible for planning and developing evaluation instruments and procedures and for carrying out evaluation of learning processes and outcomes.
29	Program developers must involve client system members in designing and using learning/training program evaluation plans.	A	A>B	NANB	B>A	B	Program developers are responsible for designing and implementing sound evaluation plans.
30	Program administrators must work with organizational members and decision makers to analyze and interpret legislation affecting organizational learning/training programs.	A	A>B	NANB	B>A	B	Program administrators are responsible for making and presenting to organizational authorities analyses of legislation that affect organizational learning/training programs.

SCORING THE INVENTORY

Directions: Circle the numbers in each column that correspond to the answers you chose on the survey (see key below) and then add down the columns. Enter the sum for each column in the box provided. You will have six scores (subtotals). Then, add the subtotals and place the sum in the total box at the bottom.

A	=	5
A>B	=	4
NANB	=	3
B>A	=	2
B	=	1

I. Learning orientation	II. Learning design	III. How people learn	IV. Learning methods	V. Program development	VI. Program admin.
1	6	11	16	21	26
5 4 3 2 1	5 4 3 2 1	5 4 3 2 1	5 4 3 2 1	5 4 3 2 1	5 4 3 2 1
2	7	12	17	22	27
5 4 3 2 1	5 4 3 2 1	5 4 3 2 1	5 4 3 2 1	5 4 3 2 1	5 4 3 2 1
3	8	13	18	23	28
5 4 3 2 1	5 4 3 2 1	5 4 3 2 1	5 4 3 2 1	5 4 3 2 1	5 4 3 2 1
4	9	14	19	24	29
5 4 3 2 1	5 4 3 2 1	5 4 3 2 1	5 4 3 2 1	5 4 3 2 1	5 4 3 2 1
5	10	15	20	25	30
5 4 3 2 1	5 4 3 2 1	5 4 3 2 1	5 4 3 2 1	5 4 3 2 1	5 4 3 2 1

TOTAL

Graphing your results

To bring your results into sharper focus regarding your andragogic or pedagogic orientation, plot your results on the following graph. Plot your total score on the Pedagogy/Andragogy continuum by placing an X at the appropriate point. Scores of 120–150 would suggest a stronger andragogical orientation. Scores of 60–30 would suggest a stronger pedagogical orientation.

Overall results: How andragogic am I?

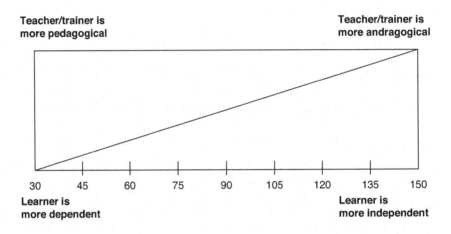

Teacher/trainer is
more pedagogical

Teacher/trainer is
more andragogical

| 30 | 45 | 60 | 75 | 90 | 105 | 120 | 135 | 150 |

Learner is
more dependent

Learner is
more independent

Component results: To what extent am I andragogical in each of the six areas?

	Pedagogically oriented	My scores	Andragogically oriented
I	5–10	_____	20–25
II	5–10	_____	20–25
III	5–10	_____	20–25
IV	5–10	_____	20–25
V	5–10	_____	20–25
VI	5–10	_____	20–25

Place each of your six component scores in the column labeled "My scores." Compare your score for each component to the pedagogy/andragogy ranges.

INTERPRETIVE GUIDE

The *Personal Adult Learning Style inventory* is a learning instrument designed to help you assess the assumptions that underlie your teaching/training activities. These assumptions may be useful or not useful, depending on the particular learner and the particular learning situation.

Teaching/learning assumptions may be categorized as *pedagogically* oriented or *andragogically* oriented. The body of theory and practice on which teacher-directed learning is based is often given the label *pedagogy*, from the Greek words *paid* (meaning child) and *agogos* (meaning guide or leader)— thus being defined as the art and science of teaching children.

The body of theory and practice on which self-directed learning is based is coming to be labeled *andragogy*, from the Greek word *aner* (meaning "adult")—thus being defined as the art and science of helping adults (or, even better, maturing human beings) learn.

Traditional learning: the pedagogical model

The pedagogical model is the one with which all of us have had the most experience. Teaching in our elementary schools, high schools, colleges, the military service, churches, and a variety of other institutions is largely pedagogically oriented. When we are asked to serve as instructors or prepare instruction for others, the pedagogical model comes quickly to mind and often takes control of our activities. That is easy to understand since pedagogy has dominated education and training practices since the seventh century.

Four assumptions about learners are inherent in the pedagogical model:

1. The learner is a dependent personality. The teacher/trainer is expected to take full responsibility for making the decisions about what is to be learned, how and when it should be learned, and whether it has been learned. The role of the learner is to carry out the teacher's directions passively.
2. The learner enters into an educational activity with little experience that can be used in the learning process. The experience of the teacher/ trainer is what is important. For that reason a variety of one-way communication strategies are employed, including lectures, textbooks and manuals, and a variety of audiovisual techniques that can transmit information to the learner efficiently.

3. People are ready to learn when they are told what they have to learn in order to advance to the next grade level or achieve the next salary grade or job level.
4. People are motivated to learn primarily by external pressures from parents, teachers/trainers, employers, the consequences of failure, grades, certificates, and so on.

CONTEMPORARY LEARNING: THE ANDRAGOGICAL MODEL

During the 1960s, European adult educators coined the term *andragogy* to provide a label for a growing body of knowledge and technology in regard to adult learning. The following five assumptions underlie the andragogical model of learning:

1. The learner is self-directing. Adult learners want to take responsibility for their own lives, including the planning, implementing, and evaluating of their learning activities.
2. The learner enters an educational situation with a great deal of experience. This experience can be a valuable resource to the learner as well as to others. It needs to be valued and used in the learning process.
3. Adults are ready to learn when they perceive a need to know or do something in order to perform more effectively in some aspect of their lives. Their readiness to learn may be stimulated by helping them to assess the gaps between where they are now and where they want and need to be.
4. Adults are motivated to learn after they experience a need in their life situation. For that reason, learning needs to be problem-focused or task-centered. Adults want to apply what they have learned as quickly as possible. Learning activities need to be clearly relevant to the needs of the adult.
5. Adults are motivated to learn because of internal factors, such as self-esteem, recognition, better quality of life, greater self-confidence, the opportunity to self-actualize, and so forth. External factors, such as pressure from authority figures, salary increases, and the like, are less important.

IMPLICATIONS OF THE MODELS FOR TEACHERS/ TRAINERS

A subscription to one model of learning or the other carries with it certain implications for the teacher/trainer. The basic concern of people with a pedagogical orientation is *content*. Teachers and trainers with a strong pedagogical orientation will be strongly concerned about what needs to be covered in the learning situation; how that content can be organized into manageable units; the most logical sequence for presenting these units; and the most efficient means of transmitting this content.

In contrast, the basic concern of people with an andragogical orientation is *process*. The andragogical process consists of eight elements: preparing the learners, considering the physical and psychological climate setting, involving the learners in planning for their learning, involving the learners in diagnosing their own needs for learning, involving the learners in formulating their own learning objectives, involving the learners in designing learning plans, helping the learners carry out their learning plans, and involving the learners in evaluating their own learning outcomes.

REFLECTION QUESTIONS

17.1 Taking the *Personal Adult Learning Style inventory*, how consistent are your results with what you imagined your style to be?

17.2 Think back about your learning style when you were age 13 and now. How has it changed?

17.3 How would you like your style to grow and change in the future?

17.4 Describe a learning situation where the person in authority allowed you to follow your learning style.

EFFECTIVE TECHNOLOGY-
BASED ADULT LEARNING

INTRODUCTION

The rapid advances in technology, the need for lifelong learning, and the growth of non-traditional students have encouraged the use of the computer as a method of instructional delivery. In fact, computer-based instruction (CBI) is fast becoming a routine part of learners' lives. Unfortunately, research on CBI has been largely atheoretical and not focused on adult learners. The model presented in this chapter is explicitly for adult learners and addresses the growing need for a planning framework to make computer-based instruction effective for them.

The rapid advances in technology, the need for lifelong learning, the learner at a distance, and the growth of non-traditional students have encouraged the use of the computer as a means of instructional delivery. Computer-based instruction (CBI) is touted as providing numerous benefits in practice. It is generally believed that CBI provides consistency of content delivery, more readily provides training to remote locations, eliminates costs associated with employees' travel, provides means of tracking learners' progress, provides standardized testing, offers learner flexibility in controlling and pacing learning, provides for diverse learning needs, provides opportunities for practice through simulation, provides greater retention, and reduces the instructional time. It is a wonder that more organizations are not using CBI as their major delivery method.

One reason may be that research on CBI effectiveness has largely consisted of fragmented studies examining small subsets of constructs (see Lowe and Holton (2005) for a more complete review of this literature and the study that served as a basis for this chapter). Thus, the constructs that are most important in affecting CBI have not been determined. Furthermore, an empirical study performed by Jones and Paolucci (1999) estimates that since 1993, less than 5 percent of published research was sufficiently empirical, quantitative, and valid to support conclusions with respect to the effectiveness of technology in education learning outcomes. Thus, there was a lack of evidence on what really impacts learning using the computer as a medium for delivery of instruction and training.

Even more troublesome is the fact that there have been only modest attempts at building a theoretical base for computer-based instruction, despite the abundance of research studies noted above. Thus, research on CBI and implementation of CBI in practice have proceeded in a largely atheoretical fashion. Our review of research shows that there is no comprehensive theory that portrays the factors leading to effective computer-based instruction. Further compounding the problem is the fact that much of the research that has been conducted has focused on CBI implementation in educational settings, not with adult learners such as would be found in work settings. It is reasonable to expect that the effectiveness of CBI for adults in work settings might be influenced by different factors.

Williams (2000), Johnson and Aragon (2002), Steinberg (1991), and Kember and Murphy (1990) reported that adopting a synthesized theory of learning could have a synergistic effect on advancing the learning environment created by CBI. Based on these studies, it is apparent that there is a need for a new theory that integrates factors affecting CBI effectiveness and provides a foundation for empirical tests of the most effective learning environments for CBI.

The purpose of this study, then, was to develop a theory of critical components that impact the effectiveness of CBI for adult learners. The methodology used to develop the CBI theory included both Dubin's (1978) deductive theory-building methodology and Patterson's (1986) criteria for evaluating theory. Space limitations prohibit a complete discussion of the process used (see Lowe and Holton, 2005).

THEORY OF COMPUTER-BASED INSTRUCTION

A theory of effective CBI for adults integrates the critical components of CBI to provide a much-needed framework for research in CBI for adults. The final theory is shown in Figure 18.1.

Units of the CBI theory

The units of the theory are the basic building blocks from which the investigator constructs the theory (Lynham, 2002). The units represent those things whose interactions constitute the realm of the theory (Dubin, 1978).

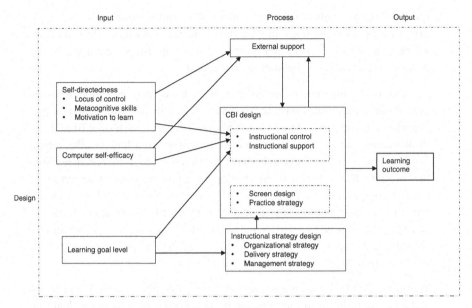

Figure 18.1 A conceptual Model of Effective Computer-based Instruction for Adults

Each unit is shown graphically as a box in Figure 18.1 and is described in the following sections.

The theory was developed using a systems approach. That is, the units are conceptualized as inputs, processes, and outputs of CBI. This approach has several advantages. First, the development of CBI is a process and, thus, lends itself to a systems model. Second, the units of the theory operate as a system to influence learning outcomes, so a systems approach is the most appropriate way to conceptualize the units. Third, a systems approach provides an elegant and logical way to organize and understand a complex system of ideas. The units of the theory will be discussed in reverse order, moving from outputs to processes to inputs.

Output units of the CBI theory

Only one output unit of the theory was identified: the learning outcome. *Learning outcome* is defined for this study simply as achieving learning goal level. Learning outcomes are the performance made possible by learning (Wager and Gagné, 1988). The learning outcome describes what the learner is able to do when learning is completed. Students' performance or learning is assessed to determine whether the designed instruction has met its design objectives (Gagné et al., 1992). The outcomes of learning are important in any theory of learning (Steinberg, 1991).

Process units of the CBI theory

The process units of the theory represent the environmental and CBI system factors expected to influence the learning outcomes.

Instructional strategy design

Instructional strategy design is defined as elemental methods for determining and sequencing content, presenting content, and decision making related to the content and its delivery. Janniro (1993) found CBI to be most effective when systematically developed and when course content follows the principles of teaching. Steinberg (1991) suggested that appropriate computer application means the application of sound instructional principles. The design of learning materials and environment is the core of educational technology (Kozma, 2000). Therefore, instructional strategy design is just as important in the development of CBI as it is in face-to-face instruction.

Reigeluth (1983) classified the components of instructional strategy design units into three types: organizational strategy, delivery strategy, and management strategy. *Organizational strategy* is the method of sequencing the subject matter content for instruction. Gagné et al.'s (1992) events of instruction should be included in the organizational strategy of the lesson or learning module. Sequencing of information within a CBI module would be determined by the objectives. For those objectives in the declarative and procedural areas, the information would be sequenced by applying principles from the learning theory in use. For higher order objectives, the sequence is based on an interaction with the learner and information (Tennyson and Foshay, 2000).

Bunderson and Inouye (1987) proposed that when designing instruction, the information can be analyzed to determine the most efficient arrangement of the knowledge for purposes of learning, not for purposes of disciplined organization. Well-organized information serves as a graphic organizer, helps in learning the information, and provides an external map-like organizer for guiding the acquisition of unfamiliar material (Dean and Kulhavy, 1981). This map links incoming information to pre-existing knowledge, processed at a deeper level of encoding, resulting in associative learning (Anderson and Archer, 1970; Craig and Lockhart, 1972; Foss and Harwood, 1975).

Once the content is organized, delivery strategies must be determined. *Delivery strategies* normally involve determining the appropriate media of instruction and grouping strategies. Because the need for CBI is an assumption of this study, one only needs to address the grouping strategy for instruction. The grouping strategy for CBI could be individual, dyad, or a small group consisting of three students. Stephenson (1991) suggested that low achievers benefit from having another human around who is aware of actions that alter the learning behavior. Carrier and Sales (1987) found that students working in pairs with CBI provided an opportunity for the students to check out understanding of concepts with their partner.

The instructional *management strategy* guides the orchestration of organizational and delivery strategies (Smith and Ragan, 1993). Scheduling of instruction and the mechanisms for delivery of instruction are guided by the management strategy. With CBI, scheduling may include providing times when a computer room is available or using resources to ensure that enough computers are available for those needing CBI. This strategy also includes the management of instruction for individuals, which provides diagnosis, prescriptions, status reports, and test scores for each individual in the CBI program. Management strategies involve the use of resources and managing individualized instruction.

CBI design

CBI design is defined as the computer programming of content and lesson design that considers the individual differences of the learner to achieve the learning goal level delivered by the computer. Critical for promoting achievement in CBI are features that provide opportunities for problem solving, corrective feedback, elaboration, visual and graphic cues, control of the routine by the learner, and appropriate wait time between input and response (Lewis, 1990). This unit of the model makes CBI different from other forms of individualized instruction. CBI design is comprised of four components: instructional control, instructional support, screen design, and practice strategy.

Three types of *instructional control* are generally considered: program controlled where the program guides the learner; learner controlled where the learner determines the options; or adaptive controlled which is a combination of program and learner controlled where control is based on the learner's responses. CBI that is adaptive or intelligent to students' responses and rate of learning is twice as effective (Gibbons and Fairweather, 2000).

Numerous researchers have found that learner control in CBI positively influences retention of information and increases test performance (Kinzie et al., 1988; Ross and Morrison, 1989; Schloss et al., 1988; Steinberg et al., 1986). Several researchers have found positive achievement results from giving learners control over elements of their instruction such as amount of contextual support (Ross et al., 1989; Shaw, 1992), amount of information and practice (Hannafin and Sullivan, 1995), amount of review (Kinzie et al.,

1988), and sequencing of the instruction (Gray, 1987). Gray (1989) concluded that CBI for single class sessions and directed at students with little background in the subject matter will be effective with minimum user control over the sequencing of instructional content.

Instructional support for the adult learner during the CBI learning process is important to the learning outcome of CBI. Instructional support enhances the understanding of the content of instruction by specific examples, glossary, procedures, help, hints, feedback, and coaching. When learners perceive instruction to be difficult, they seek out more instructional support (Tobias, 1982) such as elaborate feedback.

Feedback is one form of instructional support that influences the learning process by motivating the learner and/or by providing additional information about the task (Sales and Williams, 1988; Steinberg, 1991). Feedback is the evaluative or corrective information about an action, choice, or inquiry that the learner has made within the instructional program. Clariana (1993) found that the more information provided by feedback, the better the performance. Feedback can motivate students by encouraging them when learning is difficult (Steinberg, 1991).

Screen design research indicates that displaying information at a consistent location or relevant graphical information facilitates learning (Aspillaga, 1991). The enriched screen-control capabilities of computers provide displays that more clearly represent information in meaningful contexts (Tennyson and Foshay, 2000). Good screen design can have an important motivating role because it maintains the attention and interest of the student (Steinberg, 1991). Spatial location aids learning by providing encoding links to existing information (Bellezza, 1983). Layout has been shown to enhance transfer of information providing a second choice for the learner in arrangement of content through location (Aspillaga, 1991). CBI designers can improve learning by integrating instructional visuals designed using information-processing learning theories, and including screen design strategies to enhance the transfer of information (Janniro, 1993).

The appropriate *practice strategy* to include in CBI varies by the difficulty of the subject matter and individual learner characteristics. When faced with the decision of determining the amount of practice to include in CBI, a greater amount of practice should be provided if higher student achievement is an important goal of the instruction (Schnackenberg et al., 1998).

Schnackenberg et al. (1998) found that students who practiced more in their instructional program scored higher on the post-test than those who had a lesser amount of practice. Students preferred more practice and information in abstract or hypothetical learning situations than students working through a program in a real instructional setting. Marcoulides (1990) found that students who are "spoon-fed" sets of rules for choosing and using statistical procedures without hands-on practice in concrete examples tended to misapply or forget the rules. CBI allows for various levels of practice to achieve the desired learning goal level.

External support

External support is defined as providing for the needs of the learner with support external to the CBI program itself, but is required to promote the learning outcome of CBI. External support should provide appropriate computer equipment, technical support, period of time for the learner to participate in CBI, and support from peers, supervisors, facilitator, management, friends, and family. Tough (1967, 1979) repeatedly highlighted the strong reliance on external resources, both human and material, in the conduct of learning projects and noted that adults would like more assistance in their learning pursuits.

The necessity of considering the learning environment and its support systems has been widely recognized in education and instructional design (Tessmer, 1990). Instruction may embody the proper outcomes and strategies but lack the means to be thoroughly or successfully utilized in its intended environments. Tessmer (1990) suggested two factors that should be considered in the environmental analysis: physical and use factors.

Input units of the CBI theory

The next set of units comprises the inputs to the CBI process units.

Self-directedness

Self-directedness is defined as an approach where learners are motivated to assume personal responsibility and collaborative control of the cognitive and contextual processes in constructing and confirming meaningful and worthwhile learning outcomes (Garrison, 1997). Self-directedness is the learner's ability to independently plan, conduct, and evaluate their learning activities (Guglielmino, 1977). The level of self-directedness is different for each learner.

CBI is often referred to as self-directed learning because the learners use it at their own pace and at their own convenience with little or no human contact, and the process of learning is the responsibility of the learner. Computers can also aid in promoting self-direction and efficiency (Lewis, 1990). CBI must be designed to take different levels of self-directedness into consideration in order to influence the learning outcome. There are three dimensions to the self-directedness unit: motivation to learn, metacognitive skills, and locus of control.

Motivation to learn plays a major role in the efficacy of adult learning efforts. Carré (2000) suggested that every professional trainer knows that the typical adult learner comes to the learning/training scene with a combination of motivation, educational habit, and self-image that predisposes him or her whether or not to learn. The concept of motivation is at the core of effective adult learning. A review of motivation in adult training established the importance of motivation in the learning process (Carré, 1998, cited in Carré, 2000). For adults, the motivation to learn is internal payoffs, the personal value they will gain in solving problems, or issues in life which promote learning (Knowles et al., 2005; Wlodowski, 1985). Therefore, the adult must see value in the CBI in solving problems or providing internal payoffs. This motivation to learn will influence the CBI design and subsequently the learning outcome.

Metacognitive skills are those that help a person understand and regulate cognitive performance (Artzt and Armour-Thomas, 1992; Slife and Weaver, 1992). Chipman and Segal (1985) described metacognition as the "deliberate and reasoned deployment of cognitive resources and strategies" (p. 7). Adult metacognition is a multidimensional array of self-constructed, regulatory skills that span a variety of diverse cognitive domains (Schraw, 1998). Self-direction demands two specific characteristics (Carré et al., 1997, cited in Carré, 2000): proactivity and metacognitive competence. *Proactivity* is defined as the ability to initiate action and maintain active control. *Metacognitive competence* is the ability to reflect on the learning experience and improve the processes of learning.

Metacognitive skills enable the learner to know how and when to apply previously acquired knowledge or skills that are crucial to their performance in learning tasks (Flavell, 1980). The degree to which an individual is aware of these skills varies from person to person. Being able to recognize the cues and understanding how one learns will influence the self-directedness of the learner.

Locus of control is a person's belief in the ability to control outcomes of forces either internal or external to themselves (Rotter, 1990). Whether people attribute the cause or control of events to themselves or to an external environment is referred to as locus of control (Spector, 1982). Learners who possess internal locus of control ascribe control of events to themselves. Learners who possess internal locus of control will take responsibility for their learning with CBI, while those with external locus of control will blame the program or things external to the program for not obtaining expected learning outcomes. Providing opportunities for the learner to be in control and successful is critical to the learning outcome of CBI. In cases of internal locus of control, there would be less need for program control, while in cases of external locus of control, there would be more program control needed.

Computer self-efficacy

Computer self-efficacy is defined as the individual's belief about his or her capabilities to successfully engage in CBI. Based on the social cognitive theory developed by Bandura (1986), self-efficacy can be defined as the belief that one has the capability to perform a particular behavior. Bandura (1993) suggests that perceived self-efficacy plays an important role in affecting motivation and behavior. Theory and research on self-efficacy suggests that in contrast to individuals with low levels of self-efficacy, the highly efficacious exert more effort, persist in the face of difficulty, and achieve higher levels of performance (Jawahar et al., 1992; Wood and Bandura, 1989). Students holding a low sense of self-efficacy for achieving a task may attempt to avoid it, whereas those who feel more efficacious may attempt it more eagerly (Bandura, 1977; Schunk, 1984). Previous studies on computer self-efficacy determined that self-efficacy is essential in the learning and use of computers (Delcourt and Kinzie, 1993; Hill et al., 1987; Jorde-Bloom, 1988; Kinzie et al., 1994; Miura, 1987; Schunk, 1984).

Learning goal level

A learning goal level is defined as the activities or performance required in the affective, cognitive, and/or psychomotor learning domains that result in the desired outcome of learning (Gagné et al., 1992). To determine if the learning outcome is attained, the learning goal level must be a part of the theory (Steinberg, 1991). The learning goal level is one of the inputs into CBI. Knowing the level and type of learning that the learner must achieve impacts both the CBI design and the instructional strategy design in developing the CBI. There are three domains of behavioral learning: affective, cognitive, and psychomotor. Learning goal level is demonstrated using Bloom's Taxonomy of Educational Objectives in the Affective and Cognitive Domains (1956) and Dave's Taxonomy of the Psychomotor Domain (1970).

Laws of interaction within the CBI theory

A law of interaction is a statement of the relationship between units and shows how the units of the theory are linked. In this section, seven laws of interaction for "A Theory of Effective Computer-based Instruction for Adults" are presented.

For clarity, the units of the conceptual model in Figure 18.1 are arranged into two distinct horizontal halves. The units in the top half of the model are labeled as *support* units and the bottom half are labeled as *design* units. The units of the support half are external support, self-directedness, computer self-efficacy and the components of instructional control and instructional support of CBI design. The units of the design half are learning goal level, instructional strategy design, and the components of screen design and practice strategy of CBI design. The learning goal level influences both the support and design halves of the model. In general terms, the support and design units are expected to interact to influence CBI effectiveness. More specific interactions are identified below.

Self-directedness and CBI design

Self-directedness is expected to influence the units of instructional control and instructional support. Learners who possess internal locus of control, high metacognitive skills, and a high level of motivation to learn will be successful using learner-controlled options for CBI design and less instructional support. Learners who possess external locus of control, low metacognitive skills, and low level of motivation to learn will need program control for instruction and much instructional support. Of course, these characteristics actually exist on a continuum so various levels of instructional support and program control are possible.

Learner control may be unsuccessful for some subjects because they lack metacognitive skills (Allen and Merrill, 1985) or lack information they need about the learning progress to make meaningful decisions about how to manage learning (Tennyson and Rothen, 1979). Holden (1995) found that higher self-directed learning readiness participants had higher achievement than lower level participants, and lower level self-directed learning readiness participants with program control had higher achievement than participants with learner control. Grow (1991) identified four stages of self-directed learning and the teaching style associated with each. The four stages of self-directedness were as follows: (Stage 1) the dependent learner with the teaching style of authority and coach; (Stage 2) the interested learner with the teaching style of motivator and guide; (Stage 3) the involved learner with the teaching style of facilitator; and (Stage 4) the self-directed learner with the teaching style of consultant or delegator. The most severe problems occur when dependent learners are mismatched with the non-directive teaching styles, and when self-directed learners are mismatched with the directive teaching style. CBI can help students move from Stage 1 of dependent learner to Stage 4 of self-directed learner over their lifelong learning process.

Computer self-efficacy and CBI design

Computer self-efficacy is also expected to influence the units of instructional control and instructional support in CBI design. Learners with low computer self-efficacy must be given the opportunity to be successful. Only through experience and success with CBI will the computer self-efficacy level rise. Instructional support such as feedback and coaching needs to be available to low self-efficacy learners to enable them to be successful. An adaptive instructional control program would allow the learner to increase their level of computer self-efficacy, as they are successful with CBI. Learner control is more appropriate for the learner with high computer self-efficacy.

Low self-efficacy reflects a lack of confidence in the ability to manipulate the system to achieve desired results (Hill and Hannafin, 1997). Consequently, users are more likely to accept rather than question system-generated information or program-controlled design. High self-efficacy users tend to be more persistent in their search and more confident in their ability to locate the resources they seek (Murphy, 1988), so learner control may be more appropriate as the instructional control. There is evidence that giving learners partial control over elements of instruction yields more favorable attitudes toward CBI and produces relatively high learner achievement (Schnakerberg et al., 1998; Crooks et al., 1996). Leso and Peck (1992) found that students may encounter less frustration and gain more self-efficacy when they attempt and accomplish relatively simpler tasks and receive immediate feedback regarding their success with software application. Ertmer et al. (1994) found that enhancing the effect of the learning experience on students' efficacy through situating those experiences within a learning context that provides an acceptable means for voicing frustration and receiving encouraging feedback regarding one's developing skills was most important.

Self-directedness and external support

Self-directedness is expected to influence the unit of external support. The higher the level of self-directedness of the learner, the less external support is required. For instance, learners who possess an internal locus of control, high metacognitive skills, and high motivation to learn require less external support. Learners who possess an external locus of control will need more external support since they believe that performance is a result of the external events or environments. Low motivation to learn can be enhanced by external support. For example, management's encouragement and support could be of great importance to the learner with low motivation to learn. Dependent learners want close supervision, immediate feedback, frequent interaction, constant motivation, and continuous direction (Grow, 1991). Jawahar (2002) found that managers can positively influence employees' attitudes toward using CBI by communicating how the knowledge can enhance their productivity. Jawahar (2002) also found that goal setting had the most effect on end-user performance. External support can provide many of these elements for the dependent learner. As the learner becomes more self-directed, less external support is required.

Computer self-efficacy and external support

Computer self-efficacy is expected to influence the unit of external support. Learners who have a high level of computer self-efficacy require less external support than those with a low level of computer self-efficacy. Learners with high levels of computer self-efficacy will take it upon themselves to find the external support that is needed. However, learners with low computer self-efficacy will look to external support to facilitate learning. The low computer self-efficacy learner will need technical support, time from work to participate, and encouraging words from management to help raise their level of computer self-efficacy.

Jawahar and Elango (2001) found that managers could increase end-user performance by enhancing end users' self-efficacy beliefs. Bandura (1982) suggested self-efficacy beliefs can be enhanced through performance accomplishments, vicarious experiences, verbal persuasion, and emotional arousal. Jorde-Bloom (1988) found that organizational components and environmental considerations served as powerful motivators in determining computer-related behavior. Individuals who exhibit a low self-efficacy with technological innovations are more apt to be resistant to them (Hill et al., 1987). An individual's feeling of self-efficacy also regulates the degree of commitment that the individual is willing to invest in learning about CBI (Ertmer et al., 1994).

External support and CBI design

External support and CBI design are expected to interrelate. Strong support can be incorporated in the CBI design or be external to the program. Strong external support can offset a weak CBI design. If CBI design is a strong design that allows for the individual differences in the learner, external support can be at a minimum. However, if CBI design is weak and does not provide for the individual differences of the learner, external support must be strong. CBI design may take into account the individual differences, but some of those differences will require external support.

Instructional strategy design and CBI design

Instructional strategy design precedes the components of screen design and practice. The instructional strategy design unit influences the screen design based on the organization of the information and the practice strategy based on the level of learning goal to be accomplished. Strong instructional strategy design should influence the CBI design related to appropriate screen design and type of practice. Weak instructional strategy design will result in poor CBI design.

The organizational strategy of the instructional design influences the screen design. How the instruction is sequenced, the location of the content on the screen, and how the content is displayed impacts the learning process of the adult. Computer presentation of text can facilitate learning by providing focus (Steinberg, 1991). This occurs when the computer lesson is presented in limited amounts of text on the screen and the learner presses a key to continue reading the text at his or her own pace.

Practice provides for the learner's active participation in the learning process and assesses how learning is progressing so that remediation may be provided if the student is not learning (Smith and Ragan, 1993). Provision of instruction with explicit practice items is very important to the outcome of learning. Smith and Ragan (1993) suggested that learners should have several opportunities to practice the performance related to a specific objective to promote over-learning and automaticity of skilled performance. Student practice of instructional objectives is considered an essential element of well-designed instruction because appropriate practice during instruction gives students the opportunity to engage in activities similar to those in the objectives and to be assessed on a criterion referenced test (Gagné, 1985).

Learning goal level and instructional strategy design

Learning goal level is expected to influence the unit of instructional strategy design. The learning goal level influences how the instruction is organized and presented. CBI is judged to be successful when the essential content supports the learner's attainment of instructional goals (Hannum, 1988). Different instructional strategies are implemented based on the learning goal level to be achieved (Salisbury et al., 1985). Because different conditions are required for different learning outcomes, the nature of the events of instruction also differs for each type of learning outcome. CBI that incorporates events that are appropriate for the desired type of learning outcomes will be more likely to attain the desired learning goals (Wager and Gagné, 1988).

The learning goal level determines the type of learning for which the instructional strategy design must be developed. For example, in the first two levels of Bloom et al.'s Taxonomy of the Cognitive Domain (1956), knowledge and comprehension, learners would be required to recall verbatim, paraphrased, or summarized form facts, lists, names or organized information. The instructional strategy design would be developed for that learning outcome. In the application, analysis, synthesis, and evaluation levels of Bloom et al.'s Taxonomy of the Cognitive Domain, students learn how to recall and apply other instances not encountered during instruction. Therefore, the instructional strategy design would be developed so that the learner can discriminate, acquire concrete and defined concepts, and learn rules or principles.

Learning goal level and CBI design

Learning goal level is expected to influence the components of instructional control and instructional support of the unit domain of CBI design. Learning goal levels based on Bloom's taxonomy levels of knowledge and comprehension would be more likely to use program-controlled CBI design; while learning goal levels of application, synthesis, and evaluation would use learner controlled or adaptive controlled (Hannafin, 1984). Romiszowski (1981) found that learner control was unsuccessful for some subjects because they did not have clearly formed objectives. These objectives are developed based on the learning goals that are to be achieved. Tennyson and Foshay (2000) reported that managing the learning environment should be consistent with the defined learning goals and objectives of the instruction.

Knowledge of the outcomes guides the designer in the amount of encouragement and/or amount of instruction needed in feedback to achieve the proper results without prolonging the learning process (Sales, 1988). CBI designed for higher level learning outcomes, such as problem solving, rule learning, and defined concepts, requires that the learners generate solutions to problems, demonstrate the use of rules they have learned, and classify objects based on the instruction they have received (Briggs and Wager, 1981; Gagné and Briggs, 1979; Smith and Boyce, 1984). Instruction at this level requires the learner to acquire new knowledge and to formulate, test, and refine hypotheses on the correct use of this knowledge. Elaborative feedback that provides explanation of errors as well as additional instruction may prove to be most effective.

CBI designed for lower levels of learning outcomes, such as concrete concepts and discriminations, requires the learner to identify or to discriminate between specific members of the concept class presented in the instruction (Briggs and Wager, 1981; Gagné and Briggs, 1979; Smith and Boyce, 1984). Feedback that simply informs the learners of the correctness of their response will be sufficient in most cases. As the complexity of the information increases, the needs of the learners increase, and the level of feedback must be adjusted (Sales, 1988).

CBI design and learning outcome

The unit of CBI design precedes and influences the unit of learning outcome. When the CBI design properly incorporates all the previously discussed input and process units, learning outcomes can be expected to be achieved.

Summary of the laws of interaction

A major conclusion to be drawn from the preceding discussion is that a change in one unit of the theory brings about subsequent changes in another unit of the theory. The following Laws of Interaction are derived from the dynamic relationships among the units:

Law 1. The units of self-directedness, external support, computer self-efficacy, instructional strategy design, learning goal level, and CBI design are required for the output of the desired learning outcome.
Law 2. The units of self-directedness and computer self-efficacy influence external support.
Law 3. The units of self-directedness, external support, computer self-efficacy, instructional strategy design, and learning goal level influence CBI design.

Law 4. Self-directedness, computer self-efficacy, and learning goal level are inputs into the process of CBI design.

Law 5. Learning goal level is input into the process of instructional strategy design.

Law 6. External support and CBI design support have a two-way relationship:

    a.   Strong external support will influence the amount of CBI design support.

    b.   Strong CBI design support will influence the amount of external support.

Law 7. Instructional strategy design precedes CBI design as processes that are required for an output of the desired learning outcome.

System states of the CBI theory

System states indicate the complexity of the real world that the theory is presumed to represent and the different conditions under which the theory operates. A system state is a condition of the system being modeled in which the units of the theory interact differently (Lynham, 2002). There are three system states that reflect different values and alignments that impact the output of effective CBI. The three system states are: effective system state, ineffective system state, and moderately effective system state.

Effective system state

In the effective system state, an alignment of both the upper support half and the lower design half of the model results in effective CBI. Alignment occurs in two ways: (a) when the support units are complementary with the design units; and (b) when the support units are complementary with each other and the design units are complementary with each other.

As an example of when the support units are in alignment with the design units, consider the situation where users have weak self-directedness, and weak computer self-efficacy, but strong CBI design of instructional control and instructional support and strong external supports exist. Or, consider the case where users have weak computer self-efficacy, strong external support, strong self-directedness, and weak CBI design of instructional control and instructional support. In both cases, the support and design elements complement each other.

Alignment *within* the design unit occurs when the three units of learning goal level, instructional strategy design, and CBI design components of practice activities and screen design complement each other. The instructional strategy design should be matched with the learning goal level to be effective in the area of design. Alignment within the support unit exists when the combination of self-directedness and computer self-efficacy is correctly complemented by external and program support.

Ineffective system state

In an ineffective system state, the upper support half and the lower design half of the model are not aligned. The values of the units of support do not provide for effective support. A possible alignment would be weak self-directedness, self-efficacy, external support, combined with a weak CBI design. If computer self-efficacy is low, CBI design would not provide the instructional support needed, and external support would not be available to provide the support needed for low computer self-efficacy. If self-directedness is the weak unit, computer self-efficacy is likely to be weak as well, and poor external support and CBI design would make for an ineffective system state. Even if one unit of the support area is strong and the other three units are weak, the support area will be weak.

In the design half of the model for an ineffective system state, the instructional strategy design is not appropriate for the learning goal level. Therefore, the CBI design would be weak since the instructional strategy design is an important input into the CBI design process. A weak support area consisting of the units of low self-directedness, low computer self-efficacy, weak or no external support, and weak CBI design resulting from instructional strategy design not being appropriate for the learning goal level, will result in ineffective CBI.

Moderately effective system state

In the moderately effective system state, there is partial but not full alignment. Perhaps the most common example of this occurs with weak support and strong design. The instructional strategy design is based on the learning goal level and the CBI design uses both of these units in the design process. However, when learners have low computer self-efficacy, self-directedness and external support (a common occurrence), the support configuration does not ensure that the program will be effective. Because most CBI is purchased off the shelf and is developed by instructional designers and programmers, it will have a strong design. However, if the other components of support are not in place, no matter how good the design, the CBI will be only moderately effective.

Propositions of the CBI theory

A proposition of a theoretical model is a truth statement about the model in operation (Dubin, 1978). The propositions are aimed at the theoretical framework to explain and predict (Lynham, 2002). Proposition statements get turned into empirical indicators, then hypotheses, and finally the hypotheses are tested to match the theory with the real world (Torraco, 1994). The accuracy of a proposition is whether or not it follows logically from the model (Dubin, 1978).

Nine propositions were specified for "A Theory of Effective Computer-based Instruction for Adults." The nine proposition statements, which were logically derived from the theoretical framework, are as follows:

Proposition 1: The level of learner self-directedness will be inversely related to the external support desired.
Proposition 2: The level of learner computer self-efficacy will be inversely related to the external support desired.
Proposition 3: The level of learner self-directedness will be inversely related to the CBI design components of instructional control and instructional support.
Proposition 4: The level of learner computer self-efficacy will be inversely related to the CBI design components of instructional control and instructional support.
Proposition 5: The learning goal level is inversely related to instructional control and instructional support in CBI design.
Proposition 6: The learning goal level directly influences the instructional strategy design.
Proposition 7: The instructional strategy design directly influences screen design and practice strategy in CBI design.
Proposition 8: The level of external support is inversely related to instructional support and instructional control in CBI design.
Proposition 9: The effectiveness of CBI will be maximized when the levels of self-directedness, computer self-efficacy, learning goal level, and external support are incorporated in the CBI design.

DISCUSSION

Why do some adults start CBI but never finish? Why do some adults complete CBI without the desired learning outcome? Why hasn't CBI become the most used learning strategy for adults? This theoretical discussion brings to the forefront some of the questions pondered by CBI practitioners and researchers. Five key conclusions can be drawn from this study that may help to answer these questions.

The first conclusion drawn is that characteristics of the adult learner play an important role in the designing of CBI for adults. Clearly, there are unique characteristics of adult learners that may significantly impact the design of CBI. The adult characteristics of self-directedness and computer self-efficacy were found to be important when using CBI. Adults possess different levels of self-directedness and computer self-efficacy and these differences should be taken into consideration. Adults with lower levels of self-directedness and computer self-efficacy would require more external support and program control of instruction. Those with higher levels of self-directedness and computer self-efficacy require less external support and more learner control of instruction.

The component of instructional control of CBI design is important for those adults with a high level of self-directedness. When faced with program-controlled CBI, they may become frustrated and not complete the instruction. Even with high levels of self-directedness, program control is required for new knowledge to ensure content is covered in a low learning goal level. If the levels of self-directedness and computer self-efficacy are not aligned with the level of external support, the components of instructional control, and instructional support of CBI design, then the adult learner will not complete or obtain the desired learning outcome. CBI should be developed to respond to these individual adult differences.

A second conclusion drawn from this study is that CBI design is interwoven with the units of self-directedness, computer self-efficacy, learning goal level, instructional design strategy, and external support. This is not a simple relationship. Using software that converts face-to-face instruction to CBI is only part of the elements to be considered in developing effective CBI. Successful CBI must consider the alignment of each of the units of this theory to be effective. The support half of the model is equally as important as the design half of the model in designing effective CBI. Not only are all units required, but they must be matched to provide appropriate levels of each unit to achieve the desired learning outcomes. If both self-directedness and computer self-efficacy are at a low level, then both external support and the support part of CBI design must be at a high level for the support level to be aligned. Likewise, if the learning goal level is low and the instructional strategy design is appropriate for the learning outcome, CBI design must be aligned with the support half of the model to be effective. There are many combinations of aligning the support half with the design half, but no matter what the combination, there must be a match for effective CBI.

The third conclusion drawn from this theory is that learning goal level impacts the instructional design strategy and the component of instructional control of CBI design. This requires both the instructional designer and the instructional technologist to work together to ensure an appropriate CBI design for the learning goal level. For lower learning goal levels, CBI should be designed with more program control. The lower learning goal level is usually new knowledge or a procedure that requires learning step by step. Adults tend to demonstrate more anxiety when new material is to be learned. On the other hand, higher learning goal levels should be designed with learner control of instruction. The higher learning goal levels foster the use of metacognitive skills possessed by the adult learner. Adult learners like to share their knowledge, and a cooperative learning experience would be beneficial at the higher learning goal level. The instructional designer should use instructional design principles in developing the instructional strategy design unit.

A fourth key conclusion of this study is that both external and instructional supports are extremely important. While the literature hints at the importance of external and instruction support, there is very little research in this area. Most research in instructional support is primarily in instructional feedback. External support and instructional support in CBI design help to develop the attributes of self-directedness and computer self-efficacy in adults. By providing external support, adults receive encouragement and have opportunities for positive experiences. This may be in the form of allowing the adult learner to engage in CBI during working hours, providing a computer lab with the appropriate hardware and software for CBI, praise for the adult learner's participation in the CBI, or a peer providing positive feedback about the experience. If adults are frustrated because external support is not available to answer their questions or provide assistance, the experience becomes negative and they are not likely to engage in CBI again. The facilitator and the organization that is sponsoring the CBI should make available the external support that the adult learner needs.

Instructional support in CBI is a component of the CBI design unit in the support half of the model. Feedback is one way of providing instructional support. This support should be delivered in small doses with the opportunity to obtain more information if needed. This requires learner control for feedback to be a part of the CBI design. By giving the adult learner some control of their learning they will develop additional skills and have positive experiences that will improve their level of self-directedness and computer self-efficacy. When the adult learner can find the support they need, their computer self-efficacy level should improve.

Finally, this theory draws together the isolated variables that researchers have considered important in the adult learning process and aligns them to provide for effective CBI. This study provides a theoretical relationship and interaction between the variables. Many of these variables have been suspected as being important to CBI but have not been presented in a comprehensive and systematic manner. Many researchers have looked at these variables individually and identified small sets of variables as necessary components in CBI. However, few have attempted to develop a theory that incorporates so many variables because of the complexity of adults and CBI. This theory provides a framework for research and, when validated, will provide a guide for the practitioner.

FUTURE INVESTIGATION

There are three major implications for future investigation provided by this study: (1) developing and refining empirical indicators, (2) developing and testing hypotheses, and (3) designing empirical research.

Developing and refining empirical indicators is the first major implication for future research. Research which follows Dubin's (1978) methodology for theory building and is intended to match the theory with the real world begins by converting the propositions of the theory into hypotheses that can be tested through empirical research. This is done by first operationally defining the unit concepts of the theory with enough precision so that each concept can be measured (Torraco, 1994). Dubin (1978) refers to the specification of procedures for measuring key concepts as producing the empirical indicators. An empirical indicator is an operation employed by a researcher to secure measurement of values of the unit.

The second major implication for future research is the development of the hypotheses. Once the empirical indicators are determined or developed, the next step would be to convert the propositions into hypotheses. The hypotheses convert the propositions into testable hypotheses using the empirical indicators as variables in the hypothesis statements. They predict what will be true in the real world if the phenomena of interest behave according to the theory. Hypotheses derived from theory are known as deductive hypotheses. They drive the research process, which is ultimately intended to produce data to either support or disconfirm the theory.

For example, the first proposition states, "The level of learner self-directedness will be inversely related to the external support desired." This proposition can serve as the basis for stating a testable hypothesis by converting each key concept (learner self-directedness and external support) into variables (or empirical indicators) and by formulating a hypothesis that predicts an inverse relationship between these variables (e.g., the theory predicts that as one increases, the other decreases). This would be done for each proposition in the theory, resulting in a complete test of the model.

The third major implication for future investigation is the need for empirical research studies designed to validate this theory. As with any new theory, it will take numerous studies to reach full support.

SUMMARY

This chapter presents a new theory of CBI. It has integrated the factors affecting CBI effectiveness into a comprehensive framework and focuses exclusively on factors affecting CBI effectiveness for adult learners. It lays the foundation for tests of the most effective learning environments for CBI. It also offers the first integrated framework of the essential variables for planning and designing CBI for adults. While further investigation is needed to validate the theory, it has the potential to advance both the research and practice of CBI for adults.

PART 5

INTERNATIONAL AND FUTURE PERSPECTIVES ON ADULT LEARNING

19

EUROPEAN PERSPECTIVES ON ADULT LEARNING

This chapter was graciously contributed by Dr. John A. Henschke, Professor of Adult Education and a leading andragogy researcher at Lindenwood University, St. Charles, Missouri, USA. It was co-authored with Dr. Mary Cooper (deceased).

INTRODUCTION

While the bulk of Malcolm Knowles's work was done in the United States, andragogy has rich roots around the world, particularly in Europe. This study searched the literature providing an international research foundation for andragogy. Six themes emerged: the evolution of the term; historical antecedents shaping the concept; European and American understandings; popularizing and sustaining the worldwide concept; practical applications; and theory, research, and definition. Implications are provided for the practice of andragogy within the fields of adult, continuing, community, extension, and human resource development education.

Scholarship on andragogy since 1990 has taken two directions (Merriam, 2001). One seeks analysis of the origins of the concept for establishing it as a scientific discipline. The other critiques andragogy for its lack of attention to the learning context. Merriam (2001) asserts andragogy as one of two *pillars* of adult learning theory (self-directed learning being the other pillar) that will engender debate, discussion, research, and thus further enrich our understanding and practice of facilitating adult learning. Kapp (1833) first introduced the term (see replica on: http://www.andragogy.net). Lindeman (1926a) was the first to bring it to the USA, with the term coming into common use internationally through the work of Malcolm Knowles (1970).

On the one hand, some adult educators tended to strongly favor Knowles's version of andragogy, by using a practical approach when facilitating adults' learning within their own setting and context. Kabuga (1977) advocated using highly participative teaching/learning techniques with children as well as adults in his native Africa. Zemke and Zemke (1996) selected at least 30 ideas/concepts/techniques that they think we know for sure about adult learning. Henschke (1995) focused on describing a dozen different andragogical episodes with groups.

On the other hand, some adult educators tended to dismiss Knowles's version of andragogy as being quite inadequate and unscientific. Hartree (1984) asserted that Knowles's theory of andragogy fails to make good its claims to stand as unified theory and does not incorporate an epistemology. Davenport (1987) presented a case for questioning the theoretical and practical efficacy of Knowles's theory of andragogy. Jarvis (1984) wrote that the theory of andragogy has moved into the status of an established doctrine in adult education, but without being grounded in sufficient empirical research to justify its dominant position.

The weakness of the above picture is that both sides seem to stop short in their discussion and understanding of andragogy. In our quest, we found that most of the published material on andragogy that reaches beyond these limitations is largely untapped and not understood.

The purpose of this study was to answer the question: What are the major English works published around the world on andragogy (the art and science of helping adults learn) that may provide a clear and understandable linkage between the research on andragogy and the practice of andragogy within the fields of adult, continuing, community, extension, and human resource development education?

Two major underpinnings were relevant for the decision of what was included in this interpretive study: any material in English that presents various aspects of the concept of andragogy as viable and worth consideration for the field on a worldwide basis; and a presentation and view of the content of andragogy within any country of the world that includes no date/time boundaries. Sources included that referenced andragogy were: various databases, research and theory journal articles, practice pieces, conference proceedings, books, dissertation abstracts international, and bibliographic references within the above materials. The six major themes discovered are: evolution of the term andragogy; historical antecedents shaping the concept of andragogy; comparison of the American and European understandings of andragogy; popularization and sustaining the American and worldwide concept of andragogy; practical applications of andragogy; and theory, research, and definition of andragogy.

EVOLUTION OF THE TERM ANDRAGOGY

Van Gent (1996) asserted that andragogy has been used to designate the education of adults, an approach to teaching adults, social work, management, and community organization. Its future lies only as a generic term for adult education and as a complement to pedagogy, which has been used mainly to focus on the art and science of teaching children.

Nevertheless, in recent years pedagogy has been used to refer to the art or profession of teaching. Thus, Davenport (1987) argued that some adult educators strongly urge that adult education would simply be better off to drop the word from its lexicon. However, hooks (1994) said, "the possession of a term does not bring a process or practice into being: concurrently one may practice theorizing without ever knowing/possessing the term" (p. 61). Kaminsky (n.d.) suggested that whether we have knowledge for naming something academically or not, we may still be practicing pedagogy, andragogy, or any other "gogy" or "ism." Thus, Henschke (1998) asserted that long before the term andragogy appeared in published form in 1833, ancient Greek and Hebrew educators if not others used words that, although they were antecedents to andragogy, included elements of the concept that have come to be understood as some of the various meanings and definitions of andragogy. As an illustration of using words that may be unclear or do not have one precise definition, *Webster's* (1996) included 179 definitions of the word "run." However, we have not given up the use of that term because of the multiplicity of definitions.

Reischmann (2005) made a clear distinction in his definition between andragogy and adult education. He defined andragogy as the science of the lifelong and lifewide education/learning of adults. Adult education is focused on the practice of the education/learning of adults. Another definition is that of Zmeyov (1998) who aptly defined andragogy differently from others. He said that andragogy is "the theory of adult learning that sets out the fundamentals of the activities of learners and teachers in planning, realizing, evaluating and correcting adult learning" (p. 106).

Draper (1998), in providing an extensive, worldwide background on andragogy, reflected on and presented an overview of the historical forces influencing the origin and use of the term *andragogy*. He concluded, "Tracing the metamorphoses of andragogy/adult education is important to the field's search for identity. The search for meaning has also been an attempt to humanize and understand the educational process" (p. 24).

HISTORICAL ANTECEDENTS SHAPING THE CONCEPT OF ANDRAGOGY

Wilson (2003) researched into the historical emergence and increasing value of andragogy in Germany and the USA and discovered, among other things, a connection between a foundational element in adults' brain capacity to continue learning even into their later years—a concept labeled as *fluid intelligence*—and their brain capacity for learning being enhanced through andragogical interventions in self-directed learning. However, Allman (Allman and Mackie, 1983) predated Wilson regarding this same connection between plasticity in adult development. She asserted that this concept and research coupled with Mezirow's (1981) and Knowles's (1970, 1980b) understanding of andragogy could be linked with her ideas on group learning and then merged into a more comprehensive theory of andragogy.

Hiemstra and Sisco (1990) suggested a situation that gave rise to the emergence of andragogy as an alternative model of instruction to improve the teaching of adults. They asserted that mature adults become increasingly independent and responsible for their own actions. Thus, those adults are often motivated to learn by a sincere desire to solve immediate problems in their lives, and have an increasing need to be self-directing; in many ways the pedagogical model does not account for such developmental changes on the part of adults, and thus produces tension, resentment, and resistance. Consequently, the growth and development of andragogy is a way to remedy this situation and help adults to learn. Their article also presented an extensive list of 97 annotated bibliographical references related to andragogy.

Savicevic (1999a) suggested that Socrates, Plato, Aristotle, the Sophists, Ancient Rome, the epochs of humanism, and the Renaissance all reflect thoughts and views about the need of learning throughout life, about the particularities and manners of acquiring knowledge in different phases of life, and about the moral and aesthetic impact. Henschke (1998) went back earlier in history and claimed that the language of the Hebrew prophets, before and concurrent with the time of Jesus Christ, along with the meaning of various Hebrew words and their Greek counterparts—learn, teach, instruct, guide, lead, and example/way/model—provide an especially rich and fertile resource to interpret andragogy. Savicevic (2000) also provided a new look at some of the background and antecedents to andragogy on a much broader scale.

EUROPEAN AND AMERICAN UNDERSTANDINGS OF ANDRAGOGY

Savicevic (1999a) provided a critical consideration of andragogical concepts in ten European countries: five western (German, French, Dutch, British, Finnish), and five eastern (Soviet, Czech–Slovak, Polish, Hungarian, Yugoslav). This comparison showed common roots but results in five varying schools of thought: (1) whether andragogy is parallel to or subsumed under pedagogy in the general science of education; (2) whether agology (instead of andragogy) is understood as a sort of integrative science which not only studied the process of education and learning but also other forms of guidance and orientation; (3) whether andragogy prescribes how teachers and students should behave in educational and learning situations; (4) the possibility of founding andragogy as a science is refuted; and (5) that endeavors have been made to found andragogy as a fairly independent scientific discipline.

Savicevic (1999a) clearly aligned himself with the fifth school of thought in that this research aims toward establishing the origin and development of andragogy as a discipline, the subject of which is the study of education and learning of adults in all its forms of expression. He also declared J. A. Comenius of the seventeenth century as meriting the designation of being the father of andragogy in that he drew equal lines for man and his learning.

Knowles (1995) provided the most articulate expression and understanding of andragogy from the American perspective. The structure of the theory is comprised of two conceptual foundations: the learning theory and the design theory. The learning theory is based upon the adult and her/his desire to become and/or to express themselves as a capable human being, and has six components. (1) Adults need to know a reason that makes sense to them, for whatever they need to learn. (2) They have a deep need to be self-directing and take responsibility for themselves. (3) Adults enter a learning activity with a quality and volume of experience that is a resource for their own and others' learning. (4) They are ready to learn when they experience a need to know, or be able to do, something to perform more effectively in some aspect of their life. (5) Adults' orientation to learning is around life situations that are task-, issue- or problem-centered, for which they seek solutions. (6) Adults are motivated much more internally than externally.

Knowles's (1995) conceptual foundation of design theory is based in a process, and is not dependent upon a body of content, but helps the learner acquire whatever content is needed. There are eight components of the design process: (1) preparing the learners for the program; (2) setting a climate that is conducive to learning (physically comfortable and inviting; and psychologically mutually respectful, collaborative, mutually trustful, supportive, open and authentic, pleasurable and human); (3) involving learners in mutual planning; (4) involving learners in diagnosing their learning needs; (5) involving learners in forming their learning objectives; (6) involving learners in designing learning plans; (7) helping learners carry out their learning plans; and (8) involving learners in evaluating their learning outcomes, or re-diagnosing their additional learning needs. Active involvement seems to be the watchword of Knowles's (thus American) version of andragogy, and each step of the andragogical learning process.

The European concept of andragogy is more comprehensive than the American conception. Europeans do not use the terms andragogy and adult education synonymously, as do some Americans (Young, 1985).

THE WORLDWIDE CONCEPT OF ANDRAGOGY

Lindeman (1926a, b) was the first to bring the concept to America. Although he clearly stated that andragogy was the method for teaching adults, the term did not take hold in the new land until many years later. Knowles (1970, 1980b) infused it with much of his own meaning garnered from his already extensive experience in adult education. He then combined his expanding practice around the world with his university teaching of budding adult educators.

Dover (2006) acknowledges that Knowles was not the first to use the term. However, she suggests that his popularization of andragogy explains why Knowles is one of the most frequently cited theorists in adult education, and is often referred to as "the father of adult learning."

Henschke (2000, 2009) provides an extensive battery of works on andragogy on his andragogy websites (http://www.lindenwood.edu/education/andragogy .cfm and http://www.umsl.edu/_henschke). His hope is that it will contribute toward sustaining andragogy.

In contrast to Savicevic's (1999a) earlier-expressed concern that Knowles's misunderstanding of andragogy had caused some confusion, Savicevic (2006) reflected on his perception of Knowles as "the father of adult learning" concept of andragogy. Mezirow (1981) and Suanmali (1981) found adult educators supporting self-directed learning as forming a charter for andragogy.

THEORY, RESEARCH, AND DEFINITION OF ANDRAGOGY

Rosenstock-Huessy (1925) advanced the idea that andragogy is a necessity in which the past, present, and future merges with theory becoming practical deeds; Simpson (1964) gave four strands for the training of adult educators; Hadley (1975) developed a 60-item questionnaire assessing an adult educator's andragogical and pedagogical orientation; Henschke (1989) developed an Instructional Perspectives Inventory with seven factors including teacher trust of learners; Stanton (2005) validated Henschke's instrument in line with self-directed learning readiness, resulting in an almost perfect bell-shaped curve; the Nottingham Andragogy Group (1983) addressed their beliefs about adults and adults' abilities to think creatively and critically in learning settings; Poggeler (1994) listed the ten trends which he hopes will help future andragogical research; Schugurensky (2005) did not understand the scope of andragogy in general and Knowles's idea of andragogy in particular; Zemyov (1994) saw Knowles's view of andragogy as being the fundamental scientific foundation of the theory base of adult education in Russia; Delahaye et al. (1994) found an orthogonal relationship between adult students' andragogical and pedagogical orientation; Christian (1982) developed a 50-item instrument to measure students' andragogical and pedagogical orientation; Connor (1997–2003) pressed us to become more self-reliant and give up our teacher-reliance; the Hoods Woods (1998) perceived andragogy as being based on four environmental influences active in every being; Boucouvalas (1999) posited the importance of the researcher in the research process; Johnson (2000) saw andragogy as fulfilling all the criteria of a theory; Rachal (2000, 2002) provided seven criteria for empirical research in andragogy; Ovesni (1999) supported the idea that andragogy is to generate its own knowledge and is able to offer something to other sciences in scientific cooperation; Aspell (2003) encouraged us to change from pedagogy to andragogy even though it may be a slow transition; Ross (1988) connects some of andragogy's value with its similarity to research in teacher effectiveness; Monts (2000) articulated the need for basic instruction of both teachers and students in andragogy; Reischmann (2005) represented a shift of understanding in the direction of andragogy; Henschke (1998) called for andragogy to be a scientific discipline of study; Furter (1971) proposed that andragogy be recognized in universities as a science for the training of man throughout his life; Akande and Jegede (2004) hold that andragogy is one of the new sciences of education that is now gaining ground in many areas; Merriam (2001) posited that scholarship on andragogy is one of the two major pillars of adult learning research and theory; Reischmann (2005) offered some historical perspective on the various periods that the term *andragogy* emerged and later receded; Pinheiro (2001) found that international students in American universities prefer learning experiences with the andragogical themes of engagement and connectedness; St Clair (2002) allowed that andragogy is one theory for the twenty-first century that will maintain its role as a necessary component of the field's shared knowledge; Savicevic (1999b) added another element to the scientific foundation and design of andragogy by searching its roots; Kajee (n.d.) reported that with ESL students, the major impact of andragogy and technology is on learner autonomy and self-directedness; Wilson (2006) offered a new paradigm of the function of the brain and its anatomy being much more closely allied with andragogy and learning than previously thought; Milligan (1999) summarized andragogy as contributing vastly to the enhancement of human abilities of autonomy, self-direction, and critical thinking; Mazhindu (1990) established a foundational link between andragogy and contract learning; Ovesni (2000) proposed three concepts and models of andragog professional preparation based upon scientific research in andragogy; Krajinc (1989) provided a very succinct and pointed definition of andragogy; Hiemstra and Sisco (1990), and Hiemstra (n.d.) contribute an annotation of 97 works related to andragogy; Savicevic's work in andragogy is the most comprehensive to date (1999a); Savicevic (2000) also provided a new look at some of the background and antecedents to andragogy on a much broader scale; Cooper and Henschke (2006) provided an ongoing investigation into the comprehensive concept of andragogy.

SUMMARY

Although it has not been possible to go into the depth needed for a full understanding of andragogy, hopefully the six major themes that have emerged are enough to encourage the adult, continuing, community, extension, and human resource development educator to continue his or her exploration (theory, practice, and/or research) of the concept of andragogy.

The first important implication is that much of the research on andragogy emerged out of practice, and thus there is a strong connection for applying these findings to the improvement of practice and theory. A second important and striking implication is that the strength of the andragogical theory, research, and definition foundation may advance the practice of helping adults learn in adult, continuing, community, extension, and human resource development education. A third implication is the benefit to be derived by those adult, continuing, community, extension, and human resource development educators who are willing to intentionally use andragogy as a means for finding out, learning, and ascertaining new things for their growth. Thus, it may help them understand fresh ways to enhance the enlightenment and illumination of the adult constituents they serve on the journey to their full degree of humaneness.

REFLECTION QUESTIONS

19.1 What are some of the antecedents to modern-day adult learning theory and practice?

19.2 How do European and American perspectives on andragogy differ?

19.3 Do you think it is important to have an international view of andragogy? Explain.

ANDRAGOGY

INTERNATIONAL HISTORY, MEANING, CONTEXT, AND FUNCTION

20

This chapter was graciously contributed by Dr. Jost Reischmann, Professor of Andragogy at Bamberg University in Germany. It is based on Reischmann and Jost (2004): *Andragogy. History, Meaning, Context, Function*. Internet publication: http://www.andragogy.net (version September 9, 2004).

INTRODUCTION

Andragogy, rooted in European thinking, has present-day commonalities and differences around the world. The term *andragogy* has been used in different times and countries with various connotations. Nowadays, mainly three understandings exist:

1. In many countries there is a growing conception of *andragogy* as the scholarly approach to the learning of adults. In this connotation, andragogy is the science of understanding (= theory) and supporting (= practice) lifelong and lifewide education of adults.
2. Especially in the USA, andragogy in the tradition of Malcolm Knowles labels a specific theoretical and practical approach, based on a humanistic conception of self-directed and autonomous learners and teachers as facilitators of learning.
3. Widely, an unclear use of andragogy can be found, with its meaning changing (even in the same publication) from *adult education practice* or *desirable values* or *specific teaching methods*, to *reflections* or *academic discipline* and/or "opposite to childish pedagogy," claiming to be "something better" than just *adult education*.

Terms make sense in relation to the object they name. Relating the development of the term to the historical context may explain the differences.

HISTORICAL PERSPECTIVES OF ANDRAGOGY

The first use of the term *andragogy*—as far as we know today—was by the German high school teacher, Alexander Kapp, in 1833 (see Figure 20.1). In a book entitled *Platon's Erziehungslehre* (Plato's Educational Ideas) he describes the lifelong necessity to learn. Starting with early childhood he comes, on page 241 (of 450), to adulthood with the title *Die Andragogik oder Bildung im m.nnlichen Alter* (Andragogy or Education in the Man's Age). In about 60 pages, he argues that education, self-reflection, and educating the character are the first value in human life. He then refers to vocational education of the healing profession, soldier, educator, orator, ruler, and man as family father. So already here we find patterns which repeatedly can be found in the ongoing history of andragogy: included and combined are the education of inner, subjective personality (*character*) and outer, objective competencies (what is later discussed under *education vs. training*) and learning happens not only through teachers, but also through self-reflection and life experience, which is more than *teaching adults*.

Kapp does not explain the term *Andragogik*, and it is not clear whether he invented it or whether he borrowed it from somebody else. He does not develop a theory, but justifies *andragogy* as the practical necessity of the

Figure 20.1 Platon's Erziehungslehre

education of adults. This may be the reason why the term lay fallow: other terms and ideas were available, and the idea of adult learning was not unusual in that time around 1833. In Europe (enlightenment movement, reading societies, workers' education, educational work of churches, for example, the Kolping-movement), and in America (Franklin Institute in Philadelphia, Lowell Institute in Boston, Lyceum movement, town libraries, museums, agricultural societies) all these initiatives had important dates between 1820 and 1840 and their own terminology, so a new term was not needed.

In the 1920s in Germany, adult education became a field of theorizing. In particular, a group of scholars from various subjects, the so-called *Hohen-rodter Bund*, developed in theory and practice the *Neue Richtung* (new direction) in adult education. Here some authors gave a second birth to the term *Andragogik*, now describing sets of explicit reflections related to the why, what for, and how of teaching adults. However, *Andragogik* was not used as "the Method of Teaching Adults," as Lindeman (1926a) mistakenly suggested in reporting his experiences at the Academy of Labor, Frankfurt, Germany. It was a sophisticated, theory-oriented concept, being an antonym to *demagogy*—too difficult to handle, not really shared. So again it was forgotten. But a new object was shining up: a scholarly, academic reflection level "above" practical adult education. The scholars came from various disciplines, working in adult education as individuals, not representing university institutes or disciplines. The idea of adult education as a discipline was not yet born.

It is not clear where the third wave of using andragogy originated. In the 1950s andragogy can suddenly be found in publications in Switzerland (Hanselmann), Yugoslavia (Ogrizovic), the Netherlands (ten Have), and Germany (Poggeler). Still the term was known only to insiders, and was sometimes more oriented to practice, sometimes more to theory. Perhaps this mirrors the reality of adult education of that time: there was little or no formal training for adult educators, some limited theoretical knowledge, no institutionalized continuity of developing such knowledge, and no academic course of study. In this reality *adult education* still described an unclear mixture of practice, commitment, ideologies, reflections, theories, mostly local institutions, and some academic involvement of individuals. As the reality was unclear, the term itself could not be clear; but the now increasing and shared use of the term signaled that a new differentiation between *doing* and *reflecting* was developing, perhaps needing a separate term.

ANDRAGOGY: A BANNER FOR IDENTITY

The great times of the term *andragogy* for the English-speaking adult education world came with Malcolm Knowles, a leading scholar of adult education in the USA. He describes his encounter with the term *andragogy*:

> I replied, "Whatagogy?" because I had never heard the term before. He explained that the term had been coined by a teacher in a German grammar school, Alexander Kapp, in 1833. . . . The term lay fallow until it was once more introduced by a German social scientist, Eugen Rosenstock, in 1921, but it did not receive general recognition. Then in 1957 a German teacher, Franz Poggeler, published a book, *Introduction into Andragogy: Basic Issues in Adult Education*, and this term was then picked up by adult educators in Germany, Austria, the Netherlands, and Yugoslavia.
>
> (Knowles, 1989b, p. 9)

Knowles published his first article (1968) about his understanding of andragogy with the provocative title "Andragogy, Not Pedagogy." In a short time, the term "andragogy," now intimately connected to Knowles's concept, received general recognition throughout North America and other English-speaking countries; "within North America, no view of teaching adults is more widely known, or more enthusiastically embraced, than Knowles's description of andragogy" (Pratt et al., 1998, p. 13).

Knowles's concept of andragogy—"the art and science of helping adults learn"—"is built upon two central, defining attributes: first, a conception of learners as self-directed and autonomous; and second, a conception of the role of the teacher as facilitator of learning rather than presenter of content" (Pratt et al., 1998, p. 12), emphasizing learner choice more than expert control. Both attributes fit into the specific socio-historic thoughts during and after the 1970s, for example, the deschooling theory (Illich, Reimer), Rogers's person-centered approach, Freire's *conscientizacao*. Perhaps a third attribute added to the attraction of Knowles's concept: constructing andragogy as opposing pedagogy (*Farewell to Pedagogy*, 1970; later reduced) provided opportunity to be on the "good side," not a *pedagog*, seen as "a teacher, especially a pedantic one" (*Webster's Dictionary*, 1982, p. 441). This flattered adult educators in a time when most were andragogical amateurs, carrying out adult education based on their content expertise, experience; a mission they felt not to be based on trained or studied educational competence. To be offered now understandable, humanistic values and beliefs, some specific methods and a good-sounding label strengthened a group that felt inferior to comparable professions. This came coincidentally along with a significant growth in the field of practice plus an increased scholarly approach, including the emerging possibility to study adult education at universities. All these elements document a new period (*art and science*) in adult education; it made sense to concentrate this new understanding in a new term.

Providing a unifying idea and identity, connected with the term andragogy, to the amorphous group of adult educators, certainly was the main benefit Knowles awarded to the field of adult education at that time. Another was that he strengthened the already-existing scholarly access to adult education by publishing, theorizing, carrying out research, educating students (who themselves, through academic research, became scholars), and by explicitly defining andragogy as science (Cooper and Henschke, 2003).

ISSUES WITH ANDRAGOGY

Over the years, critique developed against Knowles's understanding of andragogy. A first critique argues that Knowles claimed to offer a general concept of adult education, but like all educational theories in history it is but one concept, born into a specific historic context. For example, one of Knowles's basic assumptions is that becoming an adult means becoming self-directed. However, other genuine concepts of adult education do not accept this "American" type of self-directed lonesome fighter as the ultimate educational goal: in family, church, or civic education, for instance, the *we* is more important than the *self*. Similarly an instructor who presents (= teaches) the name of the stars in a hobby-astronomy class would not work andragogically because this is not autonomous learning. Consequently, the Dutch scholar Van Gent (1996) criticizes that the andragogy concept of Knowles is not a general descriptive, but a "specific, prescriptive approach" (p. 116). Another critique is Knowles's conceiving of *pedagogy* as "pedantic schoolmasters' practice" (*Webster's Dictionary*, 1982), not as an academic discipline. This hostility toward pedagogy had two negative outcomes: on a strategic level, scholars of adult education could make no alliances with the colleagues from pedagogy; on a content level, knowledge developed in pedagogy through 400 years could not be made fruitful for andragogy (for more critical remarks, see Merriam and Caffarella, 1999, p. 273ff.; Savicevic, 1999a, p. 113ff.). Thus, attaching *andragogy* exclusively to Knowles's specific approach means that the term is lost for including pedagogical knowledge and those who do not share Knowles's specific approach.

In most European countries, the Knowles discussion played no or, at best, a marginal role. The use and development of *andragogy* in the different countries and languages were more hidden, dispersed, and uncoordinated, yet steady. *Andragogy* nowhere described one specific concept or movement, but was, from 1970 on, connected with academic and professional institutions, publications, programs, triggered by a similar growth of adult education in practice and theory as in the USA. Andragogy functioned here as a header for (places of) systematic reflections, parallel to other academic headers like biology, medicine, physics. Examples of this use of andragogy are:

*   The Yugoslavian (scholarly) journal for adult education, named *Andragogija* in 1969; and the "Yugoslavian Society for Andragogy."
*   At Palacky University in Olomouc (Czech Republic) in 1990 the *Katedra sociologie a andragogiky* was established, managed by Vladimir Jochmann, who advanced the use of the term *andragogy* (andragogika) against *adult education* ("Vychova a vzdelavani dospelych"), which was discredited by communistic use. Also Prague University has a "Katedra Andragogiky."
*   In 1993, Slovenia's "Andragoski Center Republike Slovenije" was founded with the journal *Andragoska Spoznanja*.
*   In 1995, Bamberg University (Germany) named a *Lehrstuhl Andragogik*.
*   The Internet address of the Estonian Adult Education Society is *andra.ee*.

On this formal level "above practice" and specific approaches, the term andragogy could be used in communistic as well as in capitalistic countries, relating to all types of theories, for reflection, analysis, training, in person-oriented programs as well as human resource development.

A similar professional and academic expansion developed worldwide, sometimes using the term andragogy more or less demonstratively: Venezuela has the "Instituto Internacional de Andragogia," and since 1998 the Adult & Continuing Education Society of Korea has published the journal *Andragogy Today*. This documents a reality with new types of professional institutions, functions, roles, with full-time employed and academically trained professionals. Some of the new professional institutions use the term *andragogy*—meaning the same as adult education, but sounding more demanding and science based. Yet, throughout Europe, the terms *adult education, continuing education, further education*, or *adult pedagogy* are still used more than *andragogy*.

ADULT EDUCATION OR EDUCATION OF ADULTS?

Some writers limit andragogy to a teaching situation (or more in the jargon: helping-adults-learn situation). An early example is Lindeman (1926a), when reporting from his experiences at the Academy of Labor, Frankfurt, Germany: he connects Andragogik (using the German term) with teaching by giving his article the title "Andragogik: The Method of Teaching Adults." Knowles, who brought the Americanized version andragogy into discussion, also uses this limiting understanding: "Andragogy is the art and science of teaching adults." This definition is generalized by Krajinc (1989, p. 19) from Slovenia in a British international handbook: "Andragogy has been defined as ... the art and science of helping adults learn and the study of adult education theory, processes, and technology to that end." Other authors include "education and learning of adults in all its forms of expression" (Savicevic, 1999a, p. 97). Reischmann (2003) offers the term "lifewide education" to describe the opening of this new field, thus encompassing formal and informal, intentional and en passant, institution supplied and autodidactic learning (see Figure 20.2).

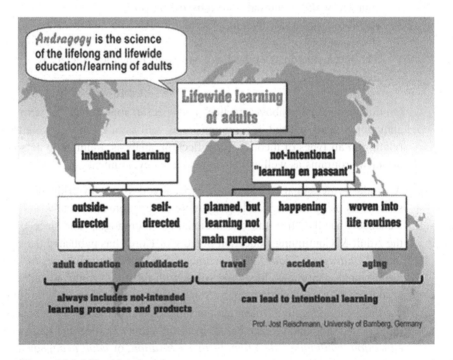

Figure 20.2 Lifewide education

These differences in understanding have to be seen as part of a historic development of the perception of adult education: what was perceived as adult education in 1833 or 1926 was different from 1969 or 2001. While until the 1970s the interest in adult education was focused on the action-oriented question, "How can teachers/facilitators support the learning of adults?" now a new, more analytical-descriptive perspective was added. From the 1970s on, it was increasingly perceived and discussed that adult learning did not only happen in more or less institutionalized or traditional settings, arranged specifically for the learning of adults. In North America, Allen Tough's research into adult learning projects provided evidence that only the "tip of the iceberg" of adult learning was adult education. In Germany, the perception of learning in social movements like self-help groups or citizen initiatives (peace movement, feminist groups) started the discussion about the *Entgrenzung* (de-bordering) of adult education. Distance and e-learning, assessment of prior learning, learning in non-traditional forms, life situations as learning opportunities, and other non-school-oriented forms and situations where adults learn, widened the perception that the education of adults happens in more situations than just in adult education. As a consequence, today many experts understand adult education only as a segment of the wider field of the education of adults.

SUMMARY

Besides this widened perception of adult learning another development challenged the understanding of adult education in the last decades: the field of adult education worldwide went through a process of growth and differentiation, in which a scholarly, scientific approach emerged. Also, a new type of adult educator was born, who was not qualified by his or her missions and visions, but by academic studies. In addition, writing a thesis or dissertation is a quite different task than educating adults: reflection, critique, analysis, and historical knowledge qualified this new type of academic professional.

An academic discipline with university programs, professors, students, focusing on the education of adults, exists today in many countries. However, in the membership list of the Commission of Professors of Adult Education of the USA (2003), not one university institute uses the name andragogy; in Germany 1 out of 35; in Eastern Europe 6 out of 26. Many actors in the field seem not to need the label andragogy. However, other scholars, for example, Dusan Savicevic, who provided Knowles with the term andragogy, explicitly claim "andragogy as a discipline, the subject of which is the study of education and learning of adults in all its forms of expression" (Savicevic, 1999a, p. 97; similarly Henschke, 2003; Reischmann, 2003). This claim is not a mere definition, but includes the prospective function to influence the coming reality: to challenge *outside* (demanding a respected discipline in the university context), to confront *inside* (challenging the colleagues to clarify their understanding and consensus of their function and science), overall to stand up to a self-confident academic identity.

Again, here this claim only makes sense when an object exists worthy of being labeled. It is not the term that makes a (sub-)discipline, but a reality with sound university programs, professors, research, disciplinarian knowledge, and students. If, where, and when this exists, a clarifying label like andragogy will make sense. The coming reality will show whether the ongoing differentiation in institutions, functions, and roles will need a term andragogy for conceptual clarification.

REFLECTION QUESTIONS

20.1 Discuss the idea of many sources of thinking about how adults learn.

20.2 Andragogy as a term: is it important, or are the ideas around adult learning important?

21

THE FUTURE OF ANDRAGOGY

INTRODUCTION

Although andragogy has a long history, there remain abundant opportunities and challenges ahead in terms of research and practice. This chapter examines some key issues in the development of the concept and philosophy of andragogy, future research needs, and developing applications in practice. This chapter is not meant to be all-inclusive, but rather to identify the key issues that will shape the research and practice of andragogy in the coming years.

THE CONCEPT AND PHILOSOPHY OF ANDRAGOGY

The concept and philosophy of andragogy has taken on distinctly different meanings depending on what part of the world one is discussing. In the United States, andragogy is clearly associated with, and shaped by, Malcolm Knowles. Debates have raged about what to call it, but in his last writings Knowles (1989b) called it a "conceptual framework that serves as a basis for an emergent theory" (p. 112). In the United States, andragogy is best identified as one perspective or theory on how adults learn, but it is not synonymous with the field of adult learning or adult education.

In Europe and other parts of the world, andragogy has a distinctly different meaning. Reischmann (2004) describes it this way:

> In most countries of Europe the Knowles discussion played at best a marginal role. The use and development of *andragogy* in the different countries and languages was more hidden, disperse, and uncoordinated—but steady. Andragogy nowhere described one specific concept, but was from 1970 on, connected with the coming

academic and professional institutions, publications, and programs and triggered by a similar growth of adult education in practice and theory; and in the U.S.A. *Andragogy* functioned in Europe as a header for (places of) systematic reflections, parallel to other academic headers like "biology," "medicine," "physics." Examples of this use of andragogy are: the Yugoslavian (scholarly) journal for adult education, named *Andragogija* in 1969; the "Yugoslavian Society for Andragogy"; in 1993, Slovenia's *Andragoski Center Republike Slovenije* was founded with the journal *Andragoska Spoznanja*; Prague University (Czechia) has a *Katedra Andragogiky*; in 1995, Bamberg University (Germany) named a *Lehrstuhl Andragogik*; the Internet address of the Estonian adult education society is *andra.ee*. On this formal level "above practice" and specific approaches, the term andragogy could be used in communistic countries as well as in capitalistic, relating to all types of theories, for reflection, analysis, training, in person-oriented programs as well as human resource development.

A similar professional and academic expansion developed worldwide, sometimes using more or less demonstratively the term andragogy: Venezuela has the Instituto Internacional de *Andragogia*, since 1998 the Adult & Continuing Education Society of Korea publishes the journal *Andragogy Today*. This documents a reality with new types of professional institutions, functions, roles, with full-time employed and academically trained professionals. Some of the new professional institutions used the name andragogy— meaning the same as "adult education," but sounding more demanding, science-based. But throughout Europe still *adult education, further education*, or *adult pedagogy* is used more than *andragogy*.

An academic discipline with university programs, professors, students, focusing on the education of adults, exists today in many countries. But in the membership list of the Commission of Professors of Adult Education of the U.S.A. (2003) not one university institute uses the name *andragogy*, in Germany one out of 35, in Eastern Europe six out of 26. Many actors in the field seem not to need a label *andragogy*. However, other scholars, for example Dusan Savicevic, who provided Knowles with the term andragogy, explicitly claim "andragogy as a discipline, the subject of which is the study of education and learning of adults in all its forms of expression" (Savicevic, 1999a, p. 97, Henschke, 2003, Reischmann 2003). This claim is not a mere definition, but includes the prospective function to influence the coming reality: to challenge *outside* (demanding a respected discipline in the university context), to confront *inside* (challenging the colleagues to clarify their understanding and consensus of their function and science), overall to stand to a self-confident academic identity.

The professional challenge is to acknowledge and coordinate these two views while maintaining their independence. The era in which the field of adult education in the United States debated adopting andragogy as its defining theory has passed and it seems unlikely that the term *andragogy* will ever have the broad meaning in the United States that it does in Europe.

RESEARCH ON ANDRAGOGY

The opportunities ahead related to research on andragogy are numerous. As Rachal (2002) points out, "Empirical examinations of andragogy—its science one might say—have tended to be inconclusive, contradictory, and few" (p. 211). He goes on to say that "the extensive anecdotal, expository, and polemical writing on the subject has tended to obscure empirical investigations, and most of the latter have been dissertations which rarely reach a wide audience" (p. 211). Yet, he notes that there have been persistent calls for more and better research on andragogy in the literature over the last 20 years (Cross, 1981; Davenport and Davenport, 1985; Merriam and Caffarella, 1991; Pratt, 1993). We see three clear directions necessary to enhance the science of andragogy.

Establish a clearer theoretical definition

As stated above, Knowles labeled andragogy as an "emergent theory," which led Rachal (2002) to declare that one of the chief impediments to strong empirical research is a lack of a clear definition of what constitutes andragogical practice. As discussed in Chapter 5, arriving at a clear definition is complicated by the fact that the application of andragogy in practice is governed by situational factors and the goals of the learning intervention. Thus, it is rare to encounter a "pure" application of andragogy. Rather, it is clear from Knowles's writings that there are degrees of *andragogyness* (Rachal, 2002) present in adult learning situations.

However, degree of application is not an excuse for inadequate theoretical development. Rather, it demands more precise theoretical explication for the conditions and variables that influence andragogical practice. The *andragogy in practice* (see Chapter 5) model is a first step toward a more precise theoretical framework that accounts for variable application.

Future research must extend this conceptual framework toward a more precise theoretical model with researchable propositions to advance the science of andragogy.

Develop a psychometrically sound measurement tool

One of the primary reasons stronger empirical research on andragogy has not emerged is that there is no psychometrically valid instrument to measure the andragogical constructs. Calls for better measurement have existed for some time; as Conti (1978) noted, a key prerequisite to growing the body of knowledge in the field of adult education was the development of measurement instruments. Unfortunately, research has yet to produce an instrument with sound psychometric qualities that validly measures both andragogy's six principles and its eight process design elements.

Clearly, no strong empirical research on the theory of andragogy is possible if researchers don't have a tool to measure it in field studies. A valid and reliable measurement instrument is essential to advancing our understanding of andragogy and must include evaluation of both andragogical principles and process design elements. Additionally, establishing an instrument's validity is critical for its use in empirical examinations. It seems odd that despite almost 50 years of use, andragogy remains more art than science. We suggest that it is critical for andragogy to move beyond philosophical or practice-based rhetoric to strong empirical testing so that practitioners in the field of human resource development (HRD) more thoroughly understand knowledge acquisition which will lead to the design and delivery of adult-appropriate curriculums.

This is not just an issue for researchers. Adult learners are not a monolithic group and educational settings span across wide contextual spectrums. For HRD practitioners, it is vital that there be a stronger empirical base for identifying and developing best practices in adult learning instructional strategies. Indeed andragogy may be the most widely practiced approach to adult education, and its tenets are well known to most adult educators. Yet, the truth is that such practice is based on shaky empirical evidence at best. Our long-term goal therefore is to provide adult educators with stronger evidence-based theory and principles.

History of measurement research

The most significant first step in the study of andragogy was the development of the *Educational Orientation Questionnaire* (EOQ) by Hadley (1975). It measured differences in beliefs amongst adult educators and effective learning strategies, including both pedagogical and andragogical orientations to learning. Knowles (1984a) noted that the contribution of the EOQ was its ability to provide a way for teachers to examine their approach to adult education. Evidence from the study indicated that teachers tend to view themselves as more andragogical than their students (Hadley, 1975, p. 421).

Kerwin (1979) remarked that the EOQ was "the first instrument to empirically study teaching behaviors of andragogically and pedagogically oriented educators" (p. 3). Hadley (1975) described his study as an "operational hypothesis based upon a theoretical construct that andragogy–pedagogy differences in attitudes toward adult education can be operationalized in terms of respondents' agreement or disagreement with relevant statements" (p. 99). To that end, he created a 60-item questionnaire designed to "discriminate among adult educators with respect to their andragogical–pedagogical orientation" (p. 127).

Hadley (1975) solicited feedback on the instrument's design from Malcolm Knowles, a member of his doctoral committee, and the questionnaire was administered to 409 teachers/educators from public and private educational institutions, as well as from business, religious institutions, and government agencies. Of the 60 items on the questionnaire, 30 were described as likely to be favored by pedagogically oriented educators and 30 were likely to be favored by andragogically oriented educators. Hadley (1975) stated that the questionnaire's underlying constructs or sub-dimensions along the pedagogy–andragogy continuum included: (1) philosophy of education; (2) purpose of education; (3) nature of learners; (4) characteristics of learning experience; (5) management of learning experience; (6) evaluation; and (7) relationships between educator and learner and among learners. Through factor analysis, eight factors emerged including: (1) pedagogical orientation; (2) andragogical orientation; (3) competitive motivation; (4) pedagogical teaching; (5) social distance; (6) student undependability; (7) standardization; and (8) self-directed change. The EOQ was found to be reliable with a test–retest measurement of 0.89 and a coefficient alpha of 0.94 (Hadley, 1975, p. vi).

The EOQ has been used and/or slightly modified by other researchers since its introduction (Christian, 1982; Kerwin, 1979; Smith, 1982). Davenport (1984) noted that the EOQ instrument had become the primary instrument for measuring the construct of education orientation and was useful because it demonstrated that educational orientations of instructors vary by gender, department, institutional setting, and academic discipline; but more research was needed to identify if these variances were related to important variables such as achievement. However, it is important to note that andragogical orientation loaded on a single factor and the other factors were not part of the andragogical model.

Two other instruments have been used by the adult learning community as tools to measure the theory of andragogy. Each is based on the Hadley instrument, including Kerwin's (1979) *Educational Description Questionnaire* (EDQ), and Christian's (1982) *Student Orientation Questionnaire* (SOQ). Kerwin (1979) modified Hadley's Educational Orientation Questionnaire (EOQ) and created his Educational Description Questionnaire (EDQ) as a means to be able to "discriminate among adult educators with respect to their andragogical–pedagogical orientation's instrument about education or effective learning situations to statements describing educator behavior" (Kerwin, 1979, p. 35). It measured behaviors or conditions that occurred in the classroom. The factorial categories included: (1) student involvement; (2) control; (3) distrust and detachment; (4) professionalism; (5) counseling; (6) individual inattention; and (7) organization. The instrument was initially tested on 74 instructors and 961 students at two community colleges (one rural and one urban) along with two technical institutes (one rural and one urban). Kerwin (1979) noted that of all the factors extracted from the EDQ, only one factor, student involvement, corresponded to a factor identified in the Hadley's EOQ. Kerwin (1979) stated that by comparing the two instruments' factors, andragogical orientation and student involvement were similar (p. 55).

Davenport (1984) noted that by identifying the factor, student involvement, the instrument was successful in reinforcing Knowles's concept of andragogy. However, the study's instrument, like the EOQ, failed to adequately measure each of the six principles of andragogy, thus limiting its ability to provide adult education researchers with the adequate data needed to move the theory to the next level of development. However, the Hadley (1975) and Kerwin (1979) instruments have been important to the field.

Christian's (1982) 50-item Student Orientation Questionnaire was a measurement tool for identifying student preferences, attitudes, and beliefs about education. His instrument was created by modifying both the Hadley (1975) and the Kerwin (1979) instruments. He studied 300 military and civilian personnel enrolled in mandatory management training at a US military base, as well as adults attending voluntary education programs being conducted on the base by a local university. Findings revealed that military personnel preferred more andragogical teaching methods as compared to civilian personnel. The researcher noted that his study was the first to isolate and examine military personnel preferences in the learning environment. Christian (1982) suggested that his instrument was significant because it aided adult education instructors in identifying the most appropriate instructional strategies based on the preferences indicated by students' responses. However, the lingering problem with the Christian (1982) instrument's ability to advance the theory of andragogy is that, like the Hadley and Kerwin instruments, it too failed to measure all six principles of andragogy.

The *Andragogy in Practice Inventory* (API), created by Suanmali (1981) as part of a doctoral study, examined leading adult educators and their beliefs regarding conceptual approaches in the andragogical process. The self-reported instrument examined conceptual agreement with the principles of andragogy held by members of the Commission of the Professors of Adult Education Association in the USA. It measured instructor acceptance of, and agreement with, andragogical concepts, specifically the concept of self-directed learning. Suanmali's (1981) 10-item inventory also examined the role of the educators, especially in terms of their contribution to helping adults become self-directed learners. Although it attempted to specifically examine congruence with andragogical principles, the API was "an instrument designed to test the presence of effective facilitation in practice, rather than providing empirical measures of forms of adult learning—or in other words, whether or not teachers are behaving as effective facilitators" (Brookfield, 1986, p. 34). Suanmali (1981) concluded that "there was a low degree of agreement among professors of adult education regarding the relative importance of the concepts used in andragogy" (p. 140); and indicated a wide variance in degrees of agreement amongst respondents regarding andragogy's significance in the adult learning environment. This variance may be due in part to the multiple disciplines amongst respondents and the wide populations adult education serves. There was some degree of agreement with the following inventory items as andragogy's impact in the learning setting including: (1) decrease learners' dependency; (2) help learners use learning resources; (3) learners define their own learning needs; (4) assist learners to define, plan, and evaluate their own learning; and (5) reinforce self-concept as a learner (Suanmali, 1981).

Knowles (1987) created his own andragogical measurement instrument, the *Personal HRD Style Inventory*, as a way to aid instructors and trainers in their general orientation to adult learning. As Knowles (1987) described it, the Personal HRD Style Inventory was designed as a self-assessment tool that would "provide insight into an instructor's general orientation to adult learning, program development, learning methods, and program administration" (p. 1). The instrument has yet to undergo academic testing and thus its potential to further understand the theory of andragogy and andragogy's impact on adult learning remains unknown.

The *Principles of Adult Learning Scale* (PALS) was developed as a 44-item instrument that "measured the frequency with which one practices teaching/learning principles that are described in the adult education literature" (Conti, 1991, p. 82). Its focus was on teaching styles, not an examination of andragogy per se. However, it can be considered one of the best instruments in the field from a psychometric quality perspective. Even though it was not created as a way to directly measure andragogy, it measures teaching methodologies which are closely associated with the principles of the theory. According to the instrument's creator, teaching styles are not randomly selected, do not change over time, and are linked to an instructor's educational philosophy (Conti, 1991, p. 89). Scores on the PALS indicate the level of learner-centered versus a teacher-centered approach to teaching.

Seven factors were embedded in the instrument. The first, learner-centered activities, evaluated preference for standardized testing, exercising control over the learning environment, determining educational objectives for each student, supporting collaboration, and encouraging students to take responsibility for their own learning. Personalizing instruction, the second factor, included limiting lecturing, supporting cooperation rather than competition, and applying different methods, materials, and types of assignments. The third factor, relating to experience, included planning learning activities that encourage students to relate their new learning to experiences, make learning relevant, and organize learning episodes according to real-life problems. The fourth factor assessed student needs which included the extent to which an instructor assists students in assessing short- and long-term range objectives through student conferences and formal as well as informal counseling. The fifth factor, climate building, included ways in which instructors eliminate learning barriers, propose dialog, encourage interaction in the classroom, facilitate student exploration and experimentation related to their self-concept and problem-solving skills via a friendly and informal setting. The sixth factor, participation in the learning process, included the extent to which instructors encourage adult-to-adult relationship building between teacher and student, involve students in developing criteria for assessing classroom performance, and allow students to determine the nature of content material. The seventh and final factor, flexibility for personal development, includes the extent to which an instructor facilitates learning versus being a provider of knowledge to students, the level of rigidity and sensitivity to students, and openness to adjusting classroom environment and curriculum to meeting changing needs of the students.

The *Adapted Principles of Adult Learning Styles* (APALS) was designed as a measurement tool for student perceptions of their instructors' teaching styles (McCollin, 1998). It met content validity testing by two juries of experts for analysis and content validity testing by field testing (Conti, 1978). The APALS has been used, according to Conti (1991), to determine teaching style and its impact on student performance in continuing education, a prison, and a tribally controlled community college. Results indicated that a learner-centered approach was positive for students. However, it has been suggested that the PALS may not be applicable in a higher education research setting due to higher education's unique *situational factors* including curriculum constraints, evaluation methodologies, and institutional goals (McCollin, 1998, p. 110).

Perrin (2000) created an instrument as part of his doctoral study which examined the extent to which adults prefer educators who subscribe to an andragogical teaching style and the extent to which andragogy adequately reflects the learning characteristics of adults. The study resulted in the creation of a seven-item, self-report instrument that was derived "directly from Knowles' 1984 final statements of descriptions of adult learners" (p. 10). The study's findings supported only a few of the seven adult learner assumptions, including a desire for self-directed learning, and skill enhancement. Unfortunately, this instrument had no psychometric validity.

By examining previous instruments used in adult learning research, it becomes evident that the field continues to fall short of developing a psychometrically sound instrument that directly measures the six andragogical principles and eight process design elements. The inability to integrate all andragogical elements into a single instrument remains problematic, and thus hampers improving adult learning. Without a valid measure of andragogy, it is impossible to conduct predictive studies. Without such studies, the theory of andragogy remains at a philosophical and theoretical level. Without rigorously designed studies, the field of adult education will continue to rely on intuition and anecdotal evidence rather than empirical foundations for critical curriculum design and instructional delivery strategies.

Recent measurement research

Recently, Holton et al. (2009) made huge strides in developing a psychometrically sound measurement instrument that measures both the andragogical principles and design elements. In their initial test of the instrument, the *Andragogical Practices Inventory* (API), they validated scales to measure five of six andragogical principles and six of eight andragogical process design elements through factor analysis. This study was more successful than any previous study in measuring andragogical constructs (principles and process design elements). The authors concluded that it was premature to assume that the missing constructs don't exist empirically as their absence could well be due to measurement issues as well.

Tables 21.1 and 21.2 show sample items and reliabilities for the scales developed in the first version of the instrument. At press time for this book the authors have developed a second version of the instrument and research tests are underway to validate the new version. They are hopeful that the new version will yield an instrument that measures all six assumptions and eight design elements. (Readers interested in obtaining a copy of the API for their own research can contact Dr. Ed Holton at: eholton2@lsu.edu.)

Conduct criterion measurement studies

The "holy grail" of research on andragogy is to empirically demonstrate that andragogical techniques lead to better outcomes. These outcomes should be in three areas: affective (learner satisfaction and motivation); learning; and learning utilization after the learning event, particularly in HRD settings.

As Rachal (2002) points out, criterion studies in andragogy are a particular challenge because of the conflicts it creates with learning assessment. In its purest form, andragogy is widely believed to advocate learner self-assessment of learning outcomes. Such an approach would be considered a weak measure in a research study. However, Rachal (2002) correctly clarifies this when he states that Knowles primarily advocated that the learning assessment (1) be mutually agreed to by the learners and facilitator, and (2) be performance based rather than a traditional schooling-oriented paper-and-pencil-type test. In this form, it is entirely possible to construct valid research-quality measures of learning outcomes to conduct a strong test of andragogy.

Rachal (2002) goes on to suggest six other criteria for andragogical empirical studies, including (1) voluntary participation, (2) adult status, (3) collaboratively determined objectives, (4) measuring satisfaction, (5) appropriate adult learning environment, and (6) random assignment of participants if possible.

Having a measurement instrument opens the door for a wide array of empirical research to strengthen the empirical research base on andragogy. Perhaps most important are the predictive studies that can now be conducted to examine the effect of andragogical practices on critical adult learning outcomes such as learning and student satisfaction. In addition, this

Table 21.1 Andragogical assumptions: principles

Scale name	Item number and descriptions	Scale reliability
Motivation	This learning experience motivated me to give it my best effort.	$\alpha = 0.933$
Experience	I felt my prior life and work experiences helped my learning.	$\alpha = 0.839$
Need to know	It was clear to me why I needed to participate in this learning experience.	$\alpha = 0.760$
Readiness	This learning experience was just what I needed given the changes in my life/work.	$\alpha = 0.811$
Self-directedness	I felt I had control over my learning in this learning experience.	$\alpha = 0.739$

Table 21.2 Andragogical assumptions: process design elements

Scale name	Item number and descriptions	Scale reliability
Setting of learning objectives	Learners were encouraged to set their own individual learning objectives.	$\alpha = 0.903$
Climate setting	The climate in this learning experience can be described as collaborative.	$\alpha = 0.910$
Evaluation	The methods used to evaluate my learning in this learning experience were appropriate.	$\alpha = 0.863$
Prepare the learner	Sufficient steps were taken to prepare me for the learning process.	$\alpha = 0.875$
Designing the learning experience	There were mechanisms in place to collaboratively design which learning activities would be used.	$\alpha = 0.943$
Learning activities	The facilitator/instructor relied too heavily on lecture during the learning experience (reverse coded).	$\alpha = 0.682$

instrument opens the door to test more complex structural models that examine the process by which andragogy affects outcomes. The API and its future iterations are a promising first step toward sophisticated empirical study of andragogy.

THE PRACTICE OF ANDRAGOGY

There are two key opportunities for the practice of andragogy: adapting andragogy to the varying conditions encountered in practice, and optimizing the application of andragogy in technology-mediated learning.

Adapt andragogy to different contexts and conditions

Just as criterion studies are the "holy grail" of andragogical research, adapting andragogy to different contexts is the "holy grail" of andragogical practice. As we argue in Chapter 5, Knowles's thinking on andragogy evolved later in life to the realization that it would rarely be applied in pure form. Rather, he realized that each situation and group of learners would require practitioners to make adjustments to apply it in different ways. In some instances, this might entail beginning with a pedagogical approach in order to develop learners toward an andragogical approach over time. In other instances, only a partial implementation of andragogy would be achievable. Of course in some instances, a complete andragogical strategy would work.

Still poorly defined is the issue of which modifications are demanded by certain conditions and circumstances. Today, this is clearly left to the art of professional practice. The andragogy in practice model provides new conceptual guidance to that art, but it is only a first step. One key new direction we see for the practice of andragogy is to develop a more clear definition as to how to vary the application of andragogy to fit varying circumstances. One example Knowles commonly used was that when leading a group of learners who are totally new to a body of information, then pedagogical strategies are often necessary until the learners have mastered the basics. Or, when leading learners with low levels of confidence, then strategies more appropriate for dependent learners would be recommended.

Our vision is something like a decision tree of key questions that practitioners ask about their learners and the learning situation, leading to adjusted andragogical strategies. Although this might offend andragogical "purists" [as Knowles wrote (1980a, p. 49)] as we argue in Chapter 5, this is the way Knowles intended for andragogy to be used and realized later in his life that it would work best. The challenge now is to put more structure to the artistry of professional application of andragogy to different contexts.

Andragogy and technology-mediated learning

Knowles (1989b) foresaw technology as one of the major forces shaping adult learning in the twenty-first century and a force that would be consistent with andragogy. We now see technology as a force that presents both great opportunities for andragogical adult learning, as well as presenting special challenges.

Technology presents bold new opportunities for providing adults with rich learning experiences in the andragogical tradition. First, it directly caters to adults' desire to be self-directed in their learning. Technology is inherently a self-directed learning medium that enables adults to access learning in a just-in-time, just-enough format under conditions of full learner control. In many ways it can provide adult learners with the complete self-directed learning experience.

Second, well-developed computer-based instruction enables adults to tailor the learning experience to fit their prior experiences. Of course we are not talking about the simple *information put online*-type instruction, but rather technology-based learning that allows users to select alternative paths through learning based on their prior learning and experiences. Although this requires more up-front investment in the technology, the result is more effective learning for adults.

Third, if properly designed, technology-based instruction easily allows learners to tailor the learning to their real-world problems; because it is usually used in the learner's natural work or life setting, learners can immediately apply the learning to their problem settings. Furthermore, it often allows them to access "just enough" to solve the problems that led them to the learning in the first place.

Along with the opportunities come special challenges, primarily in the area of self-directed learning through the use of the Internet. The Internet is increasingly the first stop as a source of information for technology-rich nations, but this fact alone does not ensure learning. Side-effects of the Internet appear to include learner impatience and shortened attention spans. Using the Internet as a primary tool for self-directed learning demands that the learners have very well-developed self-directed learning skills. In this technological context, self-directed learning and andragogy are not optional. Whereas facilitators in a classroom setting have the option of adapting andragogy to fit the developmental stage of the adult learners, including being supportive or pedagogical if necessary, technology-based learning demands that learners be ready for self-directed learning. It is not uncommon for organizations implementing technology-based learning to discover that the intended learners do not have the metacognitive skills, motivation, or confidence to engage in the required level of self-directed learning.

Thus, not only does information technology allow for andragogy, but it requires that learners be ready for andragogy and for controlling their own learning. This puts special importance on the first step of Knowles's program planning model (see Chapter 4), "Preparing the Learners," to make sure learners are ready to capitalize on the opportunities technology presents and have the more fundamental skills of learning how to learn.

SUMMARY

Andragogy remains one of the pre-eminent models of adult learning and is often the first to be encountered by newcomers to adult learning. Despite the limitations, there are many opportunities ahead for andragogy in both research and practice. Although healthy debates about the process and purposes of adult learning will certainly continue, important substantive advances through research and practice are likely to occur that will continue to shape both the art and science of andragogy.

REFLECTION QUESTIONS

21.1 What are the relative strengths of the US and European views of andragogy?

21.2 Propose a study focused on andragogy that you think is important and explain why it is important.

21.3 Discuss a specific strategy you would propose to advance andragogical concepts in the context of adults using the Internet for learning purposes.

BIBLIOGRAPHY

Adams-Webber, J. R. *Personal Construct Theory: Concepts and Application.* New York: Wiley-Interscience, 1979.

Adult Education Association. *Psychology of Adults.* Washington, DC: Adult Education Association, 1963.

Adult Education Association. *Adult Learning.* Washington, DC: Adult Education Association, 1965a.

Adult Education Association. *Processes of Adult Education.* Washington, DC: Adult Education Association, 1965b.

Akande, J. O., and Jegede, P. O. "Andragogy and Computer Literacy: The Nigerian Perspective." *The African Symposium: An On-Line Educational Research Journal, 4(2),* July 2004.

Alford, H. J. *Continuing Education in Action: Residential Centers for Lifelong Learning.* New York: Wiley, 1968.

Allen, B. S., and Merrill, M. D. "System-Assigned Strategies and CBI." *Journal of Educational Computing Research, 1(1),* 1985, 3–21.

Allender, J. S. "New Conceptions of the Role of the Teacher." *The Psychology of Open Teaching and Learning.* M. L. Silberman, et al. (eds). Boston, MA: Little, Brown, 1972.

Alliger, G. M., and Janak, E. A. "Kirkpatrick's Levels of Training Criteria: Thirty Years Later." *Personnel Psychology, 42,* 1989, 331–340.

Alliger, G. M., Tannenbaum, S. I., Bennett, W., Traver, H., and Shotland, A. "A Meta-Analysis of the Relations Among Training Criteria." *Personnel Psychology, 50,* 1997, 341–358.

Allman, P., and Mackie, K. J. (eds). *Towards a Developmental Theory of Andragogy.* Nottingham: University of Nottingham, Department of Adult Education, 1983.

Allport, G. *Becoming.* New Haven, CT: Yale University Press, 1955.

Allport, G. *Personality and Social Encounter.* Boston, MA: Beacon, 1960.

Allport, G. *Pattern and Growth in Personality.* New York: Holt, Rinehart, and Winston, 1961.

Anderson, C. R. "Locus of Control, Coping Behaviors, and Performance in a Stress Setting: A Longitudinal Study." *Journal of Applied Psychology, 62,* 1977, 446–451.

Anderson, R. C., and Archer, C. S. "Imagery and Sentence Learning." *Journal of Educational Psychology, 62,* 1970, 526–530.

Anderson, S., et al. *Encyclopedia of Educational Evaluation.* San Francisco, CA: Jossey-Bass, 1974.

Apps, J. W. *Improving Practice in Continuing Education.* San Francisco, CA: Jossey-Bass, 1985.

Apps, J. W. *Higher Education in a Learning Society.* San Francisco, CA: Jossey-Bass, 1988.

Archer, R. P. "Relationships Between Locus of Control, Trait Anxiety, and State Anxiety: An Interactionist Perspective." *Journal of Personality, 47,* 1979, 305–316.

Arends, R. I., and Arends, J. H. *System Change Strategies in Educational Settings.* New York: Human Sciences Press, 1977.

Argyris, C. *Interpersonal Competence and Organizational Effectiveness.* Homewood, IL: Dorsey, 1962.

Argyris, C. *Integrating the Individual and the Organization.* New York: Wiley, 1964.

Argyris, C. *Intervention Theory and Method: A Behavioral Science View.* Reading, MA: Addison-Wesley, 1970.

Argyris, C. *Increasing Leadership Effectiveness.* New York: WileyInterscience, 1976.

Argyris, C. *Reasoning, Learning and Action.* San Francisco, CA: Jossey-Bass, 1982.

Argyris, C., and Schon, D. *Organizational Learning: A Theory of Action Perspective.* San Francisco, CA: Jossey-Bass, 1978.

ARL Inquiry. "Developing an Infrastructure for Individual and Organizational Change." *Proceedings of the 1996 Academy of Human Resource Development Annual Meeting.* Baton Rouge, LA, 1996.

Arlin, P. K. "Adolescent and Adult Thought: A Structural Interpretation." *Wisdom: Its Nature, Origins, and Development.* M. L. Commons, F. A. Richards, and C. Armos (eds). Cambridge: Cambridge University Press, 1990.

Artzt, A. F., and Armour-Thomas, E. "Development of a Cognitive–Metacognitive Framework for Protocol Analysis of Mathematical Problem Solving in Small Groups." *Cognition and Instruction,* 9, 1992, 137–175.

Ashford, S. J., and Taylor, M. S. "Adaptation to Work Transition: An Integrative Approach." *Research in Personnel and Human Resources Management, Vol. 8.* G. R. Ferris, and K. M. Rowland (eds). Greenwich, CT: JAI Press, 1990.

Ashton-Warner, S. *Teacher.* New York: Simon and Schuster, 1963.

Aspell, D. D. "Andragogy: Adult Learning." San Antonio: University of Texas, 2003. Unpublished paper.

Aspillaga, M. "Screen Design: Location of Information and its Effects on Learning." *Journal of Computer-Based Instruction, 18(3),* 1991, 89–92.

ASTD-USDL. *America and the New Economy.* Washington, DC: American Society for Training and Development and the US Department of Labor, 1990.

Ausubel, D. P. *The Psychology of Meaningful Verbal Learning: An Introduction to School Learning.* New York: Grune and Stratton, 1963.

Ausubel, D. P. *Educational Psychology: A Cognitive View.* New York: Holt, Rinehart and Winston, 1968.

Axford, R. W. *Adult Education: The Open Door.* Scranton, PA: International Textbook Co., 1969.

Baldridge, J. V., and Deal, T. S. *Managing Change in Educational Organizations.* Berkeley, CA: McCutchan, 1975.

Baldridge, J. V., et al. *Policy Making and Effective Leadership: A National Study of Academic Management.* San Francisco, CA: Jossey-Bass, 1978.

Baldwin, T. T., Magjuka, R. J., and Loher, B. T. "The Perils of Participation: Effects of Choice of Training on Trainee Motivation and Learning." *Personnel Psychology, 44*, 1991, 51–65.

Baltes, P. *Life-Span Development and Behavior*, Vol. 1. New York: Academic Press, 1978.

Baltes, P. "On the Incomplete Architecture of Human Ontogeny: Selection, Optimization, and Compensation as Foundations of Developmental Theory." *American Psychologist, 52(4)*, 1997, 366–380.

Baltes, P., Dittman-Kohli, F., and Dixon, R. "New Perspectives on the Development of Intelligence in Adulthood: Toward a Dual Process Conception and a Model of Selective Optimization with Compensation." *Life-Span Development and Behavior*, Vol. 6. P. B. Baltes, and O. G. Brim, Jr. (eds). New York: Academic Press, 1984, pp. 33–76.

Bandura, A. *Principles of Behavior Modification*. New York: Holt, Rinehart and Winston, 1969.

Bandura, A. *Social Learning Theory*. Englewood Cliffs, NJ: Prentice-Hall, 1977.

Bandura, A. "Self-Efficacy Mechanism in Human Agency." *American Psychologist, 37*, 1982, 122–147.

Bandura, A. *Social Foundations of Thought and Action: A Social Cognitive Theory*. Englewood Cliffs, NJ: Prentice-Hall, 1986.

Bandura, A. "Perceived Self-Efficacy in Cognitive Development and Functioning." *Educational Psychologist, 28(2)*, 1993, 117–148.

Bandura, A., and Walters, R. H. *Social Learning and Personality Development*. New York: Holt, Rinehart and Winston, 1963.

Bany, M. A., and Johnson, L. V. *Classroom Group Behavior*. New York: Macmillan, 1964.

Bard, R., Bell, C. R., Stephen, L., and Webster, L. *The Trainer's Professional Development Handbook*. San Francisco, CA: Jossey-Bass, 1987.

Barker, R. G. (ed.). *The Stream of Behavior*. New York: Appleton-Century Crofts, 1963.

Barker, R. G. *Ecological Psychology: Concepts and Methods for Studying the Environment of Human Behavior*. Stanford, CA: Stanford University Press, 1968.

Barker, R. G. *Habitats, Environments, and Human Behavior*. San Francisco, CA: Jossey-Bass, 1978.

Barker, R. G., and Gump, P. V. *Big School, Small School: High School Size and Student Behavior*. Stanford, CA: Stanford University Press, 1964.

Barney, J. B., and Ouchi, W. G. *Organizational Economics*. San Francisco, CA: Jossey-Bass, 1986.

Barrett, J. H. *Gerontological Psychology*. Springfield, IL: Charles C. Thomas, 1972.

Barron, E. *Creativity and Psychological Health*. New York: Van Nostrand, 1963.

Bassi, L. *The 3 Flavors of HR – Which One Are You?* Golden, CO: McBassi & Company, 2014.

Bates, R., Holton, E., and Seyler, D. "Factors Affecting Transfer of Training in an Industrial Setting." *Proceedings of the 1997 Academy of Human Resource Development Annual Meeting*. Baton Rouge, LA, 1997.

Baughart, E. W. *Educational Systems Analysis*. New York: Macmillan, 1969.

Baum, H. S. *Organizational Membership*. Albany: State University of New York, 1990.

Becker, G. S. *Human Capital: A Theoretical and Empirical Analysis with Special Reference to Education*, 3rd edn. Chicago, IL: University of Chicago Press, 1993.

Becker, J. (ed.). *Architecture for Adult Education*. Washington, DC: Adult Education Association, 1956.

Beckhard, R. *Organization Development: Strategies and Models*. Reading, MA: Addison-Wesley, 1969.

Beder, H. (ed.). "Marketing Continuing Education." *New Directions for Continuing Education*, CE#31. San Francisco, CA: Jossey-Bass, 1986.

Beder, H. "Purposes and Philosophies of Adult Education." *Handbook of Adult and Continuing Education*. S. B. Merriam, and P. M. Cunningham (eds). San Francisco, CA: Jossey-Bass, 1989, pp. 37–50.

Bee, H. L. *The Journey of Adulthood*, 3rd edn. Upper Saddle River, NJ: Prentice-Hall, 1996.

Bell, C. R., and Nadler, L. *The Client–Consultant Handbook*. Houston, TX: Gulf, 1979.

Bellezza, F. S. "The Spatial Arrangement Mnemonic." *Journal of Educational Psychology*, 75, 1983, 830–837.

Benack, S., and Basseches, M. A. "Dialectical Thinking and Relativistic Epistemology: Their Relation in Adult Development." *Adult Development*. M. L. Commons, J. D. Sinnott, F. A. Richards, and C. Armon (eds). New York: Praeger, 1989.

Bengston, V. L. *The Social Psychology of Aging*. Indianapolis, IN: BobbsMerrill, 1973.

Benne, K. D., and Chin, R. *The Planning of Change*. New York: Holt, Rinehart and Winston, 1968.

Bennis, W. G. *Changing Organizations*. New York: McGraw-Hill, 1966.

Bennis, W. G. *Organization Development: Its Nature, Origins, and Prospects*. Reading, MA: Addison-Wesley, 1969.

Bennis, W. G., and Slater, P. E. *The Temporary Society*. New York: Harper and Row, 1968.

Bennis, W. G., Benne, K. D., and Chin, R. *The Planning of Change*. New York: Holt, Rinehart and Winston, 1968.

Bereiter, C. "Moral Alternatives to Education." *Interchange*, 1972, 25–41.

Bergevin, P. *A Philosophy for Adult Education*. New York: Seabury, 1967.

Bergevin, P., and McKinley, J. *Participation Training for Adult Education*. St. Louis, MI: Bethany Press, 1965.

Bette, N. R. "Individualizing Education by Learning Contracts." *New Directions for Higher Education*, no. 10. San Francisco, CA: Jossey-Bass, 1975.

Bierema, L. L. "Development of the Individual Leads to More Productive Workplaces." *Workplace Learning: Debating Five Critical Questions of Theory and Practice*. R. W. Rowden (ed.). San Francisco, CA: Jossey-Bass, 1996.

Billington, D. D. "Seven Characteristics of Highly Effective Adult Learning Programs." *New Horizons for Learning*. Seattle: New Horizons, 2000. http://www.newhorizons.org.

Birren, J. E. *The Psychology of Aging*. Englewood Cliffs, NJ: Prentice-Hall, 1964.

Bischoff, L. L. *Adult Psychology*. New York: Harper and Row, 1969.

Blake, R. R., and Mouton, J. S. *The Managerial Grid*. Houston, TX: Gulf, 1964.

Blake, R. R., and Mouton, J. S. *Consultation*. Reading, MA: Addison-Wesley, 1976.

Blank, W. E. *Handbook for Developing Competency-Based Training Programs*. Englewood Cliffs, NJ: Prentice-Hall, 1982.

Block, J. H. *Mastery Learning: Theory and Practice.* New York: Holt, Rinehart and Winston, 1971.

Bloom, B. S., Hastings, J. T., and Madaus, G. F. *Handbook on Formative and Summative Learning.* New York: McGraw-Hill, 1969.

Bloom, B. S., Engelhart, M. D., Furst, E. J., Hill, W. H., and Krathwohl, D. R. "Taxonomy of Educational Objectives." *The Classification of Educational Goals: Handbook 1: Cognitive Domain.* New York: Longmans, Green, 1956.

Bonham, L. A. "Learning Style Instruments: Let the Buyer Beware." *Lifelong Learning, 11(6)*, 1988, 12–16.

Boone, E. J. *Developing Programs in Adult Education.* Englewood Cliffs, NJ: Prentice-Hall, 1985.

Boone, E., and associates. *Serving Personal and Community Needs Through Adult Education.* San Francisco, CA: Jossey-Bass, 1980.

Borich G. D. (ed.). *Evaluating Educational Programs and Products.* Englewood Cliffs, NJ: Educational Technology Publications, 1974.

Botkin, J. W., Elmandjra, M., and Salitza, M. *No Limits to Learning. A Report to the Club of Rome.* New York: Pergamon, 1979.

Botwinick, J. *Cognitive Processes in Maturity and Old Age.* New York: Springer, 1967.

Boucouvalas, M. "Advances in the Neurosciences: Implications and Relevance for Lifelong Learning Professionals." *Lifelong Learning Research Conference Proceedings.* College Park: University of Maryland, February 1988, pp. 16–20.

Boucouvalas, M. "Comparative Thinking and the Structures of Adult Cognition: An Epistemological and Methodological Challenge for Comparative Adult Education." *Comparative Adult Education 1998: The Contribution of ISCAE to an Emerging Field of Study.* J. Reischmann, Z. Jelenc, and M. Bron (eds). Bamberg, Germany: ISCAE Proceedings, 1999, pp. 65–76.

Boud, D. *Developing Student Autonomy in Learning.* New York: Nichols Publishing, 1981.

Bower, E. M., and Hollister W. G. (eds). *Behavioral Science Frontiers in Education.* New York: Wiley, 1967.

Boyd, R. D., Apps, J. W., and associates. *Redefining the Discipline of Adult Education.* San Francisco, CA: Jossey-Bass, 1980.

Brache, A. P. *How Organizations Work: Taking a Holistic Approach to Enterprise Health.* New York: Wiley, 2002.

Bradford, L. P., Benne, K. D., and Gibb, R. *T-Group Theory and Laboratory Method.* New York: Wiley, 1964.

Brady, H. G. *Research Needs in Adult Education.* Tampa: University of South Florida, 1982.

Breivik, P. S. (ed.). "Managing Programs for Learning Outside the Classroom." *New Directions for Higher Education*, HE#56. San Francisco, CA: Jossey-Bass, 1986.

Brethower, D. M. "Specifying a Human Performance Technology Knowledgebase." *Performance Improvement Quarterly, 8(2)*, 1995, 17–39.

Brethower, D., and Smalley, K. *Performance-Based Instruction: Linking Training to Business Results.* San Francisco, CA: Jossey-Bass, 1998.

Briggs, K., and Meyers, I. *Myers-Briggs Type Indicator.* Palo Alto, CA: Consulting Psychologists Press, 1977.

Briggs, L. J., and Wager, W. W. *Handbook of Procedures for the Design of Instruction*, 2nd edn. Englewood Cliffs, NJ: Educational Technology Publications, 1981.

Brinkerhoff, R. O. *Achieving Results from Training.* San Francisco, CA: Jossey-Bass, 1987.

Britton, J. H., and Britton, J. O. *Personality Changes in Aging.* New York: Springer, 1972.

Brockett, R. G. (ed.). "Continuing Education in the Year 2000." *New Directions for Continuing Education,* CE#36. San Francisco, CA: Jossey-Bass, 1987.

Bromley, D. B. *The Psychology of Human Aging.* Baltimore, MD: Penguin, 1966.

Bronfenbrenner, U. *The Ecology of Human Development.* Cambridge, MA: Harvard University Press, 1979.

Brookfield, S. D. "The Contribution of Eduard Lindeman to the Development of Theory and Philosophy in Adult Education." *Adult Education Quarterly, 34,* 1984a, 185–196.

Brookfield, S. D. "Self-Directed Adult Learning: A Critical Paradigm." *Adult Education Quarterly, 35,* 1984b, 59–71.

Brookfield, S. D. *Understanding and Facilitating Adult Learning.* San Francisco, CA: Jossey-Bass, 1986.

Brookfield, S. D. *Developing Critical Thinkers.* San Francisco, CA: Jossey-Bass, 1987.

Brookfield, S. D. "Conceptual, Methodological and Practical Ambiguities in Self-Directed Learning." *Self-Directed Learning: Application and Theory.* H. B. Long (ed.). Athens: University of Georgia Press, 1988.

Brown, G. *Human Teaching for Human Learning.* New York: Viking, 1971.

Bruner, E. S. *An Overview of Adult Education Research.* Washington, DC: Adult Education Association, 1959.

Bruner, J. S. *The Process of Education.* Cambridge, MA: Harvard University Press, 1960.

Bruner, J. S. "The Act of Discovery." *Harvard Educational Review, 31,* 1961, 21–32.

Bruner, J. S. *Toward a Theory of Instruction.* Cambridge, MA: Harvard University Press, 1966.

Bryson, L. *Adult Education.* New York: American Book Co., 1936.

Bryson, L. *The Next America.* New York: Harper, 1952.

Buber, M. *I and Thou,* 2nd edn. New York: Scribner's, 1958.

Buford, T. O. *Philosophy for Adults.* Washington, DC: University Press of America, 1980.

Bullmer, K. *The Art of Empathy.* New York: Human Sciences Press, 1975.

Bunderson, V., and Inouye, D. K. "The Evaluation of Computer-Aided Educational Delivery Systems." *Instructional Technology: Foundations.* R. R. Gagné (ed.). Hillsdale, NJ: Erlbaum, 1987, pp. 283–318.

Burnside, I. M. *Working with the Elderly: Group Process and Techniques.* Belmont, CA: Duxbury, 1978.

Burton, W. H. "Basic Principles in a Good Teaching–Learning Situation." *Readings in Human Learning.* L. D. Crow, and A. Crow (eds). New York: McKay, 1963, pp. 7–19.

Bushnell, D., and Rappaport D., (eds). *Planned Change in Education: A Systems Approach.* New York: Harcourt, Brace, Jovanovich, 1972.

Caffarella, R. S. "Self-Directed Learning." *New Directions for Adult and Continuing Education, no. 57—An Update on Adult Learning Theory.* S. B. Merriam (ed.). San Francisco, CA: Jossey-Bass, 1993.

Caffarella, R., and O'Donnell, J. "Research in Self-Directed Learning: Past, Present and Future Trends." *Self-Directed Learning: Application and Theory.* H. B. Long (ed.). Athens: University of Georgia Press, 1988.

Caine, G., and Caine, R. N. "Meaningful Learning and the Executive Functions of the Brain." *New Directions for Adult and Continuing Education, 100,* 2006, 53–62.

Caine, R. N., Caine, G., McClintic, C., and Klimek, K. J. *12 Brain/Mind Learning Principles in Action: Developing Executive Functions of the Human Brain.* Thousand Oaks, CA: Corwin Press, 2009.

Campbell, J. P. "Training Design for Performance Improvement." *Productivity in Organizations.* San Francisco, CA: Jossey-Bass, 1988, pp. 177–215.

Candy, P. C. *Self-Direction for Lifelong Learning.* San Francisco, CA: Jossey-Bass, 1991.

Canfield, A. *Learning Styles Inventory Manual.* Los Angeles, CA: Western Psychological Services, 1988.

Carkhuff, R. R. *Helping and Human Relations: A Primer for Lay and Professional Helpers,* 2 vols. New York: Holt, Rinehart and Winston, 1969.

Carnevale, A. P. *Human Capital: A High Yield Corporate Investment.* Washington, DC: American Society for Training and Development, 1983.

Carnevale, A. P., Gainer, L. J., and Meltzer, A. S. *Workplace Basics: The Essential Skills Employers Want.* Alexandria, VA: American Society for Training and Development, 1990.

Carré, P. "From Intentional to Self-Directed Learning." *Conceptions of Self-Directed Learning: Theoretical and Conceptual Considerations.* G. A. Straka (ed.). Munster: Waxmann Verlag, 2000, pp. 49–57.

Carrier, C. A., and Sales, G. C. "Pair Versus Individual Work on the Acquisition of Concepts in a Computer-Based Instruction Lesson." *Journal of Computer-Based Instruction, 14,* 1987, 11–17.

Cascio, W. F. *Costing Human Resources: The Financial Impact of Behavior in Organizations,* 2nd edn. Boston, MA: Kent, 1987.

Cascio, W., and Boudreau, J. *Investing in People: Financial Impact of Human Resource Initiatives,* 2nd edn. Upper Saddle River, NJ: Pearson Education, 2007.

Casner-Loote, J., and associates. *Successful Training Strategies.* San Francisco, CA: Jossey-Bass, 1988.

Cattell, R. B. "Theory of Fluid and Crystallized Intelligence: A Critical Approach." *Journal of Educational Psychology, 54(1),* 1963, 1–22.

Cervero, R. M. *Effective Continuing Education for Professionals.* San Francisco, CA: Jossey-Bass, 1988.

Cervero, R. M., and Wilson, A. L. *Planning Responsibly for Adult Education: A Guide to Negotiating Power and Interests.* San Francisco, CA: Jossey-Bass, 1994.

Chakiris, B. J., and Rolander, R. *Careers in Training and Development.* Alexandria, VA: American Society for Training and Development, 1986.

Chalofsky, N., and Lincoln, C. I. *Up the HRD Ladder: A Guide for Professional Growth.* Reading, MA: Addison-Wesley, 1983.

Chao, G. T., O'Leary-Kelly, A., Wolf, S., Klein, H. J., and Gardner, P. D. "Organization Socialization: Its Content and Consequences." *Journal of Applied Psychology, 79,* 1994, 450–463.

Charters, A. N., and associates. *Comparing Adult Education Worldwide.* San Francisco, CA: Jossey-Bass, 1981.

Chatman, J. A. "Matching People and Organizations: Selection and Socialization in Public Accounting Firms." *Administrative Science Quarterly, 36*, 1991, 459–484.

Cheren, M. E. *Learning Management: Emerging Directions for Learning to Learn in the Workplace.* Columbus, OH: ERIC, National Center for Research in Vocational Education, 1987.

Cherrington, B. M. *Journal of Adult Education, 11*, June 3, 1939, 244–245.

Chickering, A. W. *Education and Identity.* San Francisco, CA: Jossey-Bass, 1976.

Chickering, A. W. *An Introduction to Experiential Learning.* New Rochelle, NY: Change Magazine Press, 1977.

Chickering, A. W., and associates. *The Modern American College.* San Francisco, CA: Jossey-Bass, 1981.

Chipman, S. F., and Segal, J. W. "Higher Cognitive Goals for Education: An Introduction." *Thinking and Learning Skills: Relating Instruction to Research*, Vol. 1. J. W. Segal, S. F. Chipman, and R. Glaser (eds). Hillsdale, NJ: Erlbaum, 1985, pp. 1–19.

Christian, A. *A Comparative Study of the Andragogical–Pedagogical Orientation of Military and Civilian Personnel* (UMI No. 8315684), 1982.

Clariana, R. B. "A Review of Multiple-Try Feedback in Traditional and Computer-Based Instruction." *Journal of Computer-Based Instruction, 20*(3), 1993, 67–74.

Clark, C. S., Dobbins, G. H., and Ladd, R. T. "Exploratory Field Study of Training Motivation." *Group and Organization Management, 18*, 1993, 292–307.

Clark, M. C. "Transformational Learning." *New Directions for Adult and Continuing Education, no. 57—An Update on Adult Learning Theory.* S. B. Merriam (ed.). San Francisco, CA: Jossey-Bass, 1993.

Clark, R. (ed.). *Learning from Media: Arguments, Analysis, and Evidence*, 2nd edn. Charlotte, NC: Information Age Publishing, 2012.

Cleland, D. (ed.). *Systems, Organization Analysis, Management.* New York: McGraw-Hill, 1969.

Coan, A. W., et al. *The Optimal Personality.* New York: Columbia University Press, 1974.

Collins, Z. W. *Museums, Adults and the Humanities.* Washington, DC: American Association of Museums, 1981.

Combs, A. W., and Snygg, D. *Individual Behavior*, rev. edn. New York: Harper, 1959.

Combs, A. W., et al. *Helping Relationships: Basic Concepts for the Helping Professions.* Boston, MA: Allyn and Bacon, 1971, 1978.

Commission on the Skills of the American Workforce. *America's Choice: High Skills or Low Wages.* Rochester, NY: National Center on Education and the Economy, 1990.

Conner, M. L. "Andragogy + Pedagogy." *Ageless Learner, 1997–2003.* http://agelesslearner.com/intros/andragogy.html.

Conti, G. J. *Principles of Adult Learning Scale: An Instrument for Measuring Teacher Behavior Related to Collaborative Teaching—Learning Mode* (UMI No. 7912479), 1978.

Conti, G. J. "Identifying your Teaching Style." *Adult Learning Methods.* M. Galbraith (ed.). Malabar, FL: Krieger Publishing, 1991, pp. 79–96.

Cookson P. S. (ed.). *Recruiting and Retaining Adult Students: New Directions for Continuing Education*, CE#41. San Francisco, CA: Jossey-Bass, 1989.

Cooper, M. K., and Henschke, J. A. "An Update on Andragogy: The International Foundation for Its Research, Theory and Practice." Paper presented at the CPAE Conference, Detroit, Michigan, November, 2003.

Cooper, M. K., and Henschke, J. A. "Toward a Thorough Understanding: The International Foundation of Andragogy in HRD and Adult Education." Paper presented at the Food 'N Thought Session of the Academy of Human Resource Development International Research Conference, Columbus, OH, June 2, 2006.

Copeland, S. T., and Wiswell, A. K. "New Employee Adaptation to the Workplace: A Learning Perspective." *Academy of Human Resource Development 1994 Proceedings*, 1994, pp. 35–40.

Cornwell, J. M., and Manfredo, P. A. "Kolb's Learning Style Theory Revisited." *Educational and Psychological Measurement, 54*, 1994, 317–327.

Costa, P. T., and McCrae, R. R. *Revised NEO Personality Inventory (NEO–PI-R) and NEO Five-Factor Inventory (NEOOFFI) Professional Manual.* Odessa, FL: Psychological Assessment Resources, 1992.

Craig, F. I. M., and Lockhart, R. S. "Levels of Processing: A Framework for Memory Research." *Journal of Verbal Learning and Verbal Behavior, 11*, 1972, 671–684.

Craig, R. L., and Bittel, L. R. *Training and Development Handbook.* New York: McGraw-Hill, 1967, 1976.

Cranton, P. *Planning Instruction for Adult Learners.* Toronto: Wall and Thompson, 1989.

Cronbach, L. J. *Educational Psychology*, 2nd edn. New York: Harcourt, Brace and World, 1963.

Cronbach, L. J. *Toward Reform of Program Evaluation.* San Francisco, CA: Jossey-Bass, 1980.

Crooks, S. M., Klein, J. D., Jones, E. E. K., and Dwye; H. "Effects of Cooperative Learning and Learner-Control Modes in Computer-Based Instruction." *Journal of Research on Computing in Education, 29(2)*, 1996, 109–123.

Cropley, A. J. *Towards a System of Lifelong Education.* Hamburg, Germany: UNESCO Institute for Education, 1980.

Cross, K. P. *Accent on Learning.* San Francisco, CA: Jossey-Bass, 1976.

Cross, K. P. *Adults as Learners.* San Francisco, CA: Jossey-Bass, 1981.

Crow, L. D., and Crow, A. (eds). *Readings in Human Learning.* New York: McKay, 1963.

Crutchfield, R. S. "Nurturing Cognitive Skills of Productive Thinking." *The Psychology of Open Teaching and Learning.* M. L. Silberman, J. S. Allender, and J. M. Yanoff (eds). Boston, MA: Little, Brown, 1972, pp. 189–196.

Crystal, J. C., and Bolles, R. N. *Where Do I Go From Here With My Life?* New York: Seabury, 1974.

Csikszentmihalyi, M. *Beyond Boredom and Anxiety.* San Francisco, CA: Jossey-Bass, 1975.

Cummings, T. G., and Worley, C. *Organization Development and Change*, 6th edn. Cincinatti, OH: Southwestern Publishing, 1997.

Daloz, L. A. *Effective Teaching and Mentoring.* San Francisco, CA: Jossey-Bass, 1986.

Darkenwald, G., and Larson, G. (eds). *Reaching Hard-to-Reach Adults.* San Francisco, CA: Jossey-Bass, 1980.

Darkenwald, G. G., and Merriam, S. B. *Adult Education: Foundations of Practice.* New York: Harper & Row, 1982.

Dave, R. H. "Psychomotor Domain." *Developing and Writing Behavioral Objectives.* R. J. Armstrong (ed.). Tucson, AZ: Educational Innovators Press, 1970, pp. 20–21.

Dave, R. H. *Lifelong Education and School Curriculum.* Monograph No. 1. Hamburg, Germany: UNESCO Institute for Education, 1973.

Dave, R. H. (ed.). *Reflections on Lifelong Education and the School.* Monograph No. 3. Hamburg, Germany: UNESCO Institute for Education, 1975.

Davenport, J. "Adult Educators and Andragogical–Pedagogical Orientations: A Review of the Literature." *MPAEA Journal,* spring, 1984.

Davenport, J. "Is There a Way Out of the Andragogy Morass?." *Lifelong Learning, 11,* 1987, 17–20.

Davenport, J., and Davenport, J. A. "A Chronology and Analysis of the Androgogy Debate." *Adult Education Quarterly, 35,* 1985, 152–159.

David, T. G., and Wright, B. D. (eds). *Learning Environments.* Chicago, IL: University of Chicago Press, 1975.

Davis, G. A., and Scott, J. A. *Training Creative Thinking.* New York: Holt, Rinehart, and Winston, 1971.

Davis, R. C. *Planning Human Resource Development.* Chicago, IL: Rand-McNally, 1966.

Day, C., and Baskett, H. K. "Discrepancies between Intentions and Practice: Re-examining Some Basic Assumptions about Adult and Continuing Professional Education." *International Journal of Lifelong Education,* 1982, 143–156.

Deal, T. E., and Kennedy, A. A. *Corporate Cultures: The Rites and Rituals of Corporate Life.* Reading, MA: Addison-Wesley, 1982.

Dean, R. S., and Kulhavy, R. W. "Influences on Spatial Organization in Prose Learning." *Journal of Educational Psychology, 73,* 1981, 57–64.

Delahaye, B. L., Limerick, D. C., and Hearn, G. "The Relationship between Andragogical and Pedagogical Orientations and the Implications for Adult Learning." *Adult Education Quarterly, 44(4),* 1994, 187–200.

Delcourt, M. A., and Kinzie, M. B. "Computer Technologies in Teacher Education: The Measurement of Attitudes and Self-Efficacy." *Journal of Research and Development in Education, 27,* 1993, 35–41.

Dentwhistle, N. *Styles of Learning and Teaching.* New York: Wiley, 1982.

Dewey, J. *How We Think.* Boston, MA: Heath, 1933.

Dewey, J. *Experience and Education.* New York: Macmillan, 1938.

Dirkx, J. M. "Human Resource Development as Adult Education: Fostering the Educative Workplace." *Workplace Learning: Debating Five Critical Questions of Theory and Practice.* R. W. Rowden (ed.). San Francisco, CA: Jossey-Bass, 1996, pp. 41–47.

Dirkx, J. M., and Prenger, S. M. *A Guide to Planning and Implementing Instruction for Adults: A Theme-Based Approach.* San Francisco, CA: Jossey-Bass, 1997.

Di Vesta, F. J. "Cognitive Development." *Encyclopedia of Educational Research,* 5th edn. New York: Macmillan and Free Press, 1982.

Dixon, G. *What Works at Work: Lessons from the Masters.* Minneapolis, MI: Lakewood, 1988.

Dixon, N. "Relationship between Training Responses on Participant Reaction Forms and Post Test Scores." *Human Resource Development Quarterly, 1(2),* 1991, 129–137.

Dobbs, R. C. *Adult Education in America: An Anthological Approach.* Cassville, MO: Litho Printers, 1970.

Donahue, W., and Tibbitts, C. *The New Frontiers of Aging.* Ann Arbor: University of Michigan Press, 1957.

Dover, K. H. "Adult Learning Theorist: Malcolm S. Knowles—Biography." *Adult/ Continuing Education: A Free Newsletter Guide*, 2006.

Draper, J. A. "The Metamorphoses of Andragogy." *Canadian Journal for the Study of Adult Education, 12(1)*, 1998, 3–26.

Dressel, P. L. *Handbook of Academic Evaluation.* San Francisco, CA: Jossey-Bass, 1976.

Drews, E. M. "Self-Actualization. A New Focus for Education." *Learning and Mental Health in School.* W. B. Waetjen, and R. R. Leeper (eds). Washington, DC: Association for Supervision and Curriculum Development, NEA, 1966, pp. 99–124.

Drucker, P. E. *The Effective Executive.* New York: Harper and Row, 1967.

Dubin, R. *Theory Building: A Practical Guide to the Construction and Testing of Theoretical Models.* New York: The Free Press, 1969.

Dubin, R. *Theory Building*, rev. edn. New York: The Free Press, 1978.

Dubin, R., and Raveggia, T. C. *The Teaching–Learning Paradox: A Comparative Analysis of College Teaching Methods.* Eugene: Center for the Advanced Study of Educational Administration, University of Oregon, 1968.

Duffy, T. M., and Jonassen, D. H. *Constructivism and the Technology of Instruction: A Conversation.* Hillsdale, NJ: Erlbaum, 1992.

Dunn, K., and Dunn, R. Learning Style as a Criterion for Placement in Alternative Programs. *Phi Delta Kappa, 36*, 1974, 275–279.

Dunn, K., Dunn, R., and Price, G. E. *Learning Styles Inventory.* Lawrence, KS: Price Systems, 1989.

Dykes, A. R. *Faculty Participation in Academic Decision Making.* Washington, DC: American Council on Education, 1968.

Eble, K. E. *The Craft of Teaching.* San Francisco, CA: Jossey-Bass, 1976.

Edvinsson, L., and Malone, M. S. *Intellectual Capital.* New York: HarperCollins, 1997.

Eiben, R., and Milliren, A. (eds). *Educational Change: A Humanistic Approach.* La Jolla, CA: University Associates, 1976.

Elias, J. L. "Andragogy Revisited." *Adult Education, 29*, 1979, 252–255.

Elias, J. L., and Merriam, S. *Philosophical Foundations of Adult Education.* Huntington, NY: Krieger, 1980.

Erikson, E. H. *Childhood and Society.* New York: W. W. Norton, 1950.

Erikson, E. H. *Identity and the Life Cycle.* New York: International Universities Press, 1959.

Erikson, E. H. *Insight and Responsibility.* New York: W. W. Norton, 1964.

Ertmer, P. A., and Newby, T. J. "Behaviorism, Cognitivism, Constructivism: Comparing Critical Features from a Design Perspective." *Performance Improvement Quarterly, 6*, 1993, 50–72.

Ertmer, P. A., Evenbeck, E., Cennamo, K. S., and Lehman, J. D. "Enhancing Self-Efficacy for Computer Technologies through the Use of Positive Classroom Experience." *Educational Technology Research and Development, 42(3)*, 1994, 45–62.

Estes, W. J. "The Statistical Approach to Learning Theory." *Psychology: A Study of a Science*, Vol. II. S. Koch (ed.). New York: McGraw-Hill, 1959.

Etzioni, A. *Complex Organizations.* New York: The Free Press, 1961.

Etzioni, A. *A Sociological Reader on Complex Organizations.* New York: Holt, Rinehart and Winston, 1969.

Eurich, N. P. *Corporate Classrooms: The Learning Business.* Lawrenceville, NJ: Princeton University Press, 1985.

Even, M. J. "Adapting Cognitive Style Theory in Practice." *Lifelong Learning; The Adult Years*, *5(5)*, 1982, 14–16.

Ewell, P. T. (ed.). *Assessing Educational Outcomes*. San Francisco, CA: Jossey-Bass, 1985.

Farmer, D. W. *Enhancing Student Learning*. Wilkes-Barre, PA: King's College, 1988.

Faure, E., et al. *Learning to Be: The World of Education Today and Tomorrow*. Paris: UNESCO, 1972.

Feldman, D. C. "Socialization, Resocialization, and Training: Reframing the Research Agenda." *Training and Development in Organizations*. I. L. Goldstein (ed.). San Francisco, CA: Jossey-Bass, 1989, pp. 376–416.

Felker, D. W. *Building Positive Self-Concepts*. Minneapolis, MN: Burgess Publishing, 1974.

Feur, D., and Gerber, B. "Uh-oh. . . Second Thoughts about Adult Learning Theory." *Training*, *25(12)*, 1988, 125–149.

Fields, H. *Journal of Adult Education*, *12*, January 1940, 44–45.

Fingeret A., and Jurmo P. (eds). *Involving Learners in Literacy Education*. San Francisco, CA: Jossey-Bass, 1989.

Fisher, C. D. "Organizational Socialization: An Integrative Review." *Research in Personnel and Human Resources Management, Vol. 4*. G. R. Ferris, and K. M. Rowland (eds). Greenwich, CT: JAI Press, 1986, pp. 101–145.

Flanders, N. A., and Simon, A. *Teacher Influence, Pupil Attitudes, and Achievement*. US Department of Health, Education and Welfare, Office of Education. Cooperative Research Monograph No. 12 (OE-25040). Washington, DC: Government Printing Office, 1965.

Flannery, D. D. "Global and Analytical Ways of Processing Information." *New Directions in Adult and Continuing Education: Applying Cognitive Learning Theory to Adult Learning*. D. D. Flannery (ed.). San Francisco, CA: Jossey-Bass, 1993.

Flavell, J. H. "Cognitive Changes in Adulthood." *Life-Span Development Psychology*. L. R. Goulet, and P. B. Bakes (eds). New York: Academic Press, 1970, pp. 247–253.

Flavell, J. H. "Metacognition and Cognitive Monitoring: A New Area of Cognitive Developmental Inquiry." *American Psychologist*, *34*, 1980, 906–911.

Foss, D. G., and Harwood, D. A. "Memory for Sentences: Implications for Human Associative Memory." *Journal of Verbal Learning and Verbal Behavior*, *14*, 1975, 1–16.

Freedman, R. D., and Stumpf, S. A. "Learning Style Theory: Less Than Meets the Eye." *Academy of Management Review*, *5*, 1980, 445–447.

Freire, P. *Pedagogy of the Oppressed*. New York: Herder and Herder, 1970.

Froland, C., et al. *Helping Networks and Human Services*. Beverly Hills, CA: Sage, 1981.

Furter, P. *Grandeur et Misere de la Pedagogie*. University of Neuchatel, 1971.

Gage, N. L. *Teacher Effectiveness and Teacher Education*. Palo Alto, CA: Pacific Books, 1972.

Gage, N. L., and Berliner, D. C. *Educational Psychology*, 4th edn. Houston, TX: Houghton Mifflin, 1988.

Gagné, R. M. *The Conditions of Learning*. New York: Holt, Rinehart and Winston, 1965.

Gagné, R. M. "Policy Implications and Future Research. A Response." *Do Teachers Make a Difference?* A Report on Research on Pupil Achievement. US Department of Health, Education and Welfare, Office of Education. Washington, DC: Government Printing Office, 1970.

Gagné, R. M. "Domains of Learning." *Interchange*, 1972, 1–8.

Gagné, R. M. *The Conditions of Learning*, 4th edn. New York: Holt, Rinehart and Winston, 1985.

Gagné, R. M. "Introduction." *Instructional Technology: Foundations.* Hillsdale, NJ: Erlbaum, 1987, pp. 1–9.

Gagné, R., and Briggs, L. *Principles of Instructional Design*, 2nd edn. New York: Holt, Rinehart and Winston, 1979.

Gagné, R., Briggs, L., and Wager, W. *Principals of Instructional Design*, 3rd edn. New York: Holt, Reinhart and Winston, 1988.

Gagné, R. M., Briggs, L. J., and Wager, W. W. *Principles of Instructional Design*, 4th edn. Fort Worth, TX: Harcourt Brace College Publishers, 1992.

Gale, R. *The Psychology of Being Yourself.* Englewood Cliffs, NJ: Prentice-Hall, 1974.

Gambrill, E. D. *Behavior Modification: Handbook of Assessment, Intervention, and Evaluation.* San Francisco, CA: Jossey-Bass, 1977.

Gardner, H. *Frames of Mind.* New York: Basic Books, 1983.

Gardner, J. *Self-Renewal: The Individual and the Innovative Society.* New York: Harper and Row, 1963.

Garrision, D. R. "Self-Directed Learning: Toward a Comprehensive Model." *Adult Education Quarterly, 48,* 1997, 18–33.

Gayeski, D. "Changing Roles and Professional Challenges for Human Performance Technology." *Performance Improvement Quarterly, 8(2),* 1995, 6–16.

Gent, van Bastian. "Andragogy." *International Encyclopedia of Adult Education and Training.* A. C. Tuijnman (ed.). Oxford: Pergamon, 1996, pp. 114–117.

Gessner, R. (ed.). *The Democratic Man: Selected Writings of Eduard C. Lindeman.* Boston, MA: Beacon, 1956.

Getzels, J. W., and Jackson, P. W. *Creativity and Intelligence.* New York: Wiley, 1962.

Getzels, J. W., Lipham, J. M., and Campbell, R. F. *Educational Administration as a Social Process.* New York: Harper and Row, 1968.

Gibbons, A. S., and Fairweather, P. G. "Computer-Based Instruction." *Training & Retraining: A Handbook for Business, Industry, Government, and the Military.* S. Tobias, and J. D. Fletcher (eds). New York: Macmillan Reference USA, 2000, pp. 410–442.

Gibbons, M. "A Working Model of the Learning How to Learn Process." *Learning How to Learn across the Life Span.* R. Smith, and associates (eds). San Francisco, CA: Jossey-Bass, 1990.

Gill, S. J. "Shifting Gears for High Performance." *Training and Development, 49(5),* 1995, 25–31.

Gilley, J., and Eggland, S. A. *Principles of Human Resource Development.* Reading, MA: Addison–Wesley, 1989.

Glaser, R. (ed.). *Training Research and Education.* Pittsburgh: University of Pittsburgh Press, 1962.

Glick, M. *The Instructional Leader and the Brain: Using Neuroscience to Inform Practice.* Thousand Oaks, CA: Sage, 2011.

Goble, F. *The Third Force: The Psychology of Abraham Maslow.* New York: Pocket Books, 1971.

Godbey, G. C. *Applied Andragogy: A Practical Manual for the Continuing Education of Adults.* College Station: Continuing Education Division, Pennsylvania State University, 1978.

Goldstein, K. M., and Blackman, S. *Cognitive Style: Five Approaches and Relevant Research.* New York: Wiley-Interscience, 1978.

Goodlad, J. I. *The Dynamics of Educational Change.* New York: McGraw–Hill, 1975.

Gordon, I. J. *Criteria for Theories of Instruction.* Washington, DC: Association for Supervision and Curriculum Development, NEA, 1968.

Goswami, U. "Principles of Learning, Implications for Teaching: A Cognitive Neuroscience Perspective." *Journal of Philosophy of Education, 42*, 2008, 3–4.

Gould, S., Chairman of the Commission on Nontraditional Study. *Diversity by Design.* San Francisco, CA: Jossey-Bass, 1973.

Goulet, L. R., and Baltes, P. B. *Life-Span Developmental Psychology.* New York: Academic Press, 1970.

Gowan, J. C., et al. *Creativity: Its Educational Implications.* New York: Wiley, 1967.

Gowan, J. C., and associates. *Preparing Educators of Adults.* San Francisco, CA: Jossey-Bass, 1981.

Grabowski, S. M. (ed.). *Adult Learning and Instruction.* Syracuse, NY: ERIC Clearinghouse on Adult Education, 1970.

Grabowski, S. M., and Mason, D. W. *Learning for Aging.* Washington, DC: Adult Education Association of the USA, 1974.

Grace, A. P. "Striking a Critical Pose: Andragogy—Missing Links, Missing Values." *International Journal of Lifelong Education, 15*, 1996, 382–392.

Grady, C. "The Cognitive Neuroscience of Ageing." *Nature Reviews, 13*, 2012, 491–505.

Graen, G. B. "Role-Making Processes within Complex Organizations." *Handbook of Industrial and Organizational Psychology.* M. D. Dunnette (ed.). Chicago, IL: Rand McNally, 1976, pp. 1201–1245.

Granick, S., and Patterson, R. D. *Human Aging II.* US Department of Health, Education, and Welfare, National Institute of Mental Health (HSM 71–9037). Washington, DC: Government Printing Office, 1971.

Grant, G., et al. *On Competence.* San Francisco, CA: Jossey-Bass, 1979.

Grattan, G. H. *In Quest of Knowledge: A Historical Perspective of Adult Education.* Chicago, IL: Follett, 1955.

Gray, S. H. "The Effect of Sequence Control on Computer Assisted Learning." *Journal of Computer-Based Instruction, 14(2)*, 1987, 54–56.

Gray, S. H. "The Effect of Locus of Control and Sequence Control on Computerized Information Retrieval and Retention." *Journal of Educational Computing Research, 5(4)*, 1989, 459–471.

Greiner, L. E. (ed.). *Organizational Change and Development.* Homewood, IL: Irwin, 1971.

Gregorc, A. F. "Style as a Symptom: A Phenomenological Perspective." *Theory into Practice, 23*(1), 1984, 51–55.

Griffiths, D. E. (ed.). "Behavioral Science and Educational Administration." *Sixty-Third Yearbook of the National Society for the Study of Education.* Chicago, IL: NSSE, 1964.

Grippin, P., and Peters, S. *Learning Theory and Learning Outcomes.* New York: University Press of America, 1984.

Gross, C. G. "Neurogenesis in the Adult Brain: Death of a Dogma." *Nature Reviews, 11,* 2000, 7–73.

Gross, R. *The Lifelong Learner: A Guide to Self-Development.* New York: Simon and Schuster, 1977.

Gross, R. *Invitation to Lifelong Learning.* Chicago, IL: Follett, 1982.

Grow, G. O. "Teaching Learners to Be Self-Directed." *Adult Education Quarterly, 41,* 1991, 125–149.

Guba, E. G., and Lincoln, Y. S. *Effective Evaluation.* San Francisco, CA: Jossey-Bass, 1981.

Gubrium, J. E. (ed.). *Time, Roles, and Self in Old Age.* New York: Human Sciences Press, 1976.

Gubrium, J. E., and Buckholdt, D. R. *Toward Maturity: The Social Processing of Human Development.* San Francisco, CA: Jossey-Bass, 1977.

Guglielmino, L. M. "Development of the Self-Directed Learning Readiness Scale" (Doctoral dissertation, University of Georgia, 1977). *Dissertation Abstracts International, 38,* 1977, 6467A.

Guilford, J. P. *The Nature of Human Intelligence.* New York: McGraw-Hill, 1967.

Hadley, H. *Development of an Instrument to Determine Adult Educators' Orientation: Andragogical or Pedagogical* (UMI No. 75–12, 228), 1975.

Hagen, M. and Park, S. "We Knew It All Along! Using Cognitive Science to Explain How Andragogy Works." *Proceedings of the 2014 Academy of Human Resource Development International Research Conference,* 2014.

Haggard, E. A. "Learning a Process of Change." *Readings in Human Learning.* L. D. Crow, and A. Crow (eds). New York: McKay, 1963, pp. 19–27.

Hall, G. E., and Jones, H. L. *Competency-Based Education: A Process for the Improvement of Education.* Englewood Cliffs, NJ: Prentice-Hall, 1976.

Handy, H. W., and Hussain, K. M. *Network Analysis for Educational Management.* Englewood Cliffs, NJ: Prentice-Hall, 1969.

Hannafin, M. J. "Guidelines for Using Locus of Instructional Control in the Design of Computer-Assisted Instruction." *Journal of Instructional Development, 7(3),* 1984, 6–10.

Hannafin, R. D., and Sullivan, H. J. "Learner Control in Full and Lean CAI Programs." *Educational Technology Research and Development, 43(1),* 1995, 19–30.

Hannum, W. "Designing Courseware to Fit Subject Matter Structure." *Instructional Designs for Microcomputer Courseware.* D. H. Jonassen (ed.). Hillsdale, NJ: Lawrence Erlbaum, 1988, pp. 275–296.

Hare, P. *Handbook of Small Group Research.* New York: Free Press of Glencoe, 1962.

Hare, P. *Small Group Process.* New York: Macmillan, 1969.

Hare, V. C., Jr. *Systems Analysis. A Diagnostic Approach.* New York: Harcourt, Brace, and World, 1967.

Harman, D. *Illiteracy: A National Dilemma.* New York: Cambridge, 1987.

Harrington, F. H. *The Future of Adult Education.* San Francisco, CA: Jossey-Bass, 1977.

Harris, D., and Bell, C. *Assessment and Evaluation for Learning.* New York: Nichols, 1986.

Harris, P. R., and Moran, R. T. *Managing Cultural Differences*, 4th edn. Houston, TX: Gulf, 1996.

Harris, T. L., and Schwahn, W. E. *Selected Readings on the Learning Process.* New York: Oxford University Press, 1961.

Hartley, H. I. *Educational Planning–Programming–Budgeting: A Systems Approach.* Englewood Cliffs, NJ: Prentice-Hall, 1968.

Hartree, A. "Malcolm Knowles' Theory of Andragogy: A Critique." *International Journal of Lifelong Education, 3,* 1984, 203–210.

Havighurst, R. *Developmental Tasks and Education,* 2nd edn. New York: McKay, 1972.

Hayes, C. D. *Self-University.* Wasilla, AK: Autodidactic Press, 1989.

Heerman, B. (ed.). *Personal Computers and the Adult Learner.* San Francisco, CA: Jossey-Bass, 1986.

Heerman, B. (ed.). *Teaching and Learning with Computers.* San Francisco, CA: Jossey-Bass, 1988.

Hefferlin, J. B. L. *Dynamics of Academic Reform.* San Francisco, CA: Jossey-Bass, 1969.

Heifernan, J. M., Macy, E. L., and Vickers, D. E. *Educational Brokering: A New Service for Adult Learners.* Washington, DC: National Center for Educational Brokering, 1976.

Hendrickson, A. (ed.). *A Manual for Planning Educational Programs for Older Adults.* Tallahassee: Department of Adult Education, Florida State University, 1973.

Henschke, J. A. "Identifying Appropriate Adult Educator Practices: Beliefs, Feelings and Behaviors." *Proceedings of the Eighth Annual Midwest Research-To-Practice Conference in Adult, Continuing and Community Education.* St. Louis: University of Missouri, 1989.

Henschke, J. A. "Theory and Practice on Preparing Human Resource Development Professionals." *Proceedings of Academy of Human Resource Development Research Conference.* St. Louis: University of Missouri, 1995, pp. 1–11.

Henschke, J. A. "Historical Antecedents Shaping Conceptions of Andragogy: A Comparison of Sources and Roots." Paper presented at the International Conference on Research in Comparative Andragogy, September 1998, Radovljica, Slovenia.

Henschke, J. A. http://www.lindenwood.edu/education/andragogy.cfm and http://www.umsl.edu/-henschke. 2000ff.; 2009.

Henschke, J. A. Andragogy Website, 2003. http://www.umsl.edu/-henschke.

Herzberg, F. *Work and the Nature of Man.* Cleveland, OH: World Publishing, 1966.

Herzberg, F., et al. *The Motivation to Work.* New York: Wiley, 1959.

Hesburgh, T. M., Miller, P. A., and Wharton, C. R., Jr. *Patterns for Lifelong Learning.* San Francisco, CA: Jossey-Bass, 1973.

Heyman, M. M. *Criteria and Guidelines for the Evaluation of Inservice Training.* Washington, DC: Social and Rehabilitation Service, Department of Health, Education and Welfare, 1967.

Hickcox, L. K. "Learning Styles: A Survey of Adult Learning Style Inventory Models." *The Importance of Learning Styles: Understanding the Implications for Learning, Course Design, and Education.* R. R. Sims, and S. J. Sims (eds). Westport, CT: Greenwood, 1995.

Hicks, W. D., and Klimoski, R. J. "Entry into Training Programs and Its Effects on Training Outcomes: A Field Experiment." *Academy of Management Journal, 30,* 1987, 542–552.

Hiemstra, R. "Three Underdeveloped Models of Adult Learning." *New Directions for Adult and Continuing Education no. 57—An Update on Adult Learning Theory.* S. B. Merriam (ed.). San Francisco, CA: Jossey-Bass, 1993.

Hiemstra, R. *Moving from Pedagogy to Andragogy; With Annotated Bibliography of Sources Related to Andragogy.* Retrieved October 2, 2006. N.d.

Hiemstra, R., and Sisco, B. *Individualizing Instruction: Making Learning Personal, Empowering, and Successful.* San Francisco, CA: Jossey-Bass, 1990.

Hilgard, E. R., and Bower, G. H. *Theories of Learning.* New York: Appleton-Century-Crofts, 1966.

Hill, J. E., and Nunhey, D. N. *Personalizing Educational Programs Utilizing Cognitive Style Mapping.* Bloomfield Hills, MI: Oakland Community College, 1971.

Hill, J. R., and Hannafin, M. J. "Cognitive Strategies and Learning from the World Wide Web." *Educational Technology Research & Development, 45(4)*, 1997, 37–64.

Hill, T., Smith, N. D., and Mann, M. F. "Role of Efficacy Expectations in Predicting the Decision to use Advanced Technologies: The Case of Computers." *Journal of Applied Psychology, 72(2)*, 1987, 307–313.

Holden, A. M. "The Effects of Metacognitive Advice and Control of Sequence on Student Achievement and Attitude toward Computer-Assisted Instruction and Content." Unpublished doctoral dissertation, Louisiana State University, Baton Rouge, LA, 1995.

Holton, E. F. *The New Professional.* Princeton, NJ: Peterson's Guides, 1991, 1998.

Holton, E. F. "College Graduates' Experiences and Attitudes during Organizational Entry." *Human Resource Development Quarterly*, 1995.

Holton, E. F. "New Employee Development: A Review and Reconceptualization." *Human Resource Development Quarterly, 7*, 1996, 233–252.

Holton, E. F. "Newcomer Entry into Organizational Cultures: A Neglected Performance Issue." *Pursuing Performance Improvement.* P. Dean (ed.). Washington, DC: International Society for Performance Improvement, 1998a.

Holton, E. F. "Performance Domains: Bounding the Theory and Practice." *Advances in Developing Human Resources.* R. Swanson (series ed.) and R. Torraco (vol. ed.). Washington, DC: ISPI Press, 1998b.

Holton, E. F. *The Senior Year: A Beginning, Not an End.* J. Gardner, and G. Vander Veer (eds). San Francisco, CA: Jossey-Bass, 1998c.

Holton, E., Wilson, L., and Bates, R. "Toward Development of a Generalized Instrument to Measure Andragogy." *Human Resource Development Quarterly, 20(2)*, 2009, 169–193.

Holton, E., Bates, R., Seyler, D., and Carvalho, M. "Toward Construct Validation of a Transfer Climate Instrument." *Human Resource Development Quarterly, 8*, 1997.

Homey, K. *Feminine Psychology.* New York: W. W. Norton, 1967.

Hoods Woods. *Andragogy: The Act, Process, or Art of Imparting Knowledge and Skill to Adults.* 1998. http://www.survival.com/gogy.htm. Retrieved October 23, 2007.

hooks, b. "Theory as Liberatory Practice." *Teaching to Transgress.* b. hooks. New York: Routledge, 1994, pp. 59–76.

Horn, J. L., and Cattell, R. B. "Refinement and Test of the Theory of Fluid and Crystallized Intelligence." *Journal of Educational Psychology, 57*, 1966, 253–270.

Hornstein, H. A., et al. *Social Intervention: A Social Science Approach.* New York: The Free Press, 1971.

Hospital Continuing Education Project. *Training and Continuing Education.* Chicago, IL: Hospital Research and Educational Trust, 1970.

Houle, C. O. *The Effective Board.* New York: Association Press, 1960.

Houle, C. O. *The Inquiring Mind.* Madison: University of Wisconsin Press, 1961.

Houle, C. O. *Continuing Your Education.* New York: McGraw-Hill, 1964.

Houle, C. O. *The Design of Education.* San Francisco, CA: Jossey-Bass, 1972.

Houle, C. O. *The External Degree.* San Francisco, CA: Jossey-Bass, 1973.

Houle, C. O. *Continuing Learning in the Professions.* San Francisco, CA: Jossey-Bass, 1980.

Houle, C. O. *Patterns of Learning: New Perspectives on Life-Span Education.* San Francisco, CA: Jossey-Bass, 1984.

Houle, C. O. *Governing Boards.* San Francisco, CA: Jossey-Bass, 1989.

Houle, C. O. *The Literature of Adult Education: A Bibliographic Essay.* San Francisco, CA: Jossey-Bass, 1992.

Howe, M. J. A. *Adult Learning: Psychological Research and Applications.* New York: Wiley, 1977.

Huber, R. L. "Memory Is Not Only About Storage." *Applying Cognitive Learning Theory to Adult Learning.* D. D. Flannery (ed.). San Francisco, CA: Jossey-Bass, 1993, pp. 35–46.

Hultsch, D. F., and Deutsch, E. *Adult Development and Aging: A Life Span Perspective.* New York: McGraw-Hill, 1981.

Hunkins, F. P. *Involving Students in Questioning.* Boston, MA: Allyn and Bacon, 1975.

Hunt, M. *The Universe Within: A New Science Explores the Human Mind.* New York: Simon and Schuster, 1982.

Hutchings, P., and Wutzdorff, A. (eds). *Knowing and Doing: Learning through Experience. New Directions for Teaching and Learning*, TL#35. San Francisco, CA: Jossey-Bass, 1988.

Ickes, W., and Knowles, E. S. *Personality, Roles, and Social Behavior.* New York: Springer-Verlag, 1982.

Illich, I. *Deschooling Society.* New York: Harper and Row, 1970.

Illich, I. *Tools for Conviviality.* New York: Harper and Row, 1973.

Illsley, P. (ed.). *Improving Conference Design and Outcomes.* San Francisco, CA: Jossey-Bass, 1985.

Immordino-Yang, M. H., and Faeth, M. "The Role of Emotion and Skilled Intuition in Learning." *Mind, Brain and Education: Neuroscience Implications for the Classroom.* D. A. Sousa (ed.). Bloomington, IN: Solution Tree Press, 2010.

Ingalls, J. *Human Energy: The Critical Factor for Individuals and Organizations.* Reading, MA: Addison-Wesley, 1976.

Ingalls, J. D., and Arceri, J. M. *A Trainer's Guide to Andragogy.* Social and Rehabilitation Service. US Department of Health, Education, and Welfare (SRS 72–05301). Washington, DC: Government Printing Office, 1972.

Iscoe, I., and Stevenson, W. W. (eds). *Personality Development in Children.* Austin: University of Texas Press, 1960.

Jacks, L. P. *Journal of Adult Education, I*, February 1, 1929, pp. 7–10.

Jacobs, R. L. "Structured On-the-Job Training." *Handbook of Human Performance Technology.* H. Stolovitch, and E. Keeps (eds). San Francisco, CA: Jossey-Bass, 1992.

Jacobs, R. L., and Jones, M. J. *Structured On-the-Job Training.* San Francisco, CA: Berrett-Koehler, 1995.

James, W. B., and Blank, W. E. "Review and Critique of Available Learning-Style Instruments for Adults." *Applying Cognitive Learning Theory to Adult Learning.* D. D. Flannery (ed.). San Francisco, CA: Jossey-Bass, 1993.

James, W. B., and Galbraith, M. W. "Perceptual Learning Styles: Implications and Techniques for the Practitioner." *Lifelong Learning, 8,* 1985, 20–23.

Janniro, M. J. "Effects of Computer-Based Instruction on Student Learning of Psychophysiological Detection of Deception Test Question Formulation." *Journal of Computer-Based Instruction, 20(2),* 1993, 58–62.

Jaques, D. *Learning in Groups.* Dover, NH: Croom-Helm, 1984.

Jarvis, P. "Andragogy: A Sign of the Times." *Studies in the Education of Adults, 16,* 1984, 32–38.

Jarvis, P. *Adult Learning in the Social Context.* London: Croom-Helm, 1987a.

Jarvis, P. "Towards a Discipline of Adult Education?" *Twentieth Century Thinkers in Adult Education.* P. Jarvis (ed.). London: Routledge, 1987b, pp. 301–313.

Jawahar, I. M. "The Influence of Dispositional Factors and Situational Constraints on End User Performance: A Replication and Extension." *Journal of End User Computing, 14(4),* 2002, 17–37.

Jawahar, I. M., and Elango, B. "The Effect of Attitudes, Goal Setting and Self-Efficacy on End User Performance." *Journal of End User Computing, 13(2),* 2001, 40.

Jawahar, I. M., Stone, T. H., and Cooper, W. H. "Activating Resources in Organizations." *Research in Organizational Change and Development.* R. W. Woodman, and W. A. Passmore (eds). Greenwich, CT: JAI Press, 1992, pp. 153–196.

Jensen, G., Liveright, A. A., and Hallenbeck, W. *Adult Education: Outlines of an Emerging Field of University Study.* Washington, DC: Adult Education Association, 1964.

John, M. T. *Geragogy: A Theory for Teaching the Elderly.* Reading, MA: Addison-Wesley, 1987.

Johnson, D. W., and Johnson, E. P. *Learning Together and Alone: Cooperation, Competition, and Individualization.* Englewood Cliffs, NJ: Prentice-Hall, 1975.

Johnson, L. *Understanding and Managing Conflict.* 1991, 1992, 1993.

Johnson, L. F. "Dialogues in Andragogy." Paper presented to a Doctoral Research Graduate Credit Seminar on Andragogy, University of Missouri–St. Louis. Winter Semester, 2000.

Johnson, L., Adams Becker, S., Estrada, V., and Freeman, A. *NMC Horizon Report: 2014 Higher Education Edition.* Austin, TX: New Media Consortium, 2014.

Johnson, S. D., and Aragon, S. R. "An Instructional Strategy Framework for Online Learning Environments." *Proceedings of the Academy of Human Resource Development Annual Conference (41–1).* T. M. Egan and S. A. Lynham (eds). Bowling Green, OH: Academy of Human Resource Development, 2002.

Johnstone, J. W. C., and Rivera, W. *Volunteers for Learning: A Study of the Educational Pursuits of American Adults.* Chicago, IL: Aldine, 1965.

Jonassen, D. H., and Grabowski, B. L. *Handbook of Individual Differences, Learning, and Instruction.* Hillsdale, NJ: Erlbaum, 1993.

Jones, G. B., et al. *New Designs and Methods for Delivering Human Developmental Services.* New York: Human Sciences Press, 1977.

Jones, H. E. "Intelligence and Problem Solving." *Handbook of Aging and the Individual*. J. E. Birren (ed.). Chicago, IL: University of Chicago Press, 1959, pp. 700–738.

Jones, K. *Simulations: A Handbook for Teachers*. New York: Nichols, 1980.

Jones, R. M. *Fantasy and Feeling in Education*. New York: New York University Press, 1968.

Jones, T. H., and Paolucci, R. "Research Framework and Dimensions for Evaluating the Effectiveness of Educational Technology Systems on Learning Outcomes." *Journal of Research on Computing in Education, 32(1)*, 1999, 17–27.

Jorde-Bloom, P. "Self-Efficacy Expectations as a Predictor of Computer Use: A Look at Early Childhood Administrators." *Computers in the Schools, 5*, 1988, 45–63.

Joughin, G. "Cognitive Style and Adult Learning Principles." *International Journal of Lifelong Education, 11(1)*, 1992, 3–14.

Jourard, S. M. "Fascination. A Phenomenological Perspective on Independent Learning." *The Psychology of Open Teaching and Learning*. M. L. Silberman, et al. (eds). Boston, MA: Little, Brown, 1972, pp. 66–75.

Joyce, B., and Weil, M. *Models of Teaching*. Englewood Cliffs, NJ: Prentice-Hall, 1972.

Jung, C. *The Nature of the Psyche*. Translated by R. E. C. Hull. Bollingen Series XX, Vol. 8. Princeton, NJ: Princeton University Press, 1969.

Kabanoff, B., and O'Brien, G. E. "Work and Leisure: A Task Attributes Analysis." *Journal of Applied Psychology, 65*, 1980, 596–609.

Kabuga, C. "Why Andragogy in Developing Countries?" *Adult Education and Development: Journal for Adult Education in Africa, Asia, and Latin America*, 1977.

Kagan, J. (ed.). *Creativity and Learning*. Boston, MA: Houghton-Mifflin, 1967.

Kagan, J., and Moss, H. A. *Birth to Maturity: A Study in Psychological Development*. New York: Wiley, 1962.

Kahle, L. R. "Stimulus Condition Self-Selection by Males in the Interaction of the Locus of Control and Skill–Chance Situations." *Journal of Personality and Social Psychology, 36*, 1980, 50–56.

Kajee, L. "Making Waves, Not Just Surfing the Net: ICT and Learning in the ESL Classroom." Johannesburg, South Africa: University of the Witwatersrand. Unpublished paper. N.d.

Kaminsky, S. *Comparing Pedagogy and Andragogy for Both Common and Dissimilar Meanings*. http://www.usm.maine.edu/~dlarson/kaminsky2.htm. N.d.

Kaplan, A. *The Conduct of Inquiry*. San Francisco, CA: Chandler, 1964.

Kapp, A. "Die andragogik ober bildung im mannlichen alter." *Platons Erziehungslehre, als Padagogik fur die Einzelnen und als Staatspadagogik*. Germany: Minden und Leipzig, 1833.

Kast, F. E., and Rosenzweig, J. E. *Organization and Management: A Systems Approach*. New York: McGraw-Hill, 1970.

Kastenbaum, R. (ed.). *New Thoughts on Old Age*. New York: Springer, 1964.

Kastenbaum, R. (ed.). *Contributions to the Psycho-Biology of Aging*. New York: Springer, 1965.

Katz, D., and Kahn, R. L. *The Social Psychology of Organizations*. New York: Wiley, 1966.

Katz, R. "Organizational Stress and Early Socialization Experiences." *Human Stress and Cognition in Organizations.* T. A. Beehr, and R. S. Bhagat (eds). New York: Wiley, 1985, pp. 117–139.

Kaufman, A. S. *Assessing Adolescent and Adults Intelligence.* Boston, MA: Allyn and Bacon, 1990.

Kaufman, R. *Educational System Planning.* Englewood Cliffs, NJ: Prentice-Hall, 1972.

Keeton, M. T., et al. *Experiential Learning: Rationale, Characteristics, Assessment.* San Francisco, CA: Jossey-Bass, 1976.

Kelly, G. S. *The Psychology of Personal Constructs.* New York: W. W. Norton, 1955.

Kember, D., and Murphy, D. "Alternative New Directions for Instructional Design." *Educational Technology, 30(4)*, 1990, 42–47.

Kember, D., and Murphy, D. "The Impact of Student Learning Research and the Nature of Design on ID Fundamentals." *Instructional Design Fundamentals: A Reconsideration.* B. B. Seels (ed.). Englewood Cliffs, NJ: Educational Technologies, 1995.

Kempfer, H. H. *Adult Education.* New York: McGraw-Hill, 1955.

Kerwin, M. *The Relationship of Selected Factors to the Educational Orientation of Andragogically and Pedagogically-Oriented Educators Teaching in Four of North Carolina's Two-Year Colleges* (UMI No. 7915566), 1979.

Kidd, J. R. *How Adults Learn.* New York: Association Press, 1959, 1973.

Kidd, J. R. *How Adults Learn.* Englewood Cliffs, NJ: Prentice-Hall, 1978.

Kingsley, H. L., and Garry, R. *The Nature and Conditions of Learning*, 2nd edn. Englewood Cliffs, NJ: Prentice-Hall, 1957.

Kinzie, M. B., Sullivan, H. J., and Berdel, R. L. "Learner Control and Achievement in Science Computer-Assisted Instruction." *Journal of Educational Psychology, 80(3)*, 1988, 299–303.

Kinzie, M. B., Delcourt, M. A., and Powers, S. M. "Computer Technologies: Attitudes and Self-Efficacy across Undergraduate Disciplines." *Research in Higher Education, 35*, 1994, 745–768.

Kirkpatrick, D. L. *A Practical Guide for Supervisory Training and Development.* Reading, MA: Addison-Wesley, 1971.

Kirkpatrick, D. L. *Evaluating Training Programs.* Madison, WI: American Society for Training and Development, 1975.

Knowles, M. S. *Informal Adult Education.* New York: Association Press, 1950.

Knowles, M. S. "Andragogy, not Pedagogy." *Adult Leadership, 16*(10), 350–352, 1968.

Knowles, M. S. *The Modern Practice of Adult Education: Andragogy versus Pedagogy.* New York: Association Press, 1970, 1980.

Knowles, M. S. *The Adult Learner: A Neglected Species.* Houston, TX: Gulf, 1973.

Knowles, M. S. *Self-Directed Learning: A Guide for Learners and Teachers.* New York: Association Press, 1975.

Knowles, M. S. *The Adult Education Movement in the United States*, 2nd edn. Huntington, NY: Krieger, 1977.

Knowles, M. S. *The Adult Learner: A Neglected Species*, 2nd edn. Houston, TX: Gulf, 1978.

Knowles, M. S. "Andragogy Revisited II." *Adult Education*, fall, 1979, 52–53.

Knowles, M. S. "My Farewell Address: Andragogy—No Panacea, No Ideology." *Training and Development Journal*, August, 1980a.

Knowles, M. S. *The Modern Practice of Adult Education: From Pedagogy to Andragogy.* Englewood Cliffs, NJ: Cambridge, 1980b.

Knowles, M. S. *The Adult Learner: A Neglected Species*, 3rd edn. Houston, TX: Gulf, 1984a.

Knowles, M. S. *Andragogy in Action.* San Francisco, CA: Jossey-Bass, 1984b.

Knowles, M. S. *Using Learning Contexts.* San Francisco, CA: Jossey-Bass, 1986.

Knowles, M. S. "Adult Learning." *Training and Development Handbook.* R. L. Craig (ed.). New York: McGraw–Hill, 1987, pp. 168–179.

Knowles, M. S. *The Adult Learner: A Neglected Species*, 3rd edn. Houston, TX: Gulf, 1988.

Knowles, M. S. "Adult Learning: Theory & Practice." *The Handbook of Human Resource Development*, 2nd edn. L. Nadler, and Z. Nadler (eds). New York: John Wiley & Sons, 1989a.

Knowles, M. S. *The Making of an Adult Educator.* San Francisco, CA: Jossey-Bass, 1989b.

Knowles, M. S. *The Adult Learner: A Neglected Species*, 4th edn. Houston, TX: Gulf, 1990.

Knowles, M. S. *Designs for Adult Learning.* Alexandria, VA: American Society for Training and Development, 1995.

Knowles, M. S. "Adult Learning." *ASTD Training & Development Handbook: A Guide to Human Resource Development*, 4th edn. R. L. Craig (ed.). New York: McGraw-Hill, 1996.

Knowles, M. S., and Knowles, H. *Introduction to Group Dynamics.* New York: Cambridge University Press, 1972.

Knowles, M. S., and Hulda, F. *Introduction to Group Dynamics.* Chicago, IL: Follett, 1973.

Knowles, M. S., Holton, E. F., and Swanson, R. A. *The Adult Learner*, 5th edn. Houston, TX: Gulf, 1998.

Knowles, M. S., Holton, E. F., and Swanson, R. A. *The Adult Learner*, 6th edn. New York: Butterworth-Heinemann, 2005.

Knox, A. B. *Adult Development and Learning.* San Francisco, CA: Jossey-Bass, 1977.

Knox, A. B. *Helping Adults Learn.* San Francisco, CA: Jossey-Bass, 1986.

Knox, A. B., and associates. *Developing, Administering, and Evaluating Adult Education.* San Francisco, CA: Jossey-Bass, 1980.

Kohlberg, L. "Continuities in Childhood and Adult Moral Development Revisited." *Developmental Psychology: Personality and Socialization.* P. Bakes, and K. Schaie (eds). Orlando, FL: Academic Press, 1973.

Kohler, W. *Gestalt Psychology.* New York: Meridian, 1947.

Kolb, D. A. *The Learning Style Inventory.* Boston, MA: McBer, 1976.

Kolb, D. A. "Experiential Learning Theory and the Learning Style Inventory: A Reply to Freedman and Stumpf." *Academy of Management Review*, *6*, 1981, 289–296.

Kolb, D. A. *Experiential Learning: Experience as the Source of Learning and Development.* Englewood-Cliffs, NJ: Prentice-Hall, 1984.

Kozma, R. B. "Reflections on the State of Educational Technology Research and Development." *Educational Technology Research and Development*, *48(1)*, 2000, 5–15.

Krajinc, A. "Andragogy." *Lifelong Education for Adults: An International Handbook.* C. J. Titmus (ed.). Oxford: Pergamon, 1989, pp. 19–21.

Kramer, D. A. "Development of an Awareness of Contradiction across the Life Span and the Question of Postformal Operations." *Adult Development.* M. L. Commons, J. D. Sinnott, F. A. Richards, and C. Armon (eds). New York: Praeger and Dare Association, 1989, pp. 133–157.

Kreitlow, B. W., and associates. *Examining Controversies in Adult Education.* San Francisco, CA: Jossey-Bass, 1981.

Labouvie-Vief, G. *Models of Cognitive Functioning in the Older Adult: Research Need in Educational Gerontology: An Introduction to Educational Gerontology,* 3rd edn. R. H. Sherron, and D. B. Lumsden (eds). New York: Hemisphere, 1990, pp. 243–263.

Laird, D., Naquin, S. S., and Holton, E. F. *Approaches to Training and Development,* 3rd edn. New York: Basic Books, 2003.

Latham, G. P. "Behavioral Approaches to the Training and Learning Process." *Training and Development in Organizations.* I. L. Goldstein, and associates (eds). San Francisco, CA: Jossey-Bass, 1989, pp. 256–295.

Laughary, J. W., and Ripley, T. M. *Helping Others Help Themselves.* New York: McGraw-Hill, 1979.

Leagans, J. P., Copeland, H. G., and Kaiser, G. E. *Selected Concepts from Educational Psychology and Adult Education for Extension and Continuing Educators.* Syracuse, NY: University of Syracuse Press, 1971.

Lefcourt, H. M. *Locus of Control: Current Trends in Theory and Research.* New York: Wiley, 1976.

Leibowitz, Z. B., Farren, C., and Kaye, B. L. *Designing Career Development Systems.* San Francisco, CA: Jossey-Bass, 1986.

Leibowitz, Z. B., Schlossberg, N. K., and Shore, J. E. "Stopping the Revolving Door." *Training and Development Journal,* February 1991, 43–50.

Leigh, R. D. *Journal of Adult Education, II,* April 2, 1930, p. 123.

Lengrand, P. *An Introduction to Lifelong Education.* Paris: UNESCO, 1970.

Lenning, F. W., and Many, W. A. (eds). *Basic Education for the Disadvantaged Adult: Theory and Practice.* Boston, MA: Houghton Mifflin, 1966.

Leonard, G. B. *Education and Ecstasy.* New York: Delacorte, 1968.

Leonard-Barton, D. *The Wellspring of Knowledge: Building and Sustaining the Sources of Innovation.* Boston, MA: HBR Press, 1995.

Leso, T., and Peck, K. L. "Computer Anxiety and Different Types of Computer Courses." *Journal of Educational Computing Research, 8(4),* 1992, 469–478.

Levering, R., and Moskowitz, M. *The 100 Best Companies to Work for in America.* New York: NAL-Dutton, 1994.

Levinson, D. J. *The Seasons of a Man's Life.* New York: Knopf, 1978a.

Levinson, D. J. "A Theory of Life Structure Development in Adulthood." *Higher Stages of Human Development.* C. N. Alexander, and E. J. Langer (eds). New York: Oxford University Press, 1978b, pp. 35–54.

Levinson, D. J. "A Conception of Adult Development." *American Psychologist, 41,* 1986, 3–13.

Levinson, H., et al. *Men, Management, and Mental Health.* Cambridge, MA: Harvard University Press, 1963.

Lewin, K. *Field Theory in Social Science.* New York: Harper, 1951.

Lewis, L. H. (ed.). *Experiential and Simulation Techniques for Teaching Adults.* San Francisco, CA: Jossey-Bass, 1986.

Lewis, L. H. "Computer-Enriched Instruction." *Adult Learning Methods: A Guide for Effective Instruction.* M. W. Galbraith (ed.). Malabar, FL: Robert E. Krieger Publishing, 1990, pp. 303–328.

Lewis, L. H., and Williams, C. J. "Experiential Learning: Past and Present." *Experiential Learning: A New Approach.* L. Jackson and R. S. Caffarella (eds). San Francisco, CA: Jossey-Bass and *New Directions for Adult and Continuing Education, 62,* 1994, 5–16.

Leypoldt, M. M. *Forty Ways to Teach in Groups.* Valley Forge, PA: Judson, 1967.

Likert, R. *New Patterns of Management.* New York: McGraw-Hill, 1961.

Likert, R. *The Human Organization: Its Management and Value.* New York: McGraw-Hill, 1967.

Lindeman, E. C. "Andragogik: The Method of Teaching Adults." *Workers' Education, 4,* 1926a, 38.

Lindeman, E. C. *The Meaning of Adult Education.* New York: New Republic, 1926b.

Lippitt, G. L. *Organization Renewal.* New York: Appleton-Century-Crofts, 1969.

Lippitt, G. L. *Visualizing Change.* Somerset, NJ: Wiley, 1978.

Lippitt, G. L., and Lippitt, R. *The Consulting Process in Action.* La Jolla, CA: University Associates, 1978.

Liveright, A. A. *A Study of Adult Education in the United States.* Boston, MA: Center for the Study of Liberal Arts, 1968.

Loevinger, J. *Ego Development: Concepts and Theories.* San Francisco, CA: Jossey-Bass, 1976.

London, M. *Change Agents: New Roles and Innovative Strategies for Human Resource Professionals.* San Francisco, CA: Jossey-Bass, 1988.

Long, H. B. *Are They Ever Too Old to Learn?* Englewood Cliffs, NJ: Prentice-Hall, 1971.

Long, H. B. *The Psychology of Aging: How It Affects Learning.* Englewood Cliffs, NJ: Prentice-Hall, 1972.

Long, H. B., et al. *Changing Approaches to Studying Adult Education.* San Francisco, CA: Jossey-Bass, 1980.

Long, H. B., and associates. *Self-Directed Learning: Application and Theory.* Athens: Department of Adult Education, University of Georgia, 1988.

Louis, M. R. "Surprise and Sense Making: What Newcomers Experience in Entering Unfamiliar Organizational Settings." *Administrative Science Quarterly, 25,* 1980, 226–251.

Louis, M. R. "Managing Career Transition: A Missing Link in Career Development." *Organizational Dynamics,* spring, 1982, 68–77.

Louis, M. R. "Acculturation in the Workplace: Newcomers as Lay Ethnographers." *Organizational Climate and Culture.* B. Schneider (ed.). San Francisco, CA: Jossey-Bass, 1990, pp. 85–129.

Lowe, J. S., and Holton, E. F. III. "A Theory of Effective Computer-Based Instruction for Adults." *Human Resource Development Review, 4,* 2005, 159–188.

Luiten, J., Ames, W., and Ackerman, G. A. "Meta-Analysis of the Effects of Advance Organizers on Learning and Retention." *American Educational Research Journal, 17,* 1980, 211–218. 291, 405.

Lumsden, D. B., and Sherron, R. H. *Experimental Studies in Adult Learning and Memory.* New York: Wiley, 1975.

Luo, L. and Craik, F. "Aging and Memory: A Cognitive Approach." *Canadian Review of Psychiatry*, *53(6)*, 2008, 346–353.

Lynham, S. A. "Quantitative Research and Theory Building: Dubin's Method." *Advances in Developing Human Resources*, *4(3)*, 2002, 242–276.

McCarthy, B. *The 4-MAT System: Teaching to Learning Styles with Right/Left Mode Techniques*. Barrington, IL: EXCEL, Inc., 1987.

McClelland, D. C. *Power: The Inner Experience*. New York: McGraw-Hill, 1975.

McClelland, D. C., Atkinson, J. W., Clark, R. A., and Lowell, E. I. *The Achievement Motive*. New York: Appleton-Century-Crofts, 1953.

McCollin, E. D. *Faculty and Student Perceptions of Teaching Styles: Do Teaching Styles Differ for Traditional and Nontraditional Students?* (UMI No. 9901343), 1998.

McDonald, F. J. "The Influence of Learning Theories on Education." *Theories of Learning and Instruction*. Sixty-third Yearbook of the National Society for the Study of Education, Part I. E. R. Hilgard (ed.). Chicago, IL: University of Chicago Press, 1964, pp. 126.

McGarrell, E. J., Jr. "An Orientation System that Builds Productivity." *Personnel*, *60(6)*, 1983, 32–41.

McGraw-Hill. "Photocopying Processes." *McGraw-Hill Encyclopedia of Science and Technology*, 10th edn, Vol. 13. New York: McGraw-Hill, 2007.

McGraw-Hill. *How to Judge the Reliability of Internet Information*. 2014. http://www.mhhe.com/mayfieldpub/webtutor/judging.htm.

McGregor, D. *The Human Side of Enterprise*. New York: McGraw-Hill, 1960.

McGregor, D. *Leadership and Motivation*. Cambridge, MA: Massachusetts Institute of Technology Press, 1967.

Mackaye, D. L. *Journal of Adult Education*, *III*, June 3, 1931, pp. 293–294.

McKenzie, L. *The Religious Education of Adults*. Birmingham, AL: Religious Education Press, 1982.

McLagan, P. A. *Models for Excellence*. Washington, DC: American Society for Training and Development (ASTD), 1983.

McLagan, P. A. "Models for HRD Practice." *Training and Development*, *43(9)*, 1989, 49–59.

Mager, R. E. *Preparing Instructional Objectives*. Palo Alto, CA: Fearon, 1962.

Mager, R. E. *Goal Analysis*. Palo Alto, CA: Fearon, 1972.

Mager, R. E., and Pipe, R. *Analyzing Performance Problems*. Palo Alto, CA: Fearon, 1970.

Major, D. A., Kozlowski, S. W. J., Chao, G. T., and Gardner P. D. "A Longitudinal Investigation of Newcomer Expectations, Early Socialization Outcomes, and the Moderating Effects." *Journal of Applied Psychology*, *80(3)*, 1995, 418–431.

Mangham, I. *Interactions and Interventions in Organizations*. New York: Wiley, 1948.

Marcoulides, G. A. "Improving Learner Performance with Computer Based Programs." *Journal of Educational Computing Research*, *6(2)*, 1990, 147–155.

Marquardt, M. J. *Building the Learning Organization*. New York: McGraw-Hill, 1996.

Marrow, A. J., Bowers, D. G., and Seashore, S. E. *Management by Participation*. New York: Harper and Row, 1968.

Martinko, M. J., and Gardern, W. L. "The Leader/Member Attribution Process." *Academy of Management Review*, *12*, 1987, 235–249.

Martorana, S. V., and Kuhns, E. *Managing Academic Change.* San Francisco, CA: Jossey-Bass, 1975.

Maslow, A. H. *Motivation and Personality.* New York: Harper and Row, 1970.

Maslow, A. H. "Defense and Growth." *The Psychology of Open Teaching and Learning.* M. L. Silberman, et al. (eds). Boston, MA: Little, Brown, 1972, pp. 43–51.

Mazhindu, G. N. "Contract Learning Reconsidered: A Critical Examination of the Implications for Application in Nursing Education." *Journal of Advanced Nursing, 15,* 1990, pp. 101–109.

Menges, R. J., and Mathis, B. C. *Key Resources on Teaching, Curriculum, and Faculty Development.* San Francisco, CA: Jossey-Bass, 1988.

Merriam, S. B. *Case Study Research in Education.* San Francisco, CA: Jossey-Bass, 1988.

Merriam, S. B. "Adult Learning: Where Have We Come From? Where Are We Headed?" *New Directions for Adult and Continuing Education,* No. 57. San Francisco, CA: Jossey-Bass, 1993.

Merriam, S. B. "Andragogy and Self-Directed Learning: Pillars of Adult Learning Theory. The New Update on Adult Learning Theory." *New Directions for Adult and Continuing Education.* S. Imel (Ed. in Chief). San Francisco, CA: Jossey-Bass, No. 89, spring, 2001, pp. 3–13.

Merriam S., and Cunningham P. M. (eds). *Handbook of Adult and Continuing Education.* San Francisco, CA: Jossey-Bass, 1989.

Merriam, S., and Caffarella, R. S. *Learning in Adulthood.* San Francisco, CA: Jossey-Bass, 1991.

Merriam, S., and Brockett, R. G. *The Profession and Practice of Adult Education: An Introduction.* San Francisco, CA: Jossey-Bass, 1997.

Merriam, S., and Caffarella, R. S. *Learning in Adulthood,* 2nd edn. San Francisco, CA: Jossey-Bass, 1999.

Merriam, S., Caffarella, R. S., and Baumgartner, L. M. *Learning in Adulthood: A Comprehensive Guide.* San Francisco, CA: Jossey-Bass, 2007.

Merrill, M. D. "Constructivism and Instructional Design." *Constructivism and the Technology of Instruction.* T. M. Duffy, and D. H. Jonassen (eds). Hillsdale, NJ: Erlbaum, 1992.

Merton, R. *Journal of Adult Education, XI,* April, 1939, 178.

Messick, S. "The Nature of Cognitive Styles: Problems and Promise in Educational Practice." *Educational Psychologist,* 19, 1984, 59–74.

Messick, S., et al. *Individuality in Learning.* San Francisco, CA: Jossey-Bass, 1976.

Mezirow, J. "A Critical Theory of Adult Learning and Education." *Adult Education, 32(1),* 1981, 3–27.

Mezirow, J. *Transformative Dimensions of Adult Learning.* San Francisco, CA: Jossey-Bass, 1991.

Mezoff, B. "Cognitive Style and Interpersonal Behavior: A Review with Implications for Human Relations Training." *Group and Organization Studies, 7(1),* 1982, 13–34.

Michael, D. *On Learning to Plan and Planning to Learn: The Social Psychology of Changing toward Future-Responsive Societal Learning.* San Francisco, CA: Jossey-Bass, 1973.

Miles, M. W., and Charters, W. W., Jr. *Learning in Social Settings.* Boston, MA: Allyn and Bacon, 1970.

Millenson, J. R. *Principles of Behavioral Analysis.* New York: Macmillan, 1967.

Miller, H. L. *Teaching and Learning in Adult Education.* New York: Macmillan, 1964.

Millett, J. D. *Decision Making and Administration in Higher Education.* Kent, OH: Kent State University Press, 1968.

Millhollan, F., and Forisha, B. E. *From Skinner to Rogers.* Lincoln, NE: Professional Educators Publications, 1972.

Milligan, F. "Beyond the Rhetoric of Problem-Based Learning: Emancipatory Limits and Links with Andragogy." *Nursing Education Today, 19,* 1999, 548–555.

Miura, I. T. "The Relationship of Computer Self-Efficacy Expectations to Computer Interest and Course Enrollment in College." *Sex Roles, 16,* 1987, 303–311.

Mizuno, S. (ed.). *Managing for Quality Improvement: The Seven New QC Tools.* Cambridge, MA: Productivity Press, 1988.

Monts, B. "Andragogy or Pedagogy: A Discussion of Instructional Methodology for Adult Learners." Illinois State University. Unpublished paper, 2000.

Moore, M. G., and Willis, N. P. (eds). *New Developments in Self-Directed Learning. New Directions in Continuing Education,* CE#42. San Francisco, CA: Jossey-Bass, 1989.

Moos, R. E. *The Human Context: Environmental Determinants of Behavior.* New York: Wiley, 1976.

Moos, R. E. *Evaluating Educational Environments.* San Francisco, CA: Jossey-Bass, 1979.

Moos, R. E., and Insel, P. M. *Issues in Social Ecology: Human Milieus.* Palo Alto, CA: National Press Books, 1974.

Moran, R. T., and Harris, P. R. *Managing Cultural Synergy.* Houston, TX: Gulf, 1982.

Moreland, R. L., and Levine, J. M. "Socialization in Small Groups: Temporal Changes in Individual–Group Relations." *Advances in Experimental Psychology,* Vol. 15. L. Berkowitz (ed.). New York: Academic Press, 1982, pp. 137–192.

Moustakas, C. *Finding Yourself, Finding Others.* Englewood Cliffs, NJ: Prentice-Hall, 1974.

Mouton, J. S., and Blake, R. R. *Synergogy: A New Strategy for Education, Training, and Development.* San Francisco, CA: Jossey-Bass, 1984.

Murphy, C. A. *Assessment of Computer Self-Efficacy: Instrument Development and Validation.* ERIC Document Reproduction Service No. ED 307 317, 1988.

Nadler, L., and Nadler, Z. *Developing Human Resources.* Houston, TX: Gulf, 1970.

Nadler, L., and Nadler, Z. *The Conference Book.* Houston, TX: Gulf, 1977.

Nadler, L., and Nadler, Z. *Corporate Human Resource Development.* New York: Van Nostrand Reinhold, 1980.

Nadler, L., and Nadler, Z. *Designing Training Programs: The Critical Events Model,* 2nd edn. Houston, TX: Gulf, 1994.

Nadler, L., Nadler, Z., and Wiggs, G. *Managing Human Resources Development.* San Francisco, CA: Jossey-Bass, 1986.

Neimi, J. A., and Gooler, D. D. (eds). *Technologies for Learning Outside the Classroom.* San Francisco, CA: Jossey-Bass, 1987.

Neugarten, B. L. (ed.). *Personality in Middle and Later Life.* New York: Atherton Press, 1964.

Neugarten, B. L. (ed.). *Middle Age and Aging.* Chicago, IL: University of Chicago Press, 1968.

New Oxford Dictionary. Oxford: Oxford University Press, 2010.

Noe, R. *Employee Training and Development,* 6th edn. New York: McGraw-Hill, 2012.

Noe, R. A., Hollenbeck, J. R., Gerhart, B., and Wright, P. M. *Human Resource Management: Gaining a Competitive Advantage.* Burr Ridge, IL: Irwin, 1994.

Norris, N. A. (ed.). *Community College Futures: From Rhetoric to Reality.* Stillwater, OK: New Forums Press, 1989.

Nottingham Andragogy Group. "Towards a Developmental Theory of Andragogy." *Adults: Psychological and Educational Perspective No. 9.* Nottingham, UK: University of Nottingham Department of Adult Education, 1983.

Optner, S. *Systems Analysis for Business and Industrial Problem Solving.* Englewood Cliffs, NJ: Prentice-Hall, 1965.

Organization for Economic Cooperation and Development (OECD). *Understanding the Brain: The Birth of a Learning Science.* Paris: OECD, Centre for Educational Research and Innovation, 2007.

Ormrod, J. *Human Learning Principles, Theories, and Educational Applications.* Columbus, OH: Merrill, 1990.

Osborn, R. H. *Developing New Horizons for Women.* New York: McGraw-Hill, 1977.

Ostroff, C., and Kozlowski, S. W. J. "Organizational Socialization as a Learning Process: The Role of Information Acquisition." *Personnel Psychology, 45,* 1992, 849–874.

Ovesni, K. *Andragogy as an Integral Part of Educational Sciences.* Belgrade, Yugoslavia: Faculty of Philosophy, 1999. Website, http://ifets.gmd.de/.

Ovesni, K. *Concepts and Models of Professional Preparation of Andragogues,* 2000. Retrieved July 12, 2005, from: http://www.geocities.com/ kowesni.geo/ indexma.html?200512.

Parker, B. K. *Health Care Education: A Guide to Staff Development.* Norwalk, CT: Appleton-Century-Crofts, 1986.

Parsons, T. *The Social System.* New York: Free Press of Glencoe, 1951.

Pascual-Leone, J. "Growing into Maturity: Toward a Metasubjective Theory of Adulthood Stages." *Lifespan Development and Behavior,* Vol. 5. P. B. Bakes, and O. G. Brim, Jr. (eds). New York: Academic Press, 1983.

Patterson, C. H. *Theories of Counseling and Psychotherapy,* 4th edn. New York: Harper & Row, 1986.

Patton, M. Q. *Qualitative Evaluation.* Beverly Hills, CA: Sage, 1980.

Patton, M. Q. *Creative Evaluation.* Beverly Hills, CA: Sage, 1981.

Patton, M. Q. *Practical Evaluation.* Beverly Hills, CA: Sage, 1982.

Pearlin, L. I. "Life Strains and Psychological Distress among Adults." *Themes of Work and Love in Adulthood.* N. J. Smesler, and E. H. Erikson (eds). Cambridge, MA: Harvard University Press, 1980, pp. 174–192.

Penland, P. "Self-initiated Learning." *Adult Education, 29(3),* 1979, 170–179.

Perrin, A. L. *The Fit between Adult Learner Preferences and the Theories of Malcolm Knowles* (UMI No. 9998105), 2000.

Perry, P., and Downs, S. "Skills, Strategies, and Ways of Learning." *Programmed Learning and Educational Technology, 22,* 1985, 177–181.

Perry, W. "Cognitive and Ethnical Growth: The Making of Meaning." *Forms of Intellectual and Ethnical Developments with the College Years: A Scheme.* New York: Holt Rinehart and Winston, 1970, pp. 76–116.

Peters, J. M., and associates. *Building an Effective Adult Education Enterprise.* San Francisco, CA: Jossey-Bass, 1980.

Pfeiffer, W. J., and Jones, J. E. *A Handbook of Structured Experiences for Human Relations Training,* vols I, II, III, IV, V. San Diego, CA: University Associates Press, 1969–1976.

Phares, E. J. *Locus of Control in Personality.* Morristown, NJ: General Learning Press, 1976.

Phillips, J. J. *Handbook of Training Evaluation and Measurement Methods,* 3rd edn. Houston, TX: Gulf, 1997.

Piaget, Jean. *Science of Education and the Psychology of the Child.* New York: Viking, 1970.

Pike, R. *Creative Training Techniques Handbook.* Minneapolis, MN: Lakewood, 1989.

Pinheiro, S. O. *Perceptions Versus Preferences: Adult International Students' Teaching Learning Experiences in an American University,* 2001. Retrieved October 24, 2005 from: http://nccrestedreform.nte/resounce/7101.

Pirsig, R. M. *Lila: An Inquiry into Morals.* New York: Bantam, 1991.

Pittenger, O. E., and Gooding, C. T. *Learning Theories in Educational Practice.* New York: Wiley, 1971.

Podeschi, R. L. "Andragogy: Proofs or Premises?" *Lifelong Learning, 11,* 1987, 14–20.

Poggeler, F. *Einf hrung in die Andragogik. Grundfragen der Erwachsenenbildung.* Ratingen: Henn Verlag, 1957.

Poggeler, F. "Introduction—Trends of Andragogical Research in Europe." *Developments in the Education of Adults in Europe.* P. Jarvis and F. Poggeler (eds). Frankfurt am Main: Peter Lang, Studies in Pedagogy, Andragogy and Gerontology, Poggeler, F. (ed.), Vol. 21, 9–15. (1994).

Pollack, O. *Human Behavior and the Helping Professions.* New York: Wiley, 1976.

Postman, N., and Weingartner, C. *Teaching as a Subversive Activity.* New York: Dell, 1969.

Powell, J. W. *Learning Comes of Age.* New York: Association Press, 1956.

Powers, D. R., Powers, M. E., and Aslanian, C. B. *Higher Education in Partnership with Industry.* San Francisco, CA: Jossey-Bass, 1988.

Pratt, D. D. "Andragogy as a Relational Construct." *Adult Education Quarterly, 38,* 1988, 160–181.

Pratt, D. D. "Andragogy after Twenty-Five Years." *New Directions for Adult and Continuing Education, No. 57—An Update on Adult Learning Theory.* S. B. Merriam (ed.). San Francisco, CA: Jossey-Bass, 1993.

Pratt, D. D., and associates. *Five Perspectives on Teaching in Adult and Higher Education.* Malabar, FL: Krieger, 1998.

Premack, P. L., and Wanous, J. P. "Meta-Analysis of Realistic Job Preview Experimenters." *Journal of Applied Psychology, 70,* 1985, 706–719.

Pressey, S. L., and Kuhlen, R. G. *Psychological Development Through the Life Span.* New York: Harper and Row, 1957.

Rachal, J. R. "Taxonomies and Typologies of Adult Education." *Lifelong Learning: An Omnibus of Practice and Research, 12(2),* 1988, 20–23.

Rachal, J. "Effectiveness of Andragogy Concurrent Session Presentation." American Association for Adult and Continuing Education Conference, Providence, RI, November, 2000.

Rachal, J. "Andragogy's Detectives: A Critique of the Present and a Proposal for the Future." *Adult Education Quarterly: A Journal of Research and Theory, 22(3),* 2002.

Rae, L. *How to Measure Training Effectiveness.* New York: Nichols, 1986.

Rankel, P., Harrison, R., and Runkel, M. *The Changing College Classroom.* San Francisco, CA: Jossey-Bass, 1969.

Rasmussen, W. D. *Taking the University to the People: 75 Years of Cooperative Extension.* Ames: Iowa State University Press, 1989.

Raths, L., et al. *Teaching for Learning.* Columbus, OH: Charles E. Merrill, 1967.

Raths, L., Harmin, H., and Simon, S. *Values and Teaching.* Columbus, OH: Charles E. Merrill, 1966.

Reber, R. A., and Wallin, J. A. "The Effects of Training, Goal Setting, and Knowledge of Results on Safe Behavior: A Component Analysis." *Academy of Management Journal, 27,* 1984, 544–560.

Reese, H. W., and Overton, W. E. "Models of Development and Theories of Development." *Life-Span Developmental Psychology.* L. R. Gottlet, and P. B. Baltes (eds). New York: Academic Press, 1970, pp. 115–145.

Reigeluth C. M. (ed.). *Instructional-Design Theories and Models: An Overview of their Current Status.* Hillsdale, NJ: Lawrence Erlbaum Associates, 1983.

Reischmann, J. *Why Andragogy?* Bamberg University, Germany, 2003. http://www.andragogy.net

Reischmann, J. *Andragogy: History, Meaning, Context, Function.* Version February 25, 2004. www.andragogy.net.

Reischmann, J. "Andragogy: History, Meaning, Context, Function." *International Encyclopedia of Adult Education.* L. M. English (ed.). Houndsville, NY: Palgrave Macmillan, 2005.

Reynolds, M. "Learning Styles: A Critique." *Management Learning, 28,* 1997, 115–133.

Richey, R. C. "Instructional Design Theory and a Changing World." *Instructional Design Fundamentals: A Reconsideration.* B. B. Seels (ed.). Englewood Cliffs, NJ: Educational Technologies, 1995.

Riegel, K. F. "The Dialectics of Human Development." *American Psychologist, 31,* 1976, 689–700.

Robertson, D. L. *Self-Directed Growth.* Muncie, IN: Accelerated Development, 1988.

Robinson, A. G., and Stern, S. *Corporate Creativity: How Innovation and Improvement Actually Happen.* San Francisco, CA: Berrett-Koehler, 1997.

Robinson, D., and Robinson, J. S. *Training for Impact.* San Francisco, CA: Jossey-Bass, 1989.

ROCOM. *Intensive Coronary Care Multimedia System Program Coordinator's Manual.* Nutley, NJ: Hoffman-LaRoche, 1971.

Rogers, C. R. *Client-Centered Therapy.* Boston, MA: Houghton-Mifflin, 1951.

Rogers, C. R. *On Becoming a Person.* Boston, MA: Houghton-Mifflin, 1961.

Rogers, C. R. *Freedom to Learn.* Columbus, OH: Merrill, 1969.

Rogers, C. R. *A Way of Being.* Boston, MA: Houghton Mifflin, 1980.

Rogers, M. *Journal of Adult Education,* X, October, 1938, 409–411.

Romiszowski, A. J. *Designing Instructional Systems.* London: Kogan Page, 1981.

Rosenblum, S., and Darkenwald, G. G. "Effects of Adult Learner Participation in Course Planning on Achievement and Satisfaction." *Adult Education Journal, 20(2),* 1983, 67–87.

Rosenshine, B. "Enthusiastic Teaching. A Research Review." *School Review, 78,* 1970, 499–514.

Rosenshine, B. V. "Effective Teaching in Industrial Education and Training." *Journal of Industrial Teacher Education, 23,* 1986, 5–19.

Rosenstock-Huessy, E. *Andragogy-1925.* Retrieved October 26, 2005 from: http://www.argobooks.org/feringer-notes/t24.html.

Rosenthal, R., and Jacobson, L. *Pygmalion in the Classroom*. New York: Holt, Rinehart and Winston, 1968.

Rosow, J. M., and Zager, R. *Training—The Competitive Edge*. San Francisco, CA: Jossey-Bass, 1988.

Ross, B. E. "Integrating Andragogy with Current Research on Teaching Effectiveness." *Proceedings of the Lifelong Learning Research Conference*. 1988, pp. 29–33.

Ross, S. M., and Morrison, G. R. "In Search of a Happy Medium in Instructional Technology Research: Issues Concerning External Validity Media Replications and Learner Control." *Educational Technology Research and Development*, *37*, 1989, 19–33.

Ross, S. M., Morrison, G. R., and O'Dell, J. K. "Uses and Effects of Learner Control of Context and Instructional Support in Computer-Based Instruction." *Educational Technology Research and Development*, *37(4)*, 1989, 29–39.

Rossi, P. H., and Biddle, B. J. *The New Media and Education*. Chicago, IL: Aldine, 1966.

Rossing, B. E., and Long, H. B. "Contributions of Curiosity and Relevance to Adult Learning Motivation." *Adult Education*, *32(1)*, 1981, 25–36.

Rotter, J. B. "Generalized Expectations for Internal Versus External Control of Reinforcement." *American Psychologist*, *80(1)*, 1966, 1–28.

Rotter, J. B. "Internal Versus External Control of Reinforcement: A Case History of a Variable." *American Psychologist*, *45(4)*, 1990, 489–493.

Rountree, D. *Teaching Through Self-Instruction: A Practical Handbook for Course Developers*. New York: Nichols, 1986.

Royal Society. *Brain Waves Module 2: Neuroscience: Implications for Education and Lifelong Learning*. London: The Royal Society Science Policy Centre, 2011.

Rudwick, B. H. *Systems Analysis for Effective Planning*. New York: Wiley, 1969.

Rummelhart, D. E., and Norman, D. A. "Accretion, Tuning and Restructuring: Three Models of Learning." *Semantic Factors in Cognition*. J. W. Cotton, and R. L. Klatzky (eds). Hillsdale, NJ: Erlbaum, 1978.

Rummler, G. A., and Brache, A. P. *Improving Performance: How to Manage the White Space on the Organization Chart*, 2nd edn. San Francisco, CA: Jossey-Bass, 1995.

St Clair, R. "Andragogy Revisited: Theory for the 21st Century." *Myths and Realities 19*, 2002. http://www.cete.org/acvekestonly/docgen.asp?tbl-mr8cid=109.

Sales, G. C. "Designing Feedback for CBI: Matching Feedback to the Learner and Learner Outcomes." *Computers in the Schools*, *5(1/2)*, 1988, 225–239.

Sales, G. C., and Williams, M. D. "The Effect of Adaptive Control of Feedback in Computer-Based Instruction." *Journal of Research on Computing in Education*, *20*, 1988, 97–111.

Salisbury, D. F., Richards, B. F., and Klein, J. D. "Designing Practice: A Review of Prescriptions and Recommendations from Instructional Design Theories." *Journal of Instructional Development*, *8(4)*, 1985, 9–19.

Savery, J. R., and Duffy, T. M. "Problem Based Learning: An Instructional Model and Its Constructivist Framework." *Constructivist Learning Environments: Case Studies in Instructional Design*. B. G. Wilson (ed.). Englewood Cliffs, NJ: Educational Technology Publications, 1996.

Savicevic, D. "Modern Conceptions of Andragogy: A European Framework." *Studies in the Education of Adults*, *23(2)*, 1991, 179–191.

Savicevic, D. "Understanding Andragogy in Europe and America: Comparing and Contrasting." *Comparative Adult Education 1998: The Contribution of ISCAE to an Emerging Field of Study.* J. Reischmann, M. Bron, and J. Zoran (eds). Ljubljana: Slovenian Institute for Adult Education, 1999a, pp. 97–119.

Savicevic, D. "Adult Education: From Practice to Theory Building." *Studies in Pedagogy, Andragogy, and Gerontagogy*, Vol. 37. F. Poggeler (ed.). Frankfurt am Main: Peter Lang, 1999b.

Savicevic, D. *The Roots and Evolution of Andragogical Ideas* [Koreni I razvoj andragoskih ideja—in the Serb language]. Beograd: Serbia, Institut za pedagogiju I andragogiju Andragosko drustvo Srbije, 2000.

Savicevic, D. "Convergence or Divergence of Ideas on Andragogy in Different Countries." *Papers presented at the 11th Standing International Conference on the History of Adult Education (IESVA).* Bamberg, Germany, September 27–30, 2006, pp.1–24.

Schaie, K. W. "The Course of Adult Intellectual Development." *American Psychologist*, *49*, 1994, 304–313.

Schein, E. "Organizational Socialization and the Profession of Management." *Industrial Management Review*, winter, 1968, 1–16.

Schein, E. *Process Consultation: Its Role in Organization Development.* Reading, MA: Addison-Wesley, 1969.

Schein, E. "Organizational Culture." *American Psychologist*, *45*, 1990, 102–119.

Schein, E. *Organizational Culture and Leadership*, 2nd edn. San Francisco, CA: Jossey-Bass, 1992.

Schein, E., and Bennis, W. G. *Personal and Organizational Change through Group Methods.* New York: Wiley, 1965.

Schindler-Rainman, E., and Lippitt, R. *The Volunteer Community: Creative Use of Human Resources.* Washington, DC: Center for a Voluntary Society, 1971.

Schloss, P. J., Wisniewski, L. A., and Cartwright, G. P. "The Differential Effect of Learner Control and Feedback in College Students' Performance on CAI Modules." *Journal of Educational Computing Research*, *4(2)*, 1988, 141–150.

Schlossberg, N. K., et al. *Perspectives on Counseling Adults.* Monterey, CA: Brooks/Cole, 1978.

Schlossberg, N. K., Lynch, A. Q., and Chickering, A. W. *Improving Higher Education Environments for Adults.* San Francisco, CA: Jossey-Bass, 1989.

Schnackenberg, H. L., Sullivan, H. J., Leader, L. F., and Jones, E. E. K. "Learner Preferences and Achievement under Differing Amounts of Learner Practice." *Educational Technology Research and Development*, *46(2)*, 1998, 5–15.

Schon, D. A. *Beyond the Stable State.* San Francisco, CA: Jossey-Bass, 1971.

Schon, D. A. *Educating the Reflective Practitioner.* San Francisco, CA: Jossey-Bass, 1987.

Schraw, G. "On the Development of Adult Metacognition." *Adult Learning and Development: Perspectives from Educational Psychology.* M. C. Smith, and T. Pourchot (eds). Mahwah, NJ: Lawrence Erlbaum Associates, 1998.

Schugurensky, D. *Selected Moments of the 20th Century.* Department of Adult Education, Community Development and Counseling Psychology, Ontario Institute for Studies in Education of the University of Toronto, Canada, 2005.

Schunk, D. H. "Self-Efficacy Perspective on Achievement Behavior." *Educational Psychologist*, *19*, 1984, 48–58.

Schuttenberg, E. "The Development of a General Purpose Organizational Output Instrument and Its Use in Analysis of an Organization." Unpublished doctoral dissertation, Boston University School of Education, 1972.

Schwab, J. J. "The Practical: Arts of Eclectic." *School Review, 79*, August, 1971, 493–542.

Seay, M. F., et al. *Community Education: A Developing Concept.* Midland, MI: Pendell Publishing, 1974.

Seiler, J. A. *Systems Analysis in Organizational Behavior.* Homewood, IL: Irwin and Dorsey, 1967.

Senge, P. *The Fifth Discipline: The Art and Practice of the Learning Organization.* New York: Doubleday, 1990.

Seyler, D., Holton, E., and Bates, R. "Factors Affecting Motivation to Use Computer-Based Training." *The Academy of Human Resources 1997 Conference Proceedings.* R. J. Toracco (ed.). Baton Rouge, LA: Academy of Human Resources, 1997.

Shaw, D. S. "Computer-Aided Instruction for Adult Professionals: A Research Report." *Journal of Computer-Based Instruction, 19(2)*, 1992, 54–57.

Shaw, N. (ed.). *Administration of Continuing Education.* Washington, DC: National Association for Public and Continuing Education, NEA, 1969.

Sheehy, G. *Passages: Predictable Crises of Adult Life.* New York: Dutton, 1974.

Silberman, C. E. *Crisis in the Classroom.* New York: Vintage, 1971.

Silberman, M. L., Allende; J. S., and Yahoff, J. M. *The Psychology of Open Teaching and Learning: An Inquiry Approach.* Boston, MA: Little, Brown, 1972.

Sillars, R. *Seeking Common Ground in Adult Education.* Washington, DC: Adult Education Association of the USA, 1958.

Simerly, R. G., and associates. *Strategic Planning and Leadership in Continuing Education.* San Francisco, CA: Jossey-Bass, 1987.

Simerly, R. G., and associates. *Handbook of Marketing for Continuing Education.* San Francisco, CA: Jossey-Bass, 1989.

Simon, H. A. *Administrative Behavior.* New York: Macmillan, 1961.

Simon, S., Howe, L. W., and Kirschenbaum, H. *Values Clarification.* New York: Hart, 1972.

Simonson, M., Smaldino, S., Albright, M., and Zvacek, S. *Teaching and Learning at a Distance: Foundations of Distance Education*, 2nd edn. Columbus, OH: Merrill Prentice Hall, 2003.

Simpson, J. A. "Andragogy." *Adult Education, 37(4)*, 1964, 186–194.

Skinner, B. F. "The Science of Learning and the Art of Teaching." *Harvard Educational Review, 24*, 1954, 86–97.

Skinner, B. F. *The Technology of Teaching.* New York: Appleton-Century-Crofts, 1968.

Sleezer, C. M. "Performance Analysis for Training." *Performance Improvement Quarterly*, 1992.

Slife, B. D., and Weaver, C. A. III. "Depression, Cognitive Skill, and Metacognitive Skill in Problem Solving." *Cognition and Emotion, 6*, 1992, 1–22.

Smith, B. B. "Model and Rationale for Designing and Managing Instruction." *Performance and Instruction*, April, 1983a, 20–22.

Smith, B. B. "Designing and Managing Instruction." *Performance and Instruction*, May, 1983b, 27–30.

Smith, M. A. *Practical Guide to Value Clarification.* La Jolla, CA: University Associates, 1977.

Smith, M. C., and Pourchot, T. (eds). *Adult Learning and Development: Perspectives from Educational Psychology.* Mahwah, NJ: Erlbaum, 1998.

Smith, P. L., and Boyce, B. A. "Instructional Design Considerations in the Development of Computer-Assisted Instruction." *Educational Technology, 24(7),* 1984, 5–11.

Smith, P. L., and Ragan, T. J. *Instructional Design.* New York: Merrill, 1993.

Smith, R. M. *Learning How to Learn.* Englewood Cliffs, NJ: Cambridge, 1982.

Smith, R. M. (ed.). *Theory Building for Learning How to Learn.* Chicago, IL: Educational Studies Press, 1988.

Smith, R. M., Aker, G. E., and Kidd, J. R. (eds). *Handbook of Adult Education.* New York: Macmillan, 1970.

Snow, R. E. "Aptitude–Treatment Interaction as a Framework for Research on Individual Differences in Learning." *Learning and Individual Differences: Advances in Theory and Research.* P. L. Ackerman, R. J. Sternberg, and R. Glaser (eds). New York: W. H. Freeman, 1989.

Solomon, L., and Berzon, B. (eds). *New Perspectives on Encounter Groups.* San Francisco, CA: Jossey-Bass, 1972.

Sorenson, H. *Adult Abilities.* Minneapolis: University of Minnesota Press, 1938.

Sousa, D. A. "How Science Met Pedagogy." *Mind, Brain and Education: Neuroscience Implications for the Classroom.* D. A. Sousa (ed.). Bloomington, IN: Solution Tree Press, 2010.

Sousa, D. A. *How the Brain Learns,* 4th edn. Thousand Oaks, CA: Sage, 2011.

Spector, P. A. "Behavior in Organization as a Function of Employee's Locus of Control." *Psychological Bulletin, 91(30),* 1982, 482–497.

Spelman, M. S., and Levy, P. "Knowledge of Lung Cancer and Smoking Habits." *British Journal of Social and Clinical Psychology, 5,* 1966, 207–210.

Srinivasan, L. *Perspectives on Non-formal Adult Learning.* New York: World Education, 1977.

Stanage, S. M. *Adult Education and Phenomenological Research.* Malabar, FL: Krieger, 1987.

Stanton, C. "A Construct Validity Assessment of the Instructional Perspectives Inventory." Unpublished Doctoral Dissertation at the University of Missouri–St. Louis, Division of Educational Leadership and Policy Studies, April, 2005.

Steele, S. M., and Brack, R. E. *Evaluating the Attainment of Objectives: Process, Properties, Problems, and Projects.* Syracuse, NY: Syracuse University Publications in Continuing Education, 1973.

Steinberg, E. R. *Computer-Assisted Instruction: A Synthesis of Theory, Practice, and Technology.* Hillsdale, NJ: Lawrence Erlbaum Associates, 1991.

Steinberg, E. R., Baskin, A. B., and Hofer, E. "Organizational/Memory Tools: A Technique for Improving Problem Solving Skills." *Journal of Educational Computing Research, 2(2),* 1986, 169–187.

Stephens, J. M. *The Process of Schooling.* New York: Holt, Rinehart and Winston, 1967.

Stephenson, S. D. *The Effect of Instructor–Student Interaction on Achievement in Computer-Based Training (CBT)* (AL-TP-1991–0002, pp 1–7). Brooks Air Force Base, TX: Human Resources Directorate, Technical Training Research Division, 1991.

Sternberg, R. J. *The Triachic Mind: A New Theory of Human Intelligence.* New York: Viking, 1988.

Sternberg, R. J. "The Concept of Intelligence and Its Role in Lifelong Learning and Success." *American Psychology, 52,* 1997, 1030–1037.

Stevens-Long, J. *Adult Life: Developmental Processes.* Palo Alto, CA: Mayfield, 1979.

Stewart, D. W. *Adult Learning in America: Eduard Lindeman and His Agenda for Lifelong Education.* Malabar, FL: Krieger, 1987.

Stewart, T. A. *Intellectual Capital: The New Wealth of Organizations.* New York: Doubleday, 1997.

Stokes, K. (ed.). *Faith Development in the Adult Life Cycle.* New York: William H. Sadlief, 1983.

Stolovich, H. D., Keeps, E. J., and Rodrigue, D. "Skills Sets for the Human Performance Technologist." *Performance Improvement Quarterly, 8(2),* 1995, 40–67.

Storey, W. D. *Orientation to Your Career Development Program.* Ossining, NY: General Electric Company Management Development Institute, 1972.

Stumpf, S. A., and Freedman, R. D. "The Learning Style Inventory: Still Less than Meets the Eye." *Academy of Management Review, 6,* 1981, 297–299.

Suanmali, C. *The Core Concepts of Andragogy* (UMI No. 8207343). 1981.

Suchman, E. A. *Evaluative Research: Principles and Practice in Public Service and Social Action Programs.* New York: Russell Sage Foundation, 1967.

Suchman, J. R. "The Child and the Inquiry Process." *The Psychology of Open Teaching and Learning.* M. L. Silberman, et al. (eds). Boston, MA: Little, Brown, 1972, pp. 147–159.

Swanson, R. A. "Industrial Training." *Encyclopedia of Educational Research.* H. E. Mitzel (ed.). New York: Macmillan, 1982, pp. 864–869.

Swanson, R. A. "Ready–Aim–Frame." *Human Resource Development Quarterly, 2(3),* 1991, 203–205.

Swanson, R. A. "Demonstrating Financial Benefits to Clients." *Handbook of Human Performance Technology.* H. Stolovitch, and E. Keeps (eds). San Francisco, CA: Jossey-Bass, 1992, pp. 602–618.

Swanson, R. A. "Human Resource Development: Performance Is Key." *Human Resource Development Quarterly, 6(2),* 1995, 207–213.

Swanson, R. A. *Analysis for Improving Performance: Tools for Diagnosing Organizations and Documenting Workplace Expertise.* San Francisco, CA: Berrett-Koehler, 1996.

Swanson, R. A. *Assessing Financial Benefits of Human Resource Development.* Cambridge, MA: Perseus, 2001.

Swanson, R. A. *Analysis for Improving Performance: Tools for Diagnosing Organizations and Documenting Workplace Expertise,* 2nd edn. San Francisco, CA: Berrett-Koehler, 2007.

Swanson, R. A., and Fentress, J. "The Effect of Instructor Influential Tactics on Evaluation by University Students." *Journal of Industrial Teacher Education, 13(1),* 1975, 5–16.

Swanson, R. A., and Gradous, D. B. *Forecasting Financial Benefits of Human Resource Development.* San Francisco, CA: Jossey-Bass, 1988.

Swanson, R. A. and Law, B. "Whole–Part–Whole Learning Model." *Performance Improvement Quarterly, 6(1),* 1993, 43–53.

Swanson, R. A., and Arnold, D. E. "The Purpose of Human Resource Development is to Improve Organizational Performance." *Debating the Future of Educating Adults in the Workplace.* R. W. Rowden (ed.). San Francisco, CA: Jossey-Bass, 1996, pp. 13–19.

Swanson, R. A., and Holton, E. F. *Human Resource Development Handbook: Linking Research and Practice.* San Francisco, CA: Berrett-Koehler, 1997.

Swanson, R. A., and Holton, E. F. *Results: How to Assess Performance, Learning and Perceptions in Organizations.* San Francisco, CA: Berrett-Koehler, 1999.

Swanson, R. A., and Holton, E. F. *Foundations of Human Resource Development,* 2nd edn. San Francisco, CA: Berrett-Koehler, 2009.

Swanson, R. A., and Chermack, T. J. *Theory Building in Applied Disciplines.* San Francisco, CA: Berrett-Koehler, 2013.

Taba, H. *Curriculum Development Theory and Practice.* New York: Harcourt, Brace and World, 1962.

Tannenbaum, S. I., Mathieu, J. E., Salas, E., and Cannon-Bowers, J. A. "Meeting Trainees' Expectations: The Influence of Training Fulfillment on the Development of Commitment, Self-Efficacy, and Motivation." *Journal of Applied Psychology, 76,* 1991, 739–769.

Taylor, B. and Lippitt, G. L. *Management Development and Training Handbook.* New York: McGraw-Hill, 1975.

Taylor, K. "Brain Function and Adult Learning: Implications for Practice." *New Directions for Adult and Continuing Education, 100,* 2006, 71–85.

Taylor, K,. and Lamoreaux, A. "Teaching with the Brain in Mind." *New Directions for Adult and Continuing Education, 119,* 2008, 49–59.

Tedeschi, J. T. (ed.). *The Social Influence Process.* Chicago, IL: Arline-Atherton, 1972.

Tennant, M. "An Evaluation of Knowles' Theory of Adult Learning." *International Journal of Lifelong Education, 5,* 1986, 113–122.

Tennant, M. *Psychology and Adult Learning.* London: Routledge, 1997.

Tennant, M., and Pogson, P. *Learning and Change in the Adult Years: A Developmental Perspective.* San Francisco, CA: Jossey-Bass, 1995.

Tennyson, R. D., and Rothen, W. "Management of Computer-Based Instruction: Design of an Adaptive Control Strategy." *Journal of Computer-Based Instruction, 5(3),* 1979, 63–71.

Tennyson, R. D., and Foshay, W. R. "Instructional Systems Development." *Training & Retraining: A Handbook for Business, Industry, Government, and the Military.* S. Tobia, and J. D. Fletcher (eds). New York: Macmillan Reference USA, 2000, pp. 111–147.

Tessmer, M. "Environment Analysis: A Neglected Stage of Instructional Design." *Educational Technology Research and Development, 38(1),* 1990, 55–64.

Tessmer, M., and Richey, R. C. "The Role of Context in Learning and Instructional Design." *Educational Technology Research and Development, 45,* 1997, 85–115.

Thayer, L. (ed.). *Affective Education: Strategies for Experiential Learning.* La Jolla, CA: University Associates, 1976.

Thomas, R. "Conclusions and Insights Regarding Expertise in Specific Knowledge Domains and Implications for Research and Educational Practice." *Thinking Underlying Expertise in Specific Knowledge Domains: Implications for Vocational Education.* R. G. Thomas (ed.). St. Paul: University of Minnesota, Minnesota Research and Development Center, 1988, pp. 85–95.

Thomas, W. *Journal of Adult Education, XI,* 4, October, 1939, 365–366.

Thompson, J. R. "Formal Properties of Instructional Theory for Adults." *Adult Learning and Instruction.* S. M. Grabowski (ed.). Syracuse, NY: ERIC Clearing House on Adult Education, 1970, pp. 28–45.

Thorndike, E. L. *Adult Learning.* New York: Macmillan, 1928.

Thorndike, E. L. *Adult Interests.* New York: Macmillan, 1935.

Tobias, S. "When Do Instructional Methods Make a Difference?" *Educational Researcher, 11,* 1982, 4–9.

Toffler, A. (ed.). *Learning for Tomorrow: The Role of the Future in Education.* New York: Random House, 1974.

Tokuhama-Espinosa, T. *Mind, Brain, and Education Science: A Comprehensive Guide to the New Brain-Based Teaching.* New York: Norton and Company, 2011.

Tolman, E. C. "Principles of Purposive Behavior." *Psychology: A Study of a Science,* Vol. 2. S. Koch (ed.). New York: McGraw-Hill, 1959.

Torraco, R. J. "A Theory of Work Analysis." Unpublished doctoral dissertation, University of Minnesota, St. Paul, 1994.

Torraco, R. J. "Theory Building Research Methods." *Human Resource Development Research Handbook.* R. A. Swanson, and E. F. Holton III (eds). San Francisco, CA: Berrett-Koehler, 1997, pp. 114–137.

Torraco, R. J., and Swanson, R. A. "The Strategic Roles of Human Resource Development." *Human Resource Planning, 18(4),* 1995, 11–21.

Totshen, K. P. *The Mastery Approach to Competency-Based Education.* New York: Academic Press, 1977.

Tough, A. *Learning without a Teacher.* Toronto: Ontario Institute for Studies in Education, 1967.

Tough, A. *The Adult's Learning Projects.* Toronto: Ontario Institute for Studies in Education, 1971, 1979.

Tough, A. *Intentional Changes: A Fresh Approach to Helping People Change.* Chicago: Follett, 1982.

Tracey, W. R. *Managing Training and Development Systems.* New York: American Management Associations, 1974.

Trecker, H. B. *Citizen Boards at Work.* New York: Association Press, 1970.

Tyler, L. *Individuality: Human Possibilities and Personal Choice in the Psychological Development of Men and Women.* San Francisco, CA: Jossey-Bass, 1978.

Tyler, R. W. *Basic Principles of Curriculum and Instruction.* Chicago, IL: University of Chicago Press, 1950.

University of Illinois. CSL *Quarterly Report for June, July, August 1960.* Coordinated Science Laboratory, University of Illinois. Champaign-Urbana, IL, 1960.

Van Enckevort, G. "Andragology: A New Science," Nederlands Centrum Voor Volksontwikkeling, Amersfoort, The Netherlands, April, 1971 (mimeographed).

Van Gent, B. "Andragogy." *The International Encyclopedia of Adult Education and Training.* A. C. Tuijnman (ed.). Oxford: Pergamon, 1996, pp. 114–117.

Van Maanen, J., and Dabbs, J. M. *Varieties of Qualitative Research.* Beverly Hills, CA: Sage, 1982.

Vermilye, D. W. (ed.). *Lifelong Learners—A New Clientele for Higher Education.* San Francisco, CA: Jossey-Bass, 1974.

Verner, C. *A Conceptual Scheme for the Identification and Classification of Processes.* Washington, DC: Adult Education Association, 1962.

Verner, C., and Booth, A. *Adult Education.* New York: Center for Applied Research in Education, 1964.

Von Bertalanffy, L. *General System Theory.* New York: Braziller, 1968.

Vroom, V. H. *Work and Motivation* (Classic reprint). San Francisco, CA: Jossey-Bass, 1995.

Waetjen W. B., and Leeper, R. R. (eds). *Learning and Mental Health in the School.* Washington, DC: Association for Supervision and Curriculum Development, NEA, 1966.

Wager, W., and Gagné, R. M. "Designing Computer-Aided Instruction." *Instructional Designs for Microcomputer Courseware.* D. H. Jonassen (ed.). Hillsdale, NJ: Lawrence Erlbaum Associates, 1988, pp. 35–60.

Walberg, H. J. (ed.). *Evaluating Educational Performance: A Sourcebook of Methods, Instruments, and Examples.* Berkeley, CA: McCutchan, 1974.

Wanous, J. P. *Organizational Entry: Recruitment, Selection, Orientation and Socialization of Newcomers*, 3rd edn. Reading, MA: Addison-Wesley, 1992.

Wanous, J. P., and Colella, A. "Organizational Entry Research: Current Status and Future Directions." *Research in Personnel and Human Resources Management.* G. R. Ferris, and K. M. Rowland (eds). Greenwich, CT: JAI Press, 1989, pp. 59–120.

Wanous, J. P., Reichers, A. E., and Malik, S. D. "Organizational Socialization and Group Development: Toward an Integrative Perspective." *Academy of Management Review, 9*, 1984, 670–683.

Watkins, K., and Marsick, V. *Sculpting the Learning Organization.* San Francisco, CA: Jossey-Bass, 1993.

Watkins, K., and Marsick, V. "The Case for Learning." *Academy of Human Resource Development 1995 Conference Proceedings.* E. F. Holton (ed.). Austin, TX: AHRD, 1995.

Watson, G. "What Do We Know about Learning?" *Teachers College Record*, 1960–1961, 253–257.

Watson, G. (ed.). *Concepts for Social Change.* Washington, DC: National Training Laboratories Institute for Applied Behavioral Science, NEA, 1967.

Webster's Encyclopedic Unabridged Dictionary of the English Language—Updated Revised Deluxe Edition. New York: Random House Value Publishing, 1996.

Webster's New World Dictionary of the American Language. New York: Warner Books, 1982.

Weiler, N. W. *Reality and Career Planning: A Guide for Personal Growth.* Reading, MA: Addison-Wesley, 1977.

Weinstein, C. E., and Mayer, R. E. "The Teaching of Learning Strategies." *Handbook of Research on Teaching*, 3rd edn. M. C. Wittrock (ed.). New York: Macmillan, 1986.

Weiss, H. M. "Subordinate Imitation of Supervisor Behavior: The Role of Modeling in Organizational Socialization." *Organizational Behavior and Human Performance, 19*, 1977, 89–105.

White, R. H. "Motivation Reconsidered. The Concept of Competence." *Psychological Review, 66*, 1959, 297–333.

Willems, E. P., and Rausch, H. L. (eds). *Naturalistic Viewpoints in Psychological Research.* New York: Holt, Rinehart and Winston, 1969.

Williams, S. W. "Towards a Framework for Teaching and Learning in an Online Environment: A Review of the Literature." *Proceedings of the Academy of Human Resource Development Annual Conference (1–2)*. K. P. Kuchinke (ed.). Baton Rouge, LA: Academy of Human Resource Development, 2000.

Willis, J. "The Current Impact of Neuroscience on Teaching and Learning." *Mind, Brain and Education: Neuroscience Implications for the Classroom*. D. A. Sousa (ed.). Bloomington, IN: Solution Tree Press, 2010.

Wilson, C. "A Comparative Study of the Historical Development of Andragogy and the Formation of its Scientific Foundation: In Germany and the United States of America, 1833–1999." Tulsa, OK: Oral Roberts University. Unpublished Doctoral Dissertation, 2003.

Wilson, C. *No One is Too Old to Learn: Neuroandragogy: A Theoretical Perspective on Adult Brain Functions and Adult Learning*. New York: iUniverse, 2006.

Wislock, R. F. "What Are Perceptual Modalities and How Do They Contribute to Learning?" *Applying Cognitive Learning Theory to Adult Learning*. D. D. Flannery (ed.). San Francisco, CA: Jossey-Bass, 1993.

Wiswell, B., and Ward, S. "Combining Constructivism and Andragogy in Computer Software Training." *Proceedings of the 1997 Academy of Human Resource Development Annual Conference*. R. Torraco (ed.). Baton Rouge, LA: Academy of Human Resource Development, 1997.

Witkin, H. A., Monroe, O. A., Goodenough, D. R., and Cox, P. W. "Field-Dependent and Independent Cognitive Styles and Their Educational Implications." *Review of Educational Research, 47(1)*, 1977, 1–64.

Wlodowski, R. J. *Enhancing Adult Motivation to Learn*. San Francisco, CA: Jossey-Bass, 1985.

Wolf, P. "The Role of Meaning and Emotion in Learning." *New Directions for Adult and Continuing Education, 100*, 2006, 35–41.

Wood, R. E., and Bandura, A. "Impact of Conceptions of Ability on Self-Regulatory Mechanisms and Complex Decision-Making." *Journal of Personality and Social Psychology, 56*, 1989, 407–415.

Woodruff, D. S., and Birren, J. E. (eds). *Aging*. New York: Van Nostrand, 1975.

Yelon, S. L. "Classroom Instruction." *Handbook of Human Performance Technology*. H. Stolovitch, and E. Keeps (eds). San Francisco, CA: Jossey-Bass, 1992.

Young, G. "Andragogy and Pedagogy: Two Ways of Accompaniment." *Adult Education Quarterly, 35(3)*, 1985, 160–167.

Zadeh, L. *Systems Theory*. New York: McGraw-Hill, 1969.

Zahn, J. C. *Creativity Research and Its Implications for Adult Education*. Syracuse, NY: Library of Continuing Education, Syracuse University, 1966.

Zander, A. *Groups at Work*. San Francisco, CA: Jossey-Bass, 1977.

Zander, A. *Making Groups Effective*. San Francisco, CA: Jossey-Bass, 1982.

Zemke, R., and Zemke, S. "Thirty Things We Know for Sure about Adult Learning." *Training, 25(7)*, 1988, 57–61.

Zemke, R., and Zemke, S. "Adult Learning: What Do We Know for Sure?" *The New Training Library: Adult Learning in Your Classroom, Chapter 2: Understanding and Motivating the Adult Learner*. D. Zielinski (ed.). Minneapolis, MN: Lakewood Books, 1996, pp. 71–74.

Zmeyov, S. I. "Perspectives of Adult Education in Russia." *Developments in the Education of Adults in Europe. Vol. 21 of Studies in Pedagogy, Andragogy and Gerontology.* P. Jarvis, and F. Poggeler (eds). Bern, Switzerland: Peter Lang, 1994, pp. 35–42.

Zmeyov, S. I. "Andragogy: Origins, Developments and Trends." *International Review of Education, 44(1)*, 1998, 103–108.

Zurcher, L. A. *The Mutable Self: A Concept for Social Change.* Beverly Hills, CA: Sage, 1977.

INDEX

Page numbers in **bold** refer to figures, page numbers in *italic* refer to tables.